THE WAR OF MY GENERATION

THE WAR OF MY GENERATION

Youth Culture and the War on Terror

EDITED BY

DAVID KIERAN

RUTGERS UNIVERSITY PRESS
New Brunswick, New Jersey, and London

Library of Congress Cataloging-in-Publication Data

The war of my generation : youth culture and the War on Terror / edited by David Kieran.
       pages cm
    Includes bibliographical references and index.
    ISBN 978-0-8135-7262-8 (hardcover : alk. paper)—ISBN 978-0-8135-7261-1 (pbk. : alk. paper)—ISBN 978-0-8135-7263-5 (e-book (web pdf))
       1. War on Terrorism, 2001–2009—Social aspects—United States. 2. Youth—United States—Social conditions—21st century. 3. Popular culture—United States—History—21st century. 4. Political culture—United States—History—21st century. 5. War on Terrorism, 2001–2009—Influence. 6. War and society—United States. I. Kieran, David, 1978- editor, author.

HV6432.W3717 2015
   306.2'70973090511—dc23
   2014040919

A British Cataloging-in-Publication record for this book is available from the British Library.

Visit our website: http://rutgerspress.rutgers.edu

Manufactured in the United States of America

For my mother, and in memory of my father

CONTENTS

ACKNOWLEDGMENTS

More than most books, a collection of essays represents the work of many hands, and so I begin the acknowledgements by thanking my contributors. As one contributor told me after I shared the table of contents with her, "It's too bad this is an edited collection and not a party, because it would be fun to get all of these smart people in the same room." The contributors to this collection have not only written thoughtful and important work—including several essays that authors graciously agreed to tackle after I approached them about contributing to this collection—but did so with unfailing patience and good cheer over many months that alternately included multiple, lengthy revisions and the occasional need for almost instantaneous responses to queries.

The idea for this collection emerged after the panel "The War on Terror in Youth Culture" at the 2010 Annual Meeting of the American Studies Association in San Antonio, Texas. Thanks to my copanelists Rebecca Adelman and Aaron DeRosa and to our chair and commenter Wendy Kozol for an inspiring conversation that helped move my thinking forward. My colleagues in the American studies department at Franklin and Marshall College made completing this collection easier. Particular thanks go to my chair, Alison Kibler, who made sure that I had time to work on my scholarship during the academic year, and to Dennis Deslippe, who read several drafts of the introduction. Ann Wagoner and her staff of work-study students cheerfully completed a number of administrative tasks for me, and the interlibrary loan staff at Shadek-Fackenthal library tracked down a number of obscure books and articles for me. Thanks as well to the entire Posse crew that helped me have fun amid all of the editing.

Claire Potter first suggested that Rutgers University Press might be a good home for this collection, and she was right. Leslie Mitchner was open to the collection from the beginning, and Lisa Boyajian was a tireless advocate for its publication, an incisive reader of drafts and a patient editor. Thanks for believing in these essays as much as I did. Lisa also arranged for two rounds of external review by an anonymous reviewer who offered encouragement and rigorous critique that improved the collection more than I could have imagined. Brian King's copyediting made the collection much more coherent and readable. Derek Gottlieb prepared the index.

My essay was first published in Children's Literature Association Quarterly 37.1 (2012), 4–26. Copyright © 2012 Children's Literature Association. Reprinted with permission by Johns Hopkins University Press. I am grateful for this permission.

My family, especially Kathy Dolley, Kathleen Kieran, Susan Gilmore, Carrie and Rob Wagner, and Jamie and Elsbeth Iannone, deserve credit for the large and small ways that they have encouraged me along the way. This collection is dedicated to my mother, Mary Anne Kieran, and in memory of my father, Richard J. Kieran, because it was from them that I learned the value of education, hard work, and compassion and that the work that we do should improve the lives of those around us.

My final thanks, as always, are reserved for Emma Gilmore Kieran, who has supported and encouraged me in all of my endeavors, academic and otherwise. Thanks again for always being there for me. We've had a lot of adventures, and there will be many more.

THE WAR OF MY GENERATION

INTRODUCTION

"The War of My Generation"

DAVID KIERAN

On August 13, 2006, ample evidence made clear that the events of September 11, 2001, and the subsequent wars in Iraq and Afghanistan continued to shape American public life. The *New York Times* published an editorial complaining that on September 11, 2001, "civil aviation authorities, the military and the highest officials in the Bush administration [had] failed to respond quickly enough to avert catastrophe."[1] Fifty-seven Iraqi civilians died in the sectarian violence.[2] And far from either New York or Iraq, sixteen-year-old Janel Weathow visited the Flight 93 National Memorial in Somerset County, Pennsylvania. At the time, the memorial consisted of a sparse gravel lot that overlooked the impact site and a chain-link fence on which visitors often hung items in remembrance of the passengers and crew who had revolted against the hijackers on September 11. Weathow used one of the four-by-six-inch index cards that the National Park Service provided for visitors to write a note that declared, "I've been told by my mom that this is the war of my generation. Thank you for being brave and fighting back. You'll always be remembered by me and everyone else."[3] (Fig. 1)

Weathow's comment joined many others. At Christmastime 2001, Kristen Starkey and Katie Dunmore, middle-school students from Mt. Prospect, Illinois, wrote holiday cards to American soldiers and sent them to the memorial. "Everyone here in the U.S. is praying for you and we appreciate all that you are doing for us," one declared; the other read, "I also wanted to thank for you fighting for our country."[4] In 2004, thirteen-year-old Sam Weiser left a note reading, "We are in a solemn prayer for those who died in the 9/11 attacks. Our troops are dying for you and our freedom. We love this beautiful nation called the United States and the attacks changed the nation in a positive way. We are now more brotherly and we banded together to stop terrorism."[5]

Parents also used the memorial as a place to consider the relevance of the September 11 attacks and the Iraq and Afghanistan Wars in their children's lives.

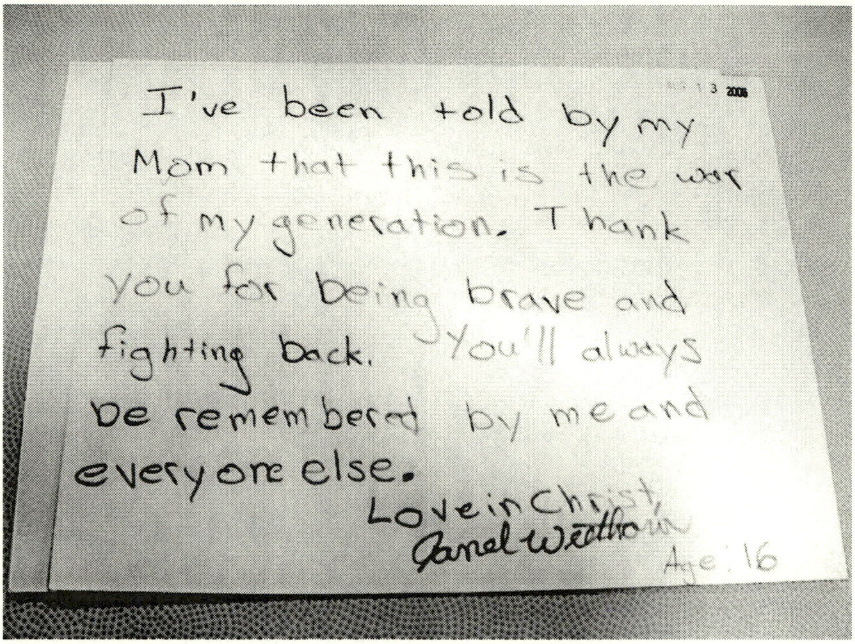

FIGURE 1. Note left by Janel Weathow at the Flight 93 Memorial, Somerset County, Pennsylvania. National Park Service, Flight 93 National Memorial. (Photograph by the author.)

The photographs of children pledging to the flag with an inscription that reads, "Thank you for giving us a future" or of a child in a miniature marine uniform with a card that has "You are my heroes in heaven. My aunt is my hero in the Marine Corp [sic]. I love you all—Semper Fi" suggest that many children have been encouraged to embrace dominant narratives that celebrate American militarism. Other parents, though, have been more ambivalent. While one mother wrote that "it will be a honor to keep your memory alive and teach my kids of the day you saved our country," another wrote that "as I look over the hills I wonder . . . what legacy will I leave for my children. I hope a world of peace."[6] Nor is pride universally assumed to be a child's response to a parent's deployment. A military father wrote in 2008, "Today my son learned why daddy has to keep going away to war," but someone else left behind Mr. Stuffy, a stuffed bear dressed in camouflage fatigues that comes with a book entitled *Mr. Stuffy's Uniform: A Children's Story of Comfort for Troubled Times,* and a note that reads, "Dear Friend, This is Mr. Stuffy, my good friend who always helps me when I am afraid. I will pray for you both to be safe."[7]

These items illuminate an important aspect of post-9/11 US culture. Those whose childhood and adolescence coincided with the aftermath of the terrorist attacks and the subsequent War on Terror—members of the millennial generation, which includes those born between 1982 and 2003, and the post-millennials who have followed them—have been deeply engaged with their moment's central political and cultural debates, including those about the Iraq and Afghanistan Wars, civil rights, surveillance, and memorialization.[8] They protested the wars and enlisted in the military, built memorials and staged rallies against discriminatory practices. Their responses have been informed by the culture in which they live. Children and adolescents learned about these events through school curricula, holiday parades, and teachers, parents, and other adults who care for and about them. They also consumed a growing body of popular culture from literature to videogames that is specifically intended for their consumption. Reckoning with these millennial and post-millennial experiences of and engagements with the War on Terror thus represents a critical imperative for scholars of twenty-first century US culture.

The eleven essays gathered in *The War of My Generation* offer a starting place for examining millennials' engagement with these events and issues. The contributors place young people's experiences at the center of 9/11 culture to address from varying perspectives three animating questions: What attitudes about the September 11 attacks and their aftermath have young people adopted? How have those attitudes been cultivated? What are the political stakes of their investment and engagement? The essays reveal that there are multiple answers to this query. The individuals of the millennial and post-millennial generations are diverse, and a plethora of old and new media offers a variety of perspectives on the attacks, the wars that have followed, and domestic life in their midst. These essays embrace that diversity, map the contours of these generations' encounters with post-9/11 culture, and explore the political and cultural consequences of young people's engagement with contemporary US culture and foreign policy.

The War of My Generation joins an emerging field of 9/11 studies that has paid some attention to youth culture. For example, Rebecca Adelman, whose essay on teaching atrocity photographs appears in this volume, has examined the curious phenomenon of Flat Daddies, life-size photographs of service members in uniform that families use as a stand-in for the deployed parent at family dinners, soccer games, and other events.[9] Reebee Garofalo, in "Pop Goes to War, 2001–2004: U.S. Popular Music after 9/11" in Jonathan Ritter and J. Martin Daughtry's *Music in the Post-9/11 World*, offers a useful overview of how popular music and Top 40 radio engaged with, and often supported, the patriotic and militaristic discourses of the early years of the War on Terror. Stephen Packard's "Whose Side Are You On?" and Matthew J. Costello's "Spandex Agonistes"—both in Veronique Bragard, Christophe Dony, and Warren Rosenberg's *Portraying 9/11: Essays on Representation in Comics, Literature, Film, and Theatre*—and Joseph Michael Summers essay "The Traumatic Revision of Marvel's Spider-Man: From 1960s Dime-Store Comic Book to Post-9/11 Moody Motion Picture Franchise" seriously consider how Marvel Comics responded to the September 11 attacks, and the attention to superhero and horror films in books like Tom Pollard's *Hollywood 9/11: Superheroes, Supervillains, and Super Disasters* and Aviva Briefel and Sam J. Miller's *Horror After 9/11: World of Fear, Cinema of Terror* treat genres that certainly attract young audiences.[10] Yet the study of popular culture for young people is far from complete. For example, while Henry Jenkins proposes that "studying comics allows us not only to map the immediate response but also to measure the long-term impact of these events on American popular culture," he quickly calls the genre "a fringe (even an *avant garde*) medium, one which appeals primarily to college students and college-educated professionals."[11] Similarly, Stacy Takac's *Terrorism TV: Popular Entertainment in Post-9/11 America* offers one of the most comprehensive accounts of the War on Terror in popular culture but makes only passing references to popular culture for children and adolescents.[12] Oral histories have similar gaps. Damon DiMarco's collection, *Tower Stories,* begins from the premise that "if we give our grandchildren free access to our history, maybe they'll come up with better answers than we have," but it does not include the voices of children whose parents were in the towers; similarly, a collection of essays by New York City teachers, *Forever After: New York City Teachers on 9/11,* provides a lot of reflection of what happened in classrooms during and after the attacks but only from the perspective of adults.[13] Indeed, within this body of scholarship, only Sunaina Maira's ethnography of South Asian youth, *Missing: Youth, Citizenship, and Empire After 9/11,* offers a sustained, book-length examination of young people's experiences and activism.

There has also been substantial work on pedagogy, particularly in the form of lesson plans available from online sources as diverse as the US Department of Education, the National September 11 Memorial and Museum, and the scholarly publisher Scholastic. In addition, a few scholarly journals have offered thorough meditations on classroom practice and the challenges inherent in teaching this history to students who have lived through it and who often have strong feelings about it, such as the essays by Jeffrey Melnick and Magide Shihade in *Radical History Review* and by Claire Potter, Martin Flaherty, and Lary May in the *OAH Magazine of History.*[14]

The War of My Generation adds to this growing body of work that takes seriously young people's experiences and actions related to the attacks and their aftermath. Drawing on a variety of disciplinary perspectives—ethnography, sociology, cultural studies, literary studies—these essays constitute the first collection to focus specifically on the September 11 attacks and their aftermath in millennial and post-millennial culture. Rather than offering a comprehensive assessment of youth culture—an impossibility for a single volume—this collection has three primary aims: First, it highlights the diversity of millennial and post-millennial experiences and attitudes. Second, it offers case studies that illustrate how popular culture has shaped young people's understandings of the War on Terror and adult understandings of young people's experience. Finally, it discusses the practical and theoretical challenges inherent in teaching this complicated history to students who have lived through much of it.

This collection first challenges any universalizing notion of the "9/11 Generation" by highlighting the diversity of engagements and responses of young people of different ages and ethnicities. The millennial generation spans two decades, which means that it includes both adults who were in basic training on September 11, 2001, and children who were in utero when the United States invaded Iraq on March 20, 2003. In the more than twelve years since the 9/11 attacks, approximately four million Americans have turned eighteen each year and more than fifty million children have been born.[15]

This population has embraced, resisted, and offered alternatives to the dominant narratives of patriotism and militarism that dominated post-9/11 culture. Many, like Janel Weathow, visited memorials and engaged in commemorative celebrations, regularly attending, choreographing, and participating in memorial services at their schools and in their communities. On September 11, 2002, for example, elementary-school students in St. Petersburg, Florida, held a daylong memorial ceremony.[16] In several schools, students built memorials that incorporated materials from the World Trade Center.[17] In Bloomington, Indiana, a student outraged at the anti-war movement organized a rally in support of the Iraq War; more than a few others have sought to join the military against their parents' wishes.[18]

Other young people embraced progressive and anti-war politics. In 2006 and 2007, for example, students in Brattleboro, Madison, Denver, Omaha, St. Paul, and elsewhere walked out of class to protest the Iraq War.[19] In Frederick, Maryland, students were escorted from school by police "after staging a 'die-in' in front of a Marine Corps recruiting booth during an on-campus job fair," while a suburban Chicago district threatened students with expulsion for staging an anti-war sit-in.[20] Other youth have worked diligently to address anti-Muslim sentiment and to help their fellow students opt out of military recruitment.[21]

Young people's experiences thus vary not only by age but also by region, gender, ethnicity, political affiliation, and citizenship. The three ethnographies in this collection's first section, "Experiences and Attitudes of the 9/11 Generations," illustrate the diversity, revealing that whether in pre-school, high school, or college; in homogenously white or ethnically diverse neighborhoods; or in the middle or the working class, young people have actively sought to understand these events and have alternately questioned, embraced, and resisted the policies of the War on Terror. Holly Swyers begins the collection with "*Starship Troopers*, School Shootings, and September 11," which calls into question the utility of the category "the millennial generation" in understanding so broad and numerous a population. She argues that children born in the 1980s and who reached adolescence around the time of the 2001 terrorist attacks constitute a "sandwich generation"; neither members of Generation X nor millennials, they grew up in a moment dominated not by the ethics of the Cold War—the sense of looming external threats that the nation must unify to defeat—but rather in one marked by the relatively progressive politics of liberal humanitarianism, multiculturalism, and conflict resolution. As Swyers demonstrates in her study of suburban Illinois high-school students, the political culture and school curricula of the 1990s led many adolescents to resist the anti-Muslim sentiments and the rush to war that followed the September 11 attacks. She argues that a nuanced engagement with this history will allow scholars and teachers to better analyze this cohort's subsequent political engagement.

Younger Americans have not shared this skepticism, as Cindy Dell Clark shows in "Summer, Soldiers, Flags, and Memorials: How US Children Learn Nation-Linked Militarism from Holidays" her ethnography of suburban Philadelphia children's experiences at Memorial Day and Independence Day celebrations between 2005 and 2012. While these holidays are often reductively viewed as opportunities for summer recreation, Clark shows that both formal and informal celebrations of these holidays teach even very young children that militarism is a central component of American culture, that maintaining a militarized posture is necessary to defend freedom and "the American way of life" that children putatively enjoy on those holidays, and that celebrating militarism is a defining attribute of good citizenship.

The third ethnography, Sunaina Maira's essay "Fighting with Rights and Forging Alliances," examines the ways in which youth who have been subjected to marginalization, racism, and surveillance have responded with activism of their own. Maira examines how Muslim youth in California's Silicon Valley have embraced the discourses and rhetoric of civil rights and of human rights as they have sought to address both the extralegal harassment and violence and the governmental surveillance and denial of rights that has plagued Muslim communities in the aftermath of the 2001 attacks. Like Swyers, she is keenly interested in understanding the investments that young people bring to their consideration of the cultural politics of the War on Terror, and she helps illuminate the range of responses that subgroups of the millennial and post-millennial generation have made.

Read together, these three essays encourage a more complicated assessment of the contours of the 9/11 generation. They reveal that their historical consciousness and their previous cultural encounters provided some young people with tools through which they could question or resist the culture of militarism, surveillance, and xenophobia that followed in the wake of the attacks. They also reveal, however, that powerful currents in American culture work to interpellate young people into discourses of patriotic orthodoxy and an embrace of militarism. Together, the three essays suggest that there is in fact not a monolithic "9/11 generation," but rather many cohorts within the two post-9/11 generations, and they demonstrate that any study of young people's engagement with the War on Terror must begin by asking which young people and in what moment.

Millennials and post-millennials have learned about and engaged with their world in a variety of ways, but popular culture remains among the most important. The second section of *The War of My Generation*, "Post-9/11 Militarism in Old and New Media" gathers essays that examine how both old and new media have represented the Iraq and Afghanistan Wars to young people. Rather than offering a comprehensive account of every genre of popular culture available to young people, this section explicitly focuses on popular culture produced for young people and provides four essays arranged in pairs—two about traditional media (children's literature) and two about new media (video games)—that take as their topic a single issue: the military responses to the September 11 attacks. These essays provide a case study of how popular culture contributes to debates regarding the legitimacy of the United States' post-9/11 military interventions and encourages and facilitates military service. Taken together, these essays provide one model of how scholars might examine other facets of popular culture through a multidisciplinary approach to both old and new media.

In the first of the two essays on children's and young-adult literature, "How to Tell a True War Story . . . for Children: Children's Literature Addresses Deployment," Laura Browder examines the surprisingly robust body of literature written for the children of deployed service members. In an essay that resonates with both Clark's assessment of how young people come to embrace militarism and Benjamin Cooper's assessment in a later essay that innocence, suffering, and resilience provide the lens through which younger children apprehend the War on Terror, Browder finds that many of these books encourage children to treat the parent's absence as a struggle and sacrifice that they must endure for the greater good and alternately sanitize and depoliticize the war and implicate the child within the interventionist logic that underlies the war. At the same time, however, Browder illustrates that several young-adult novels offer surprisingly complex accounts of the struggles that military families face.

My own essay, "'What Young Men and Women Do When Their Country Is Attacked': Interventionist Discourse and the Rewriting of Violence in Adolescent Literature of the Iraq War," follows Browder's and engages with literature written for older children. Reading two well-received novels and a memoir, I maintain that this literature not only embraces the logic that the Bush administration used to cultivate support for the war in Iraq but also systematically revises the most troubling aspects of the Iraq War—military sexual trauma, the Abu Ghraib Scandal, and the killing of Iraqi civilians chief among them—in ways that sanitize the war, valorize the US military presence, and encourage an uncritical embrace of American military adventurism. Together, these two essays provide an overview of how contemporary children's literature informs young people's engagement in the cultural politics of the War on Terror from birth through high school. In doing so, they help address a gap in scholarship on post-9/11 literature, which has focused almost exclusively on novels written for adults and primarily on the work of major literary figures.

The next two essays examine a cultural form increasingly central to young people's experience—electronic games. Though other scholars have recognized that products that take both the current and earlier wars as their topic— including popular *America's Army* game that the army produced as a recruiting tool or the *Medal of Honor* series—there has yet to be a sustained analysis of their production and content in relation to the critical issues of their moment. The essays partner to examine these games' engagement with the political rhetoric that has surrounded the wars and the realities of fighting wars that have become evident over the past thirteen years. Jeremy Saucier's essay "Calls of Duty: The World War II Combat Video Game and the Construction of the 'Next Great Generation'" shows how invoking the collective remembrance of the Second World War and the enduring veneration of the so-called Greatest Generation became a critical rhetorical trope within efforts to cultivate young peoples' support for the Iraq and Afghanistan Wars. He then examines recent first-person shooter games about the Second World War, arguing that they encourage the embrace of contemporary militaristic narratives by allowing players to virtually engage in battles widely understood as having preserved democracy and defined the United States' role as a global superpower.

In contrast to Saucier's cultural analysis of first-person shooter games, Robertson Allen offers "Software and Soldier Life Cycles of Recruitment, Training, and Rehabilitation in the Post-9/11 Era," an ethnography that examines how developers of the army's wildly popular *America's Army* series have conceptualized and adapted the platform to address the army's needs across soldiers' careers. Allen complicates simplistic critiques of the game as a exploitative recruiting tool by detailing developers' struggles to create a "realistic" game that accurately represents Army life while also appealing to a young audience. More importantly, he locates the game within the army's larger efforts to meet the varying needs of this generation of soldiers and shows that the game platform has been adapted for uses as diverse as virtually training soldiers to use expensive equipment and providing therapy for post-traumatic stress disorder. Read together, Saucier and Allen's essays place a critical spotlight on one of most important cultural forms for twenty-first century American youth.

For many adults, the September 11 attacks and the wars that followed raised questions about how that these events would impact young people. Parents and parenting experts have alternately imagined young people as infantilized innocents who demand protection from the events' most disturbing realities and as emerging citizens who require instruction in order to become appropriately patriotic young people. Within weeks of September 11, for example, *Parenting* magazine encouraged parents to "try not to watch the news when [their] infant, toddler, or preschooler is in the room" and maintained that there was "no need to share the anxiety producing details."[22] Others, though, hoped that children would adopt particular notions of national subjectivity and citizenship as they learned about the attacks. A teacher planning a memorial service in September 2002 declared that its purpose was "to remind the kids about America" and "give them a highlighted awareness of the freedoms they have as Americans."[23] The major memorials to the attacks, in contrast, have encouraged young people to become civically engaged and more egalitarian. The recently opened National September 11 Memorial and Museum implicitly took the position that telling children about the attacks was unpleasant but necessary and that parents should "help [their] children recognize how their own compassion can prevent future acts of intolerance and violence."[24]

The presence of military recruiters in schools and the No Child Left Behind Act's provision that schools provide students' demographic data to recruiters was another source of debate and anxiety.[25] Some parents, teachers, and school boards have viewed recruiters' presence as an appropriate way to cultivate patriotism and provide career opportunities; others have seen it as exploitative, as when parents in New York and Maine questioned the presence of uniformed troops in middle schools and an Austin-area parent complained about the presence at her son's high school of a "sleek, $2 million, 18-wheeler military Cinema Van that . . . offered free access to the most sophisticated high-tech battle-simulation computer games" for students willing to "give the recruiters their personal information."[26] These debates are unsurprisingly rooted in issues of race and class as much as in attitudes toward the war; in 2005, a Pittsburgh parent told a recruiter, "Military service isn't for our son. It isn't for our kind of people," while in San Antonio a guidance counselor told a recruiter that he had "'a lot of kids who needed to be talking to him. . . . It's their best option.'"[27]

The third section of this collection, "Coming of Age Stories and the Representation of Millennial Citizenship during the War on Terror," approaches the relationship between popular culture and young Americans' experiences of the War on Terror from a slightly different perspective than the four essays that precede it. The two essays in this section examine how the challenges facing young people living in the post-9/11 United States have been represented in coming of age stories that appeal to both children and young adults. Reading different genres of popular culture, each engages with the question of what kind of citizens young people were able, or expected, to become after September 11 and what responsibilities, opportunities, and dangers attend those formal and informal enactments of citizenship. Jo Lampert argues in "Coming of Age in 9/11 Fiction: Bildungsroman and Loss of Innocence" that post-9/11 literature about young adults should be read within the tradition of the bildungsroman, or the coming of age story. In these novels, the United States emerges, through the adolescent protagonists of each novel, as "a nation forced against its will to grow up in the wake of an uncertain future" in which "allegiance to country is equated with maturity." Healing after September 11, Lampert suggests, consists not of pursuing any meaningful social change but of recuperating the perceived stability of the pre-9/11 moment. Her essay thus carries the observations that Laura Browder and I make about literature written for young people into a discussion of literature *about* young people while suggesting how this literature encourages adults to think about young people's experience.

In "'Army Strong': Mexican American Youth and Military Recruitment in *All She Can*," Irene Garza discusses the cultural representation of one of the most significant issues of contemporary militarism: the increasing recruitment of rural, nonwhite youth into the US military. Her analysis of the 2011 film *All She Can* places it within the larger debates that attend race, class, citizenship, and military recruiting. In her reading, the film offers an interrogation of the myriad pressures that many Latino youth face—the desire for economic opportunities outside of small, rural towns; familial and community pressures to embrace military service; and the likelihood that such service will result in grievous injury. While clearly a film intended for adult audiences, it gives voice to the issues central to many young people's experience. These two essays, like the four that precede them, offer a pairing that highlights from contrasting perspectives the challenges faced by young people living in the post-9/11 United States and analyze how popular culture contributes to debates about their resolution.

The intellectual questions that animate the first three sections of this collection—What histories and investments shape millennial and post-millennial attitudes and activism? How has popular culture represented the War on Terror to these generations? What struggles do these young people face, and how have they been imagined in contemporary popular culture?—lead to two additional crucial questions: How can the War on Terror be meaningfully taught to a generation that has lived through much of it? What are the political consequences of instructors' pedagogical approaches?

Questions about what material is appropriate for K-12 and college classrooms and which pedagogical approaches teachers should embrace have emerged since the earliest moments of the War on Terror. In Lincoln, Nebraska, a teacher was asked to resign after showing the anti-war documentary *Baghdad ER* to his class, but in Wilmot, Iowa, the school board determined that Michael Moore's *Fahrenheit 9/11* was suitable for classroom use.[28] In late May 2004, school districts in California, North Carolina, Georgia, Texas, Nebraska, and Arkansas suspended teachers who had shown students videos of beheadings in Iraq and Afghanistan, but a New Mexico teacher won a lawsuit after being fired for teaching anti-war poetry, as did a Massachusetts teacher disciplined for showing the Abu Ghraib photos to his class.[29] In North Carolina, a teacher was criticized for inviting a speaker who distributed "a handout titled 'Do Not Marry a Muslim Man,'" while anti-war veterans' 2006 visits to a San Francisco Bay area high school were seemingly less controversial.[30]

The two essays in *The War of My Generation*'s final section, "Politics and Pedagogy" address these questions. In an essay that recalls and builds upon Swyer's discussion of intergenerational differences in imagining the cultural context of the War on Terror, Benjamin Cooper's "In This War But Not of It: Teaching, Memory, and the Futures of Children and War" discusses his experience teaching a course on children's war literature and reflects on his misplaced assumption that his students would share his perception of the relationship between the War on Terror and the larger history of the United States' wars—one that he acknowledges is, like Swyers's, tied to his own childhood during the late Cold War and the 1991 Gulf War. Rather, Cooper finds students' "lived memories" of the attack led them to dismiss the trajectory of innocence and disillusionment that shapes many older Americans' remembrances of earlier wars and instead to link the September 11 attacks to the Holocaust as moments in which innocent people suffered but resiliently persevered. From this experience, Cooper deduces that a critical classroom project is deconstructing the narratives and shared memories that students bring to their reading, and he proposes how the analysis of different kinds of shared remembrance—lived memories, generational memories, and postmemories—can encourage young people to become more reflective consumer of popular culture.

Rebecca Adelman closes this section with "'Coffins after Coffins': Screening Wartime Atrocity in the Classroom," an exploration of the problematic use of atrocity images in high-school and college classrooms. She begins by recounting incidents in which teachers were disciplined for showing photographs of prisoner abuse at Abu Ghraib and videos of Nicholas Berg's beheading to explore the cultural politics of spectatorship and the ethics of teaching controversial visual culture. The focus on whether students in US classrooms have been disturbed by these images, Adelman insists, is misplaced, given the multiple levels of violence inherent in the images themselves; as such, she proposes a set of strategies that can lead to ethical viewing practices and to students' deeper consideration of the cultural work that such images perform. Together, Cooper and Adelman ask those of us who teach this generation to consider how we might best do so—how can we help students unpack the narratives that they bring to our classrooms, and how can we teach complicated issues in an ethical manner?

The essays in this collection raise important questions and address them through the focused consideration of a few topics. There are, however, several genres of popular culture for young people that don't receive attention in this collection. The afterword offers a brief bibliographic essay that highlights some of the best scholarship available elsewhere on the culture of the 9/11 generations and suggests directions for further research.

The September 11 attacks and the subsequent War on Terror—the Iraq and Afghanistan Wars and domestic policies that have resulted in the marginalization and mistreatment of many living in the United States—have not been insignificant in the lives of or absent from the concerns of young people. Rather, young people grew up in a culture saturated with cultural products, organizations, and institutions that shaped their vision of the attacks and of the United States' response to them. They used the lessons they had learned in school and at public ceremonies to cultivate their own opinions about these events and to engage in various forms of protest and support. And they engaged with adults deeply concerned with their experience of these events and their relationship to the nation in its aftermath.

The imperative to understand how young people have experienced these events and defined their relationship to them is been nowhere more evident than in the death of nineteen-year-old Kevin Cardoza of Mercedes, Texas, who was one of five US Army soldiers killed by an improvised explosive device in Kandahar, Afghanistan, on May 4, 2013. The oldest was twenty-eight, and thus would likely have been sixteen on September 11, 2001; Cardoza, the youngest among those killed, had been seven, and his family told reporters that he had "fulfilled a lifelong dream when he joined the U.S. Army after graduating [from high school] in 2011."[31] To understand Kevin Cardoza's death, the war in which it occurred, and the culture that sent him to it requires a substantial reckoning with the experiences of his generation and the one that followed, one that grew up entirely in the shadow of the attacks and amid the wars that followed them. These essays are a step toward doing so.

NOTES

1. "Our Porous Air Defenses on 9/11," *New York Times*, August 13, 2006.
2. Paul von Zielbauer, "Five Bombs Rip through South Baghdad, Killing at Least 57 as Apartments Collapse," *New York Times*, August 14, 2006.
3. Visitor Comment Card, August 13, 2006. Flight 93 National Memorial Visitor Comment Cards 7-31-06 to 10-29-06, Flight 93 National Memorial, Somerset, PA (hereafter cited as FLNI).
4. Kristen Starkey to "American Hero" and Katie Dunmore to "American Hero," Folder FLNI 1202 Box 7 FF8 FS 5-3-02, Box 7, FLNI.
5. Visitor Comment Card, July 10, 2004. Flight 93 National Memorial Visitor Comment Cards 11-2-03 to 7-29-04, FLNI.
6. Visitor Comment Card, September 9, 2006. Flight 93 National Memorial Visitor Comment Cards 7-31-06 to 10-29-06, FLNI; Visitor Comment Card, September 27, 2004. Flight 93 National Memorial Visitor Comment Cards 8-7-04 to 5-29-05, FLNI.
7. Visitor Comment Card, May 23, 2008. Flight 93 National Memorial Visitor Comment Cards 8-11-07 to 5-27-08, FLNI; Uncatalogued Item, SL 10-27-03, Group 2003.65, FLNI.
8. The periodization of millennials is taken from Worley Winograd and Dr. Michael Hais, "How Millennials Could Upend Wall Street and Corporate America," Brookings Institution, 2014,

http://www.brookings.edu/~/media/research/files/papers/2014/05/millennials%20wall%20st/brookings_winogradfinal.pdf.

9. Rebecca A. Adelman, "'Thank You for Our Flat Daddy': Photography, Imagination, and Citizenship as Child's Play," *Photography and Culture* 6, no. 1 (2013): 65–80.

10. Joseph Michael Summers, "The Traumatic Revision of Marvel's Spider-Man: From 1960s Dime-Store Comic Book to Post-9/11 Moody Motion Picture Franchise," *Children's Literature Association Quarterly* 37, no. 2 (2012): 188–209.

11. Henry Jenkins, "Captain America Sheds His Mighty Tears," in *Terror, Culture, Politics: Rethinking 9/11*, ed. Daniel J. Sherman and Terry Nardin (Bloomington: Indiana University Press, 2006), 69, 72.

12. Stacy Takacs, *Terrorism TV: Popular Entertainment in Post-9/11 America* (Lawrence: University of Kansas Press, 2012), 9–11, 54–55, 102–103.

13. Damon DiMarco, *Tower Stories: An Oral History of 9/11* (Santa Monica: Santa Monica Press, 2007); *Forever After: New York City Teachers on 9/11* (New York: Teachers College Press, 2006).

14. Jeffrey Melnick, "'Get Your War On!': Teaching the Post-9/11," *Radical History Review* 111 (2011): 217–224; Magid Shihade, "Teaching 9/11: Lessons from Classrooms in the United States and Pakistan," *Radical History Review* 111 (2011): 225–231; Claire Potter, "Because It Is Gone Now: Teaching the September 11 Digital Archive," *OAH Magazine of History* 25, no. 3 (2011): 31–34; Martin S. Flaherty, "Human Rights Law, American Justice, and the 'War on Terror,'" *OAH Magazine of History* 25, no. 3 (2011): 35–40; and Lary May, "Teaching American Politics and Global Hollywood in the Age of 9/11," *OAH Magazine of History* 25, no. 3 (2011): 45–49.

15. United States Census Bureau, "Earlier Editions—The 2012 Statistical Abstract," March 5, 2013, http://www.census.gov/compendia/statab/past_years.html; United States Census Bureau, "Table 78. Live Births, Deaths, Marriages, and Divorces: 1960 to 2008," 2012, https://www.census.gov/compendia/statab/2012/tables/12s0078.pdf.

16. Jeffrey S. Solochek, "Students Reflect on a Day of Terror: Chime Reflects Nation's Losses," *St. Petersburg Times*, September 12, 2002.

17. Rick Hampson, "Americans Rush to Build Memorials to 9/11," *USA Today*, May 22, 2003.

18. Sharon K. Wolfe, "Message of Teen's Rally: Win in Iraq," *The Pantagraph* (Bloomington, IN), August 28, 2007; Anne Hull, "Call to Duty: In a Community Where Many Roads Lead to the Military, Deciding Whether to Enlist Becomes a Turning Point," *Washington Post*, April 9, 2006; *Associated Press*, "Parents Challenge Pentagon's Pursuit of Records," July 6, 2005; and Jack Kelly, "Parent-Trap Snares Recruiters: The Tune Changes at Some Homes When They Hear 'Sign Here,'" *Pittsburgh Post-Gazette*, August 11, 2005. On parental anxieties about recruitment, see Beth Bailey, *America's Army: Building the All-Volunteer Force* (Cambridge: Harvard University Press, 2009), 251.

19. Howard Weiss-Tisman, "School Disciplines Protesting Students," *Brattleboro Reformer*, November 27, 2007; Susan Troller, "Speaking Up for Peace: Memorial Students Pass on Class to Protest War," *Capital Times*, October 13, 2007; Gabriela Resto-Montero, "Students' Walkout Forms Army against War," *Denver Post*, March 23, 2007; Qianna Bradley, "Taking a Stand against Iraq War; Students Cut Classes in a Protest at the City-County Building," *Omaha World-Herald*, November 9, 2006; and David Hawley, "Rain Dampens Anti-War Protest: Student Walkout Is Second in Six Months," *St. Paul Pioneer Press*, April 29, 2006.

20. Associated Press, "Md. High Schoolers Suspended after Protest," April 27, 2006; United Press International, "Students Face Expulsion for Protest," November 9, 2007.

21. Tara Bahrampour, "Young U.S. Muslims Strive for Harmony: 9/11 Spurred Action, Helped Define Beliefs," *Washington Post*, September 4, 2006; Jennifer Gollan, "Marin Teenagers Say 'No Way' to Uncle Sam," *Marin Independent Journal*, November 27, 2005.

22. "How to Help Kids Feel Safe in Unsettled Times," *Parenting* 15, no.10 (2001/02): 76.

23. "Students Show Spirit, Resolve in Sept. 11th Ceremonies," *South Bend Tribune*, September 12, 2002.

24. Amanda Cochran, "How to Talk to Your Kids About 9/11," *CBS News*, September 10, 2011, http://www.cbsnews.com/8301-504744_162-20103884-10391703/how-to-talk-to-your-kids -about-9-11/; 9/11 Memorial, "Talking to Your Children About 9/11," 911memorial.org. n.d., http://www.911memorial.org/sites/all/files/TalkingToChildren_FINAL4.pdf.

25. Michael Dobbs, "Schools and Military Face Off: Privacy Rights Clash with Required Release of Student Information," *Washington Post*, June 19, 2005.

26. *Portland Press Herald*, "Guard's Seventh Grade Program Draws Heat," September 25, 2006; Jennifer Wederkind, "The Children's Crusade: Military Programs Move into Middle Schools to Hunt for Future Soldiers," *Washington Post*, June 12, 2005.

27. Tom Mooney, "Luring Reluctant Recruits," *Providence Journal*, June 20, 2005; Kelly, "Parent-Trap Snares Recruiters"; and Damien Cave, "San Antonio Proudly Lines Up behind the Military Recruiter," *New York Times*, October 7, 2005. See also Kathleen Lucadamo, "Army of Recruiters Target Hallways: Prefer Large Schools With So-So Students," *New York Daily News*, March 5, 2006; Dogen Hannah, "Bay Area Enlisting Can Be a Battle," *Contra Costa Times*, March 16, 2008.

28. Margaret Reist, "Teacher's Departure Prompts Debate," *Lincoln Journal Star*, May 13, 2007; Associated Press, "District Says Film Can Be Shown in Class," December 7, 2004.

29. Marla Jo Fisher, "Fourth 'R': Restrictions: Districts Have Rules about What Can Be Shown in Class," *Orange County Register*, May 15, 2004; Associated Press, "Mount Airy Teacher Suspended for Watching Berg Video in Classroom," May 20, 2004; Hugh Aynesworth, "School Suspends Teachers for Video: Students Shown Berg's Beheading," *Washington Times*, May 21, 2004; Associated Press, "Fort Worth Teachers Who Showed Beheading Will Keep Jobs," May 20, 2004; Associated Press, "Second North Platte Teacher Suspended for Showing Berg Video," May 20, 2004; Associated Press, "Teachers Who Showed Beheadings Will Keep Jobs," May 21, 2004; Tawnell D. Hobbs, "More Teachers in Trouble for Showing Berg Images to Students," *Dallas Morning News*, May 23, 2004; Associated Press, "Second North Platte Teacher Suspended for Showing Berg Video," May 20, 2004; Associated Press, "Another Arkansas Teacher Suspended over Beheading Pictures," May 23, 2004; Heather Clark, "Former Rio Rancho Teacher Settles Lawsuit with District for $205,000," Associated Press, August 2, 2004; and "Teacher Wins Lawsuit on Use of Iraq Prison Photos in Class," *Education Week*, September 8, 2004, 2.

30. Associated Press, "Teacher Allowed Distribution of Anti-Islam Materials in High School Class, Activists Say," February 22, 2007; Jennifer Gollan, "Anti-War Veterans to Discuss Stories at High Schools," *Marin Independent Journal*, February 27, 2006, http://www.marinij .com/marin/ci_3551690.

31. Jared Janes, "Mercedes Soldier Killed in Afghanistan Had a 'Passion' to Serve," *Monitor*, May 6, 2013, http://www.themonitor.com/news/local/article_16ea0f00-b68c-11e2-9448-0019 bb30f31a.html.

PART I EXPERIENCES AND ATTITUDES OF THE 9/11 GENERATIONS

1 · *STARSHIP TROOPERS,* SCHOOL SHOOTINGS, AND SEPTEMBER 11

Changing Generational Consciousnesses and Twenty-First-Century Youth

HOLLY SWYERS

In 2011, as the tenth anniversary of the terrorist attacks of September 11 loomed, one question frequently repeated in US media was how to talk to children about the events of that day in 2001. The media conversation was couched in a tone of near surprise; as one blogger observed: "A story on my local NPR station this morning reminded me of something I'd not yet really been aware of: kids up to 8th grade don't really remember 9/11."[1] The discovery that "for most students, the memories will primarily be secondhand stories. To them, 9/11 is history," prompted much reflection on media exposure, changes in US culture, and sudden awareness of how quickly an event can become history.[2] Should people shield their children from the inevitable replay of the images of jetliners plowing into the twin towers of the World Trade Center? For children in their teens, would the images trigger forgotten traumas? As Brodsky Schur commented in an article by *Scientific American* writer, Katherine Harmon, "Even now . . . seeing footage of the Twin Towers in flames . . . children might wonder: 'Is this happening now? All over again?'"[3]

I watched this discussion unfold in the media as a college professor teaching a first-year seminar on social memory. Unsurprisingly, when assigned to develop a final project on an event that produced social memory, one group of students elected to research 9/11. As they presented their project in December, I confess to my own sudden awareness of history. My students chose to focus on their own generation's social memory of 9/11. Using their own memories as a starting point, they described common motifs of confusion around what they thought was a movie trailer that kept playing, unexpectedly shortened school days, and most poignantly, the vivid memories of their parents crying. The students explained that they realized that "a shocking event that we could not fully grasp and comprehend happened." What meaning did they ascribe to the events ten years later? They agreed that September 11 was a drastic event that had changed their worlds, but they differed in their interpretations, ranging from "no matter who you are or where you're from, someone doesn't like you and wants to see you fall," to "it was a horrible, horrible, tragic event that was used by the government as the perfect excuse to start a war." They recognized that within their small group, their perspectives varied according to their geographic proximity to Ground Zero in New York City, and that their understandings of what 9/11 meant were shaped by how their later education helped them make sense of the strong yet confused impressions left in their then eight-to-nine-year-old minds.

This set of reactions was jarring to me, in large part because my college teaching career began in the fall of 2001. That fall, in the days after September 11, I was confronted with a very different set of reactions from students, all of whom were around the same age as the students in my then just-concluding dissertation research on American high-school culture. Both my new college students and the high-school students with whom I was working baffled me in an entirely different way than their juniors would in 2011. Rather than seeing a world suddenly full of "haters" of the United States and cynical uses of power, my 2001 students were perplexed by the reactions of adults to the attacks. Many of them reflected with anxiety on what they saw as a xenophobic kind of patriotism inflecting the new "war on terror" unfolding around them. If there was hating going on, by their logic, it was on the part of older Americans connecting acts of terror to all Muslims. With the exception of those from the poorest inner-city areas and isolated rural communities—particularly those with little to no racial integration—the idea of someone being categorizable as "enemy" on the basis of some preexisting trait was generally viewed as abhorrent and beyond comprehension for the young Americans I worked with in the late 1990s and early 2000s.

But why was the idea so incomprehensible? The 1990s were not absent of examples of group hatred that students would have heard about. Both the Bosnian and Rwandan genocides had made headlines in the United States in the mid-1990s. The students had been taught about the Holocaust and the American Jim Crow era. Yet to their minds, it seemed such examples were evidence of "backward" thinking no longer possible in what they saw as the enlightened post–civil rights America in which they grew up. When first confronted by these ideas from my students, I saw them as charmingly naive, although I also saw them as a reason for hope. In the aftermath of September 11, I comforted myself by looking to my students and seeing in them a willingness to think deeply about causes and to think critically about received wisdom. I also fell into the trap of assuming that the views I was hearing from my students reflected a general trend of youth, not realizing until my student presentations in 2011 that what I was witnessing was a particular generational moment produced by a specific convergence of world historical events and American educational goals of the 1990s. I have since concluded that a small slice of Americans, primarily born in the 1980s, represent what Raili Nugin referred to as a "sandwich generation."[4] Fitting neither the media-generated view of Generation X nor of millennials, this subset of Americans could be viewed as existing in an "intermediate zone"[5] between generations. However, as Nugin pointedly asks, "Do we, as researchers, have the capacity to label an age group as a twilight or intermediate generation, if the members of the birth cohort clearly feel they form a separate generation?"[6] I argue that Americans who were between the ages of about fourteen and twenty-three on September 11, 2001, experienced the events of that day through a generationally specific worldview created by the historical conditions, policy decisions, and general cultural milieu in which they were raised. Their experience has been elided by media narratives of American generational dynamics, but closer examination of this cohort can help us think more carefully about the circumstances that create generational self-awareness and the consequences for potential social change.

My method of argument entails a mix of ethnographic vignettes, reviews of changing educational and geopolitical policy in the 1990s, media examples, and historical reflection. Going back over my field notes from 1998 through 2003 and reviewing the work of Karl Mannheim and others, I trace out the way in which Americans born in the 1980s, like the Estonians born in the 1970s that Nugin studied, experienced "rapid changes in socialization patterns and memory,"[7] which leave them distinct from members of the immediately preceding generation (Generation X), but not entirely in tune with the teens coming of age in the 2010s.[8] Will they continue to exist as a "generation in actuality" as described by Karl Mannheim, with a "concrete bond . . . [formed] by their being exposed to the social and intellectual symptoms of a process of dynamic destabilization"?[9] Or has a moment of unique generational consciousness ("entelechy" in Mannheim's conceptualization) been swallowed up by social change proceeding at "too greatly accelerated a tempo," leading to "destruction of embryo entelechies"?[10] There is not yet enough historical distance to say, but I contend that for Americans coming of age in the few years to either side of 2001, the war of their generation was experienced in distinctly different ways than it was by other Americans. This difference is one with generative potential, producing not just different ways of seeing events, but also a range of potential responses and long-term decision making that could, if allowed to foment, produce novel solutions to the challenges of the twenty-first century. However, the potential for unique and possibly impasse-breaking insight can as easily be subsumed in our cultural rush to generalize about young Americans of the twenty-first century, leaving a substantial portion of that population feeling misunderstood and voiceless. If for only this reason, the social forces producing generational consciousness deserve our attention against the facile idea that arbitrary twenty-year spans distinguish one generational from another.

SEPTEMBER 11

To begin to grasp the distinctiveness of the generational mindset I have encountered, it is best to start from my field notes in the immediate aftermath of 9/11. On September 14, 2001, I was sitting in the library of the high school where I had been doing fieldwork for a year and a half. There were perhaps ten of us gathered around a round table, talking in hushed tones but with great intensity. It had taken us forty minutes of careful conversation, veiled questions, and hinted perspectives to get to what we all wanted to talk about: the events of September 11. The students gathered around were a study of urban diversity. They included immigrants from Eastern Europe, South Asia, and Mexico, as well as American-born Latinos and African Americans. At least two of the students had close family members who had been working in the World Trade Center on September 11, all of whom had fortunately survived the attack and subsequent building collapse. The students were shocked and scared, as were many people throughout the United States. For the immigrant students, the shock and fear were almost more palpable than that expressed by the American-born teens at the table. There were obvious causes for concern regarding potential changes in Immigration and Naturalization Service policies, but their worries ran to something even deeper. This particular set of immigrant students had consciously embraced the "American Dream"—one had even been instrumental in persuading her parents to immigrate to the United States. The symbolic value of the attacks of September 11 was not lost at all on them: had they pinned their hopes on an idea and ideal that might have been destroyed?

They also, however, had quickly discovered that there was little space in school or in their neighborhoods to talk about what had happened. Only three days after the World Trade Center collapsed, they had figured out that there were limits to the ways they could express their worries. They could be shocked, yes. They could be confused. They could fear for their lives. They could not, however, be "unpatriotic." They could not ask how the events of September 11 might have been a response to American foreign policy. They could not be too vocal about their fear and disappointment at the surge in racist and anti-Islamic rhetoric. They could ask if the United States had been irrevocably changed, but they could not question whether that change was for the better.

The students spent a half hour sounding me out before they began to tell me these things, this despite the fact that many of them had known me for long enough to predict my reaction. Most conversations would start around the personal dimensions of the tragedy, generally accompanied with a sense of relief that the hurdle of starting the discussion was over. With few exceptions, however, the tension would begin building almost immediately as the students broached some variant of three questions: Why did it happen? What's the government doing? And what did I think about it? These questions were almost always preceded by decreasing eye contact and more guarded scrutiny of my face. The uneasiness from that point continued in each conversation until I made any comment that expressed my concern for potential ethnic persecution or my interest in making sure we were sure of the who and why of the attacks before the United States reacted.

Once I had made such a comment, the floodgates would open, and the young people began pouring out concerns about racial/ethnic profiling, mischaracterizations of Islam, their fears that striking back would only escalate other nations' hatreds of Americans, their concern that we might dishonor America's place as an international role model if we reacted the wrong way. Similar ideas show up in their peers' reflections on 9/11. A survey conducted by Patricia Somers at the University of Texas-Austin of students at five universities who had been in high school at the time of 9/11 revealed that 45 percent of students reported feeling a "direct reaction of anger toward the U.S. government and the media" in response to 9/11.[11] One blogger, an undergraduate at Columbia University in 2001, wrote, "Days after the attack, the *Village Voice* put out a cover showing the second plane hitting the towers, under the headline, '*THE BASTARDS!*' I remember a friend angrily objecting that this was irresponsible, that it would foment anti-Muslim feeling."[12]

When this discussion about negative American reactions emerged in a one-on-one setting, I found I could scarcely get a word in edgewise. In small group settings, students talked almost over one another, building on each other's points, and when in a semipublic place (i.e., the school library), the conversation at this point would draw in more students. While the teens I talked to expressed a belief that the people who were responsible for the acts needed to be found and punished, they also wanted to make sure we discovered what grievance was so great that it would prompt someone to die and kill for it. If we could understand and resolve the grievance, they thought, we would prevent future attacks. The nuance of their arguments and their willingness to see multiple sides of the story defy contemporary readings of so-called millennials as entitled, self-centered narcissists.[13] Their engagement in debates beyond those perceived as "allowed" also defies earlier descriptions of 1990s youth as characterized by "apathy, alienation, and disaffection."[14]

Some of their comments seemed cavalier. One high-school student I talked to opined: "The best way to deal with these things is get back to normal as fast as possible; you can't know when they're going to happen." Lest this response be read too much as a reflection of George W. Bush's frequently lampooned (and ultimately apocryphally attributed)[15] suggestion that we should all go shopping to avert economic catastrophe after the September 11 attacks, such comments were couched in larger conversations about the need to get down to the business of conflict resolution. Such resolution, the teens and young adults of 2001 pointed out, was impossible when emotions were still running high, and many of them expressed to me that it was the US government's responsibility to discover why the parties responsible for the attacks felt so aggrieved that they had to take such violent action. Violence, to their minds, was a response to provocation even if such provocation were unwittingly offered—an idea I will explore in more depth later in this chapter.

These responses show a critical difference between these young people and either the Gen Xers that preceded them or the millennials that followed them. I, a Gen Xer, found my 2001 informants' emphasis on discovering the source of provocation en route to conflict resolution to be a confusing response. Like most people my age and older in the immediate aftermath of September 11, I was struck by the Cold War-esque turn of public discourse. I recognized the tropes and turns of phrase, the ease with which "communist" could be replaced by "terrorist" in all the rhetoric from my own teenage years. Like Elaine Tyler May, I felt that "the terrorists seemed to have brought into reality national nightmares that dated back more than half a century . . . the villains seemed to personify the characteristics of the Communist threat."[16] From my own understanding of history at the time, I saw that the United States was reentering a time of having a national enemy. I had been eighteen when the Berlin Wall fell and twenty-one when the Soviet Union collapsed. While I had marveled before that my young informants treated these world-changing events in my lifetime as ancient history, I had not quite realized that their life experience did not include the idea of a "national enemy." Communists to them had been defeated long ago and were never a credible threat in their lifetimes; they could not so easily swap "terrorist" into the space "communist" had held in the United States' national imagination, and "terrorist" entered their vocabularies too late to seem self-evident as a category. The idea of a named security threat was novel in their lived American experience in a way it could not be if they had been born a few years earlier or later, and many of them seemed to feel it as a point of generational tension. The point was driven home forcefully in the months and years after September 11, but it was visible far before then.

STARSHIP TROOPERS

I was teaching high-school enrichment classes in the summer of 1998 when I got my first taste of how different the world was for children born in the 1980s. The students were still drifting into my classroom when I decided to ask them what they thought about the movie *Starship Troopers*,[17] released the previous summer.

The movie had been marketed toward a teen audience, and my suspicion was that it had missed the mark with kids, but I was curious to hear what they had to say. I was not surprised that almost all the students had seen it, nor was I entirely surprised that they gave it at best mixed reviews. When I expressed that I "kinda liked it" and asked them to explain what was bad about it, a student explained, "It was just too incredible, y' know." This assertion was met by general agreement.

Intrigued, I pressed the point. I wondered if it was an issue of it being science fiction, or of the future world presented by the film, or of the ways the characters were making decisions. As I speculated aloud, the students shook their heads and explained that while some of the things I mentioned were pushing the envelope of credibility, that really wasn't it. Finally a student in the back raised his hand and said, "You know that scene with the kids? You know, and the cockroaches?"

I thought for a minute, then nodded. The scene in question is fairly fleeting in the film, a piece of stereotypical war-propaganda footage of a type that frames the entire movie. In the clip, people are exhorted to "do their part" in the war as a video rolls of children on a playground viciously stomping on bugs (the war in the movie is between humans and bug-like aliens). "You mean of them stomping on the bugs?" I asked by way of confirmation.

"Yeah," the student replied. "That was the bit that did it for me. I mean, I just can't believe people could hate something like that."

The issue, as I discovered with further probing, was that the students were deeply troubled by the idea that the insects in the clip were being destroyed for the explicit reason that they had some physical semblance to the actual enemy being fought. It was clear that the bugs being squished were "just ordinary bugs, y' know. They didn't have anything to do with it [the war]," and yet the media/government in the movie was effectively telling people to go out of their way to kill the bugs anyway. "People just aren't like that," one student contributed. "You don't just hate people for something someone else did."

While not explicitly mentioning it, the student's comment clearly was critiquing what he saw as a phenomenon parallel to racial profiling. His expressed dismay matches pre-9/11 American attitudes reported by Leti Volpp, who noted, "Before September 11, national polls showed such overwhelming opposition to racial profiling that both U.S. Attorney General John Ashcroft and President George W. Bush felt compelled to condemn the practice. There was a strong belief that racial profiling was inefficient, ineffective, and unfair."[18] Clearly, the student recognized the unfairness, but the idea that people not only should not, but simply *did* not think that way in his world was surprising.

The moment, obviously, stuck with me. The class was exclusively white, primarily middle class, and drawn from a large town in the heart of a Great Lakes state almost two hours from any urban center. The students were a mixed group, some struggling to pass classes, others straight-A students who were taking my summer enrichment course to get an edge in future classes. As we worked through the day's lesson (ironically on World War II), the theme of persecution on the grounds of similarity to a sworn enemy returned. The students still regarded it as not only morally outrageous, but as almost *unthinkable*. Punishment for one's own actions was well within the students' purview, but to punish someone for an at best tenuous connection to some wrongdoing, it seemed, was not.

This is not to suggest that the students in my class were innocent of cliquishness and casual slights based on their group orientations. However, the notion of a national enemy—of a whole people defined as an enemy—struck them as utterly foreign. Ideologically, at least, for this group of students, enemies spoke only for themselves and could not be dealt with by blanket attacks on their "type." The question is, how did this ideology come about? How could they so blithely dismiss a view of the world that I, only ten or twelve years their senior, had been raised within and recognized as part of the American conception of reality?

As a starting point, the students who objected so strongly to *Starship Troopers* were all born in the early 1980s, in the twilight of the Cold War. Most of them knew that Reagan had been president when they were born and were vaguely able to identify his political party (strikingly, given the political polarization that characterized the latter part of the 2000s, they generally seemed bewildered by the notion that party affiliation had any real meaning). The oldest among them was nine when the Berlin Wall fell; the youngest was six. They were old enough to remember the Gulf War, which they universally described as "that war about oil." They made no mention of Kuwait or the politics of national sovereignty that justified the war at the time. Notably, all of them entered junior high after the start of the Clinton presidency; "it's the economy, stupid"[19] was likely the first political catchphrase they were old enough to remember. At the time they were in class with me (1998), the largest threats they saw to the United States were internal, characterized to a greater or lesser degree by Waco, the Unabomber, and the Murrah Building bombing. They also worried about the economy, a concern made real to them by the autoworkers strike in full swing and felt locally during the time that I was teaching them.

These historical realities are significant, as Max Weber has pointed out: "The stream of immeasurable events flows unendingly toward eternity. The cultural problems which move men form themselves ever anew and in different colors, and the boundaries of that area in the infinite stream of concrete events which acquires meaning and significance for us, i.e., which becomes an 'historical individual,' are constantly subject to change."[20] In other words, the things which human beings pick out as important and world shaping are conditioned by their own experiences within the world, limited to some degree by what a person experiences as concretely real. While the Cold War is definitely a historical event that has effects upon the students whom I taught, to them the effects were not apparent and that epoch, in the very present-centered world of an American high schooler, was as a remote a piece of history as the Industrial Revolution or the defeat of the Spanish Armada. It was impossible for them to imagine that the fall of the Berlin Wall meant more than the obvious truth that communism was a failed experiment, if they even connected that much importance to it. They saw that event *through the eyes of an established historical narrative* with the end already obvious and predetermined, rather than having lived it as a moment of triumph and as a destabilization of a long-standing mode of understanding world affairs.

But what sense did they make of this narrative? Eviatur Zerubavel offers a useful way of thinking about this question: "I believe that the historical meaning of events basically lies in the way they are situated in our minds vis-à-vis other events. Indeed, it is their structural position within such *historical scenarios* (as 'watersheds,' 'catalysts,' 'final straws') that leads us to remember past events as we do. This is how we come to regard the foundation of the State of Israel, for example, as a 'response' to the Holocaust, and the Gulf War as a belated 'reaction' to the U.S. debacle in Vietnam."[21] When events occur before we are old enough to be conscious of them, the story is effectively already written and to imagine that there was a time when the outcome of any historical event was in doubt requires a conscious effort of imagination quite different from that of memory. While young people born after 1980 might revisit the significance of the Cold War in shaping the present world, they will never be able to know how they themselves would have reacted had they lived through the events of that time. They will not be able to imagine how participating in the events of the Cold War could shape how their elders think. Instead, they will see the fixed ideas of their parents and grandparents and will be unable to grasp the dynamic process through which those ideas emerged. They will be left resentful of the charge of naïveté leveled against them when they critique what they perceive as outdated thinking. Here we see a manifestation of a generation gap.

It may seem unduly facile to focus on the fact that the young people of any given era are experiencing history differently than their older counterparts. However, it becomes an important consideration when the question before us is one of how a culture/society produces generations with distinct identities. As Mannheim notes, "While the older people may still be combating something in themselves or in the external world in such fashion that all their feelings and efforts and even their concepts and categories of thought are determined by that adversary, for the younger people this adversary may be simply nonexistent: their primary orientation is an entirely different one."[22] He goes on to observe, "The possibility of really questioning and reflecting on things only emerges . . . around about the age of 17. . . . It is only then that life's problems begin to be located in a 'present' and are experienced as such."[23] The students I was teaching, just shy of seventeen, were no less Americans for having at best dim memories of the Cold

War. Their reticence to buy into ideas of "national enemies" had become part of what it is to "be American," as we shall see. In fact, during the late 1990s and 2000s, I was increasingly encountering in high schools and colleges a tendency that at one time would have been categorized as profoundly *un*American—an active curiosity and quest for information about communism. The term that had denoted "the enemy" to my generation and the one before me, the one that I had so easily supplanted with "terrorism," was clearly already understood very differently by them. They had been coached to understand themselves as products of a new era, freed from the prejudices of the past. To see those prejudices return in the War on Terror could not fit their historical narratives to that point.

The importance of the end of the Cold War for Americans was captured by George H. W. Bush in his 1990 State of the Union address. As he announced: "Nineteen forty-five provided the common frame of reference, the compass points of the postwar era we've relied upon to understand ourselves. And that was our world, until now. The events of the year just ended, the Revolution of '89, have been a chain reaction, changes so striking that it marks the beginning of a new era in the world's affairs."[24] In light of this "new era," Bush directed the nation to focus its energies on education (both at home and abroad)—a striking contrast to the previous year's State of the Union address, in which the United States was exhorted to stand unified before the world and "stay strong to protect the peace."[25] Rather than confronting the world with a "reluctant fist,"[26] Bush told the American story of the impending decade as one where "America stands at the center of a widening circle of freedom—today, tomorrow, and into the next century."[27]

One might argue that the words of a president do not make the attitudes of a nation, but from the presidential addresses of the 1990s, we can get a feel for the kind of sea change that was occurring in the United States at the time. The narratives suggested by the State of Union addresses fit a larger national narrative, a restructuring of world understandings to fit new historical conditions. The emphasis on American unity in the face of a national threat was played down in favor of a previously existing idea of pluralism. The image of America as the embattled freedom fighter underwent a dramatic shift—now the United States was learning to see itself as benevolent leader to the world. By 1992, with the Soviet Union in collapse, President Bush was describing this new world order: "A world once divided into two armed camps now recognizes one sole and preeminent power, the United States of America. And they regard this with no dread. For the world trusts us with power, and the world is right. They trust us to be fair and restrained. They trust us to be on the side of decency. They trust us to do what's right."[28]

The emphasis on trust and fairness was not one limited to American's relationship to the world. It was also directed purposefully toward the education of America's youth. In contrast to the previous decade's concern with the "Nation at Risk" from an education system failing to keep pace with world standards, the rhetoric around education in the 1990s became much more about fairness, pluralism, and equal opportunity in "the kindest nation on Earth".[29] With the change of the federal administration in 1993, Bill Clinton formalized the nature of this "kindest nation" into a call for community: "I challenge a new generation of young Americans to a season of service: to act on your idealism by helping troubled children, keeping company with those in need, reconnecting our torn communities. . . . In serving, we recognize a simple but powerful truth: We need each other, and we must care for one another."[30]

From these excerpts from the State of the Union addresses we can see a shift in the historical narrative of the United States toward the ideas I found so naive among my students in 1998. The philosophies of pluralism and community had been present during the Cold War, but they had been subsumed under the over-riding worldview of democracy/capitalism[31] versus communism. As this latter basis for organizing American knowledge was rendered obsolete (at least in perception), notions of fairness in absolute leadership surfaced to replace the old model of keeping the "world safe for democracy."[32] Domestic policy and foreign policy became curiously intermingled ("There is no longer a clear division between what is foreign and what is domestic"[33]) as a new "role model" sensibility became predominant in American rhetoric. Education became a site for simultaneously inculcating a revised vision of a future in a no longer embattled free world *and* for "setting the American house in order" as an exemplar for other nations.

The turn toward education in a time of national uncertainty is a common pattern within the United States and arguably within any nation-state. An effort to instill the values viewed as crucial for coping with an uncertain future in the "crowd of starlings and protoplasmic creaturely potential"[34] who will take up the mantle of power in that future accompanies nearly every dramatic challenge to the existing worldview. For example, we see a decided effort to "fix" education in the aftermath of both world wars during the twentieth century. Interestingly, the mood of reform efforts of post–Cold War America tend to parallel those after World War I more closely than those of the early Cold War years. After the fall of the USSR, the idea that the "day of conquest and aggrandizement is gone by"[35] seemed more real than at any previous point and was reinforced by an increasing sense of globalism. By 1999, the kinds of battles being waged for world peace and prosperity—in the American context—were a struggle for the future in the form of education. Then-Chicago Public Schools CEO Paul Vallas, in a March 1999 meeting with University of Chicago students that I taught, put it bluntly: "World War III is happening in your generation, and it is a war to fix education." The rootedness of this attitude by the last year of the 1990s is worth noting; Vallas's remarks came a scant six weeks before the notion of schools as a battlefield took on a literal dimension in Littleton, Colorado, and the way the reactions played out over time showed strongly the peace-keeping, conflict resolution orientation that characterized the last decade of the twentieth century.

SCHOOL SHOOTINGS

On April 20, 1999, the midday news was dominated by the story of a hostage crisis with shots fired at Columbine High School in Littleton, Colorado.[36] By the end of the day, Americans were still reeling from the story of massacre that had come out of white middle-class America, a place where, it was thought, people just didn't go around senselessly killing each other. As the details unfolded about the shootings, the story became one of alienated teens, of broad-based revenge against stereotyped groups (as opposed to previous narratives of school violence based on personally motivated revenge), of untempered rage against an established order. Dozens of potential causes for the shootings were fingered in their aftermath: video games, violent media, inattentive parents, casual school attitudes toward certain types of bullying, easy access to firearms, Internet sites for bomb building. For all this, though, as Erika Doss points out, the larger media focus was on the grief rather than the causes of the shootings: "the lack of analysis accorded the most often repeated lament expressed by Columbine's mourners—'I don't understand why this happened'—suggests the mostly superficial nature of mass media's 'coverage' of grief."[37] The consequence of this focus was the emergence of what Marita Sturken calls a "narrative of innocence" that "helped to perpetuate the myth that American society is not violent."[38] These observations help explain how the events of Columbine did not work to derail the "new era" rhetoric we saw in the previous section; rather, Columbine and its aftermath helped cement ideas regarding the dangers of racial profiling and anxieties about the consequences of terrorism for individual self-expression that I saw from young people in response to 9/11.

The focus of school-related stories in US media experienced a sudden shift away from questions of school success to those of school safety, a trend reinforced when the one-month anniversary of the Columbine shootings was marked by an apparent copycat crime in at a school in Conyers, Georgia. The question of the United States as a global role model was suddenly translated into one of American role modeling for American children. A stunned educational system, unified only by parental and student fears, geared itself up to prevent repeat occurrences. Metal detectors, long commonplace in inner-city high schools, became standard fixtures in supposedly "safer" suburban schools. Sophisticated video systems were installed in some well-off schools, and search and seizure became routine. Suspicious behavior was more stringently monitored, and zero-tolerance policies enjoyed renewed popularity. Meanwhile, the adult world saw an increase in attempted legislation to regulate popular media and political pressure to reduce violence in entertainment, as well as the passage of more stringent gun-control laws. Parents and teachers were entreated to monitor their own behavior more closely, to be aware of what messages they were sending children regarding the kinds of reactions appropriate to frustrating situations.

Not surprisingly, many of the measures and much of the advice given in the days and weeks following Columbine and Conyers began to meet resistance as life settled back to normal. Many teenagers found themselves unjustly coming under suspicion or questioned for their taste in music or clothing, and during the early 2000s, students in my college classes often told stories of Columbine-related targeting they had encountered while in high school. While few had stories this extreme, one example posted to a public forum on CNN captures the way many zero-tolerance and related surveillance policies were experienced on the ground by some high-school students:

> I have nothing that can be said to compare to what the students and faculty experienced that dark day on April 20, 1999. What I can say is what I experienced in the aftermath of the media frenzy. I lived three states away, wore all black and kept to myself. I was in high school at the time. I was already getting bullied all the time by the students, and even the teachers. . . . An incident happened when my car was broken into and stereo stolen out of my car, when I called the police, the officer that showed up refused to file a report, called me names, said I was the next Columbine, and all I could do was stand there and cry, as he mocked me more and more.[39]

Witnessing experiences like this likely changed the way my 1998 students viewed the possibility of profiling happening in the United States, but it is equally likely that such experiences hardened their distaste for profiling practices, helping explain the strength of some of their specific reactions to 9/11.

In the fall of 1999, several months after Columbine, zero-tolerance policies drew fire in the media after the controversial suspension of six Decatur, Illinois, high-school students. The local response to a bleacher fight at a high-school football game made Decatur the center of a media storm, complete with protest marches and national news coverage. The beleaguered Decatur school board sought desperately to justify their effort to ensure the safety of their students. Despite their attempts, they were portrayed in the media as the perpetrators of general injustice and of discipline run amok. In framing his objections to the expulsions, Rev. Jesse Jackson said: "The byproduct of discipline should be of some educational value. You reprimand them . . . and you redeem, and let them go on with their lives."[40] By implication, Decatur had failed in this task.

In light of the events surrounding the situation in Decatur, some of the more quietly advocated responses to the problem of school violence moved center stage. By the first anniversary of the Columbine shooting, conflict-resolution programs and community involvement, already quietly at work throughout the

1990s and temporarily displaced by zero-tolerance, had become the central components of school-safety reform. Plans regarding disciplinary responses to crimes already committed or planned were supplanted by preventive-education efforts. In a press release announcing government grants supporting such prevention-oriented programs in April of 2000, then secretary of education Richard Riley pointed out: "We know from experience that a comprehensive communitywide and schoolwide approach works best to promote healthy child development and reduce school violence and drug use. The safety and well-being of our children can be enhanced through the work of partnerships that bring together schools, families and community organizations and offer a broad-based preventive approach to violence and drug use."[41]

The unfolding of public reaction and policy decision making in the months and years after the Columbine shootings is noteworthy on several fronts. The first is the shift from the immediate "bunker mentality" following the attacks to the more systematic approaches to finding root causes for outbreaks of violence. For children in school during this time, this progress was not only watched, but felt. As much as the apparent escalation in school violence[42] had alarmed American parents and put them on alert, students tended to be savvy to the causes of such violence and regarded the disruptions to their routines with varying degrees of frustration or approval. A Discovery Channel/TIME Magazine poll,[43] conducted in the early months of 2000 and discussed in more detail below, revealed sharp disagreements in perception of school violence, its causes, and its solutions between parents and students. Children of high-school age at this time were rough contemporaries of the students I had taught a year and a half before, the ones who had—prior even to the Columbine shooting—demonstrated a marked disapproval of stereotyping and violence toward nonaggressive parties.

At the time of the 2000 poll, nearly eight years of citizenship pedagogy geared toward the creation of global, pluralistic citizens was showing its effects. In addition to a focus on conflict resolution at the local level, children coming of age in the 1990s grew accustomed to seeing US military power deployed for "peacekeeping" reasons.[44] Students were being presented with a world where both ethno-national conflict and individual profiling were increasingly distasteful and often presented as morally wrong. At home and in the international arena, or so young people were taught, Americans had learned peaceful, tolerant multiculturalism was a noble goal that US policy and culture could enforce. The exuberant triumphalism that came in the wake of the Cold War led to an air of paternalism in the explanations of these overseas conflicts, and schools helped promote the idea of enlightened development from the "bad old days." Young people, lacking a frame of reference that included the sharp divisions of the Cold War and drilled in the lessons of the civil rights movement, took this sentiment to heart and internalized it.

The Discovery/TIME poll shows this internalization as generational difference between student and parent responses to poll questions. The very definition of violence elicited generational distinction. As the poll reported:

- Two of three teenagers (66%) define verbal insults or threats as violence compared to only one-third (35%) of parents.
- (39%) of teens are more likely than parents (24%) to believe that even if you are defending yourself in response to being hit, this is still considered violence.[45]

While opinion polls have their own limitations in revealing prevailing sentiments, these reactions correspond to my own field notes and research over the course of the period from 1998 to 2003. Students generally regarded violence as a nonconstructive response to a situation, ultimately leading to more violence. While some violent actions were more forgivable than others in their worldview, the kinds of lack of respect and empathy that allowed for violence in the first place (lack of respect was the top cause of violence cited by teens in the poll) were widely decried and seen as the product of "ignorance." During my fieldwork, I often saw students attacked as "ignorant" by their peers when they stereotyped anyone, and I repeatedly met with the idea that only a person lacking in education could be a "hater."[46]

With this context, it is less surprising that the reactions of younger Americans to the aftermath of September 11 were at variance with those of their older counterparts. In fact, in many ways, the aftermath of Columbine gave adolescents a framework for understanding September 11 that their parents could not possess. Unlike the adult experience of April 20, 1999, students were struck by a powerful blow to their sense of personal safety. The shootings in Littleton provided students with a microcosmic prelude to the strike against the United States. The events had similar qualities—sudden, tragic interruptions of daily life that seemed to come out of the blue. Whereas September 11 managed to shake nearly all Americans with a sense that no place was safe, Columbine had already impressed students with the idea that no *school* was safe. Since schools are very much the place where students are supposed to be, their sense of personal security—on a concrete level—was as affected by Columbine as by September 11. For many of the students I worked with, the national reactions to the shootings and the aftermath in many ways served as a template for what they thought they could expect in the weeks and months after 9/11. They were surprised and disappointed when the older adults around them demonstrated that they had failed "learn the lessons" of Columbine. Neither they nor the adults around them were in a position to recognize that when the phrase "the American way of life" was used in the aftermath of 9/11, it meant something very different to the generation coming of age than it did to their elders. Nor could either group anticipate that the emergent, post-9/11 "American way of life" would shape the reality of younger children, a theme I will return to later in this chapter.

WAR PROTESTS

I have proposed that in the immediate aftermath of 9/11, young people responded in ways that reflected their experience of what it meant to be American *sans* any living memory of the Cold War. I contend that as time went on the Americans born in the 1980s became increasingly conscious of their unique generational viewpoint. Eighteen months after 9/11, on April 5, 2003, I was once again in the field with high-school students. This time the setting was not a school library but the plaza outside the federal building in downtown Chicago. I was there at the behest of a group of students from a Chicago suburb who were involved in one of the large protest marches against the war in Iraq organized by the Campus Antiwar Network.[47] The young African American woman who had invited me to join the protest had grown increasingly frustrated with the US government's War on Terrorism. Her high-school research on the civil rights movement had motivated her to try to *do* something about the way she felt that the United States had changed, and she was not only leading the group from her high school, but she had been chosen to speak at the rally before the protest march. The content of her speech was striking, as she asked: "Will we rest our hate, when we can prove that no ethnicity has gone unhated, has gone unrepressed, has not been impoverished or dehumanized? And even then, will we continue until that hate has been equally distributed? Will we continue our destruction, creating weapons, until the only thing left to destroy is ourselves?" Her words reflected the image I had developed of young people in the post-9/11 moment: sensitive, multiculturally aware, resistant to hate mongering, shaped in large part by a youth spent during the relative peace and prosperity of the 1990s.

The speech she gave on April 5 is worth more examination, as it offers both an illustration of the kinds of things I was hearing from young people who remained in correspondence with me from my fieldwork and from my college students, and it demonstrates some of the nascent generational consciousness I saw within them. For example, the young speaker couched her arguments in an explicitly generational frame: "Do not let this be yet another generation after which the next generation will say, 'we will learn from their mistakes.' . . . Having learned from the generations before us, the time for action is now! Being unwilling to learn from our past dooms us to repeat it. This is our chance." Her words echo similar sentiments expressed in the 1962 "Port Huron Statement of the Students for a Democratic Society": "Our work is guided by the sense that we may be the last generation in the experiment with living. . . . As students, for a democratic society, we are committed to stimulating this kind of social movement, this kind of vision and program is campus and community across the country. If we appear to seek the unattainable, it has been said, then let it be known that we do so to avoid the unimaginable."[48] The parallel between these two statements, issued forty years apart, is the sense of generational self-awareness, a potential "participation in the common destiny of this historical and social unit" that Mannheim argues as necessary to the production of a "generation in actuality."[49] While a cynic might argue that there will always be young people in the United States ready to protest against what the powers-that-be are doing, I contend that closer examination shows something historically contingent and specific that unites my vocal protestors with the hesitant students in the library of an inner-city high school.

We can find hints of this generationally specific spirit later in the protest speech: "In a nation of immigrants, I find it interesting that so many of us feel that it is just to look down on other immigrants. I find it interesting that certain ethnic groups would feel they have the right to claim that they are better, smarter, richer or less of a 'threat' than others, even after each of these ethnic groups have been hated, despised and looked upon with disgust at some point in the past." The rhetoric presented in this speech undoubtedly sounds familiar; it is borrowed from two themes I've already identified as prominent in high-school classrooms throughout the United States in the 1990s and early 2000s: global pluralism and conflict resolution.

The student protestors, like their peers, were raised to *believe* what George H. W. Bush and later Bill Clinton argued—that the United States, having established itself as the world's preeminent superpower, had a *responsibility* to the rest of the world. Having established that freedom and equality, the virtues of liberal democracy, must be the organizing principles of the world, the United States needed to protect and/or nurture freedom and equality for other peoples. No child—of any race, creed, or color—should be left behind. That this message would take on a different valence in US school reform[50] was not yet visible to them, nor could they anticipate that children not much younger than them would read a very different lesson from a world that was characterized by the constant risk of attack.

The principles of multicultural understanding and global cooperation, drilled into high-school students through messages about global pluralism in the years leading up to September 11, helped establish for teenagers a paradigm for global affairs that, for many of them, made the war on Iraq seem literally un-American. The sentiment was reinforced by the effects of their post-Columbine lives, which highlighted the risk of doing harm in the name of being safe. Throughout the 1990s and up until the events of September 11, 2001, the American educational system was gearing itself toward producing a new type of citizen—an empathetic, global citizen. While this effort was not uniformly applied or successful, many of the messages about cultural relativity, human rights, and interpersonal tolerance made an impression. Unlike their elders, who came of age in the Cold War with a firm understanding of what it means to have a national enemy, the young people protesting in 2003 were having difficulty conceiving of an aggressive United States as anything other than a bully. At best they might find a military action punitive yet deserved; for them, the obvious unrivalled power of the United States gave the nation a potential for global tyranny that we as its citizens must be prepared to check. As one college student told a reporter during the March 5, 2003, protests in New York: "We kind of felt like making a statement on war," said Hudson, a Stuyvesant sophomore. "I think it's amazing that so many people from throughout the city have come here to take a stand against the war. This war is unjust and immoral. I think we are doing it just because we want to get their oil."[51] This critique sounds in some ways like one of the comments of my 2011 college students referenced at the beginning of this chapter, that 9/11 was used as an excuse to start a war. What is notably different is that the student in 2003 does not show the same sense of historical inevitability of the war, nor does he tie it to justice for 9/11 in the way my current students do.

I bring us back to my current college students, those born in the 1990s, to highlight the ways in which their response to the world post-9/11 does not accord with those born in the 1980s. Their consciousness, as children coming of age during the War on Terror, is tempered in many ways like mine was as a child of the Cold War, in full awareness of an ongoing national threat. The Americans coming of age now have been subject to new arguments about global dynamics, and the version of cultural pluralism they received has been tempered by security concerns. They do not know the version of America where young people only a few years older than they grew up expecting to be the vanguard in a new era of peace. As noted above, Mannheim claimed that generational consciousness tends to develop when a cohort is around seventeen years of age. Mannheim's claim has been supported by later research by Howard Schuman and Jacqueline Scott, who discovered that specific world and political events were most likely to be remembered as particularly significant "by those in a narrow age band of teens to middle 20s when each occurred."[52]

It is perhaps the problem of where the memory of 9/11 falls into the life course that has made the so-called millennials so difficult to puzzle out. Are they ironic[53] or sincere?[54] Are they self-obsessed narcissists[55] or family-engaged social activists?[56] Barbara Misztal argues, "Generational habitus, which is the foundation of generational memory, and therefore identity, can be seen as a system of practice-generating schemes rooted in the uniqueness of the sociohistorical location of a particular generation."[57] In other words, how the cohort of Americans born in the 1980s lead their lives will be crucially shaped by the ways in which they experienced, talked about, and reacted to 9/11. That shared memory of disillusionment with adult responses to life-changing events, characteristic of many of them, will guide how they respond to things in their future. In a similar way, children born in the 1990s will share a memory of "a shocking event that we could not fully grasp"—and children born in the 2000s will not remember 9/11 at all. Research on millennials has flattened these clear age-based distinctions, defining the generation as "those born after 1980—the first generation to come of age in the new millennium."[58]

The 1980s birth cohort may retain something of their distinctiveness as they continue to age, and this may assert itself as they rise into positions of power and influence in their forties. However, the persistent failure of mass media and popular culture to recognize and validate their experience of September 11 may erode any consciousness of themselves as distinct from the larger body of millennials. From my experiences with them in the late 1990s and the early 2000s, the war of their generation was configured completely differently than that which many of the rest of us—both younger and older—could possibly have experienced. Free from the idea of national enemies, they were able to imagine different responses to 9/11 than those made by American pundits and political leaders. If the United States had been able to deploy on the world stage the tools we had taught American children and teens during the 1990s, perhaps the War on Terror would not have been a war at all. Alas, it seems that the state of war following 9/11 is a war of my and my elders' generations and, save for a small and relatively invisible cohort, we are making it the war of our children's generations.

NOTES

1. Meghan Murphy-Gill, "How Do You Teach Kids About 9/11?," *U.S. Catholic*, http://www .uscatholic.org/blog/2011/09/how-do-you-teach-kids-about-911. See also John Farley, "How to Teach 9/11 to Those Too Young to Remember It?," *Thirteen: WNET New York Public Media*, August 24, 2011, http://www.thirteen.org/metrofocus/2011/08/how-do-you-teach-911-to -those-too-young-to-remember-it/.

2. Pamela R. Moran and Ira D. Socol, "Why September 11, 2001 Must Be in Our Classrooms," *New York Times*, August 29, 2011, http://learning.blogs.nytimes.com/2011/08/29/teaching -911-why-how/.

3. Katherine Harmon, "How Young Children Learn about Terrorism and 9/11," *LiveScience*, September 11, 2011, http://www.livescience.com/15993-children-terrorism-9-11.html.

4. Raili Nugin, "Social Time as the Basis of Generational Consciousness," *Trames: Journal of the Humanities and the Social Sciences* 14, no. 4 (2010): 361–362.

5. Ibid., 361.

6. Ibid., 362.

7. Ibid.

8. Generation X (Gen X) presents its own set of problems as a small cohort that gained generational consciousness largely through media representations. The disappearance of Gen X from a national conversation focused on Baby Boomers and millennials has not appeared to affect the generational self-awareness of members of Gen X, but a thorough examination of the case of Gen X and its implications for the "sandwich generation" described here is

outside the scope of this chapter. For more on Generation X, see Sherry Ortner, "Generation X: Anthropology in a Media-Saturated World," *Cultural Anthropology* 13, no. 3 (1998): 414–440.

9. Karl Mannheim, "The Problem of Generations," *Psychoanalytic Review* 57, no. 3 (1972): 395.

10. Ibid., 402.

11. Kay Randall, "Generation 9/11," University of Texas at Austin Office of Public Affairs, September 12, 2005, http://www.utexas.edu/features/2005/generation/.

12. E.G. "The Response from the Young," *The Economist*, September 11, 2011, http://www .economist.com/blogs/democracyinamerica/2011/09/remembering-911-0.

13. Jean M. Twenge, *Generation Me*, (New York: The Free Press, 2006).

14. James E. Côté and Anton L. Allhar, *Generation on Hold: Coming of Age in the Late Twentieth Century*, (Toronto: Stoddart Publishing Co. Limited, 1994), 130.

15. Tom Murse. "Did President Bush Really Tell Americans to 'Go Shopping' after 9/11?" About.com, September 14, 2010, http://usgovinfo.about.com/od/thepresidentandcabinet/ a/did-bush-say-go-shopping-after-911.htm. Note that the White House did encourage consumerism as part of an idea of preserving the "American way of life." More on this can be found in Marita Sturken, *Tourists of History: Memory, Kitsch and Consumerism from Oklahoma City to Ground Zero* (Durham, NC: Duke University Press, 2007), 58–92.

16. Elaine Tyler May, "Echoes of the Cold War: The Aftermath of September 11 at Home," in *September 11 in History: A Watershed Moment?*, ed. M. L. Dudziak (Durham, NC: Duke University Press, 2003), 42.

17. Edward Neumeier, *Starship Troopers*, DVD, directed by Paul Verhoeven (Culver City, CA: TriStar Pictures, 1997).

18. Leti Volpp, "The Citizen and the Terrorist," *UCLA Law Review* 49 (2002): 1576.

19. This phrase was famously used by Clinton campaign strategists in 1992 and was frequently repeated and riffed upon throughout the 1990s and into the 2000s.

20. Max Weber, "'Objectivity' in the Social Sciences," in *The Methodology of the Social Sciences*, ed. and trans. E. A. Shils and H. A. Finch (New York: The Free Press, 1949), 84.

21. Eviatur Zerubavel, *Time Maps: Collective Memory and the Shape of the Past* (Chicago: The University of Chicago Press, 2003), 12.

22. Mannheim, "The Problem of Generations," 390.

23. Ibid., 391.

24. George H. W. Bush, *Public Papers of Presidents of the United States: George Bush, Book 1 (Jan 20–Jun 30, 1990)* (Washington, DC: U.S. Government Printing Office, 1991), 130.

25. George H. W. Bush, *Public Papers of the Presidents of the United States: George Bush, Book 1 (Jan 20–Jun 3, 1989)* (Washington, DC: U.S. Government Printing Office, 1990), 3.

26. Ibid.

27. Bush, *Public Papers, (Jan 20–Jun 3, 1989),* 130.

28. George H. W. Bush, *Public Papers of the Presidents of the United States: George Bush, Book 1 (Jan 1–Jul 31, 1992)* (Washington, DC: U.S. Government Printing Office, 1993), 157.

29. Ibid., 163.

30. William J. Clinton, *Public Papers of the Presidents of the United States: William J. Clinton, Book 1 (Jan 20–Jul 31, 1993)* (Washington, DC: U.S. Government Printing Office, 1994), 2.

31. The conflation of democracy and capitalism during the Cold War has its own peculiarities and consequences and it is not clear that the idea of free markets and free government have been disaggregated in American imaginations.

32. Woodrow Wilson, "Making the World 'Safe for Democracy,'" *History Matters*, http:// historymatters.gmu.edu/d/4943/.

33. Clinton, *Public Papers*, 2.

34. Michael Taussig, *The Magic of the State* (New York: Routledge, 1997), 14.

35. Woodrow Wilson, "President Wilson's Fourteen Points," The World War I Document Archive, http://wwi.lib.byu.edu/index.php/President_Wilson's_Fourteen_Points.

36. At the writing of this chapter in 2013, the number and severity of school shootings appeared to be on the rise. The responses to these more recent shootings have their own character, and I make no claims about how they might be interpreted by children or others living through them. The Columbine events referred to here, however, occupied a clear position in the minds of students who had been in high school or middle school at the time and figured into their understands of September 11.

37. Erika Doss, *Memorial Mania: Public Feeling in America,* (Chicago: University of Chicago, 2010), 79.

38. Sturken, *Tourists of History,* 16.

39. MessyR, "My Own Columbine Hell," *CNN iReport Assignment: After Columbine,* July 20, 2012, http://ireport.cnn.com/docs/DOC-817964.

40. Valerie Wells, "Community Urged to 'Redeem' Troubled Children," *Herald Review Online* (Decatur, Illinois), November 4, 1999, http://web.archive.org/web/2000051618075,/http://herald-review.com/04/bfast1104–9.html.

41. United States Department of Education, "President Clinton Announces More than $41 Million in Community Grants to Prevent Violence Among Youth," April 15, 2000, http://www.ojp.usdoj.gov/archives/pressreleases/2000/ojp000415.html.

42. The escalation was only apparent. A Justice Policy Institute report compiled data on school crime from 1998 to 1999 and discovered that school-associated violent deaths decreased 40 percent over that time. Jessica Portner, "School Violence Down, Report Says, But Worry High." *Education Week,* April 12, 2000, 3.

43. Discovery Channel/*TIME Magazine,* "Poll on Youth Violence," Discovery Channel, April 2000, http://web.archive.org/web/20001006220849/http://www.discovery.com/stories/history/hateviolence/pollindex.html.

44. At least in terms of publicly stated goals.

45. Discovery Channel/*TIME Magazine,* "Poll on Youth Violence,"

46. The concept of a "hater" as I've encountered it in schools reflects an idea that envy manifests as hate.

47. More information about the Campus Antiwar Network can be found here: http://www.grassrootspeace.org/campus_antiwar_2.html. Details about the Chicago protest can be found here: http://grassrootspeace.org/can05apri103.html.

48. Students for a Democratic Society, "Port Huron Statement," 1962, http://coursesa.matrix.msu.edu/~hst306/documents/huron.html.

49. Mannheim, "The Problem of Generations," 394.

50. Michael W. Apple, "Ideological Success, Educational Failure?: On the Politics of No Child Left Behind," *Journal of Teacher Education* 58, no 2 (2007): 108–116.

51. Bill Vann, "New York City: Thousands of High School Students Walk Out to Protest Iraq War," *World Socialist Web Site,* March 6, 2003, http://www.wsws.org/en/articles/2003/03/nyc-m06.html.

52. Howard Schuman and Jacqueline Scott, "Generations and Collective Memories," *American Sociological Review* 54, no. 3 (June 1989): 367.

53. Christy Wampole, "How to Live without Irony," *New York Times,* November 17, 2012, http://opinionator.blogs.nytimes.com/2012/11/17/how-to-live-without-irony/.

54. Jonathan D. Fitzgerald, "Sincerity, Not Irony, Is Our Age's Ethos," *Atlantic,* November 20, 2012, http://www.theatlantic.com/entertainment/archive/2012/11/sincerity-not-irony-is-our-ages-ethos/265466/.

55. Twenge, *Generation Me.*
56. Pew Research Center, "Millennials: Confident. Connected. Open to Change," *Pew Research Social and Demographic Trends,* February 24, 2010, http://www.pewsocialtrends.org/2010/02/24/millennials-confident-connected-open-to-change/.
57. Barbara A. Misztal, *Theories of Social Remembering* (Philadelphia: Open University Press, 2003), 90.
58. Pew Research Center, "Millennials."

2 · SUMMER, SOLDIERS, FLAGS, AND MEMORIALS

How US Children Learn Nation-Linked Militarism from Holidays

CINDY DELL CLARK

Education scholar William Damon described a conversation with a friend who as a young man had emigrated from Europe to America. Damon asked his friend when in his life he had become American.[1] His friend replied that he felt American when, over a decade after his US arrival, he made a trip back to Europe. The trip set in relief for him the old ways he had left behind and the new ways in which he had become transformed into an American. For children too, the process of becoming American becomes manifest by situated reflection. Recent views of development show learning to be exuberantly complex, encompassing processes that are embodied and emplaced within a highly dynamic world, a world that learners configure using their own perceptual lenses. Humans engage with, participate in, and perceive salient environmental features, actions, habitus, and ideologies using a constellation of processes that are subject to fluidity. These processes include sensory perception used for dynamic "sensation construction," such that the senses are entwined with cognitive and cultural construction.[2] Because learning is embodied and dynamic, its study requires an analytical focus that permits a view of how discursive and sensory processes unfold within specific observable contexts.

Political socialization of the youngest Americans, of course, is touched by the flux of history, which raises intriguing issues regarding the particular experience of children in the post-9/11 generation. These children grew up in an era when American vulnerability to terrorism and the national War on Terror were foregone conditions. The study reported here uncovered that in this context, children learned early the cultural idea of militarism as a means to sustaining

American liberty, an idea that was conveyed on a visceral, sensory level through summer patriotic rituals of the era. Admittedly, the concretized iconography of soldiers, flags, and memorial rites did not start with the War on Terror. Children in prior generations were similarly ushered into the ranks of the American citizenry via ritual and totem, especially totemic uses of the flag.[3] But because children in the twenty-first century experienced America's rituals and symbols at a time when expressions of gratitude for the sacrifices made by soldiers in Iraq and Afghanistan were resonant in everyday discourse and media, these children were likely to be especially steeped in the human basis behind the symbols. Arguably, there is no better cohort for studying how nascent ideas of national belonging tie to America's root metaphor; that is, that a nation of free citizens (symbolized by the flag) endures and is sacralized through courageous sacrifice. This is the metaphor of the national anthem, and one learned early, I argue, not through language or explicit teaching but through apprehension of the mythopoetic sensoria of ritual.

This chapter reports on an ethnographic investigation of how children instantiate national meanings, observed in settings of celebration on Memorial Day and Independence Day (Fourth of July) from 2005 to 2012. The study was conducted among families living in and around Philadelphia. Methods included extensive participant observation in neighborhoods diverse in social class and ethnicity, at parades, memorial services, fireworks displays, and other public community rituals and events. Additionally, the study was bookended in the years 2005 and 2012 by twenty-two in-home informant interviews with a diverse sample of children aged six to twelve and their separately interviewed mothers or fathers.[4] The informant interviews incorporated methods known to be effective in studying children's firsthand experiences within culture, including drawing, sorting of pictures of patriotic icons related to US ritual practices, role play, and photoelicitation.[5] Photoelicitation refers to giving an informant (in this case a child) a camera to use to take snapshots of an experience; the developed photos are in turn used to "show and tell" about the experience during an in-person interview.[6] By using instant photography, children were able to take pictures of holiday experiences and have them available for an interview conducted by the author during the days immediately following each holiday. Photoelicitation supports the goal of child relevance within inquiry; the discussion is child framed based on what each young informant chooses to photograph, even as the pictures serve as visual prompts to aid the child's verbal explanation.

Community and family-based rites of American celebration on Memorial Day and the Fourth of July make up an opportune nexus for studying how children instantiate national meanings and learn nation-linked values. To be sure, research on political socialization in recent decades has had a leaning toward studying school or organizationally based socialization of political and civic values.[7] Yet the contemporary American cycle of holidays situates the most prominent nation-linked festivals in the summer, when school and after-school programs are not in session. Before a child enters kindergarten in the United States, she has already become steeped in expressive, symbolic experience linked to national meanings during the high season of patriotic celebration. This may be especially true over the post-9/11 years of this research, when both Memorial Day and Fourth of July festivities were saturated with patriotic symbols and symbolic support for the military, concurrent with ongoing American military action in Afghanistan and Iraq. Adults often assume school to be the ultimate site where civic learning takes place, but there is an adultist bias in the assumption that children passively learn what adults intend to teach when and where adults intend to teach it. Ritual, as anthropologists know well, is a universal imparter of values and meanings for humans regardless of age, communicating through mythopoetics rather than top-down directives or didactics.[8] The renowned anthropologist Victor Turner observed that ritual symbols "make visible, audible, and tangible beliefs, ideas, values, sentiments, and psychological dispositions that cannot directly be perceived."[9] Children and adults discern and cultivate deep-seated cultural notions by means of seeing, hearing, and touching the concrete tropes, artifacts, and practices of ritual. If the senses are a way to embody social categories, ritual spectacle employs a lush, value-laden, affectively laced feast for such embodiment.[10] Sensoria derived from pageantry and ritual, one might say, impart ideas and values to celebrants by rendering abstract meaning palpable and real through action and symbol.

Ritual is socially shared, and by definition, repeats its form over time or place. Fireworks I observed in one neighborhood of Philadelphia followed an underlying routine of praxis that bore marked similarity to other neighborhoods, regardless of ethnicity. Memorial Day parades in the most affluent community studied were more elaborate and expensive than in the poorest community, but there were marked consistencies: both included fire engines and other vehicles, veterans from a span of generations, and a ubiquitous presence of youth and children such as scouts, sports teams, and school marching bands. In an affluent suburb on a typical Memorial Day, candy was thrown to watching children by varied groups of parade participants, while others handed out flags for children in the audience to wave. In a starkly impoverished location not far away, parade marchers distributed lesser amounts of candy perhaps, yet at the same time a local church group distributed a toy to each child along the parade route. Both affluent and less-privileged children eagerly grabbed at the goodies sent their way. Regardless of social class, candy is perceived cross generationally as a fun treat linked to frivolity and indulgence rather than serious nourishment. Ritual draws on and reveals overriding meanings, while cutting across other social divisions.

Parades, picnics, fireworks, and such memorial tributes as gun salutes or cannon firings are not nationally mandated on national holidays but reflect the local organizing efforts of civic or community groups.[11] Yet without being centrally brokered, these rituals bring a predictable echo of concurrent, patterned expressive and symbolic activity, attended in person or watched on television. Families take initiative, as well, to celebrate these holidays surrounded by kin or fictive kin in a manner highly patterned; family gatherings are held out of doors, in open air, and with ubiquitous outdoor barbecues or picnics—a pattern that holds overall regardless of ethnicity or class.

The study reported here aims to unpack how children experience the semiotic elements within this socially shared, dynamic ritual activity and how children contribute to the meaning making of ritual in interaction with adults. Specifically, the study helps to glean the culturally situated *process* by which young children learn to link militarism with national freedom, a process that has interesting features. First, children learn early, even preverbally, through ritualized metaphors and symbols of nation. Second, children are themselves active participants who impact adults by their participation, rather than passive internalizers of explicit and unidirectional adult instruction. Third, expressive and emotional aspects, including fear and awe, convey an epistemological tone of essentialist, unquestioned, constitutive authority to the values learned.

Quantitative investigations of political socialization conducted during the mid-twentieth century identified that symbolic icons such as the American flag are elemental in priming early notions of national affiliation.[12] In some ways, this research takes up where such studies decades ago left off, exploring in situ how concretized symbolization in the context of ritual is fundamental to how children instantiate national themes, including themes related to memorialization.

MEMORIAL DAY

From its post–Civil War inception, Decoration Day—or as it is now called, Memorial Day—actively involved children in the commemoration of war heroism and sacrifice. James Redpath, an influential northern abolitionist, engaged the children of freed slaves to decorate the graves of Union soldiers in Charleston, South Carolina, in May 1865.[13] Decoration of graves tended historically to be done through localized, vernacular events, including family gatherings in which children were included. The day took on a broader meaning over time, expanding to include subsequent US-involved wars. Children continued to be part of the commemoration into the twentieth century. A 1953 account that described how a Springhill, Kentucky, family gathered to clean a family gravesite and place flowers on it went on to mention that after the commemoration children were "let loose to play in the graveyard."[14] During my eastern Pennsylvania fieldwork in the early twenty-first century, children were mainstays of public Memorial Day parades and commemorations. They were also in active attendance at private family-based gatherings that included picnics outdoors. Such picnics were planned with opportunities for children to play, swim, or visit the beach as part of the activity. Public swimming pools in this region, it might be noted, predictably open for the summer season starting on Memorial Day. In general, Memorial Day is regarded by Americans as a temporal beacon announcing summer, timed close to the end of the school year; few times are more symbolically liberating as far as children are concerned than their regained freedom of summer, away from the strictures of formal education. The start of a sun-kissed season when "you get to go outside and play instead of [staying] inside" adds to a sense of regained liberty, my informants in both generations reported.

Children, whether playing or swimming outdoors, attending a picnic, or marching in or watching a parade, made contributions to the ritualized portions of Memorial Day. Children served as witnesses at memorializing ceremonies, and some helped to place flags on soldiers' cemetery gravesites. Parading children stepped in time with vets in parades or rode on parade floats to honor combat veterans. When in the audience, kids waved flags as parading vets passed. By such acts, the young contributed actively to the systematic symbolism of memorialization. Adult informants said that they regarded children as a justifying rationale for what was being honored on Memorial Day. At more than one Memorial Day parade, I overheard adults who instructed kids to stand and applaud the passing vets. Kids stood up as flag-bearing honor guards of veterans walked by. Kids joined in when an assembled crowd stood and warmly applauded Vietnam-era vets. A single mother, employed as a Philadelphia police officer, explained that having children of one's own brings into focus the national values she took for granted, and in the process she hoped that children were grateful, through ritual remembrance, for the rights they too had.

Additionally, children impacted adults on Memorial Day in a way that could be read between the lines of adult reactions. Children's inclusion in Memorial Day events struck a note of visible pleasure for adults nearby, as if to set a positive tone or mood within the ritual, despite the day's memorializing intent. Children are generally regarded in the American cultural context as quintessentially innocent in a way that is diametrically opposed to the traumatic realities of war participation. The sight of children alongside soldiers and veterans on parade or placing flags on the graves of deceased veterans had an effect of making the very topic of war more approachable, less solemn, and more innocent by association. Thus, while adults consciously perceived children as beneficiaries of militarism, the young also served implicitly to make militarism more palatable to their elders by their invited, front-row participation at memorializing rites. Despite the solemn purpose of the day, many adults described Memorial Day in positive, upbeat terms. A mother who attended a picnic where the children went swimming, played outdoors, and danced ("like at a disco for kids") said the day was happy and relaxed given that "everyone was off of work, sitting back, laughing, while the kids are playing." Memorial Day, she surmised, initiates "fun season . . . the kids are out of school, they're free."

It is difficult to convey the nature of *children's* engagement on Memorial Day without emphasizing their sensorimotor involvement. Children see, hear, and have hands-on interaction through concrete symbolization during ritual. They *hear* and react to twenty-one-gun salutes or cannon firings. The *sight* and colors of the American flag are an ever-present visual screen, repeated in omnipresent decorations, even on cakes and cookies. By helping to adorn the home with flags and flag colors or by waving flags given to them by adults at public events, children know by *touch* that the nation emblemized by the flag is tied to the holiday's purpose. It has been advised that anthropologists should account for the senses within cultural experience.[15] This is especially astute advice when ritual engages youngest cultural members in multisensory spectacle, as it does on Memorial Day, a holiday when the citizenry vividly shows and states (with veterans present) that it valorizes combat service.

It is also worth emphasizing that the sensory experience of America's cycle of patriotic holidays is linked to an embodied sense of being "free." As mentioned, Memorial Day serves as the effective symbolic beginning of summer when pools and beaches open and school is over or nearly out. Play immigrates to the less-encumbering out of doors. Swimming, in particular, is experienced by children with a bodily sense of flowing, free movement, a refreshing haptic experience in which splashing, jumping, diving, and being underwater are all possible. Barbecues, which are explicitly associated with both Memorial Day and the Fourth of July, allow the smell of burning meat (or sweet marshmallows) to waft freely through the open air, prior to eating picnic style. At outdoor celebrations, children are free to run, let go, and make noise—the embodiment and outward display of unrestrained being. Even for those families with a member in military service, the holiday's serious meaning is ironically juxtaposed with a sense of free enjoyment and even joy; the somber intent of the day is concomitant with a show of freedom in the guise of children having fun.

Consider the case of Mrs. Morero, who was born in Puerto Rico and was mother to three kids born in the continental United States. Mrs. Morero celebrated Memorial Day with her extended family, including a teenage cousin who was scheduled to enter the army when summer ended. (Mrs. Morero and other informants' names are pseudonyms.) She also had a nephew who was in the National Guard and had served two years in combat in Iraq. The nephew had just returned home from war, and his homecoming had led relatives to display a bumper crop of flags to honor him on Memorial Day. Mrs. Morero took very seriously that her nephew had been "fighting for his life on behalf of the United States." She saw his willingness to face war and risk death as directly beneficial to the United States. "The country benefits," she said, "because we have freedom and we have a lot more choices. We are safer." In this way Mrs. Morero echoed a national root metaphor linking military sacrifice and freedom by voicing that her nephew's service had made America more secure and more free than would be the case in other countries. "If they don't go [to war]," she reasoned, "we don't have this freedom, the freedom we have here. We would be leading a different life."

Mrs. Morero said that having children play and run freely at the family's Memorial Day gathering contributed to her felt sense of protection and liberty availed by military sacrifice. Her six-year-old daughter, as she put it, "has the freedom to just be happy. She doesn't have to be worrying about [someone saying] you can't go to this part, and you can't be here. She has the freedom to do whatever it is that she wants. . . . She doesn't have to be worrying about bombing or people getting hurt or needing to be inside." Children's unencumbered playfulness composed for Mrs. Morero and others a kind of innocent veneer and deeply felt justification for military action, a redemptive joy in the face of what combat service entails. At Memorial Day, American families remember and appreciate those who died by being thankful and happy and by allowing kids to have unimpeded fun in the liberty of the open air. It is as if each family re-creates a living, enacted trope, that free action ("letting go" amid festivity) is of a piece with military service.

Still, most families did not have a family member on active duty in Afghanistan or Iraq; many had no experience or contact with military service. In many families, Memorial Day was perceived almost entirely as a day off meant for a good time or a day at the seashore. As I sat down with Mrs. Peters, for example, she mainly talked about preparing for and enjoying her holiday, which she referred to as the "seasonal kickoff" of summer. The mood of the day reflected an easy enjoyment. "Everybody is just happy, relaxed, they're off work," she described. "You just sit back, talking and laughing. Kids are playing." Part of the fun of the day to her was watching her children have fun and run around: "They keep goin' and goin'." Mr. and Mrs. Peters set up an above-ground swimming pool and a slip-and-slide water toy for the kids. The neighbors set off fireworks in the street that Memorial Day evening, and the kids watched, at least until the local police came by to stop the illegal display. Describing her family's day at length, Mrs. Peters did not once mention nation-linked ideas. She brought up in passing that the children had "little flags" and that there were red, white, and blue decorations. When I asked her about the colors of the decorations, she commented nonchalantly: "People forget about what everyone did for the country, stuff like that, but they just decorate with the colors and just swim and have fun and just celebrate. . . . I really didn't think of anything, I just relaxed." The military meanings implicit to the phrase "what everyone did for their country" were latent rather than salient for Mrs. Peters. It would seem that the militarism inherent in memorializing rituals resonates at variable and person-dependent, rather than constant, frequencies. Many adults considered the topic of war with detachment, at arm's length, rather than with an explicit sense of personal investment.

This century's so called War on Terror, of course, did not mandate a civilian effort within the United States. There was no rationing, no war bonds, not even increased taxes to concurrently fund the armaments buildup. Not everyone had a direct stake in the fight. Mr. Evans remarked that his granddad served in World War II, but no one else in his family had served since then. He recalled that a teenage son had to register for the draft recently at age eighteen, but he did not personally support a draft for military service: "That should be your God-given right to decide if you want to get up and go fight for your country. You shouldn't be forced to leave your pregnant wife or kids." As a working-class man with a disability, Mr. Evans added that economics might be involved in who did the fighting. "The rich people are still paying the poor people to do their fights for them," he pointed out, recalling how the privileged had served in far fewer numbers than the poor in recent conflicts. Mr. Evans's sense of nation extended to the idea that military sacrifice was constitutive of American freedom, but this was mostly a glossed-over platitude rather than a felt call to action. On some level, he thought Memorial Day was "solemn" and not just a "party day." But he brushed off whether children would be aware of the solemn purpose behind the day off from school and work. "They don't know the meaning when I see them celebrating with sparklers," he surmised.

CHILDREN AND MEMORIAL DAY

Mr. Evans was wrong when he doubted that children sensed the military-linked underpinnings of Memorial Day as they celebrated. Young informants sensed much more than Mr. Evans thought they did, underscoring the point that children actively construct their sense of nation apart from explicit parental intent. At eight years of age, his youngest son Kevin mentioned the tie of Memorial Day to soldiers right at the outset as we sat on the Evanses' living-room floor together to talk. "It's all about the soldiers," he began. "They have to try to survive [or] they die." Kevin Evans was an avid player of the video game, *Call of Duty*. He anticipated that he wanted to join the army when he came of age, inspired by *Call of Duty* and by an acquaintance at the end of his street who had enlisted in the army. On Memorial Day, Kevin confided, he prayed for the soldiers to survive and prayed for them to win the war. Kevin did not gloss over the violent nature of army duty, familiar to him from *Call of Duty*, a game Kevin assumed to be an accurate depiction: "In the army you shoot, kill the bad guys . . . they have people who wear bombs and you kill them, they explode." I asked Kevin to pretend aloud about an imaginary world, an entire world like Memorial Day. For him, such a place was imagined as populated by soldiers and guns. When asked, he was not sure if there were any sparklers in that world, despite having enjoyed the fun and visual spectacle of sharing a neighbor's sparklers on Memorial Day. Kevin's take was predominantly militaristic, despite his own father's speculation to the contrary. Children at a young age and under the right circumstances, Kevin's example shows, develop sympathy and common cause with US soldiers at war, a sort of militaristic affiliation that is, for them, rudimentary to being American.[16] These notions are not questioned as might be the case in reasoned teaching but rather are vividly reified by enacted ritual metaphor or, in Kevin's case, from the enacted narratives of video games as well.

My past work on family rituals at Christmas, Easter, and Halloween has demonstrated that parents often have diverging interpretations of festive celebrations compared to their children's ideas.[17] Parents' conscious attempts to socialize are not necessarily predictive of children's understandings. Memorial Day is such a case. While children's presumed innocence and relaxed playfulness added to parents' redemptive interpretations of Memorial Day as celebrating freedom, children inscribed nation-linked meanings of their own. Flags pervasively decorated both the scene and the color scheme of refreshments, and the relevance of this decorative scheme, even its military relevance, did not go unnoticed by kids as exemplified in one girl's explanation.

[Girl, 9, describing a photo:] This is a cake. It has red white and blue and it has stars because [it is] Memorial Day. We got it so we could eat it at the beach. It's kind of like the flag of the United States of America. Those are like the colors. And the stars are in the corner [of the flag in] a big rectangle, inside of it. And it has fifty stars representing the states that are in the United States. And it has stripes, red and white, coming down. [Interviewer: Why is the United States of America part of Memorial Day?] It's like freedom day. I think it's kinda the freedom that we got from Britain. It's a day that you remember all the people that are in the Navy . . . and the army and stuff. People that fight for our country. . . . They're like fighting for our country and it represents what they are doing.

Although grammar-school aged informants did not always accurately remember the lyrics of the national anthem or the correct words from the pledge of allegiance recited in school, recognition of the flag appeared elemental. The poetics of the national anthem—the sung imagery of the flag that endured in the light of battle—was echoed in children's understandings of the flag on Memorial Day, even if they could not sing or recite accurately the words.[18] A culturally recurring sensory symbol, the flag is a condensed symbol in Victor Turner's sense, representative of a union of opposed poles of meaning by which American *freedom* is invigorated through *sacrificial* acts.[19] The flag is the semiotic vehicle through which sacrifice for country is transduced to and equated with freedom.[20] Discussing a picture of Memorial Day commemorative activities at graveside, a twelve-year-old boy singled out the presence of the flag as emblematic of what was being honored. A person could tell they are honoring the dead, he explained "because of the flag . . . a flag has to do with honoring the dead of America, because without the flag we would not be free." The notion that death and freedom are instantiated within the American flag and that the flag honored soldiers presumed to make freedom possible was not lost on him. An eleven-year-old girl, upon looking at a scene of Memorial Day commemorations in a cemetery, likewise placed her attention on the flags in the scene: "Each grave has a flag, and it's America, and it has crosses on it, and a lot of people that died." I watched many a child on Memorial Day holding or waving a child-sized American flag, props that were often handed to children at public events. Adults, both relatives and strangers, advised toddlers to be careful not to drop the flag or let the flag touch the ground; toddlers took heed of this and held their flags with care, a sign that sacralizing postures toward the flag were not overlooked even by the very young. When children asked family members to pose for portraits, more than one showed the family posed with flags in hand or nearby. A seven-year-old informant, who took a photograph of a US flag hanging where her family celebrated, explained to me its relevance by referring to the flag as the "memorial flag," then correcting herself to call it "our country's flag." The flag was categorized by her as vaguely memorial linked, even as it provided a backdrop for her enjoyment of the day.

Flags and flag decals, of course, stimulate the senses of vision and touch as they are held, waved, saluted, or placed to decorate a home or car. The sensory experience at a young age of handling and seeing the national flag is broadly ritualized, as well as systematically associated with expressive significance. "On Memorial Day we put out flags," a boy who had turned ten had come to understand. "It's Memorial Day because it's praising the loved lost and the veterans, people that are no longer here [they're] in the cemetery." This boy attended a party for Memorial Day at his grandmother's house and had never attended a parade or memorial service in person. But the flag-draped environment in his community had imparted a sense that the flag connects children of the nation with veterans past.

Public displays on Memorial Day had pronounced, demonstrable impact on children in attendance. Past historic studies of American family rituals have indicated that Memorial Day patriotism sometimes has been subdued. A 1975 study of the community known as Middletown (in Indiana) identified minimal public festive attention to Memorial Day. Following the unpopular Vietnam war, Memorial Day had "passed by almost unnoticed by Middletowners," and there was a general lack of interest in civic ceremonies.[21] By contrast, during the recent War on Terror in the early twenty-first century, there have been countless public occasions replete with displays of patriotic sentiment and enacted support for soldiers.[22] To be sure, the children I interviewed at home sometimes had only seen parades or soldier-honoring ceremonies on TV rather than in person. (By contrast, many more children had attended fireworks displays in person, including some held on Memorial Day.) But for children in attendance at public memorializing events, there was demonstrable, largely sensory impact, starting at a young age. It is worth retelling as a case of one town's memorializing rites in which the young participated; the case illustrates how the discourse of ritual—its sensory symbols and narrated central myths—prime children through embodied metaphor to accept military sacrifice as unquestionably tied to the viability of a free American nation.

At a 2007 Memorial Day ceremony steeped in long tradition, held in a town tracing its roots to colonial Pennsylvania, numerous children played in the nearby playground of a public park as an hour-long public ceremony was held in the morning. The ceremony followed a long and elaborate parade, which many children had attended. Numerous children from Cub Scouts to Brownies to students from a local martial-arts school had marched in the parade, which ended at Monument Avenue, so named because it was where memorializing rituals had been held dating back to just after the Civil War. The ceremonial honors were held in the park, where children could be heard playing in a playground nearby. World War II veterans attended and began the ceremony by raising the American flag. A little girl chosen for the honor by the Daughters of the American Revolution led the pledge of allegiance, as a couple of hundred people—including some adults and children dressed in Revolutionary-era garb—held their hands over their hearts to salute the contemporary flag. A senior citizen, who had won a singing competition to earn the privilege, sang the national anthem. Uniformed Boy Scouts were present as well and listened as a local church deacon gave the invocation replete with themes about appreciating the shelter of life in America and honoring past soldiers who, to quote the pastor's phrasing, gave their lives for freedom. A local politician, a former navy admiral who held national elected office, gave a speech about the glories of sacrifice. The audience paid half attention to his tale about a heroic gunner on a World War II navy boat, who continued to engage the enemy even though mortally wounded and surrounded by death. Following the speech, a man from the local Veterans of Foreign Wars chapter read the names of recently deceased veterans, most of them serving in World War II. As a bagpipe band mournfully played "Amazing Grace," I heard a girl ask her father if they could leave. Just then, delegates dressed as colonial-era soldiers fired muskets as ceremonial honors. A female musician, dressed in colonial garb, played taps on what appeared to be a brass bugle. A profound sense of solemnity and silence came over the restless mood of the crowd following the musket firing and playing of taps. My field notes described the scene:

> A woman, dressed in the clothing of Revolutionary times, played Taps on a bugle. The crowd became dramatically silent as she played. One baby fussed, who had also cried during the musket firing, but this only set into relief the total silence of everyone else. Every soul in sight was completely attentive. On the next block, there was a playground that had quieted for a moment when the guns fired, and

now resumed whatever game had been going on. Here, standing on the grass where Taps was played, there was solemn silence. The juxtaposition of the sound of free play with the sounding of the song played at military funerals, Taps, was striking. Here was the paradox of the day, honoring solemn sacrifice on the one hand, while free play was heard in the distance, as kids on the playground carried on as usual. [Field notes, 6/3/2007]

The fussing baby nearby had been startled and cried when the muskets were fired. Young ones distressed at the muskets' noise were common over my years of participant observation at memorials and fireworks. At the memorial event just described, for example, cannons were fired later that day as part of a military "demonstration." My field notes reported on this relatively louder explosion:

The master of ceremonies announced that there would be demonstrations by military enactors. He warned people to stay away from the area and to keep a distance so that "no one will get injured." Perhaps his reminder showed that it was lost on many people that the historic cannons they were about to fire had been real weapons of death. When they fired, the cannons made a loud noise that caused me to mildly startle. Laughter by the crowd, perhaps a way to vent the momentary flinching and tensing at each boom of the cannon, occurred after each shot. Mothers and grandparents covered the ears of children with their bigger hands, and many children covered their own ears in protection from the noise. One young woman, high school aged, walked away as they fired, announcing to her friend "I do not like that." As the firing continued, dads also shielded their own ears. One father had several flags he was carrying for his children, and used them to add a layer of sound protection under his hand as he protected his ears. . . . In a kind of finale, the musket carriers all shot their guns together and then all the cannons shot together. Some children I saw continued to cover their ears many minutes after the firing had stopped, as if in momentary shock. [Field notes, 6/3/2007]

Over my years of Memorial Day fieldwork, I visited numerous locations where ear-splitting ballistics were sounded. Without exception, the noise caused younger boys and girls to flinch, become tense, or cover their ears. At every outdoor fireworks display I attended, I saw babies and tots tense up and cry at the piercing booms—yet adults did not leave the scene but stayed on watching the fireworks while their baby or tot wailed. Eye blinks and startle responses to sudden auditory noise are known to be inborn, ubiquitous, and not under intentional control.[23] Auditory eruptions are such a reliable trigger of the startle response that loud sound is the tried and true stimulus in experiments studying startle, fear, and anxiety.[24] Elevated levels of startle to acoustic disruption, research shows, are symptomatic of those with post-traumatic stress disorder[25] or anxiety disorder.[26] Some Iraq-era vets, their comrades in arms informed me, avoid going to firework shows for that reason. It is notable and significant that children are escorted to fireworks as a kind of captive audience, despite their distress. Not once did I witness an adult who left the fireworks and headed home with their crying infant.

Memorial Day, as experienced by children, delivers unplanned, unintentional sensorial lessons. These lessons carry an embodied sense of freedom (encoded by swimming, picnics, play, and good times with family) juxtaposed with more noxious discharges, which children said sounded like bombs or weapons. Children's presence in ritual activities had the effect on adults of rendering militarism as redemptive, approachable, and even quasi-innocent. At the same time, children were given to imagining and remembering the nation through a paradoxical aesthetic in which the sight of the flag and the onerous sound of explosions dialectically constructed a unity of threat and freedom. Children's senses became attuned to the fearful disruptions, and the children braced themselves. In the process, children were primed to accept that threat and explosions accompany the appreciation of US liberty, a paradox thereby held poetically and unquestioningly. As such, children's senses aided in instantiating a relatively simplistic vision of national viability, that war participation conveys the benefits of free democracy to American citizens. The vision imagined did not extend to the complexities of civic discourse or a mandate for active democratic participation.[27]

Other historical instances of sensoria conveying lasting associations have been documented. Gabriel Moshenska has written about World War II gas masks issued to British children as reifying artifacts central to later memories about the war.[28] Though the masks were never needed, British children were drilled regularly in their use and the need to carry them everywhere during the war. In some training, adults released gas around children to drive home the seriousness of the lesson. The memories of children half a century later were run through with cast-in-time sensory images. "I can still recall the feeling of this monstrous rubber object being strapped on and my face being clammy and the rubber edge fluttered against my cheeks when I blew out," was a typical testimony of a much older person reflecting on a wartime childhood.[29] The fact that adults also recalled fun uses of the gas masks is perhaps not surprising; play often is used as an elevator of mood amid threat.[30] Adults reflecting on their childhood war years recalled how gas masks and the masks' cases became items for play at the time, such as employing the mask as a scary costume when chasing one's sister or other such nonserious uses.

Children actively control and manipulate the material artifacts that fall into their hands. Emotion-laced memories of sensory artifacts carry both benign and noxious sensory traces. For contemporary US children, flag-frosted cakes and cannon firings, roast marshmallows and graves, came to be linked elementally and unquestioningly to values of flag, nation, sacrifice, and freedom. In the company of their family, and in the unencumbered open air of summertime, children in essence associated their personal liberty (to play and live freely) with a kind of vicarious, sacrificial act: the bodily courage necessary to withstand auditory startle. The meanings are poetic, conceived through direct enactment, but aligned with hegemonic national meanings equating military sacrifice and freedom. It is as if children are given a vicarious taste of the courage required by exposure to the sounds of war, which coincides with a sense of liberation and unencumbered action. Kids themselves are living enactments of the ritual's core paradox of sacrifice and liberty.[31]

FOURTH OF JULY

A book series meant for early readers by Creative Teaching Press has volumes treating diverse holidays celebrated in the pluralist United States—from Christmas to Cinco de Mayo. The volume titled *Celebrating Patriotic Holidays* implies that the Fourth of July is the favored American patriotic holiday. "My favorite American holiday comes right in the middle of summer," the text states under an illustration of a boy and his dog, seated leisurely next to a swimming pool. "We have parades and picnics. We celebrate freedom. We watch fireworks at night. We remember that America became a nation in 1776."[32] The celebration of America's birthday, like Memorial Day, is associated with summertime enjoyment and outdoor events including picnics, barbecues, parades, and other civic celebrations. Family-based festivities typified children's Fourth of July observances, with swimming, beach time, or other forms of expansive outdoor play remembered and photographed as part of the day. Just as on Memorial Day, these outdoor celebrations set a tone of, as one mother put it, "being outdoors and free, since that's what we're celebrating." Informal eating of a fire-cooked meal, while kids "sit wherever" and ditch inside table manners, was also similar to that of Memorial Day.

Fireworks, introduced into patriotic celebrations in the United States beginning in the mid-1800s, were more frequent and salient on the Fourth of July than on Memorial Day.[33] Fireworks, with sight and sound designed to be spectacular, made a pronounced sensory impact on children. In interviews, fireworks were among the most highlighted and extensively discussed memory of the Fourth of July.

Even more so than on Memorial Day, the US flag was a ubiquitous sight, decorating homes, refreshments, and public places. Some Fourth of July parades included children who rode on bikes or pulled homemade floats built on wagons, family-decorated in red, white, and blue ribbons, paper, and painted cardboard. At public events of all kinds, children were seen attired in flag colors. Children literally embodied the flag (and by association, the nation) through the hues on their shirts, shorts, and dresses. Even a few dogs were patriotically accessorized with scarves.

After a day of outdoor enjoyment and eating al fresco, it was commonplace for children to be part of the audience for fireworks, either on TV or in person. Fireworks displays were held near a city pier, on the beachside boardwalk, at organized civic events in local high schools or parks, and quite commonly in neighborhoods where pyrotechnic hobbyists launched rockets and displays for a neighborhood audience.

CHILDREN AND THE FOURTH OF JULY

As mentioned, children often began their narrative account of the Fourth of July by talking about fireworks. Fireworks displays are an exciting and lasting memory, and they occur after dark, offering kids a chance to stay up later than usual and to be outside after dark.

A form of consumer-marketed fireworks legally available to children in the area was sparklers. Handheld sparklers were person-sized but packed a combined aesthetic of combustibility and splendor. One young person referred to sparklers as "fireworks you hold in your hand." Once lit, they sparked caution and attraction simultaneously, requiring bravery to handle but paying off with an awesome visual spectacle. Children described how they held tight to the sparklers and made tracings of light. The emboldened drew their names, bright like stars.

Children recounted stories of injuries from sparklers that they heard on TV or from adult conversation. An eleven-year-old boy described a TV wrestler who reenacted a fireworks injury: "They were playing with sparklers [and] he burned his whole entire hand from here [pointing to his forearm]. It was on fire and he was [yelling] 'Get it off! Get it off!'" The same boy also told of a sparkler-related accident during a neighborhood fireworks display. "He tripped over it [on the ground] but he didn't fall. He started screaming." His comments reinforce that the visual splendor is double-edged in children's perceptions, spectacular but risky.[34]

Children often bought or brought chemical light sticks to play with before public fireworks as older family members sat and awaited the official display. Children ran tirelessly over the grass, wielding and twirling their light sticks as they went. As a form of entertainment, children of all social backgrounds were seen to chase after, catch, and release fireflies, too. The visual impact of the play with light sticks and fireflies was impressive, a kind of child-powered, moving light display. The sight seemed an informal opening act for fireworks, as kids' improvisations lit the darkening sky. Once total dark descended, children then settled in with the adults.

At the crack of the first official firework, all eyes—regardless of age—pointed skyward. The only talk that could be heard during the display was sense-involved. "See the silver/gold/red/blue!" "Awe!" "Ooh!" "Wow!" In some places, there was patriotic music playing during the display.

The noise made by fireworks was viscerally startling. Infants, toddlers, and many grade-schoolers showed startle reactions: flinching, shuddering, putting hands over ears, cuddling their parents or older cousins with tense bodies and faces, and bracing themselves for the next round. It is worth reiterating that crying tots were observed at every community fireworks I attended across a broad range of social classes and differing ethnicities. Without exception, families stayed for the duration of the spectacle even if a very young child shuddered and wailed.

According to my school-age informants, fireworks are scary because little kids are still not habituated. The frightening sound, older children said, became easier to withstand as one grew older. By implication, though, the salvos had associations connoting danger and a need for courage. One boy, age seven, explained:

> [Boy, 7:] I hear this loud noise. I used to be, I used to not like fireworks. But this year I didn't hold my ears, well I did once, but then I let them go and I watched all the other fireworks. Two nights ago there was a big storm cloud and it had all lightning in it [as he stood by a window].

Or in another exchange with an eight-year-old boy:

> CDC: What is the good part about fireworks?
> BOY, 8: Nothing happened, just fireworks.
> CDC: What would somebody think happened?
> BOY, 8: A gun shot.

Older children, who had grown more able to "stand" the noise of fireworks, were sympathetic to younger kids' fright.

> [Girl, 12:] We had two 4-year-olds, they're both my cousins. So one of them sat on my lap. . . . So then my little cousin heard the big boom, and [then] he'd go with his mom. . . . Maybe there should be fireworks that don't have any noise.

Whether fireworks were amateur affairs shot off by neighborhood hobbyists or professionally produced at the beach or community park, children consistently experienced fireworks as beautiful and tinged with visceral risk. Just as holding and moving a sparkler was somewhat like painting-with-fire, fireworks engendered paired reactions: shock and awe.

Memories of the spectacle were not suppressed once the display was finished. Children recalled during interviews both the visual dazzle and the deafening salvo of fireworks. A girl told how, during a homemade fireworks display, the sparks from one of the explosions "came right at her." On another occasion, the garbage can used to launch a rocket fell over, which directed the rocket toward the attending child, too close for comfort. Children also overheard cautionary tales about injury and mishap during fireworks from nearby adult conversations, which they retold. When I asked children to draw a picture of a planet where everything was analogous to the Fourth of July, they drew explosive rockets and noisy explosions as if it were part of the climate.

In their explanations, children gave clues that they took the mixture of shock and awe to be a relevant and significant part of ceremonies honoring America. Ceremonial explosions were taken by children as reminiscent of military bombs or gunfire and were said to emit smoke in the same manner as the weapons of war. These sensory associations in effect invoked explosive arms as part of the festivities' meaning. "You're pretty much blowing up a bunch of gunpowder" or "you're kind of setting off a bomb" youngsters' explanations disclosed. To a nine-year-old girl, fireworks sounded like "when we were at war with Britain." A home-schooled seven-year-old boy compared the appearance of a firework that moved about on wheels to a "tank."

The flag, ever-present in hues of red, white, and blue on the Fourth of July, was associated with bellicose themes by children. Writing about adult American beliefs, Carolyn Marvin and David W. Ingle have made a compelling case that America has a civil religion with blood sacrifice at its core. The flag is the central sacred object in the cult,[35] and as such, the flag flown and waved upon both Memorial Day and the Fourth of July 4 is doubly symbolic, of military sacrifice on one hand, and liberty on the other. Flags and flag colors pervaded and framed the places where fireworks occurred; in turn, the sensorial themes of the fireworks were experienced in parallel with the patriotic meanings of the flag. Thus there arose for children a gestalt sense of shock and awe, aligned with the meanings of sacrifice and freedom mediated by the flag.

Fireworks are not the only disquieting-but-awesome experience on display. Another example occurred at every parade I attended on the Fourth of July, or on Memorial Day, courtesy of the local fire department.[36] A recurring part of each parade was a fire engine, often draped in the flag, blaring its loudest siren as it swept down the street. The overwhelming noise consistently startled tots along the parade route, including many who cried or covered their ears. But in keeping with the paradoxical sensory poetics of US patriotic festival, children simultaneously experienced sensations of positive excitement along with anxiety; walking parade participants threw out goodies toward the very kids who were startled and stressed, inviting them to grab and enjoy the treats. As children stood beside the parade, then, their senses of taste, smell, sight, sound, and touch all conspired to create in them a sensory aesthetic blending shock and indulgence, parallel to the sense of shock and awe at fireworks.

To say that America is the land of the free and the home of the brave, as the national anthem asserts, is entirely consistent with the sensoria of patriotic festival on the Fourth of July. Whether fireworks or a parade, children navigated a tableau of red, white, and blue while experiencing charged feelings and sensations combining startle and expansiveness. Young celebrants are, in effect, called on to be both free and brave on patriotic ritual occasions.

DISCUSSION

At patriotic rituals, the US flag (and by association the nation) gets centrally placed within a play of opposed sensoria interpreted by children as both threatening and dazzling. If children had committed to heart and mind the words of the national anthem, they would have recalled how in the song the red glare of rockets and bombs served to give sight to the victorious flag, a trope for the nation's viability through battle. Yet without knowing the song, kids know the theme, for it is consonant with what is embodied and concretized upon holidays. "Memorial Day is a day that you celebrate about the soldiers who died in war," intoned a nine-year-old girl, who sometimes bicycled with friends to a cemetery to visit the grave of her mother's grandfather, who died in combat. I conducted my interview with her in 2005. Seven years later, another nine-year-old told me of her cousin serving in the air force. She speculated, "I think we go to the beach and have barbecues . . . because when you remember someone who's doing all this for you, it makes you smile. When you have someone in the army . . . like my cousin . . . the fun kind of mixes with it."

Blended sensoria, then, effectively usher children into the visceral, militaristic underpinnings of US national identity. Sensory associations prime even the very young to hold, unquestioningly, a deep-seated paradoxical equivalence between traumatic experience and unencumbered freedom. By contrast, any potentialities laid down by sensoria about democratic or civic values are entirely missing. There is nothing in these rituals to symbolize voting or democratic participation. When shown a picture of a voting booth, in fact, very few young interviewees recognized what it was.

The late Sharon Stephens speculated that studying children's relationships to nation is a way to think about a nation from the "inside out," a notion these findings second.[37] Children's early experiences of values rendered in reified, concretized form point to militarism, not voting, as being elemental to US freedom. This may be especially evident in the post-9/11 cohort but likely reveals a larger, general truth about how patriotism is, at root, symbolically mediated.

These findings have important implications that support broadening research-ers' frameworks of how political socialization occurs. Researchers have for too long restricted their focus to learning in schools or formal programs, assuming that children directly internalize adult didactics. (As seen earlier, children do not even recall completely or accurately the Pledge of Allegiance recited daily in school.) The seeds of nation-linked understandings, it would seem, do not sprout simply through adults' conscious socializing efforts. Nation-linked values seem, in profound ways, to be essentially preverbal, learned through embodied, poetic sensoria within ritual. For those concerned with motivating self-giving civic participation among the young, there is an implication that is hard to deny: America's mythopoetics at times of civic ceremony prime the young to make militarism, not democracy, as fundamentally constitutive of a free United States.

Extensive research of children's studies, over recent decades, has established that children are active participants in constructing their notions of nation and self. Based on this study, it seems that hegemonic cultural resources available for self-construction have an impact strikingly early, perhaps long before the onset of conscious explanatory attempts by adults. Ritual's poetics prime children at a deeply sensed level, through sensoria rather than conscious adult teaching. Ritual annually enacts a mission of metaphor with relentless and expressive fervor across the special days of summer. Right before children's eyes, it is made palpable, and takes precedent over reasoning or debate, that militarism makes Americans free.

NOTES

1. William Damon, foreword to *Bridging Cultural and Developmental Approaches to Psychology*, ed. Lene Arnett Jensen (New York: Oxford University Press, 2011), xix.
2. Vaike Fors, Asa Backstrom, and Sarah Pink, "Multisensory Emplaced Learning: Resituating Situated Learning in a Moving World," *Mind, Culture and Activity* 20, no. 2 (2013): 170–183.
3. Carolyn Marvin and David W. Ingle, *Blood Sacrifice and the Nation: Totem Rituals and the American Flag* (Cambridge: Cambridge University Press, 1999).
4. Thanks are due to my undergraduate research assistants, Jason A. Damasco, Iris DeVaughn. Demetrius Tirado, and Sherrie Culbreath. Gratitude also goes to the children and parents who participated.
5. Cindy Dell Clark, *In a Younger Voice: Doing Child-Centered Qualitative Research* (New York: Oxford University Press, 2011).
6. Cindy Dell Clark, "The Autodriven Interview: A Photographic Viewfinder into Children's Experience," *Visual Studies* 14, no. 1 (1999): 39–50; Marisol Clark-Ibanez, "Framing the Social World with Photo-Elicitation Interviews," *American Behavioral Scientist* 47, no. 12 (2004): 1507–1527; and Iris Epstein, et al., "Photo Elicitation Interview (Pei): Using Photos to Elicit Children's Perspectives," *International Journal of Qualitative Methods* 5, no. 3 (2008): 1–11.
7. Debra A. Friedman, "Becoming National: Classroom Language Socialization and Political Identities in the Age of Globalization," *Annual Review of Applied Linguistics* 30 (2010): 193–210.
8. Theodore Jennings, "On Ritual Knowledge," *Journal of Religion* 62, no. 2 (1982): 111–127.

9. Victor Turner, *The Forest of Symbols: Aspects of Ndembu Ritual* (Ithaca: Cornell University Press, 1967), 50.

10. Kathryn Linn Geurts, *Culture and the Senses: Bodily Ways of Knowing in an African Community* (Berkeley: University of California Press, 2002).

11. Matthew Dennis, *Red, White, and Blue Letter Days: An American Calendar* (Ithaca: Cornell University Press, 2005).

12. Robert Hess and Judith Torney-Purta, *The Development of Political Attitudes in Children* (New Brunswick, NJ: Transaction Publishers, 2005).

13. Dennis, *Red, White, and Blue Letter Days*, 221.

14. Jack Santino, *All around the Year: Holidays and Celebrations in American Life* (Champaign: University of Illinois Press, 1995), 119–120.

15. Constance Classen, "Foundations for an Anthropology of the Senses," *International Social Science Journal* 49, no. 153 (1997): 401–412; Sarah Pink, *Doing Sensory Ethnography* (London: Sage Publications, 2009).

16. The video-game industry, in concert with the military establishment, has a pedagogical intent in developing virtual war games for electronic play. See David Leonard, "Unsettling the Military Entertainment Complex: Video Games and a Pedagogy of Peace," *SIMILE* 4, no. 4 (2001): 1–8.

17. Cindy Dell Clark, *Flights of Fancy, Leaps of Faith: Children's Myths in Contemporary America* (Chicago: University of Chicago Press, 1998); Cindy Dell Clark, "Tricks of Festival: Children, Enculturation, and American Halloween," *Ethos* 33, no. 2 (2005): 180–205.

18. The lyrics are "Oh say can you see, by the dawn's early light, What so proudly we hailed at the twilight's last gleaming? / Whose broad stripes and bright stars, 'thro' the perilous fight, O'er the ramparts we watch'd were so gallantly streaming? / And the rockets' red glare and bombs bursting in air, Gave proof through the night that our flag was still there. / O say, does that star-spangled banner yet wave O'er the land of the free and the home of the brave?" (For a history of the anthem, originally written after a surprise American victory in the War of 1812, see Ace Collins, *Song Sung Red White and Blue* [New York: Harper Collins, 2003].)

19. Marvin and Ingle, *Blood Sacrifice and the Nation*.

20. This symbolism is enacted not only at Memorial Day, but also during military funerals. See Judith A. Cohen and Anthony P. Mannarino, "Trauma-Focused CBT for Traumatic Grief in Military Children," *Journal of Contemporary Psychotherapy* 41, no. 4 (2011): 219–227.

21. Theodore Caplow, et al., *Middletown Families: Fifty Years of Change and Continuity* (Minneapolis: University of Minnesota Press, 1982), 225.

22. For example, the flag was extensively displayed in homes, cars, or worn as pins during the post-September 11 period. See Linda J. Stitka, "Patriotism or Nationalism? Understanding Post-September 11, 2001, Flag-Display Behavior," *Journal of Applied Social Psychology* 35, no. 10 (2005): 1995–2011.

23. P. Brown, et al., "New Observations on the Normal Auditory Startle Reflex in Man," *Brain* 114, no. 4 (1991): 1891–1902; Christian Grillon and Johanna Baas. "A Review of the Modulation of the Startle Reflex by Affective States and Its Application in Psychiatry," *Clinical Neurophysiology* 114, no. 9 (2003): 1557–1579.

24. Christian Grillon, et al., "Darkness Facilitates the Acoustic Startle Reflex in Humans," *Biological Psychiatry* 42 (1997): 453–460.

25. Christian Grillon, et al., "Effect of Darkness on Acoustic Startle in Vietnam Veterans with PTSD," *American Journal of Psychiatry* 155 (1998): 812–817.

26. Christian Grillon, Lisa Dierker, and Kathleen Merikangas, "Startle Modulation in Children at Risk for Anxiety Disorders and/or Alcoholism," *Journal of the American Academy of Child and Adolescent Psychiatry* 36, no. 7 (1997): 925–932.

27. Even high schoolers in the United States, research shows, do not generally make a connection between patriotism and civic participation. Only 16 percent agreed that "if you love America, you should notice its problems and work to correct them." High-school students may have adorned themselves in patriotic symbols following 9/11, but their patriotism did not necessarily extend to their own responsibilities in the democratic process. See Joel Westheimer, "Patriotism and Education: An Introduction," *Phi Delta Kappan* 87, no. 8 (1976): 569–572.

28. Gabriel Moshenska, "Gas Masks: Material Culture, Memory and the Senses," *Journal of the Royal Anthropological Institute* 16 (2010): 609–628.

29. Ibid., 618.

30. Cindy Dell Clark, *In Sickness and in Play: Children Coping with Chronic Illness* (New Brunswick: Rutgers University Press, 2003); Cindy Dell Clark, "Therapeutic Advantages of Play," in *Play and Development: Evolutionary, Sociocultural, and Functional Perspectives*, ed. Artin Goncu and Suzanne Gaskins (Mahwah, NJ: Lawrence Earlbaum, 2007), 275–293.

31. In this way, national selfhood is upheld not by rote language, but through affectively laced social membership and personal actions in a familial context. Children's identification through vicarious sacrifice is further discussed in Lisa Silvestri, "Surprise Homecomings and Vicarious Sacrifices," *Media, War & Conflict* 6. no. 2, (2013), 101–115.

32. Joel Kupperstein, *Celebrating Patriotic Holidays* (Huntington Beach, CA: Creative Teaching Press, 1999), 11–13.

33. Diana Karter Appelbaum, *The Glorious Fourth* (New York: Facts on File, 1989); James Cross Giblin, *Fireworks, Picnics and Flags* (New York: Clarion, 1983).

34. Fireworks sold directly to consumers are a common source of injury to child bystanders and child users. From 1990 to 2003, an estimated 85,800 pediatric fireworks injuries were treated in emergency departments of US hospitals. See Rachel Witsaman, R. Dawn Comstock, and Gary Smith, "Pediatric Fireworks–Related Injuries in the United States: 1990–2003," *Pediatrics* 118 (2006): 296–303.

35. Marvin and Ingle, *Blood Sacrifice and the Nation*.

36. Fire engines carried first responders to the World Trade Center on 9/11/01, leading to extensive public honoring of the fireman who lost their lives or served.

37. Sharon Stephens, "Editorial Introduction: Children and Nationalism," *Childhood* 4, no. 1 (1997): 5–17.

3 • FIGHTING WITH RIGHTS AND FORGING ALLIANCES

Youth Politics in the War on Terror

SUNAINA MAIRA

This article is based on an ethnographic study of young people from communities targeted by the United States in its War on Terror and the forging of new political alliances in the post-9/11 era. These coalitions were formed in response to the US invasions of Iraq and Afghanistan, and US foreign policy in South and West Asia, creating new cartographies of political mobilization and affiliation. At a time when the War on Terror shifted its focus to "homegrown terrorism," and Islamophobia and Arabophobia have continued to infuse public debates about Muslim and Arab Americans, Muslim American youth of diverse ethnic and racial backgrounds have been viewed as objects of "radicalization" by fundamentalist and terrorist movements. What does "politics" look like for youth whose politicization is viewed as a potential threat to homeland security and who live with the fear of permanent surveillance in the warfare state? This article explores what it means for young Arab, South Asian, and Afghan Americans to express their dissent to the War on Terror on the terrain of rights, and how permissible and "radical" politics in the so-called 9/11 generation has been regulated.

Focusing on South Asian, Afghan, and Arab American youth in the Silicon Valley and Fremont/Hayward areas of northern California, my research explores how the 9/11 generation has created new coalitions linking Arab, South Asian, and Muslim American communities—including Afghans, Iranians, and Muslims of diverse ethnic and racial backgrounds—and grapples with the possibilities and limitations of rights talk. Arab, South Asian, and Afghan American youth have engaged with an emergent Muslim American politics that is both identity and rights based and defined by the frameworks of "Muslim civil rights" and human rights, in some cases, as well as, ethnic, national, and pan-Islamic identities, orientations that often overlap in these movements. The frame of this post-9/11 politics bridges the national and the transnational: youth from communities targeted in the War on Terror have made linkages to a domestic history and discourse of civil rights and also invoked the notion of human rights to make linkages to the experiences of others elsewhere—in Iraq, Afghanistan, Pakistan, or Palestine. In this essay, I explore the turn toward civil rights after 9/11 as a political strategy and discourse in response to the US-led War on Terror and the ways it enters a political field that regulates "good" and "bad" Muslim American politics. This "new civil rights" movement draws on a US genealogy of civil rights based on race and citizenship, as well as a framework of religious inclusion, drawing on multiculturalism and infusing interfaith alliances. What animates this new activism among youth and what are the limits of the discourse of civil liberties in response to Islamophobia, racial and religious profiling, and state violence? What forms of political subjecthood are produced by and for these youth in the context of the War on Terror?

It is important to note that young people's development of an engagement with rights talk and an awareness of state policies and state violence did not necessarily begin on 9/11. Islamophobia and also, of course, imperial racism have a long history in the United States and so shape the political subjectivities of Muslim, Arab, South Asian, and Afghan Americans throughout their lives.[1] Arab and Muslim Americans have long had to grapple with the domestic ramifications of US foreign policy—including military and political interventions—in West and South Asia and the repression of Arab nationalist and Palestinian movements in the United States.[2] This has led to a relationship to the state and the mainstream public sphere that is necessarily ambivalent and critical, if not oppositional, what Nadine Naber situates in a "diaspora of empire."[3] The post-9/11 period was thus not an exceptional era of political repression in US history nor a rupture marking a completely new politics for Arab and Muslim Americans. Some youth I spoke to were involved in Muslim student associations or antiwar movements while in high school and were engaged with Palestine solidarity or Middle East and global politics well before 2001. The 9/11 generation is enacting continuities as well as discontinuities with the public politics of previous generations of Muslim American activists, who were the founders of organizations such as the Council of American-Islamic Relations (CAIR) and the Muslim American Society. These national organizations have increasingly become involved with the US political sphere and used the framework of "Muslim civil rights" to counter Islamophobia and profiling by the homeland security state. The research illuminates the ways in which South Asian, Asian, and Arab Americans in Silicon Valley are situated in a political field that is marked by the contradictions of liberal racism and liberal multiculturalism and the figure of the "moderate" and "angry" Muslim American, powerful assemblages of ideologies and practices that shape the political engagement of youth.

THE STUDY

This article is based on an ethnographic study exploring post-9/11 political mobilization and coalition building among college-age youth in northern California between 2007 and 2011. It is situated in Silicon Valley and Fremont/Hayward where there are large concentrations of South Asian, Arab, and Afghan Americans and where a new generation of activists has increasingly engaged in antiwar and civil rights movements and in other kinds of progressive alliances.[4] I want to note that not all of the young people in this study were Muslim (there is a large Arab Christian community in the Bay Area, and although I focused on Pakistani and Indian Muslim youth, there is a large Indian Hindu and Sikh population) and those that were from Muslim families had various relationships to Islam as identity and practice; however, all engaged in some form or another with the politics of Islam and Muslim-ness. Silicon Valley is an interesting site for this research because it has an increasingly visible and highly organized Muslim American community, including Arab and South Asian immigrant families as well as Afghan refugees in San Jose and its affluent suburbs as well as the towns of Fremont/Hayward in its hinterland. These communities, which have grown since the 1990s, have established major Muslim institutions such as the Muslim Community Association (MCA) mosque in Santa Clara and Granada Islamic school, which draw a large, ethnically diverse (Sunni) Muslim population from the region, as well as a Shia mosque.

While there are sizeable communities of South Asian and Arab Americans in the larger San Jose area and Afghan Americans in the Fremont/Hayward area (in fact, these adjacent cities in the East Bay host the largest Afghan community outside Afghanistan), there has been barely any research on these groups and none from a comparative perspective. The Arab American community is a diverse one, consisting of Egyptians, Palestinians, Lebanese, Iraqis, and Yemenis, some of whom have lived in northern California for three generations. The South Asian community is generally composed of Pakistani and Indian immigrants who came to the United States after the Immigration Act of 1965 loosened restrictions on Asian immigration, particularly for technically skilled and professional emigrants. South Asian and Arab Americans in this area tend to be upwardly mobile professionals, but there are also middle-class and some lower-middle-class families. The Afghan American community consists largely of refugees who are less affluent and who came in two waves: one wave after the Soviet invasion of Afghanistan in 1979 and the other wave after the rise of the Taliban in the 1990s. The college-age youth who I interviewed in Silicon Valley were generally the children of Arab, Indian, and Pakistani immigrants who had come to the United States in the 1960s and 1970s, mostly as graduate students or technical workers, and of Afghan refugees from Afghanistan or Pakistan.

South Asian, Afghan, and Arab American youth in this area grow up in racially and ethnically diverse areas but are from communities that have largely not engaged in cross-racial alliances with other minoritized groups, because of fissures of class and race. The much-vaunted ethnic and national diversity in Silicon Valley, created by high-tech capitalism as employers lobbied for H-1B visas to "import skilled labor from India, China, Canada, the Philippines, Taiwan, Korea, Japan, the UK, Pakistan, and Russia," has been riven by class and racial divisions created in part by the recruitment of different forms of labor for the aggressively expanding industry.[5] The contradictions between the idealized narratives of liberal "tolerance" and self-reinvention in Silicon Valley and the realities of the conservative political culture in this hypercapitalist region—and of anti-Muslim, anti-Asian, and anti-Arab racism—need to be situated in the history of the production of Silicon Valley as a space emblematic of technological "progress" and cultural heterogeneity.[6] Since 9/11, young South Asian, Afghan, and Arab Americans have begun to organize with other youth of color, including Latinos, Asian Americans, and, to a lesser extent, African Americans. These youth attend the same high schools and, in the case of Muslim youth, sometimes the same Islamic schools, and so the politics of cross-ethnic coalition building are interesting to examine in a region where liberal multiculturalism is constantly invoked as a celebratory, and often self-congratulatory, image.

The intensified (re)codification of the racialization of Muslim-ness, and Arabness, has generated new forms of solidarity and new coalitional categories since 9/11. Labels such as Arab, Muslim, and South Asian (AMSA), Middle Eastern, Arab, Muslim, and South Asian (MASA), or Arab, Middle Eastern, Muslim, and South Asian (AMEMSA), and other unwieldy acronyms have been coined by activists to link communities who increasingly experienced similar processes of disciplining, exclusion, and violence in the aftermath of 9/11. These middle- to upper-middle-class youth were students at private and public universities, including community colleges, and were engaged in politics both on and off campus, sometimes through organized groups or movements (what could be described as both faith-based and secular) as well as in informal ways. Furthermore, college campuses provide a particular context for activism that shapes the kinds of alliances and movements with which these middle- and upper-middle-class youth engage and also the forms of political repression and regulation they encounter in a climate of liberal multiculturalism.

THE TURN TO CIVIL RIGHTS

The language of civil rights is one that generally resonates with the younger generation of Arab, South Asian, and Afghan Americans who find in it a framework for linking their critique of Islamophobia and racism to a larger history of struggles by other groups within the United States. For example, Aisha, a Palestinian American woman from Fremont, who was very involved with both domestic and global Arab politics as an undergraduate and after graduating from college, observed, "African Americans had their struggle, they fought for their civil rights, and now Muslim Americans have to do the same. I think it's about democracy." The narrative of black civil rights struggle offered her a framework for politics that situated Arab American activism in a national genealogy. The profiling of Muslim or Arab Americans thus becomes not exceptional but yet another instance of exclusion from the nation-state that has been experienced by other racialized minorities at various moments in US history. Activism focused on Muslim civil rights also becomes an opportunity to wage a battle for inclusion into the national community via a discourse of rights, which is framed as a test of the true nature of "democracy" as promised by the United States. This necessitates an appeal to the state as the arbiter of rights, individual as well as collective, accompanied sometimes by an assumption that the nation is the horizon of political mobilization in response to 9/11. The turn to civil rights thus becomes, in some cases, a domestication of dissenting politics.

For some youth, however, political organizing is framed in part by the nation-state but not circumscribed by it as they also engage with questions of imperialism and sovereignty—often via human rights—that transcend the issue of domestic civil rights, often simultaneously. Several youth, including Aisha, grappled with the contradictions generated by this dual approach and its implications for a critique of democracy, a notion that has been used to legitimize US invasions and occupations in the Middle East through wars for regime change and "democratization" of nations and regions presumably unfit for self-governance. The question of democracy links these domestic civil rights movements and antiwar and anti-imperial politics, and it also draws attention to the political language that is legible in the current global order. In the larger project, I discuss the ways in which these youth produce and participate in the discourse of human rights, and of humanitarianism, but here I just want to note here that youth understand on some level that in order to constitute themselves as recognizable, political subjects, they must resort to the language of rights. The struggle for rights and the "promise of rights," however, circumscribe permissible political mobilization and discourse, and fundamentally demarcate who is "civil" and also "human."[7]

After 9/11, many national Muslim American organizations that focused on political mobilization launched or intensified programs using civil rights as a response to the heightened discrimination faced by Muslims, Arabs, South Asians and "Muslim-looking" people. Given the mass detentions, deportations, and interrogations in the War on Terror, and the abrogation of constitutional rights under the USA PATRIOT Act, this was certainly a necessary and strategic response to the crisis experienced by those defined as enemies of "homeland security." I do not want to dismiss here the pragmatic need, often urgent, to resort to civil rights in the context of a crisis but to illuminate the need for critique of what it means to engage in this mobilization. The War on Terror made most vulnerable those who were not privileged enough to adequately defend themselves within the US justice system, given its newfound powers to use secret evidence, mandatory and indefinite detention, "extraordinary rendition" (abduction), and torture. Immigrants working in the service sector who were easy targets in public spaces, whether working as taxi drivers or gas-station attendants, were likely to be targets of the most violent assaults after 9/11, but even professionals and other more privileged Muslim, Arab, and South Asian Americans found themselves at risk of being harassed, losing their jobs, having their bank accounts frozen, subjected to wiretapping, or being taken off a plane.[8] Prosecution for "material support" of terrorism became an ambiguous legal dragnet into which many were trapped for charitable donations to Arab or Muslim organizations or, in the case of one Brooklyn College student, presumably for facilitating donations of socks and raincoats to Al Qaeda in Pakistan.[9] Discrimination and racialized surveillance occurred at the level of civil society and also the state; while women in hijab were harassed in stores or attacked on the street, young men were surveilled by the FBI and found GPS devices installed under their cars—as did a student from Santa Clara—and Muslim student groups have been infiltrated by FBI informants.[10]

In this context, educating targeted communities about civil and immigrant rights seemed imperative, and CAIR and other organizations began hosting Know Your Rights workshops and distributing educational materials with information about civil rights and legal resources after 9/11. For example, pamphlets translated into various languages instructed community members on what to do if an FBI agent came to their door to interview them, how to deal with the government interview program targeting Muslim males who were noncitizens ("Special Registration"), or how to respond to interrogations at airports. Some youth entered the sphere of formal "politics" via this civil rights activism. For example, Malaika, a young Pakistani American woman who was born in Santa Clara and grew up in San Jose and Tracy, attended a Know Your Rights workshop conducted by the Sacramento chapter of CAIR at her mosque while she was a high-school student. She later went on to work with CAIR in the Bay Area in their civil rights and government-relations programs, a trajectory common to many young, progressive Muslim Americans who began entering national civil rights and advocacy organizations and the legal field. She described her work as part of a larger process of community "empowerment" via greater engagement with national, electoral politics:

Part of CAIR's mission, in addition to protecting civil liberties and educating people of their rights, is empowering the community. Being politically active and engaged, and then also developing better relationships with public officials. You know, making sure that their voice is heard and that they're also aware of issues. So we're constantly scheduling meetings with city council members, with assembly members, with congressmen. . . . And then also, we go to [voter] registration drives, have workshops on an occasional danger, reaching out to the mosque and making sure the community is active.

Civil and immigrant rights are, in this view, linked to the question of citizen rights that can be addressed by participation in the political structure of representative government and that empowers the "community." Several national Muslim and Arab American organizations organized or intensified their campaigns for voter registration, political lobbying, and "civic engagement" after 9/11. For example, the Arab American Institute launched an annual Yalla [Let's Go] Vote campaign, CAIR has a Citizenship Curriculum, and the American Muslim Political Coordinating Council engages in lobbying.[11] Since 9/11, a new generation of Muslim Americans has come to the forefront of civil rights organizing across the nation. Young people participated in these campaigns and also organized on the platform of civil rights using street protests, public rallies, and alliances with larger immigrant and civil rights movements. Uniting both these strands of civil rights activism, electoral and grassroots, was a focus on pressuring the nation-state to live up to its liberal-democratic promise of constitutionally mandated rights and racial and religious equality.

This surge in civil rights activism not only exposed the racialized distribution of rights by the state but, in its reformist variant, also became the site of the possibility of nationalization. For example, a "leader" in the Arab and Muslim American community framed the mobilization against the post-9/11 assault on civil rights as redeeming belief in American justice: "People in the end did not lose hope in the sense of fairness here in the country."[12] A common refrain after 9/11 was that Muslim Americans were the latest group to fight for inclusion into the nation and that like African Americans, Latinos, and Asian Americans before them, they would become part of the national community through their struggle in the crucible of civil rights activism. The "story of racial and ethnic inclusion," as Nikhil Pal Singh points out, is central to a national narrative based on notions of "America's exceptional universalism" and "religious tolerance."[13] The 2008 election of President Barack Hussein Obama, an African American from a partly Muslim family, only reaffirmed this narrative of redemption and vindication of civil rights struggle, highlighting the ultimately inclusive and tolerant tenets of the nation for many Muslim Americans, perhaps as much as anything else.

The civilizing story that the nation tells about itself is one of a community of diverse groups of immigrants, each of which ultimately realized its dream of a better life after winning its struggle for inclusion, occluding the history of genocidal violence against indigenous peoples, slavery and Jim Crow, the colonial appropriation of other territories, and imperial interventions overseas. A national teleology of civil rights is enshrined in an American mythology of "national redemption and moral regeneration."[14] In the nationalist civil rights narrative, iconic figures such as Martin Luther King Jr. are selectively embalmed to symbolize the ability of the nation to live up to its mythic ideals of equality and tolerance and to confer inclusion on groups that engage in peaceful struggles shaped by Christian ethics and liberal democratic politics. The virtues of hard work, discipline, and a belief in the revolutionary promise are rewarded by integration into the political order.

The nationalist framework for civil rights was historically erected as a front in the United States' ascendancy to global power, and clearly the recuperation of civil rights struggles by groups who are targets of the racial state's violence and exclusion, which undermine radical struggles against US imperialism, is not new. Mary Dudziak has argued that civil rights legislation and the will to desegregation in the United States during the Cold War was shaped by the need to "sell democracy to the Third World," for "America could not save the Third World for democracy if democracy meant white supremacy."[15] Other scholars have traced the shift from radical movements for racial and economic justice that challenged the state in the 1960s and 1970s to mobilization that resorts to the "liberal multicultural state as that institution that *recognizes* and legitimizes legal and political claims based on gender and race."[16]

What this nationalist narrative of "civil liberties" obscures is the logics of white supremacy and class inequality that undergird the ethos of a settler colonial, capitalist state. As Singh and others have pointed out, critiques of this ethos that take the logic of imperialism and capitalism as their starting point, including those offered by King himself in his later years, are dismissively labeled "radical" and "anti-American"—which, indeed, if America's constitutive national logics are white supremacy and capitalist order, they are.[17] For some, the Obama moment signified the ultimate realization of King's dream of racial equality and the beginning of a "post-racial" era that would shift the image of the United States on the world stage. And yet, the War on Terror continued with ongoing and expanded mass surveillance; racial, religious, and political profiling; FBI entrapment targeting young Muslim men and government plans to root out "homegrown" terrorists; while deportations targeting immigrant communities actually increased under the new regime. Obama ratcheted up the war on Afghanistan as promised (shifting the theater of war from Iraq), stepped up the drone attacks in northwest Pakistan, and, despite his promises, did not eventually shut down the infamous prison at Guantanamo—not to mention his administration's rush to bail out the banks who had created the spiraling financial crisis. While the early euphoria about hoped-for "change" subsided among liberals and progressives, it was still difficult to acknowledge that Obama-mania had been partly driven by a current of longing for national redemption, even if the 2008 campaign was also rife with deeply racist sentiments and expressions of Islamophobia.

This redemptive sentiment tied to the desire to include worthy Muslim American subjects rested on the desire for the actualization of a multicultural America that Donald Pease argues was invoked by Bill Clinton and his New Covenant with America that neutralized the radical left and co-opted minoritized movements into neoliberal market rationalities and a multicultural security state.[18] This liberal exclusion was evident in the "Obama effect" that dampened civil rights and antiwar and civil rights organizing during the early years of Obama's presidency.[19] The strategy of liberal exclusion in the post-9/11 moment requires also a strategy of liberal inclusion of Muslim, Arab, South Asian, and Afghan Americans and not just recuperates, but desires, their struggles. In the context of the War on Terror, the staging of multicultural nationalism is an attempt to deflect accusations of racism and Islamophobia as evidence of the hollowness of US rhetoric about democratization and human rights.

In the post-9/11 climate, the notion of civil rights was re-energized by the emergence of Muslim American political subjects and campaigns waged by Muslim Americans that became a platform on which to enact the drama of Americanization for another group who could be the new canaries in the coal mine and eventually be welcomed into the national fold. Civil rights activism itself came to be seen as an act of Americanization—a battle against a legal regime and ideological climate that was seen as, in effect, guilty of "breaking American law and tradition"—and a rupture for immigrant communities with anti-democratic traditions from repressive home countries.[20] This narrative of racialized progress, including in its somewhat Orientalist variant, is evident in some studies of post-9/11 mobilization which suggest that Muslim, Arab, and South Asian American community activists had to "convince immigrants to believe in the American way of activism, advocacy, and mobilization" since they presumably came from societies lacking in civil and human rights and needed tutelage in liberal, participatory democracy.[21] Gaining recognition as modern, political subjects ("moderate" Muslim Americans) is contingent, however, on evading a radical critique of imperial interventions and neoliberal capitalism.

What I would like to argue here is that a liberal nationalist framework of "civil rights," as used in the post-9/11 era and invoked by grassroots groups, is redemptive also because of its conjuncture with "civility" and with the larger question of civilization itself, especially in the War on Terror. This is a planetary war imagined by its proponents in the United States as remaking regions of the world that need to be civilized through the project of Western liberal democracy and neoliberal governmentality and as redefining what is acceptable resistance or necessary violence.[22] The notion of the "civil," then, is an ideological helix in which a racialized and colonial logic defines what counts as "civil" disobedience and what can be deemed "uncivil" resistance, a logic that seeps into the post-9/11 culture wars and the neoconservative paradigm of the "clash of civilizations."

For some youth, however, civil rights was an inadequate framework for political activism for various reasons. According to Majed, a Palestinian American from Santa Clara whose family was very involved with CAIR, civil rights was not the fundamental strategy for opposing profiling and Islamophobia, which in his view were rooted in ignorance about Islam and Muslims. Commenting on civil rights activism, he observed:

> I definitely think it's important. Especially right after 9/11, I think it gave a boost to Muslims. I think more people wanted to learn about government in general. So civil rights work, because no matter what there are always going to be problems. But at the same time, I think what's even more important is education. Because if people are educated on religion or Islam and are not ignorant, then there's no need to have civil rights. Or that minimizes the civil rights work that you have to do.

Rights work is thus not the fundamental solution but education to convince the public that Muslims in the United States deserve rights is. The paradox is that, as Jacques Ranciere observes, one has to have rights in order to bestow rights or even to make the political, or moral argument, that all deserve civil rights.[23]

For other youth, however, civil rights is a limited response to the War on Terror because the root cause of state-sponsored or sanctioned discrimination and violence cannot be attributed only to ignorance about Arabs or Muslims, but also to a system of racial domination that is central to the nation-state and the ideology of Manifest Destiny. So while some youth I spoke invoked a liberal discourse of civil rights, others were ambivalent or, in some cases, deeply skeptical. For example, Yasser, whose father was Pakistani and mother Mexican American, attended Ohlone College in Fremont was critical of the War on Terror but felt that Muslim Americans needed to take a more radical stance:

> Muslims need to start standing up for their opinion and start attacking the credibility of the CIA and the FBI and telling them they're full of shit. Stop being scared! Unite! Who cares if they kill you or you lose your jobs? Or they do all this funny stuff like they did with the black people and their civil rights movement. If you start standing up, other people will start standing up. If we start standing up, people will follow along.

For Yasser, the role of the FBI or CIA in the War on Terror needed to be exposed and challenged by a political critique of the security state that would link the targeting of Muslim Americans by programs of surveillance and infiltration to similar repressive strategies used against African American civil rights activists, for example, during the COINTELPRO era. In this view, which is shared with Muslim American youth and young activists shaped by the legacy of radical liberation movements and figures such as Malcolm X, Muslim Americans could be at the forefront of a radical movement that would be willing to take risks in order to challenge the imperial state.[24] Commenting on Obama, Yasser said:

> He's a good guy but it's the same thing. They just put a Black guy in the white House, so what? The only way I'll believe that Obama actually did something is if in ten years, I see that America's not being imperialistic to South America by putting interest on them and taking away their money. . . . I read *Confessions of an Economic Hit Man* and how America is still collecting interest off of Latin American countries, basically using their resources. And basically because their country is paying so much interest and the leaders are puppets, people are starving and dying. . . . So I'll only acknowledge Obama's success when he fixes it for other people. When the Third World is done suffering from the U.S. hand, the European hand. If you look, America's been interfering with Nicaragua, they went to El Salvador. . . . They attacked Panama . . . and killed many civilians, they dropped bombs on them. And these are poor people who have nothing. They did the same thing to Iraq, Afghanistan. So this evil approach they have, unless it changes then [only] I can say Obama's a great guy. To me, Obama and Bush are on the same boat. And people . . . think one man runs the world. No, its still the government, still the people standing behind the curtain. . . .

I cite Yasser's critique at length because it emphasizes a systemic analysis of US racism, challenging the notion that the appointment of one African American president would change the enduring structure of an imperial state and its military, economic, and political interventions in other countries. Perhaps partly because of his mixed Latino–South Asian background, but also because of his interest in works such as John Perkins's analysis of globalization and neoliberalism, Yasser links the wars in Iraq and Afghanistan to earlier interventions in Central and Latin America and critiques the transnational apparatus of counterterrorism and counterinsurgency.[25] He points to the ways in which US imperial power has rested on proxy wars, covert operations, and client regimes and on neoliberal policies tied to the International Monetary Fund and World Bank that have imposed structural adjustment and onerous debts on the global South. This is an astute analysis because US imperialism has relied on nonterritorial, secret, and flexible forms of political, economic, and military domination, making it difficult to name and even more difficult to resist. Yasser's framework shifts the premise of imperial interventions from the liberation of women and "regime change" for democracy to the imperial state's desire for economic and political hegemony and to a larger biopolitics of violence and terror that has radically altered lives and also the very definition of who is "human," and where.

For Yasser, it seems, dissent must challenge US plans for global hegemony and link domestic and overseas repression, rather than simply seeking inclusion on the terrain of civil rights and multicultural recognition. Yasser was critical of the Muslim Student Association (MSA) on his campus, though he had been involved with organizing events with them earlier, partly, it seemed due to his general frustration with the politics of the Muslim American community and partly due to what he viewed as their lack of energetic commitment and organizing. In his view, their failure was demonstrated to some extent by the lack of non-Muslims they were able to attract to events. It is this desire to enlarge the sphere of mobilization that drove other youth to participate in interfaith programs that provided a legitimate sphere for political recognition and coalition-building in the post-9/11 era.

INTERFAITH AND INTERRACIAL COALITIONS

I found that interfaith activism provided an acceptable basis for political solidarity for Muslim Americans but existed in an uneasy relationship with cross-racial alliances in the post-9/11 era for several of the youth I spoke to in Silicon Valley. Interfaith coalitions, I argue, have been promoted as the primary form of permissible politics in the War on Terror. The turn to interfaith organizing has occurred in tandem with the turn to civil rights, and both are sites for producing a narrative of liberal inclusion and proper political subjecthood for South Asian, Arab, and Afghan American youth. Since 2001, Muslim Americans have become increasingly active in a growing interfaith movement, including an expanding interfaith youth campaign that has emerged on college campuses and rapidly spread across the United States since the early 1990s.[26] Interfaith youth programs have generally involved various kinds of workshops, forums, and volunteer activities that include participation of Muslim, Jewish, and Christian youth and attempt to connect the "Abrahamanic traditions" establishing commonalities among the religions of "the book" (the Bible). The goals of the interfaith youth movement are generally to encourage engagement across religious difference, a worthwhile goal certainly, and to create a public place for religious tradition within society through interfaith cooperation. Interfaith activism thus becomes a site for education about Islam and for cross-ethnic alliance building, within the ambit of faith-based communities.

Muslim American youth often threw themselves into organizing interfaith programs or, in some cases, found themselves positioned within what became an acceptable venue for producing a Muslim American identity in the post-9/11 United States. For example, Leila, a Pakistani American who grew up in Fremont and was attending an Islamic school when the attacks of 9/11 occurred, talked about bomb threats the school received after 9/11 and visits by Jewish Americans to show support as part of interfaith outreach activities. Other students spoke of how their public expressions of Muslim American identity were shaped by involvement or leadership in interfaith programs; for example, Malaika talked about coordinating an "interfaith club council" at her college and organizing lectures on topics such as "women in Islam" for "debunking stereotypes"; she commented wryly that the events were "boring one[s], but [they were] necessary." I am interested here in the imperative to challenge Islamophobia by creating alliances between faith-based communities, in particular, and the potential erasures or deferrals that are set in motion by this move.

Many interfaith programs tend to propound ideas of "tolerance" and "dialogue" that are deeply embedded in wider, liberal assumptions about multiculturalism and neoliberal democracy and have grown out of the Bush administration's effort to push social services out of governmental agencies and into "faith-based initiatives." Generally, interfaith alliances have flourished in liberal spheres such as the academy and nonprofit organizations where interfaith dialogue has been promoted and also in programs related to Israel/Palestine. The growing "interfaith industry" that has burgeoned since 9/11 and is sanctioned by the state has produced a liberal notion of religious multiculturalism. This has been buttressed by the simultaneous trend within the Muslim American community, and among youth, emphasizing Islam as a religion that crosses national, ethnic, and racial boundaries and therefore compatible with liberal democratic multiculturalism.

Clearly, the eviction of Muslim Americans from citizenship and political community after 9/11, which necessitated outreach and alliance-building and educational and interfaith activities, had many positive effects. However, post-9/11 religious multiculturalism obfuscates a critique of the geopolitical imperatives of the War on Terror or political conflict, reducing politics instead to issues of interreligious and intercultural tension, understanding, and acceptance that can be resolved on the terrain of faith or culture. The underlying assumptions of many of these interfaith programs involving the triad of Muslims, Christians, and Jews—or the dyad of Muslim-Jewish or Arab-Jewish dialogue—are often to remove analyses of and solutions to political conflict and structural inequity outside of the realm of the state, confining this to what Mahmood Mamdani calls "culture talk."[27] I argue that the "interfaith industry" is a response generated by the post-9/11 national crisis to contain the possibility of radical political dissent within the grammar of religious "diversity."

The growing interfaith movement has implications for the ways in which cross-racial alliances are shaped, or suppressed, in the arena of global as well as domestic politics. This was brought home to me in a conversation with Iman, a young Palestinian American woman who grew up in Santa Clara and attended Granada and then the University of California, Berkeley. Iman, whose family had a long involvement with CAIR, observed that interfaith alliances in the local Muslim American community often took precedence over cross-ethnic alliances. She lamented the lack of interracial solidarity during events such as the high-school walkouts by Latino youth during the immigrant rights marches of 2006:

> The Hispanic community in my high school was big and they organized a walk-out event when everyone left campus, and that was huge. And it would have been nice if the Muslim community made a bigger effort to participate. Because the Hispanic community in San Jose is huge. But instead I feel like we did outreach to like the Jewish community, or the Christian community. And we'd go to churches and synagogues and that was it.

Iman seemed to suggest that Muslim American youth at her high school in Santa Clara, and possibly also the local Muslim American community at large, missed an important political opportunity to forge an alliance with the growing immigrant-rights movement, failing to connect the issues that Muslim immigrant (as well as Arab, South Asian, and Afghan) communities were facing after 9/11 to those of Latinos and others targeted for detention and deportation. So while there were indeed coalitions that emerged involving Muslim American, particularly South Asian and Arab American, and immigrant-rights groups in some cases in the Bay Area, Iman points to a fissure in Muslim American groups in the South Bay, one that reveals the difficulties in producing a larger critique of the state's racial policies of immigrant labor and neoliberal capitalism.

Furthermore, despite the lure of civil rights struggle as a framework justifying Muslim American activism, there is also the vexed issue of alliances and fissures between "immigrant" Muslims (or Muslims of South Asian, Arab, Afghan, Turkish, and Iranian origin) and African American Muslims. On the one hand, it is apparent that in the larger Bay Area, there are several venues in which cross-racial identification is produced between immigrant Muslim and African American Muslim communities, using a liberal discourse of civil rights and also a more radical approach to social justice organizing. At the institutional center of these interracial alliances are charismatic figures such as Imam Zaid Shakir, an African American Muslim cleric who is a popular figure on the college lecture circuit and one of the cofounders of Zaytuna Institute in Berkeley, the first Islamic liberal arts college in the country. The affinity between Muslim American youth from immigrant communities and other US-born Muslim Americans is highlighted also in the ethnically and racially diverse Ta'leef Collective, a community organization in Hayward whose cofounder, Usama Canon, also works with incarcerated persons.[28] Ta'leef's Friday night *halaqas* (study circles) are attended by up to two or three hundred young Muslims. Abed, an Egyptian American from San Jose who has attended Ta'leef, commented, "You'll go to one of their events and you'll see a white lady in her blouse and slacks and you'll see another dude with tattoos and a guy with, like, a mohawk and they are all Muslim and they go there because they feel comfortable. You will see people [who were] born and grew up Muslim also going to that community." The social and political subcultures that crisscross in the space of Ta'leef are racially and also culturally diverse, and several young Muslim American activists I spoke to in the area, as well as Muslim youth in general, participated in Ta'leef events. The discourse about Ta'leef suggests a certain kind of multiculturalism but not one that insists on diversity for diversity's sake but rather for the sake of a larger goal, that of creating a more open Muslim community firmly situated in a specific local, generational context and not primarily in the nation. This is in contrast to liberal interfaith projects that emphasize volunteerism and use a depoliticized approach, but I also want to acknowledge that youth who attend Ta'leef do so for different reasons and have different political and faith-based investments.

Another important element of cross-racial affiliation is produced through youth culture, with the growing genre of Muslim American hip-hop playing a central role.[29] Many youth I spoke to were fans of Amir Sulaiman, an African American Muslim MC from the Bay Area known for his progressive politics who performs at local events; in 2011, Sulaiman collaborated with Arab American rap artists, such as Omar Offendum, on a song in solidarity with the Egyptian revolution, "#Jan 25 Egypt."[30] Sulaiman is also affiliated with Ta'leef, which is also the hub of a growing cross-racial Muslim American youth subculture that includes Muslim rap artists, B-boys, and B-girls. Imam Shakir noted the "crossing of lines" at Ta'leef where Afghan American youth from Fremont and Hayward regularly meet with African American, Arab American, and other young adults. For Imam Shakir, this has a political significance: "When youth begin to identify with the history of the African American struggle or the Chicano struggle, they adopt some of that militancy and it emboldens a lot of Muslim students, it allows them to push back. It is the anniversary of COINTELPRO, and we are identifying with people who were the targets of the FBI. Those people were shot at and their leaders were assassinated; today, it's wiretapping." At San Jose State, a Pakistani American student, Bassem, who was born in San Jose and has lived in Fremont, talked about an event organized by the Black Student Union on African American-Muslim connections; he said it featured an African American speaker who is a former Black Panther and is viewed by some as "very controversial" because he is "a strong advocate of getting the minorities together against the American occupation of different countries." Thus a radical or progressive Muslim American youth culture generates alliances that are built on a longer history of criminalization of targeted groups, such as COINTELPRO's surveillance and the state's violence against the Black Power movement, and resists policies of counterterrorism or counterinsurgency through cross-racial solidarity that does not exceptionalize the post-9/11 War on Terror's assault on Muslim civil rights in the United States.[31]

At the same time, it is evident that beyond spaces such as Ta'leef or the network of progressive Muslim American activists, artists, and students who are forging cross-ethnic affiliations, there are indeed tensions between African American and immigrant or non-black Muslims. Abed commented on these fissures within the Muslim American community in Silicon Valley, in relation to MCA: "The funny thing is that the largest ethnic group of Muslims is African American. I don't think a lot of people realize that. As a community, I don't think we have done enough to outreach toward the African Americans and to other communities in general. Our only focus is on the desis [South Asians] and Arabs. . . ." Malaika noted that there is frustration and disappointment among "indigenous" Muslim Americans with the racial divide among Muslim Americans. Given that the largest indigenous group of Muslims in the United States is African Americans, who constitute approximately one-third of the Muslim population, relationships between them and immigrant communities, notably from South and West Asia, are a key issue for Muslim youth in the United States at large. Jamillah Karim's research on South Asian and African American girls in Chicago and "new types of interethnic alliances and exchange in America" among Muslim youth finds that interracial tensions between African American and immigrant Muslims shape an evolving "American Muslim identity" and persist in the younger generation.[32]

Needless to say, anti-black racism in immigrant communities in Silicon Valley coexists with a class divide between the generally more affluent Muslim (particularly Arab and South Asian) American and the more impoverished African American communities; there are also class schisms within immigrant Muslim communities, which underlie the gaps between civil rights and labor rights organizing. An important flip side to the spotlight on civil rights organizing and interfaith alliances after 9/11 was the general absence of attention to cross-class alliances or labor issues among South Asian, Arab, and Afghan Americans in Silicon Valley. Indian American activist Raj Jayadev, who was involved in organizing low-wage workers in the high-tech industry, "debugs" the myths of Silicon Valley as a "new business frontier" and a "new Western city," a place where the American Dream of autonomy, private property, capitalist success, and California-style self-reinvention makes invisible working-class struggles and poverty.[33] It is a context in which South Asian and Arab immigrants, and less so Afghan Americans, are often wealthy entrepreneurs who are sometimes engaged in exploitative class relations with workers from their own ethnic communities, as Jayadev observed. For communities who are increasingly viewed only through the prism of the War on Terror and its logics of securitization and national inclusion, the basis for affiliations with other groups is a racialization paradigm centered on religion and, to some extent, nation, and so cross-class and also interracial conflict is largely underemphasized.

There were some cases in which interracial alliances were, indeed, forged by progressive South Asian, Arab, and Arab American activists after 9/11, such as immigrant-rights movements in San Francisco and Oakland that involved

Latinos, African Americans, and Muslim Americans and anti-imperial coalitions with antiwar activists and Native Americans, such as those initiated by the (former) American Arab Anti-Discrimination Committee in San Francisco. One significant instance of cross-ethnic coalition building in the Bay Area and also in Silicon Valley was the ongoing solidarity of progressive Japanese American activists in San Jose, as well as in northern California in general, with Muslim and Arab American communities after 9/11, reflective of the larger alliance forged by Japanese Americans across the nation. In most instances, this solidarity was forged through a shared history of exclusion as "enemy aliens" in wartime and a common struggle for civil and citizen rights.

I want to note here that it is evident that the Muslim American youth I spoke to were generally not as involved in these interethnic coalitions initiated by Japanese American activists as in interfaith alliances, but it was also apparent that interfaith programs did not generally stretch to include Buddhists—nor always Sikhs or Hindus. These fissures exist partly because alliances with progressive-left antiwar Japanese American activists in the Bay Area, in certain instances, did not fit comfortably within the liberal multiculturalist paradigm of mainstream interfaith alliances, as they challenge the politics of the warfare state and racialized incarceration. These different forms of solidarity and the gaps within them are part of ongoing contestations of the limits of acceptable or "moderate" and controversial or "radical" Muslim American youth politics. What it means to be "civil" is defined in a political field dominated by discourses of tolerance, dialogue, and inclusion in which "good" Muslims participate and images of "radical" youth who are subjected to surveillance, containment, and criminalization.

"GOOD" MUSLIMS AND "ANGRY" POLITICS

Cross-racial alliances that directly challenge state policies express a dissident politics that conservative segments in South Asian, Arab, and Afghan American communities would rather evade. This evasion has much to do with the politics of performing a "good" or moderate Muslim identity in a context in which the discourse of terrorism and hysteria about Islamic "radicalism" or "self-radicalization," particularly among youth, filters nearly all political expressions by Muslim Americans.[34] This dichotomy of the "good"/moderate and "bad"/radical Muslim emerges both on the fault line of class and across class and ethnic boundaries.[35] On the one hand, working-class or less affluent Muslim immigrant communities were disproportionately targeted in the mass detentions and deportations after 9/11. On the other hand, even affluent Muslim American professionals found themselves swept into the dragnet of the surveillance-security state, forcing a realization for some of the limits of the American Dream and the protections of model minorityhood. While many still clung to the defense that they were "good" Muslims—productive, peaceful citizens who believed in American democracy, civil rights, and capitalist mobility—others became skeptical and in some cases publicly critical of the War on Terror. These were often labeled the "bad" Muslims: anti-American, unpatriotic, and potentially an "internal" threat to national security that challenged the state's policies of permanent warfare, neoliberal capitalism, and racial violence.

Many of the young people I spoke to explained their activism through a progressive notion of Islam focused on social justice and defiantly challenged the parameters of "good" Muslim politics.[36] However, it is important to emphasize that the demonization of political dissent by Muslim and Arab Americans, particularly by youth, has meant that not all in fact are willing to risk becoming a "bad" Muslim. The dichotomy of "good" and "bad" Muslim politics has had an impact on the very notion of what constitutes an appropriate politics for youth in the War on Terror. For example, Yasmeen, an Afghan American from Newark (near Fremont), remarked, "I really do not like politics very much so I try not to get involved in many political activities." But she also explained that she was involved in an Afghan student group in high school and in both the MSA and the Afghan Students Association while at San Jose State—an engagement that she chose to define as not "political." Malaika was involved with creating an MSA chapter in her high school after 9/11 and reflected, "When it came to the Muslim Student Association and the activities we would do, we tried to avoid all politics. We didn't know where that would lead and we wanted to keep it strictly educational." Malaika expresses a fear about engaging in "politics" that many Muslim and Arab Americans experienced after 9/11, in a climate where political speech that was critical of US policies could be grounds for surveillance and even investigation or prosecution. When Malaika became vice president of the MSA on her campus, she continued to feel the same hesitation and anxiety about being too "political." The programs that she organized with the MSA were "mostly educational" and "interfaith type" activities, and she seemed aware that these were strategic choices in a repressive climate that deemed such programs safely outside of risky "politics." Malaika went on to become coordinator of the interfaith club and social justice club in college, and in her view: "We were a pretty harmonious campus but I think that was because we stayed away from political issues. I know that the year before I started college they had organized an Israel-Palestine awareness week. So MSA and Hillel had worked together, and I think it went over well. But in general, even in my school of international studies we would try and stay away from it." Malaika's reflections illustrate the tensions and also shifts that some young Muslim Americans experienced in their understandings of what they felt were permissible politics. At the same time, the production of "moderate" Muslim politics is a process that the state itself has been deeply invested in as it has promoted and even funded "good" Muslim leaders who assert that as "peace-loving" Muslims and loyal Americans they support the US regime and distinguish themselves from "extremists" and militants who violently oppose US policies and interventions.[37]

While there is clearly not a small degree of strategic self-defense in these performances of the "good" Muslim activist, Andrew Shryock points out the costs of what he describes as an emergent "Islamophilia" that is the flip side of Islamophobia.[38] For Shryock, the production of Islamophobia/Islamophilia is intimately intertwined with notions of modernity, citizenship, and democracy, for the "good" Muslim is one who has been made "safe" for US neoliberal democracy: "The good Muslim is also a pluralist (. . . a champion of interfaith activism); he is politically moderate (an advocate of democracy, human rights, and religious freedom, an opponent of armed conflict against the U.S. and Israel); finally, he is likely to be an African, a South Asian, or, more likely still, an Indonesian or Malaysian; he is less likely to be an Arab. . . ."[39] As Shryock observes, Muslim activists who are Arab, and who implicitly or explicitly affirm the right to resist wars and occupation by the United States and Israel, are suspicious political subjects. I should add that the "good Muslim" is as likely to be female, for the binary of the "good"/"bad" Muslims is deeply gendered. The fact that terrorism and "radicalization" are pinned largely onto Muslim males creates an increasingly public role for female Muslim spokespersons who can testify to the repressiveness of Islam and legitimize US interventions to save Muslim women.[40]

Given the criminalization of Muslims for their political activities and for their political and theological beliefs, the assertion of "moderate" Muslimness is often a strategic question for Muslim American youth. Heena, a Muslim American woman whose family is from India and who grew up in San Jose, said that when she went to the University of California, Berkeley, "I didn't feel like it made a difference to be in protests. And I could think of better ways of communicating your point. . . . I think that if you act angry all the time that's not going to help anything." Heena commented that while many Muslim American youth became "more outspoken" after 9/11, over time "people were scared of political events backfiring." She commented on protests against the war in Iraq: "Like my freshman year, we organized a big protest but then people used the images of those protests as example of how violent Muslims are. So I think that after that the MSA became less political because of that one incident." While Heena was wary of "angry" political expressions, she seemed to acknowledge that there was a demonization of political protests involving Muslim youth as inherently "violent" and threatening—ironically, for protesting state-sponsored violence, torture, and massacres, such as in Iraq. As Heena's and also Malaika's reflections on political activism suggest, there is a wariness about engaging in protest of US wars or US-backed occupations and military violence in Iraq or Palestine, for these are constituted as indices of "radical" Muslim politics. Furthermore, while broader attitudes toward the war on Iraq and later also the war on Afghanistan (which had been seen as a "just war") and drone warfare in "Af-Pak," began to shift, it continued to be the case that antiwar politics among Arab and Muslim American youth continued to be viewed with suspicion, as outside of the bounds of humanitarian solidarity and always potentially based on sympathy with "jihadists." It is also the case that solidarity with Palestinians is persistently deemed as dangerously beyond the pale of "moderate" politics for the mainstream, even for non-Muslims and non-Arabs, often through an association with terrorism and a conflation of critique of the Israeli state with anti-Semitism.

Perhaps the most egregious example of the criminalization of political protest by Muslim American youth after 9/11 is the case of the Irvine 11, a group of Arab and Muslim students from the University of California, Irvine and the University of California, Riverside who engaged in a peaceful protest at a speech by the Israeli ambassador at UC Irvine in 2010, a year after the Israeli war on Gaza in 2008–2009. The UC Irvine administration subjected the students to disciplinary action and suspended the Muslim Student Union, although the group had not sponsored the protest.[41] In an unprecedented move, the Orange County district attorney then filed criminal charges against the students and ten of the students were found guilty of misdemeanors. Given that few other instances of peaceful protest or civil disobedience on college campuses—including interruptions of speeches by George W. Bush and Barack Obama—have met with this kind of severe punishment, or any punishment at all, the exceptional criminalization of the pro-Palestinian protesters and the Muslim student group sent a chilling message that only intensified fear and self-censorship among Muslim and Arab American student activists. This was perhaps the intended effect, as the post-9/11 generation of Muslim and Arab Americans has engaged in bolder protests and in the global Boycott, Divestment, and Sanctions movement targeting Israel—particularly at UC Irvine and other California campuses where there are large, politicized Muslim and Arab student populations.

The Irvine 11 case is just one of several cases of repression and censorship in California and around the country, yet it illuminates what constitutes acceptable politics among Muslim American youth and highlights that Palestine-solidarity activism represents the threshold of "radicalism." The Palestine issue, in fact, is the model of "angry" or controversial politics par excellence, and a risky political cause for young Muslim Americans, or others, to engage with in the United States, given the limits of civil rights in selected instances of solidarity activism. The Palestine question is also at the center of the intercultural and interfaith industry, and often inserted into programs focused on Arab-Jewish or Muslim-Jewish dialogue through the fallacy of neutrality, eliding the politics of occupation and racial exclusion. "Civil disobedience," in the case of protests of occupation or state warfare supported by the United States and of boycott and divestment campaigns, is construed as inherently "uncivil" and undeserving of the protection of civil liberties and the right to freedom of expression.[42]

CONCLUSION

My discussions with youth in Silicon Valley about the experiences of grappling with the "political" in a post-9/11 landscape shaped by the counterterrorism paradigm were infused with feelings of fear, anxiety, desire, outrage, and empathy. The turn to civil rights, and the compulsion to engage in interfaith activism, are rife with paradoxes but also provide powerful frames in the context of imperial modernity and a racial state that regulates proper political subjecthood. The boundary between "angry" and "moderate" Muslim American youth politics lies in a discursive battle about the meaning of what is "civil" and who is human and in zones of war, incarceration, and surveillance stretching from San Jose to Kabul, and Fremont to Gaza City. There is a deeply racialized logic at work in institutionalized patterns of repression, a logic embedded in an imperial regime of rights that regulates which forms of politics are permissible and for whom, shaping and regulating Arab, Afghan, or South Asian political subjects.

The War on Terror has seeped into and transformed political, social, and religious identities in this generation, and it has done so by reconfiguring structures of political feeling and sentiments of dissent and solidarity. It has defined what an acceptable Muslim American male or female looks, thinks, and speaks like—within and beyond the Muslim American community itself—and which forms of, solidarity, rage, or compassion are permissible. Some youth attempt to challenge the definition of proper objects of affiliation, resisting the notion that it is natural to form affinities with those in churches but not in the streets or in prisons, while others struggle with the fear that they may be imprisoned if they mobilize in the street or even on their own campus for a politics deemed too radical. Youth culture may provide spaces where this generation can experiment with alternative frameworks for affinity and mobilization in the context of a war being fought on multiple fronts: domestic and global; military, cultural, and economic.

NOTES

1. Steven Salaita, *Anti-Arab Racism in the U.S.A.: Where It Comes from and What It Means for Politics Today* (London: Pluto Press, 2006).
2. Edward Said, "America's Last Taboo," *New Left Review* 6 (November–December 2000): 45–53.
3. Nadine Naber, *Arab America: Gender, Cultural Politics, and Activism* (New York: NYU Press, 2012), 27. See also Nabeel Abraham, "Anti-Arab Racism and Violence in the United States," in *The Development of Arab-American Identity*, ed. Ernest McCarus (Ann Arbor: University of Michigan Press, 2004), 155–214; Gregory Orfalea, *The Arab Americans: A History* (Northampton, MA: Olive Branch Press, 2006).
4. Given Afghanistan's liminal location between South and Central/West Asia, it is often not included in South Asia, partly as a result of Cold War cartographies that continue to divide and partition regions in Asia. While Afghan American youth I spoke to in many cases had

family members who had lived or had themselves spent part of their lives as refugees in Pakistan, their identification with South Asia was at best, ambivalent. Pakistani and Indian American youth also did not always identify Afghans as South Asian, so I have not subsumed Afghan Americans in the category of "South Asian American." In the larger project, I dwell on the (re)suturing of Afghanistan to Pakistan/South Asia through the violently enforced label of "Af-Pak" in the US war and drone attacks on the border region, and also on the implications of considering Arabs as West Asians.

5. J. A. English-Lueck, *Cultures@SiliconValley* (Stanford: Stanford University Press, 2002), 21, 25.

6. Stephen J. Pitti, *The Devil in Silicon Valley: Northern California, Race, and Mexican Americans* (Princeton: Princeton University Press, 2004).

7. David L. Eng, "The Civil and the Human," *American Quarterly* 64, no. 2 (June 2012): 208; Wendy S. Hesford, *Spectacular Rhetorics: Human Rights Violations, Recognitions, Feminisms* (Duke University Press, 2011), 5.

8. Tram Nguyen, *We Are All Suspects Now: Untold Stories from Immigrant Communities After 9/11* (Boston: Beacon Press, 2005); Lori A. Peek, "Reactions and Response: Muslim Students' Experiences on New York City Campuses Post 9/11," *Journal of Muslim Minority Affairs* 23, no. 2 (2003): 271–283.

9. Jeanne Theoharis, "The Legal Black Hole in Lower Manhattan: The Unfairness of the Trial of Muslim Activist Syed Fahad Hashmi," *Slate,* April 27, 2010, http://www.slate.com.

10. Chris Hawley, "NYPD Monitored Muslim Students All over the Northeast," Associated Press, February 18, 2012, http://www.ap.org/Content/AP-In-The-News/2012/NYPD -monitored-Muslim-students-all-over-Northeast; Kim Zetter, "Caught Spying on Student, FBI Demands GPS Tracking Device Back," *Wired,* October 7, 2010, http://www.wired.com/ threatlevel/2010/10/fbi-tracking-device/.

11. Amy Bakalian and Mehdi Bozorgmehr, *Backlash 9/11: Middle Eastern and Muslim Americans Respond* (Berkeley: University of California Press, 2009), 180–182, 216.

12. Cited in Ibid., 182.

13. Nikhil P. Singh, *Black Is a Country: Race and the Unfinished Struggle for Democracy,* (Cambridge, MA: Harvard University Press, 2004) 19.

14. Singh, *Black Is a Country,* 3.

15. Mary. L. Dudziak, "Desegregation as a Cold War Imperative," in *Critical Race Theory: The Cutting Edge,* ed. Richard Delgado and Jean Stefancic (Philadelphia: Temple University Press, 2000), 106, 115.

16. Andrea Smith, "Unmasking the State: Racial/Gender Terror and Hate Crimes," in *State of White Supremacy: Racism, Governance, and the United States,* ed. Moon-Kie Jung, Joao H. Costa Vargas, and Eduardo Bonilla-Silva (Stanford: Stanford University Press), 2011, 232.

17. Singh, *Black Is a Country,* 1–6.

18. Donald Pease, *The New American Exceptionalism* (Minneapolis: University of Minnesota Press, 2009), 71, 74.

19. See Andrew Shryock, "Introduction: Islam as an Object of Fear and Affection," in *Islamophobia/Islamophilia: Beyond the Politics of Enemy and Friend,* ed. Andrew Shryock (Bloomington: Indiana University Press, 2010) 1–25.

20. Bakalian and Bozorgmehr, *Backlash 9/11,* 182.

21. Ibid., 178.

22. Alain Badiou, *Polemics,* trans. Steve Corcoran (London: Verso, 2011).

23. Jacques Ranciere, *Dissensus: On Politics and Aesthetics,* ed. and trans. Steven Corcoran (London: Continuum Publishing, 2010), electronic edition.

24. See Sohail Daulatzai, *Black Star, Crescent Moon: The Muslim International and Black Freedom beyond America* (Minneapolis: University of Minnesota Press, 2012).

25. John Perkins, *Confessions of an Economic Hit Man* (San Francisco: Berrett-Koehler Publishers, 2004).

26. Eboo Patel, "Affirming Identity, Achieving Pluralism," in *Building the Interfaith Youth Movement: Beyond Dialogue to Action*, ed. Eboo Patel and Patrice Brodeur (Lanham, MD: Rowman and Littlefield, 2006), 15–41.

27. Mahmood Mamdani, *Good Muslim, Bad Muslim: America, the Cold War, and the Roots of Terror* (New York: Pantheon, 2004).

28. For more about the Ta'leef Collective: http://www.taleefcollective.org/?page_id=26.

29. See Hisham Aidi, "Jihadis in the Hood: Race, Urban Islam and the War on Terror," *Middle East Report* (2007): 224, http://www.merip.org/mer/mer224/224_aidi.html; Daulatzai, *Black Star, Crescent Moon.*

30. See video for song at: http://www.youtube.com/watch?v=sCbpiOpLwFg.

31. See Daulatzai, *Black Star, Crescent Moon*; Naber, *Arab America.*

32. Jamillah Karim, "Between Immigrant Islam and Black Liberation: Young Muslims Inherit Global Muslim and African American Legacies," *The Muslim World* 95 (October 2005): 130, 497.

33. Pitti, *The Devil in Silicon Valley*, 4, 193.

34. Sunaina Maira, "'Good' and 'Bad' Muslim Citizens: Feminists, Terrorists, and U.S. Orientalisms," *Feminist Studies* 35, no. 3 (2009): 631–656.

35. Mamdani, *Good Muslim, Bad Muslim.*

36. See Naber, *Arab America.*

37. See Hamid Dabashi, *Brown Skin, White Masks* (London: Pluto, 2011).

38. Shryock, "Introduction," 9.

39. Ibid., 10.

40. Sherene H. Razack, *Casting Out: The Eviction of Muslims from Western Law and Politics* (Toronto: University of Toronto Press, 2008).

41. For background on this, see the "Stand with the Eleven" website: http://www.irvine11.com/timeline/.

42. Steven Salaita, *Israel's Dead Soul* (Philadelphia: Temple University Press, 2011).

PART II POST-9/11 MILITARISM IN OLD AND NEW MEDIA

4 · HOW TO TELL A TRUE WAR STORY . . . FOR CHILDREN

Children's Literature Addresses Deployment

LAURA BROWDER

Is it possible, to crib a title from Tim O'Brien, to tell a true war story? For children? In *The Things They Carried*, his 1990 collection of related stories about a platoon of American soldiers fighting in Vietnam, O'Brien published a definition of a "true" war story that has since been much-cited: "War is hell, but that's not the half of it, because war is mystery and terror and adventure and courage and discovery and holiness and pity and despair and longing and love. War is nasty; war is fun. War is thrilling; war is drudgery. War makes you a man; war makes you dead."[1] O'Brien's story, of course, is resolutely male. It's about a group of soldiers in Vietnam, one of whom first tries to feed and then tortures to death a baby buffalo.

O'Brien's story is about men in a combat zone, and in his terms, women are incapable of even understanding what a war story might be since they can by definition never be involved in war. In a passage dripping with contempt, O'Brien's narrator tells us:

> Now and then, when I tell this story, someone will come up to me afterward and say she liked it. It's always a woman. Usually it's an older woman of kindly temperament and humane politics. She'll explain that as a rule she hates war stories; she can't understand why people want to wallow in all the blood and gore. But this one she liked. The poor baby buffalo, it made her sad. Sometimes, even, there are little tears. What I should do, she'll say, is put it all behind me.
>
> Find new stories to tell.
>
> I won't say it but I'll think it.
>
> I'll picture Rat Kiley's face, his grief, and I'll think, *You dumb cooze.*
>
> Because she wasn't listening.
>
> It *wasn't* a war story. It was a *love* story.[2]

Women, or "dumb coozes," have been neither the subject of nor the audience for traditional war stories. But with over 280,000 women, to date, deployed to combat zones in Iraq and Afghanistan, in wars that have passed the decade mark, war stories—and the audiences for which they are intended—have changed. The new war stories are less about the mystery and terror and manliness of war and more about what war does to families. And the new war stories are not intended for men. They are not even intended for women. They are stories for teenagers, children, and even babies.

Since the First Gulf War in 1991, but especially since the current wars in Iraq and Afghanistan, dozens of books have been written for babies and young children whose parent or parents are deployed, as well for about older kids undergoing the same experience. And in these new books, war stories are definitely also love stories. Rather than O'Brien's model of war as something that makes men men and distinguishes them from women and children, in the view of these new books, war is something that is a family affair and affects everyone.

The earliest new war stories written for youthful audiences were those published in the aftermath of the First Gulf War—a war in which women and reservists were being deployed for the first time in large numbers. Because Desert Shield/Desert Storm, was such a short conflict, these stories focused more on the novelty of families that had to reconfigure themselves—they were more sociological treatises than survival manuals—and ask the question: what does it mean when we have to change mothers into soldiers? However, the books written for babies and young children during the long conflicts in Iraq and Afghanistan ask a very different question: what happens when children have to think about themselves as soldiers and the entire family becomes militarized? Yet finally—and no doubt because of the great length of the Iraq and Afghanistan conflicts, and the repeated deployments that so many troops have experienced—a final category of these books has come to ask an even more haunting question: how does war change not only the soldiers who fight it but also the militarized families left behind? How do they help prepare children not only for the long absence of a parent but for the possibility that that parent will return from his or her deployment emotionally damaged—or not return at all? Ultimately these kids' books, through redefining war as a family affair, force all of us to rethink what a true war story might be.

FAMILY WAR STORIES

Of course, these are not the first children's books about kids left behind while a parent, typically a father, is off at war. After all, Louisa May Alcott's *Little Women*, in which the March father is gone to the Civil War for the entire book, is one of the great classics of American youth literature. Yet *Little Women* was published in

1868, years after the war was over; whereas the books discussed in this essay have been written while the wars in Iraq and Afghanistan were still taking place.

Curious about this genre, I researched children's books on this subject published in previous wars—surely World War I, World War, the Korean War, the Vietnam War, and the First Gulf War must have produced a large body of literature. I couldn't find much—a few young-adult novels published many years after the Vietnam War, a number published decades after World War II.

There were a couple of novels published in the wake of Desert Shield/Desert Storm, but that war was over so quickly—after all, the ground war lasted five days, and the entire operation a matter of months—that there was literally no time for authors to get their books out in that period. Stumped, I asked Marcia Whitehead, a humanities research librarian at the University of Richmond, if she could find any. After a fruitless search, this is the email she sent me:

> I've looked at a number of children's books web sites and searched Worldcat for books published from 1940–1970 and, while there are a few books from the 1940's about families affected by the war, they are not really focused, as far as I can tell, on the social or emotional effect on the children. I will continue to look, but I was an army brat and my father was in Vietnam during my freshman year of high school. I don't remember anyone showing the least interest in how I felt about it. That was a war fought mostly by young men without children, and the broader populace was so alienated that it wasn't interested until years later in the personal issues of the soldiers or their families. WW II was a war to which the entire country was committed; I think it was assumed that children would want their fathers to fight, just like their friends' fathers. Add to that, society as a whole was less obsessed with the happiness of its children. I think that people just expected children to suck it up and do as they were told. It wasn't about them.[3]

There's a lot to what Whitehead writes—O'Brien's "true war story" certainly has little concern for the feelings of "dumb coozes," let alone their children. Parenting has changed a great deal since the Vietnam era, and even though children of deployed troops are instructed in the current books to "be brave" and repress their feelings in order to keep functioning, at least there is a widespread acknowledgment on the part of authors that they have difficult feelings that will require managing.

CHILDREN AS HOME FRONT SOLDIERS

Now that the social novelty of mothers at war has worn off, the necessity for children to cope remains, and that is what many of the contemporary books for these children address. However, while the current crop of books focuses a great deal on children's feelings, the books are also heavily focused on how children can manage their feelings in order to become soldier-like in their own right. Depending on the age level the books are written for, children are asked to learn how to support the parent who is deployed as well as the one who is still at home.

With the enormous stresses placed on military families as the wars extend beyond the ten-year mark and as military parents deploy for the second, third, and even fifth time, a new genre of books has sprung up to help children cope with the uncertainties of deployment. The Department of Defense publishes its own materials, including checklists for children of deployed parents; and at conferences and in journal articles, military psychologists and social workers address the problems that have arisen for children in these families: high incidences of child abuse on military bases, including sexual abuse; children struggling academically and sometimes having to be held back a year in school because of anxiety problems; and a wide range of other behavioral issues. Alongside these works produced by the military and for the military are commercially published (and sometimes self-published) books aimed directly at kids and families who are affected by deployments. Many military parents see children's literature as being absolutely crucial to the mental health of their children during deployments. Former army sergeant Erica Lewis recorded herself reading stories for her four-year-old son Tariq while she was deployed to Abu Ghraib in 2003 and mailed the cassettes back to him.[4] Had she had access to the books now available to deployed troops, she might have found them extremely useful.

Indeed, before exploring what these books of fiction written for audiences ranging from babies to teenagers are about, it may be helpful to listen to a number of military parents—mothers, in this case—reflecting on their experiences of deployed parenthood, sharing their true family war stories. From their point of view, the experience often includes their feelings of guilt at leaving their children behind and concern that their children do not understand the reasons for what seems to them like parental abandonment in its purest form. These stories show the stark realities and lingering aftereffects of parental deployment for both parents and children.

As army sergeant Connica McFadden told me about her deployment to Iraq in 2003,

> I just feel, I guess, guilty in a way for having to leave her so much and I know my son, I left him too, but he was able to deal with it more, so I guess her just dealing with the problems she got now and lashing out sometimes and the way she acting, I mean, I guess I blame myself a lot for it, 'cause I know that I'm the one that's in the military, and I'm the one that left her. She didn't ask for this. I just pray that once she get older, she understand that mommy had a job to do. You know, they called, so I had to go.[5]

McFadden, who had to deploy (with her husband) against doctor's orders when her daughter Aisha was six months old and still breast-feeding, arrived home less than a year later to find that her daughter did not recognize her parents and cried inconsolably when left with McFadden or her husband. It took months of weekend visits with Aisha before they were able to take her home and have her readjust to life at home with them and her older brother. Then, less than a year later, McFadden had to deploy again for another year. Looking back several years later, she mused: "I keep letters that I wrote them, and you know, she can't read or nothing, I still wrote letters and wrote cards when I could. And I think that when she get older and I made her a little scrapbook, that she'll understand and she'll see and hopefully she'll look at me like her brother do—as a hero."[6]

Laweeda Blash, who is an army staff sergeant and a mother of four, including one daughter who is severely autistic, was deployed to Iraq three times between 2003 and 2006. As she said when I spoke to her,

> They showed strength in front of me, but they were upset. They were worried. One of my sons, he got affected so bad, he wound up staying back one grade—just couldn't concentrate. It wasn't really the teacher's fault. The different schools around Army bases—the military bases—especially the bases have units that's deployed, constantly deploying—they try to have some kind of support groups for family members and children and so on. So, you know, really, they tried to have support systems in place, but some children, you know, gravitate to it or go to it. Mine, just so happens, like I said, with my husband already being there—that was like a big weight off of me and him and the kids, but they didn't want me to go. As a matter of fact, my oldest son—the one that got sick, the one that was retained—he said, "mommy, I'm tired of you going." You know, and I said, "I know." I said, "but, you know, Jesus got a plan. He's allowed me to go for many a reason and plus that's part of my job." And so he took it with a grain of salt and he—and he just did his best. And so, they took it real hard.[7]

Blash's and McFadden's stories are emblematic of many others. Schools on military bases feature support groups and other counseling services for children of deployed parents (groups that come in for their share of discussion and even ridicule in books written for or about older kids), but Blash's kids, among others, were not particularly interested nor found these groups helpful. McFadden desperately hoped that Aisha would learn to see her deployment as an act of heroism, rather than as abandonment. For both Blash's and McFadden's kids, the experience of war and deployment was profoundly transformative and not necessarily in a good way.

To address the enormous need for parents and their children to make it through deployment together, there are books aimed directly at helping kids make it through the weeks, months, and even years of a parent's absence. At their least subversive, these books for younger children serve as manuals for how to cope with a parent's long deployment. Yet even these books, some with titles like *My Mommy Wears Combat Boots*, demonstrate just how radically US war experiences have changed since war was defined in terms more like O'Brien's. And books for and about older kids whose parents are at war delve much further into redefining war stories. While the thrust of books written for young children is certainly toward understanding and appreciating a parent's sacrifice, those written for older kids—middle-grade books and young-adult novels—additionally see a parent's deployment as an occasion for personal growth for the child.

Through close readings of these books, as well as listening to the experiences of deployed mothers, we can begin to see how completely inadequate O'Brien's truth has become for the hundreds of thousands of American children whose parents have deployed once, twice, or many more times to Iraq and Afghanistan over the past ten years. Instead of war being a rite that separates male warriors from the rest of society, war has become something that involves the whole family—and the most hard-hitting of these books stress how completely the experience of war can change children and spouses as well as the deployed troops.

The huge number of customer reviews on Amazon for the thirty or so books aimed mainly at young kids offer sometimes startling glimpses into the challenges faced by the children of deployed parents—both from the stresses of one parent's absence and, sometimes, the difficulties of another parent or caretaker's presence. As one of thirty customer reviews for Karen M. Pavlicin's *Surviving Deployment: A Guide for Military Families* noted: "One thing I liked about this book was the section on how to win cooperation from your kids and how to avoid child abuse. None of us thinks about this much because of course we would never want to hurt our kids. But deployments put a lot of pressure on a lot of single parents who are also under tremendous stress."[8]

How do these books—ranging from inspirational workbooks for kids to fill out during their parent's deployment (*Heroes!*; *Activities for Kids Dealing with Deployment*; *My Dad's Deployment: A Deployment and Reunion Activity Book for Young Children*) to warm storybooks designed to help kids feel connected to absent military parents (*A Paper Hug*; *Dear Baby, I'm Watching Over You*)— help children prepare for the unpredictability of life with a stressed parent or other caretaker?

BOOKS FOR YOUNG CHILDREN

Of course, much depends on the age level at which these books are aimed. The cover for *Dear Baby, I'm Watching Over You*, by Carol Casey (with illustrations by Mark Braught), shows a blonde, blue-eyed baby draped in an American flag.

There is no mention of war at all in the text or reference to it in the illustrations, just illustrations of men and women in uniform, delivering reassuring messages like, "On this brand new day, I think of you and pray. It's *my* way of watching over you." A saluting soldier, stands before a waving American flag and says, "Honor, duty, freedom, and pride; these are the reasons I decide that protecting my country is *my* way of watching over you."[9] The reasons for the father deploying are to "protect" his country in exactly the same way that he would protect his child—war in this construct is nothing so much as an extension of a father's role. In *Night Catch*, by Brenda Ehrmantraut, with illustrations by Vicki Wehrman, a father separated from his perhaps four-year-old son transforms their usual games played with a bat, ball, and mitt into "night catch" in which they pretend to toss the North Star back and forth. Although the father is shown in combat fatigues against a background of a desert with a camel, a couple of palm trees, and some minarets, there is nothing to indicate that a war is going on.[10]

Even when there is some acknowledgement of how difficult the separation might be, the tone of books for younger children remains resolutely upbeat. In *A Paper Hug*, written by Stephanie Skolmoski and illustrated by Anneliese Bennion, the narrator's mother cries when her husband receives his deployment orders, but his father tells her "everything [will] be all right. 'I chose to serve my country and now I am needed.'"[11] Most of the book centers on the narrator's creating of a pair of paper hands traced from his own and attached by a piece of yarn that he sends to his father—this book, as all the other book referenced so far, ends with the happy reunion between the two of them when the father arrives home.

Books for slightly older children acknowledge the war but often recast the parent as a hero capable of handling it. In *Hero Dad*, a boy explains, "My dad is a superhero. He doesn't wear rocket-propelled boots—he wears Army boots." The illustrations show the father wearing night-vision goggles against a background of tanks, carrying an M-16, and posing with his (gender-integrated) platoon. His deployment is presented as heroic, too: "Sometimes he has to go away for long trips, but that's what superheroes have to do." The final page shows a happy family reunion, with the caption "My dad is an American soldier."[12] There is no sense here that a child might feel abandoned—only proud of what his parent is doing.

Likewise, in *The Impossible Patriotism Project*, by Linda Skeers, aimed at five-to-eight-year-olds, the protagonist can't think of a theme for a school project about patriotism, since his classmates have already covered such topics as the Liberty Bell and the statue of liberty. He ends up with a more personal project about his deployed father: "'That's a picture of my dad in uniform,' Caleb said proudly. 'Patriotism means going away from your family even if you have to miss Parents' Night. It means keeping everyone in the United States safe.' He smiled and gently touched the picture. 'My dad taught me to love my country. My *dad* is patriotism.'"[13] The father has become much larger than life, on par with American icons of patriotism. Here, the text and pictures echo the message of shared sacrifice that Marcia Whitehead remembers from her father's Vietnam deployment.

Perhaps the most traditionally patriotic of all, and certainly the best-known of these books is *Don't Forget, God Bless Our Troops*, by Jill Biden, illustrated by Raul Colon, which presents the current wars as being ones that all Americans (at least all Americans known to the book's protagonist) appreciate and support. While like most of the books discussed here it is based on the author's own experience, of her son's deployment to Iraq, unlike the others, it is explicitly written as a public service for military families: "I hope Natalie's story gives readers some insight and encourages them to commit a simple act of kindness toward a military family."[14] In this book, every page ends with an injunction for Natalie, who appears to be around five: "*Be brave, Natalie.*" Natalie is surrounded by kind friends and neighbors who appreciate her father's sacrifice: as one of his friends tells her when he comes over to shovel snow, "'Your dad is sure helping our country,' Alex says. 'I want to help too!'" The celebration of her father's patriotism helps insure that "Natalie feels special. Proud." And Natalie sacrifices as well, spending a day sending hundreds of boxes overseas with her grandparents. The final image is of her father in uniform with his arms around Natalie, celebrating her bravery while in the background an American flag waves. If war is an extension of parenting in these books, then children can succeed at their own roles by supporting their parents at war and not questioning the necessity of or even the reasons for their absence.

Yet not every book completely papers over the fear and anger that children might feel when their parents deploy. In *My Dad's Deployment: A Deployment and Reunion Activity Book for Young Children*, simple, nonmilitary tasks—the kinds of sequencing that would be at home in any kindergarten classroom—mingle with instructions to "circle the things you might do when you feel angry,"[15] as well as ways to connect to a missing parent—in this case, always a father.

Occasionally there is a stark reminder that the war story may not be so easily contained. *Daddy's in Iraq, but I Want Him Back* features a three-year-old narrator and generally follows the same pattern as the others, ending with, "So, if you're sad 'cause your Daddy's in Iraq, you'll be o.k. He loves you and he's coming back!" However, an author's afterword ends the book starkly: "Some of your spouses and parents will not come back and my heart breaks for you. I think of you often with tears in my eyes and a lump in my throat knowing this could have been our story. I did not know how to integrate that scenario into this book, for it is primarily focused on helping small children deal with the anxiety and insecurity of their parent going to war."[16] Clearly, there are limitations on how much truth can be allowed into a story for young children. In fact, I have not been able to find a single book for very young children that deals with a parent's death in the Iraq or Afghanistan wars.

In *Love, Lizzie: Letters to a Military Mom*, nine-year-old Lizzie sends epistles expressing frustration at the babysitter's restrictions and asks, "How long does defending freedom take?"[17] Although the war is not explicitly referenced, Lizzie does ask, "Are you staying safe, Mommy? Please don't forget to wear your helmet. I promise I'll wear my bike helmet EVERY TIME if you wear your helmet too—O.K.?" Her mother replies, "I know you're worried that I'm in danger. Lizzie, I promise to do everything I can to stay safe." At the end of the book, Lizzie's mother—like all the other parents discussed in these books—comes home safe and sound.

When these books do not fall back on patriotism and defending freedom as reasons for a parent's absence, they sometimes connect the child's safety at home with his or her deployed parent's work to make other children safe. "When Mommy is away, she said part of her job in the Army is helping other kids and babies, like me, who live far away. Mommy said these kids don't have good food to eat or shoes to wear on their feet,"[18] says the narrator of *My Mommy Wears Combat Boots*, a young bear whose anger and fear during her mother's deployment make her struggle to behave well. Her mother, after all, is taking on a maternal role for Iraqi children as well as for her own daughter.

The book concludes, "My mommy also said she loves me no matter what, and that I should say a prayer for her every night before I go to bed. I should also pray for all the other Army babies, like me, who miss their mommies. Because there are lots of mommies who wear combat boots." Learning how to manage anger over feeling abandoned, as well as a range of other difficult emotions, is key for children dealing with a parent's deployment. And part of managing emotions means never questioning the reasons for war or for a parent's participation in it.

Of course, in real life, children often express that anger in many ways. As army staff sergeant Shawntel Lotson recollects,

One of my main concerns was my daughter, because I know when I left to go to Korea when she was three, she didn't talk to me for the first six months, and that kind of hurt, because I was leaving. You know, her mom was leaving, and "why are you leaving me to go be with somebody else" was her take on that, so—and she did the same thing when I went to Egypt. So, she was one of my main concerns because my boys, you know, boys are a little bit stronger than the girls are, so this time, it was a little bit easier for her, you know, she cried about it. But my oldest cried more this go-around, because he was like, "well what if you don't come back," and I'm like, "don't think that way, you know, I have to go do my duty, and no matter what I'm always going to be with you." So, it was hard on them.[19]

Fear of a parent's death in a combat zone, when acknowledged by these texts, makes for the most difficult moments. In Alan Madison's novel featuring a seven-year-old girl, *100 Days and 99 Nights*, Esme's father is away to an unspecified place, which is only briefly defined as a war: "I imagined him standing in the center of a giant desert. Not one person near, only sand as far as anyone could possibly see, camel looking over his shoulder, phone pressed to his ear." However, this chapter ends with Esme telling us, "The days were difficult because that was when you were told bad news. When Principal Pershing poked her partly gray, all-the-way curly head into class we all held our breaths—one girl sent home—one boy sent home. We were all so very brave. It was our duty."[20] Esme and her classmates are thoroughly militarized—familiar with the conventions of informing loved ones of a parent's death or war wounds, aware that these events can and do happen to them. And aware, too, that they have their duty to be brave, just like their parents.

Esme worries about not doing enough on the home front: like many of the characters in these deployment books, she is portrayed—and thinks of herself—as being a soldier in her own way and thinks often of the importance of being brave, of doing her duty. Yet for once this attitude is not fully endorsed by the text: when Esme asks Principal Pershing what she can do to help on the home front, the principal tells her: "All do what they can . . . and there's not much we *can* do."[21] Yet finally the principal's attitude does not count for much: Esme documents her efforts to save gas by riding her bike. As she says, "I loved helping on the home front because it made me feel like I was part of the good 'ol U.S.A., which made me feel like I was part of the army, which made me feel like I was part of my dad."[22] Esme and her friends, who all have parents deployed to the war, attempt to reenact the rituals of World War II home-front life—attempting to plant victory gardens (hard to dig a bed in the northern Virginia winter), selling bonds (not possible any more), or saving scrap metal. Their neighbor, widowed in both World War I and World War II, comments wistfully of the Great War, "That was the war to end all wars."[23] Like other books in this genre and written for this age group, the current wars are presented as being in a long line of earlier American wars—ones with the support of the whole population.

Yet there are moments when even Esme questions the idea of duty: "He had other duties—duties here with us. Which came first, the sergeant or the daddy?"[24] Esme's troublesome baby brother, Ike, asks their grandfather, "Grandpa, do all Dads come back from war?" "No, Ike, they don't."[25] And when their father finally does return home, for once the story does not end with the triumphant reunion, but later the same night, as the family is together:

> "And now you'll never have to go back again," stated Ike.
> There was a whole bowl of silence.
> "Won't lie to you, Ike. I might have to go back."[26]

Even for children as young as seven, then, the truth of the war story can break through the discussion of bravery, patriotism, and duty: the realities of death and loss are never completely at bay. However, it is the books that are not written explicitly as survival manuals for kids—the ones that often more thoroughly explore the contours of the new war stories—that most thoroughly challenge O'Brien's model for the true war story.

The challenges to O'Brien's kind of narrative are of course most evident in stories written for girls (and the vast majority of middle-grade and young-adult books are written for girls, not boys). In some respects, having a parent at war is as convenient for middle-grade plot purposes as the traditional fairy tale device of the dead parents or missing parents: it places the child protagonist in a position where he or she has to fend for himself or herself, to learn independence, and to grapple with finding a way in an unfamiliar world. With war as the backdrop, it is easy for writers to use a parent's deployment as a way for a boy protagonist to come of age in a very traditional, manly way. Such is the case in Cynthia DeFelice's 2011 novel, *Wild Life*, which begins when seventh-grader Erik Carlson learns that not one but both of his reservist parents are to be deployed to Iraq later that week, forcing him to leave his upstate New York home and travel to a remote corner of North Dakota to live with his mother's parents, whom he has only met once when he was three. All of the ingredients for a masculine coming-of-age experience are present: Erik is disappointed not so much because he will miss his parents but because he has just gotten his New York junior hunting license and was supposed to hunt for the first time the day after he is scheduled to fly to North Dakota.

The novel has the kind of dreamy quality of a myth, with an extremely linear plotline: Erik arrives to find his grandfather to be gruff and angry, his grandmother incapable of driving herself anywhere. He immediately encounters, and rescues, a beautiful hunting dog that has been stuck with porcupine quills, whom he renames Quill. When he opens the forbidden door in their house, he finds that it leads to the room of their son, Dan, who died fighting in Vietnam thirty-four years previously and whose name is never mentioned by Erik's grandparents, Oma and Big Darrell. These circumstances provide him with the opportunity to live out his fantasy: as he initially explains to his mother why he wants to hunt, he tells her "Sometimes. . . . I wish it was still pioneer times. Kids really got to *do* things back then."[27] In remarks that sound straight out of Robert Bly's popular New Age text on masculinity, *Iron John*, he talks about "the old days, when people and animals were part of the same world, you know?"[28] Interestingly, unlike the characters in most deployment fiction, Erik barely seems to give his absent parents a thought once they fly off to Iraq. The story hinges not on them but on his grandparents' grief for their lost warrior son—grief which is only resolved after Erik steals Dan's rifle and runs away with Quill to live off the land. "He thought of his parents, halfway across the world. 'They're the ones who sent me here and told me to make the best of it. And that's what I'm doing,' he told himself."[29] And this is where it gets really existential. Surveying the unpopulated North Dakota countryside,

A feeling of exhilaration rose in him. From this moment on, he realized, every decision was his to make. Not only that, these were going to be *real* decisions, important ones, having to do with staying alive. He had one simple task, he told himself, to live off the land.

The challenge quickened his blood.[30]

Symbolically, Erik comes to replace his lost uncle Dan. Rather than emphasizing his parents' dedication, toughness, and bravery, the story is about Erik's own: "He had only the supplies he could fit in his pack and his own wits and courage, and that was all he needed."[31] The novel hinges on his ability to use his gun, after all, which he does with great success, living off the pheasants he kills, field dresses, and roasts on fires that he builds. He survives drinking contaminated water and being racked with cramps, vomiting, and diarrhea. "He had been careless, and careless people didn't survive."[32] He escapes a would-be rescuer, who is anxious for the reward his grandparents have posted, and runs into a blinding snowstorm. When he finds his way back to his grandparents' house, Big Darrell thinks he is Dan. The experience of losing and then regaining Erik is as transformative to his grandparents as his walkabout is to Erik himself. As the normally undemonstrative Big Darrell gathers him in a hug, he tells Erik, "I lost one boy. Didn't think I could stand to lose another."[33] Erik has survived his war with the elements in a way that Dan did not survive the actual war, and he very explicitly comes to replace that lost son.

The terms of *Wild Life* are minimalist: his parents are so absent from the text that the grandparents don't even notify them when Erik goes missing for five days so as not to worry them. Erik does not think about them much, and the only thing we hear from them after their departure is a single letter in which his "father wrote that he was proud to be serving his country, despite the upset to their lives."[34] Erik's absence propels his grandmother to drive again, in search of him. As she tells him after he returns, "The Lord works in mysterious ways, Erik. I hope I never have to go through anything like the last five days. But something wonderful has happened, and it couldn't have happened without you running off the way you did. . . . You running off—it changed Big Darrell."[35] At the end of the book, Big Darrell offers to fix the broken step on the porch that he had built with Dan decades before. As Oma says to him, "You used to be quite the handyman." As Big Darrell tells her,

> "I guess there's a lot of things I used to do." He looked at Erik. "Maybe I just wanted a boy to do 'em with."
> "I'm ready if you are,' said Erik."[36]

Erik has symbolically transformed himself into the lost warrior son, with the help of Dan's gun, and has restored his grandparents to the world of the living. As

Oma tells him, "That's the problem with grieving. The dead can begin to matter more than the living."[37] The gender politics of the book are very different from those of many other novels in which a mother deploys. In this case, the mother joined the Army Reserves to escape from her father, whom she could not console for the loss of his son. At first when Erik comes to his grandparents' house, he is given his mother's old room, which is cluttered with old junk. It is only after he returns from his existential coming-of-age adventure that he is promoted to Dan's old room, which had been untouched since the boy's death in Vietnam. Soon, it is clear, his grandfather will be able to start hunting again—another one of the things he gave up after his son's death. *Wild Life* is an Iraq war book that resolves the Vietnam War, at least for Erik's grandfather.

THE NEW TECHNOLOGIES

When Tim O'Brien, at the end of "How to Tell a True War Story," reflects once more about the genre, he concludes that "a true war story is never about war. . . . It's about love and memory. It's about sorrow. It's about sisters who never write back and people who never listen."[38] Yet the current crop of war stories suggest the opposite—children driven crazy by their attempts to listen all the time to a parent's experience, even when a parent can't or won't talk about it.

There are a number of issues that make the experience of American children with parents deployed post-9/11 different from the experience of children in previous wars. Paramount among these is the technology that often makes communication between parents and children instantaneous, which completely changes the dynamic. Children can now use the Internet to learn much more about what is actually going on where their parent is deployed. Odetta Johnson, a sergeant major in the army reserve, was deployed to Baghdad in 2005 when her kids were nine and eleven. As she recalls:

> Well, whenever I got hurt I would tell them and I thought it was so exciting I was sending pictures home. But I had no idea they were like, "Oh. Oh." And I was like, "Oh, it's not that bad." You know, and then—but they were keeping up with me when I said, "Well, I went to the Ministry of Defense two days ago." And they were like, "Mom, that was near Suicide Cape." And I was like, "How do you know about Suicide Cape?" "It's on the internet." It's like, duh.

Eventually, Johnson made the decision not to keep in electronic or phone contact with her kids: they sent letters back and forth instead, so her children would not be overwhelmed by the tide of information they were receiving.[39]

The tantalizing, yet frustrating nature of communication between children and their deployed parents features in novels written for older children. A powerful graphic novel written for teenagers, *Refresh, Refresh* takes its title from the way its teenage boy characters constantly push the "refresh" button on their computers in the hope that their deployed fathers will have sent them emails. This novel acknowledges more than most the complexities of life for the children of deployed soldiers: it opens with the three best friends beating each other to a pulp because, as the narrator writes, "It was Cody's idea that we should fight each other. He wanted to be ready. He wanted to hurt those who hurt him. And if he went down, he would go down swinging, as he was sure his father would. This is what we all wanted: to please our fathers, to make them proud—even though they had left us."[40] *Refresh, Refresh* graphically depicts the stresses of life on a military base: the realities of dead-end factory jobs for the parents left behind, what happens when the power company shuts off the electricity, the way those left behind by deployed soldiers take out their frustrations in drinking and violence. The novel ends when the three boys' enemy, whose father has just been killed in the war, comes to inform Josh, the protagonist, "I regret to inform you. . . ." Josh, who has grown up in military culture, knows that the military never sends anyone alone to execute this duty—and beats him badly, with help from his friends. Although Josh has been accepted to college and will be the only one of the three to take a path other than military service, he enlists at the novel's end in order to avoid the threat of jail if his victim presses charges. *Refresh, Refresh* is undeniably powerful, but it is also well outside the mainstream of the genre of literature for and about the children of deployed soldiers. It had its origins in a short story published by Benjamin Percy in the *Paris Review*, an elite literary journal. It was then adapted into a screenplay by James Ponsoldt, whose first film premiered at Sundance, and then finally adapted into graphic novel form. Unlike any other text discussed here, *Refresh, Refresh* depicts life in the military as an almost inevitable dead end for its teenage characters. Although some of its characters (generally the lesser ones) might tell war stories to impress girls, it is clear that these stories are transactional only: violence is the only thing that is truly of consequence in this book.

The new technologies also form a central element in *The Summer before Boys*, a novel aimed at nine-to twelve-year-olds by Nora Raleigh Baskin, whose narrator, twelve-year-old Julia, tells readers "I would go online hoping to see an e-mail from my mother. And then I would log off and on again a second later because I knew it was daytime in Iraq and she might have written just at that second."[41] Yet more radical than its discussion of new technologies is the book's unusual admission of the costs of war, costs that extend well past the joyful parent-child reunion that ends just about every book discussed here. And perhaps most radical of all is the admission within the book that most Americans are completely disengaged from the Iraq and Afghanistan Wars and that all talk of victory gardens or saving scrap metal is worse than irrelevant.

As she accepts an expression of sympathy, Julia muses: "She was sorry my mom was so far away. Sorry there was a war and some people didn't come back, or came back without their leg, or their hand, or their eyes. Or their memories."[42] In this book, too, is an acknowledgment that few Americans care about the war or the troops—anathema in the world of children's and young-adult literature— and that when soldiers return, they are altered: "Our country was at war. It was far away from here, and most people never even thought about it, but it never rested. And every day, soldiers and doctors and military police and cooks and engineers came home different from when they left."[43] In fact, another character in the book has his father's second deployment cut short, and tells the school counselor, that "He's angry all the time. . . . He yells. He likes it quiet in the house. When my baby sister started running around the kitchen, making all this noise, he slammed his fist down on the counter. He told her to shut up. . . . And he screams. At night. In his sleep, I guess." He concludes by telling the counselor, "sometimes I wish my dad hadn't come home at all."[44] In the end, Peter's father opts to go back to the war. And Julia, who is well connected to the internet, tells the reader what the body count is in Iraq.

Yet even this book ends the first night that the deployed parent is home— and the experiences of soldiers I interviewed suggest that the post-deployment period is just as challenging for families in many ways.

CHANGING KIDS AND CHANGING PARENTS

Staff Sergeant Blash mused that upon her return home, she needed to learn how to relate to each child again.

> That was my biggest challenge, and I'm still learning, 'cause it's kind of difficult to go to a school when, you know, and teachers are telling you about the kids, and I felt very odd, 'cause I didn't know what to say to them because I've been gone— when it comes to the progression of my kids and certain things and everything, so I really felt out of place with that.[45]

It is the rare children's book that can really confront the fact that parents are going to be changed and often in ways that can be difficult for a child. As marine corps sergeant Jocelyn Proano told me, although she had been trying her best to avoid being deployed when her daughter was young, once she got her orders, her attitude—and her identity—changed: "The mommy mentality left me as soon as we got on that bus and started flying to Cherry Point to fly out. All of a sudden the Marine hit me and I'm like, alright we've got combat training."[46]

When Proano did come home at the halfway point for leave, she found that her daughter had changed as well:

> But it is so different like at the half-way point being home, 'cause I did see my daughter and she's walking and like yup and I don't even know what she's saying,

but it was so cute, because she was so different. She looked so cute, I could not believe she was my kid. It just—it felt weird. And plus, she wasn't used to me—she wanted my mom more, I think. I'm like, "hey do you want me to make you breakfast." "No, I want Nanna."

Although Proano was happy to be home with her daughter, she still felt the pull of deployment: "You want to be a Marine, and you can't be a mom all the time. I enjoy to do certain things. I feel bad for wanting to go out again, but I don't want to live my life in the marine corps thinking, 'man, I should've deployed again—I should've done this.' So, it's kind of hard."

And Staff Sergeant Lotson reflected on her own transformation as a mother:

So, it was reconnecting with my kids again. I mean, the love is still there, but it's at the same time in the back of my mind is—You hear them talking about, "oh, I did this and did that." But at the same time, it's just so sad, because I missed that. I missed it. You can't bring it back. You know, and reconnecting, because I did change a little bit. I was a little bit more calm, you know, I had some points where I would always blow up, you know, not blow up blow up, but get so angry at the person in the car in front of you "get out the way!" you know? Now, I just sit and listen to my music. Just relax a little bit.[47]

Although few of these books under consideration really get into how parents as well children change as a result of a deployment, one book written by the daughter and spouse of deployed soldiers seems most to reflect the experiences soldiers expressed in interviews with me. *High Dive*, by Tammar Stein, whose protagonist is a college freshman, comes closest of any of these books to a true war story in that it talks about how war changes the soldiers who experience it— as well as those who stay at home. In *High Dive*, Arden feels that her mother's experience gives her perspective or ought to: "What was a crappy hotel room or selling a vacation home compared to life in the barracks, working twelve-hour shifts? She had to deal with dying Iraqi babies and soldiers with missing limbs and burned-off faces. I had to deal with the fact that my vacation wasn't as fabulous as I had hoped."[48]

The plot of *High Dive* revolves around Arden, who is heading to Sardinia to close up the family vacation home in preparation for its sale. Her father has died in a car crash two and a half years previously, and her mother is deployed to Iraq, working in a combat-support hospital where two-thirds of the patients are Iraqis, many of them children and babies. Her emails to Arden reveal both how difficult her deployment is and how much she wants to be there: "I've been a nurse for twenty years. Nothing prepared me for this. I don't know what could. But if I didn't know what I was about, I would say this is the only place for me. There's no place in the world that needs me like the trauma center in Baghdad."[49]

The gritty details of managing deployment have a deep reality in this novel written by a military spouse whose reservist father deployed to Lebanon and whose husband has deployed to Central America. Arden has a cell phone but gives almost no one the number: "No one had the number but my mom, my roommate, and the dean of students. It was a phone for bad news."[50]

Unlike in the books for younger kids, patriotism is really not a motivating force here. As Arden's mother writes her,

> There's talk that they're going to launch fireworks for the Fourth of July. I told the commander what a bad idea that was. I don't think people with post-traumatic stress need more explosions, even if they're pretty ones. . . . As you can imagine, I'm on a mission to eradicate patriotic fever. I'm a nurse, after all. I'm naturally inclined against fevers.[51]

Of course, Arden worries about her mother's safety:

> Nothing could happen. Medical staff were safe.
>   Not necessarily, said the little voice that never shut up. A roadside bomb didn't care if there was a large red cross painted on the truck. Suicide bombers didn't ask bystanders their occupation before they exploded; mortars didn't care where they fell and exploded.[52]

For Arden, her identity as a military brat overrides all other forms of identity. She frequently uses military metaphors: following a rain storm, "As if a ceasefire had been declared, civilians emerged from shelters, umbrellas were put away, and life returned to Paris."[53] She sees herself as a chameleon, and we don't find out until page 69 that she is Jewish. Thus, part of the journey she takes throughout the book, then, is seeing her identity not solely in military terms: "That was another thing, like my mother being deployed or my father being dead, that I didn't usually tell people. It wasn't that I thought people were anti-Semitic. It was that it was another barrier to fitting in, another thing to make people think I was different from them."[54]

Yet when an insensitive remark from one of her "civilian" friends angers her, she reminds herself, "There was no cause to get so upset. Except it brought home again that our lives, mine and my mom's, were so affected by the war, while for everyone else it was meaningless. . . . The only signs that anyone was even aware of its existence were the yellow ribbon decals on cars saying 'Support Our Troops.' But the only 'support' these people gave was spending three bucks at the gas station to buy the damn decal. It was easy to 'support' the war when it demanded nothing of you."[55] There is zero sense that the American public is deeply engaged with the war—more a sense that, as soldiers are fond of saying, "We went to war, and America went to the shopping mall."

Arden worries about the changes that her mother is going through: "As difficult as her life was right now, when she came back, would life seem dull? How could heart attacks and sliced fingers and the occasional stabbing wound compare? How could being near me compare to the heart-pumping adrenaline thrill of saving so many lives, of being so needed? Right or wrong, the reason for the war in Iraq ceased to matter after a while."[56] The sense of disconnect Arden experiences from her mother is reality based, and her fears are never assumed to be unfounded.

Ultimately, the key to Arden's progression is her learning to give up her own identity as a military child and realize that she does not need to be endlessly adaptive. "I couldn't always blend in. But I was beginning to see that being a human chameleon wasn't necessarily a good way to go through life."[57] Like all the other books discussed here, the novel ends when Arden's mother returns safe and sound from her fourteen-month deployment: "She's home safe. And so am I."[58]

This, of all the books under consideration, may be the truest of war stories: as Stein tells us in her acknowledgments,

> The soldiers who have served or are currently serving in Iraq are making a huge sacrifice. They are brave, loyal, and strong. But they leave behind brave, loyal and strong wives and husbands, parents and children, who are forced to let their beloveds go in harm's way. . . .
>
> This is the heartache en masse that doesn't appear on the TV or in the papers. But make no mistake, the pain and longing at home is a terrible price hundreds of thousands of Americans pay whenever we go to war. I can't erase that pain, but I can bear witness.[59]

It is powerful, but it is not the last word. Perhaps the most potent children's literature is not what is published, but what the soldiers write for their children—books that are usually not intended for immediate consumption. Air force major Tabitha Stump showed me the journal she had written for her baby, who was five months old when she deployed to Afghanistan: every day she would write on a strip of paper, and then tape the strip into a loop. She eventually came home with a full chain, which she keeps hung up in a room in her house.[60] And Erica Lewis documented all of the things she was and experienced during the months she worked at Abu Ghraib as a prison guard. Her plan is to give it to Tariq when he is old enough, so that he will be able to understand her better. This is a practice that many soldiers follow, and these journals and letters, the truest war stories they can write, are sure to reverberate through the lives of their children for years and decades to come.

And this is, finally, where things get stickiest. In asking children to take on military roles like their deployed parents, the books under discussion generally ask them, although not in so many words, to accept the provisions of the Uniform Code of Military Justice that prohibit soldiers from criticizing the commander in chief—and are widely interpreted by soldiers to mean that it is illegal to criticize the mission. Thus, the soldiers I interviewed had a number of ways of dealing with risking their lives in a conflict that they may or may not believe is just or necessary. As a civilian, this was initially hard for me to understand. However, it became clear to me that even those women who may have had reservations about their role in this war took their oaths very seriously—and, more to the point, took their responsibility to the members of their units even more seriously. The children that are the intended audience for the books discussed here have taken no oaths. Yet these books, especially those written for younger children, in effect ask them to take on their parents' adherence to the Uniform Code of Justice as their own, to view their parents' deployment as an extension of their preexisting parental roles—and never, ever to question the mission. For if fighting the war is an extension of being a parent—protecting the American nation, or taking care of Iraqi children—then conversely, deployed parents and children become part of the same unit, and the distinctions between family life and wartime deployment blur to the point of elision.

NOTES

1. Tim O'Brien, *The Things They Carried* (New York: Houghton Mifflin, 1990), 86–87.
2. O'Brien, *The Things They Carried*, 90.
3. Marcia Whitehead, email message to author, January 14, 2013.
4. Erica Lewis, interview with author, July 23, 2011. http://mothersatwar.com/.
5. Connica McFadden, interview with author, November 10, 2007.
6. Ibid.
7. Laweeda Blash, interview with author, March 23, 2008.
8. R. Peters, October 15, 2005, comment on *Surviving Deployment*, Amazon.com. http://www.amazon.com/Surviving-Deployment-Guide-Military-Families/dp/0965748367/ref=sr_1_1?s=books&ie=UTF8&qid=1370352653&sr=1-1&keywords=surviving+deployment+a+guide+for+military+families.
9. Carol Casey and Mark Braught (illustrator), *Dear Baby, I'm Watching Over You* (Dear Baby Books, 2010), unpaginated.
10. Brenda Ehrmantraut and Vicki Wehrman (illustrator), *Night Catch* (Jamestown, ND: Bubble Gum Press, 2005). Similarly, in *Stars above Us* by Geoffrey Norman and E. B. Lewis (illustrator), the book jacket reads: "When Amanda's Dad has to go away, he tells her how looking at the same stars can help them feel close," (New York: G. P. Putnam's Sons, 2009).
11. Stephanie Skolmoski and Anneliese Bennion (illustrator), *A Paper Hug* (self-published, 2006), unpaginated.
12. Melinda Hardin and Bryan Langdo (illustrator), *Hero Dad* (Tarrytown, NY: Pinwheel Books, 2010), unpaginated.
13. Linda Skeers and Ard Hoyt (illustrator), *The Impossible Patriotism Project* (New York: Dial, 2007), unpaginated.
14. Jill Biden and Raul Colon (illustrator), *Don't Forget, God Bless Our Troops* (New York: Simon & Schuster, 2012), unpaginated.

15. Julie LaBelle and Christina Rodriguez (illustrator), *My Dad's Deployment: A Deployment and Reunion Activity Book for Young Children* (St. Paul, MN: Elva Resa Publishing, 2009), 37.

16. Carmen R. Hoyt, *Daddy's in Iraq, but I Want Him Back* (Victoria, BC: Trafford Publishing, 2005).

17. Lisa Tucker McElroy and Diane Paterson (illustrator), *Love, Lizzie: Letters to a Military Mom* (Morton Grove, IL: Albert Whitman & Company, 2005), unpaginated.

18. Sharon G. McBride, *My Mommy Wears Combat Boots* (Bloomington, IN: AuthorHouse, 2008) unpaginated.

19. Shawntel Lotson, interview with author, December 10, 2007.

20. Alan Madison, *100 Days and 99 Nights* (New York: Little, Brown and Company, 2008), 63.

21. Ibid., 67.

22. Ibid., 73.

23. Ibid., 82.

24. Ibid., 101.

25. Ibid., 111.

26. Ibid., 134.

27. Cynthia de Felice, *Wild Life* (New York: Farrar, Strauss and Giroux, 2011), 14.

28. Ibid., 15.

29. Ibid., 91.

30. Ibid., 95.

31. Ibid., 98.

32. Ibid., 131.

33. Ibid., 159.

34. Ibid., 172.

35. Ibid., 166.

36. Ibid., 177.

37. Ibid., 167.

38. O'Brien, *The Things They Carried*, 91.

39. Odetta Johnson, interview with author, April 29, 2008. Odetta Johnson interview with Jacki Lyden on *Tell Me More*, NPR, September 6, 2011, http://www.npr.org/2011/09/06/140214598/military-moms-how-wars-affect-families.

40. Danica Novgorodoff (adapted from the screenplay by James Ponsoldt, based on the short story by Benjamin Percy), *Refresh, Refresh* (New York: First Second, 2009), 5–7.

41. Nora Raleigh Baskin, *The Summer before Boys* (New York: Simon & Schuster, 2011), 73.

42. Ibid., 25.

43. Ibid., 29.

44. Ibid., 84–85.

45. Laweeda Blash, interview with author, December 10, 2007.

46. Jocelyn Proana, interview with author, October 26, 2007.

47. Shawntel Lotson, interview with author, December 10, 2007.

48. Tammar Stein, *High Dive* (New York: Knopf, 2008), 10.

49. Ibid., 10.

50. Ibid., 14.

51. Ibid., 43.

52. Ibid., 67.

53. Ibid., 68.

54. Ibid., 102.

55. Ibid., 114.

56. Ibid., 71.

57. Ibid., 180.

58. Ibid., 198.

59. Ibid., 199–200.

60. Tabitha Stump, interview with author, July 23, 2010. This is a common practice in military families. For a children's book in which this practice figures significantly, see Mindy L. Pelton and Robert Gantt Steele (illustrator), *When Dad's at Sea* (Park Ridge, IL: Albert Whitman & Company, 2004).

5 · "WHAT YOUNG MEN AND WOMEN DO WHEN THEIR COUNTRY IS ATTACKED"

Interventionist Discourse and the Rewriting of Violence in Adolescent Literature of the Iraq War

DAVID KIERAN

On October 30, 2001, George W. Bush appeared on the stage at Wootton High School in Rockville, Maryland. Before an audience that included students, administrators, members of the Veterans of Foreign Wars, and a uniformed school band, President Bush introduced the Lessons of Liberty initiative, a program that brought veterans to speak to school audiences. "Veterans," he intoned, "show us the meaning of sacrifice and citizenship. . . . At this moment, we especially need the example of their character."[1] Bush, unsurprisingly, had conflated citizenship with support for military intervention throughout the speech, telling students, "You're learning that to be an American in a time of war is to have duties. You're learning how a strong country responds to a crisis by being alert and calm, resolute and patient." Casting that response in particularly militarized terms, he inveighed that "we must always be . . . freedom's defender" even as he asserted a humanitarian intent: "As we pursue the enemy in Afghanistan, we feed the innocents. As we try to bring justice to those who have harmed us, we find those who need help."[2]

I do not open with this vignette because this language was unique within the president's post-9/11 rhetoric. Indeed, as Marita Sturken has shown, a dominant post-9/11 "narrative of innocence enabled the U.S. response to avoid any discussion of what the long histories of U.S. foreign policies had done to help foster a terrorist movement . . . [and] allows U.S. global interventions to be understood in a framework of benevolence rather than imperialism."³ Rather, I point to this moment as evidence of a larger discourse that insistently imagined young people as subjects whose support for the neoconservative interventionist policies that underlay the Bush administration's prosecution of the global War on Terror required cultivation. Although, as William Tuttle has shown, this phenomenon is not unique to the wars in Afghanistan and Iraq, it is nonetheless critical to note that over the past decade, the lives of young people living in the United States have consistently served as a terrain for debate over the most significant issues related to these conflicts.⁴ As students in schools, audiences at speeches, targets of military recruiters, and agents in their own acts of protest and memorialization, students of all ages insistently encountered, considered, adopted, developed, and acted according to diverse positions regarding the wars.

Young people also encountered cultural products, some specifically intended for their consumption, that took these wars as their subject. Taking seriously Eric Avila's assessment that "culture, like war, is politics by other means," in this chapter I interrogate recent young-adult literature's participation in contemporary debates over US foreign policy and militarism.⁵ Reading Ryan Smithson's memoir *Ghosts of War: The True Story of a 19-Year-Old GI* and the novels *Sunrise over Fallujah* by Walter Dean Myers and *Purple Heart* by Patricia McCormick, I argue that each contributes to the legitimization of the discourse of neoconservative humanitarian interventionism that has been central to the defense of the US intervention in Iraq.

These texts, which deal specifically with the experience of soldiers serving combat deployments in Iraq and were published as support for the Iraq War declined, are those with significant cultural capital; each novel is written by an award-winning children's author, and major publications have reviewed all three. Each, I maintain, contributes to interventionist discourse in two key ways: First, I demonstrate that they determinedly describe the war and the soldiers' experience in language that evokes that discourse's tenets, casting the Iraq War as an appropriate response to the September 11 terrorist attacks, as a humanitarian mission, and as an intervention in which it is appropriate for dutiful, patriotic young Americans to participate. Simultaneously, each text acknowledges but revises controversial moments of violence that have dominated media coverage of the Iraq War and have shaped the growing opposition to it. I demonstrate that these texts portray the Abu Ghraib prison, the practice of house-to-house search operations, the frequent incidence of military sexual trauma, and the killing of Iraqi civilians in ways that minimize their violence or define them as appropriate and necessary—or at least unavoidable—aspects of the war. In so doing, these texts prohibit a full consideration of the war's violence and undermine the political critiques that such an awareness would enable. Indeed, entirely absent from each of these texts is any consideration of the flawed logic that linked Iraq to the September 11 attacks and enabled the subsequent invasion.

My aim in making this argument is not particularly to critique either the United States' decision to intervene in Iraq in 2003—although both that decision and subsequent ones regarding the prosecution of the war certainly warrant debate—or, more broadly, the United States military. Rather, I have two central interests: First, I seek to acknowledge that these texts' representations of the war and the soldiers' experience in it do participate in the construction of positions within those political debates.[6] Second, I seek to interrogate how their participation in those debates relies upon their recalling or eliding critical elements of the discourse that has surrounded the war's history and to examine what is at stake, culturally and politically, in their contributions to adolescents' visions of the war, the military, and US foreign policy. I argue that these texts' presentation of the war buttresses a discourse that defines the Iraq intervention as necessary, appropriate, and potentially successful. They stand in contrast to what critics have identified as an antiwar tendency in recent war literature for young people, in spite of Tuttle's observations about children's popular culture during the Second World War and Julia Mickenberg's contention that "much of the familiar children's literature of the twentieth century at least implicitly supports . . . the policies of the United States abroad."[7] Critically examining the cultural work that these texts do thus becomes a vital component of interrogating the ways in which young Americans come to imagine the contours of citizenship and the role that the United States, and its military, should play in the world.

"I KNOW YOU ALL KNOW THAT WE'RE FIGHTING A WAR": ADOLESCENT CULTURE AND THE WARS IN AFGHANISTAN AND IRAQ

The three texts that I analyze appeared more than five years after the beginning of the Iraq War, and more than seven years after the start of the War on Terror. During those years, young Americans were hardly sheltered from the contentious debates that surrounded the conflicts, but were consistently exposed to and actively participated in them.[8] In speeches by politicians and veterans, students were assured that US intervention was necessary and that the nation's intentions were pure; in classrooms, they heard from pro- and antiwar teachers and colleagues; and in their hallways and lunchrooms they encountered recruiters seeking their enlistment, protesters condemning the wars, and artwork memorializing soldiers who had died. Simultaneously, students themselves grappled with the wars' meanings and impact on their lives through their own acts of protest, support, and memorialization. And as all of this transpired, both the popular press and professional educational journals chronicled the controversial legal and pedagogical issues that the wars raised. These debates reveal a contentious struggle between a discourse that positioned adolescents as citizen-subjects to be interpellated within interventionist discourses and an alternative narrative that viewed them as potential critics, if not potential victims, of those conflicts.

George W. Bush was perhaps the most significant purveyor of pro-war rhetoric in public schools. As I noted above, I do not quote Bush because his rhetoric has gone unremarked, but to emphasize the frequency with which he reprised before young audiences assertions familiar from addresses ostensibly aimed at adults, casting the intervention in Afghanistan and the planned invasion of Iraq as justified and worthwhile, and the United States' engagement in these interventions as reluctant and defined by a humanitarian intent aimed particularly at helping women and children.

In 2002, he told Atlanta high-school students that in Afghanistan "our nation has liberated . . . women and children who lived under . . . one of the most oppressive regimes in this history of mankind," and that "it's not over unless we pursue our mission."[9] Recalling Sturken's claim that "fear of reprisal for the war became quite easily justification for that war," Bush warned of "thousands of ticking time bombs ready to go off. And, therefore, we must be relentless in our pursuit . . . wherever they hide."[10] He deployed nearly identical language in La Crosse, Wisconsin, telling students that the United States had "liberated a group of people from the clutches of barbaric people who would not even educate young girls," before inveighing that "the kids in this high school have got to understand, it is worth it. . . . We fight for civilization. . . . This country is going to defend our values to the core, and we're going to win."[11] In Eden Prairie, Minnesota, he remarked that "it's hard for any American to understand how barbaric this regime was," as he sought "to assure the students who are here . . . [that] defending freedom is a noble cause, and it is a just cause."[12]

Elementary-school students heard similar remarks. "We want to be friends with Muslims and Muslim children," he said in Lanham, Maryland, but added, "It's important for the boys and girls . . . to know that we're fighting evil with good."[13] At an elementary school in Alexandria, Virginia, he told students, "We're fighting against people . . . who want to hurt us. . . . But we're fighting for more than just a war; we're fighting to help people, too."[14] At a Nashville school, Bush referred to Iraq as a place where people "simply do not adhere to the ideals we believe in," before declaring that "American history teaches us that we must lead toward a more peaceful world. . . . [A]s threats develop, we must deal with them before they become too acute."[15] Given the cultural capital of a presidential address, particularly considering the audience, these speeches reveal a concerted effort to construct the citizenship of young Americans according to particularly pro-war contours and threaten to foreclose students' consideration of other attitudes toward the interventions.

Although in his second term Bush spoke less frequently at schools and hardly mentioned the wars, young people nonetheless heard other speakers, including members of Congress and veterans.[16] The latter in particular echoed Bush's pro-war rhetoric. An army colonel told Pennsylvania high schoolers that "we can't pull out now without finishing our job," and "recommended an Army career"; a Michigan national guardsman described his visit to elementary school students as "'a chance to stand in front of people and let them know everything we're doing over there is good.'"[17] Such comments continued students' exposure to militaristic pro-war attitudes and foreshortened debate over alternative views.

Yet schools were hardly dogmatic in fomenting support of the wars. Rather, young people encountered diverse opinions about the Iraq and Afghanistan conflicts in both abstract and concrete ways: in classrooms; as the children, friends, and students of soldiers; and as protesters against, supporters of, and perhaps potential participants in the wars.[18] Even before the Iraq War began, *Education Week* reported "clashes in classrooms between students"; concluded that "schools must walk a fine line between educating students about current events, allowing students to express anti-war views, and respecting others who may have differing opinions"; and chronicled schools' and teachers' responses ranging from a Florida teacher who planned "to continue to tell students of his support for President Bush and his decision to go to war" to "the San Francisco school board . . . [which] passed a resolution in January opposing a war and authorized a teach-in on the issues associated with Iraq."[19] As the wars' popularity declined, questions persisted about how the subject should be broached in classrooms and the circumstances in which teachers and students should be disciplined.[20]

Meanwhile, activists, parents, politicians, and educators increasingly debated the presence of military recruiters in high schools and, particularly, the No Child Left Behind Act's requirement that federally funded school districts provide student data to the military.[21] A parent in suburban Montgomery County, Maryland, complained that "recruiting methods glorify careers in the military while minimizing the risks students who enlist will face if they join"; in Florida, activists convinced a school board "to implement a uniform policy . . . that regulates on-campus military recruitment."[22] Other school districts, however, were more welcoming. Suburban Philadelphia teachers attended a miniature boot camp— complete with parachute training and a trip to the rifle range—"intended to create positive impressions of the Army that would be shared with students, parents, and fellow faculty members."[23] New York City mayor Michael Bloomberg remarked, "A lot of people, in this day and age, want to go into the military, and we will make sure they have that option."[24]

Students, of course, were hardly idle witnesses to these debates or passive recipients of these discourses. Rather, adolescents expressed diverse views about the Iraq War in a variety of forums.[25] Many protested the war, as when hundreds of Seattle-area high-school students staged a walkout and "planned to march to Seattle Public Schools headquarters."[26] Others, however, continued to support the war. Near Los Angeles, "Junior ROTC cadets raised $3,500 to install a 950-pound black granite monument to honor a former student who died . . . in

Iraq," and Orange County students installed thirty-five banners in school hallways, showing the faces of servicemen killed in the wars, as a means of "'rais[ing]
awareness for what they're doing for our country.'"[27]

These vignettes offer only a few examples of the multivalent ways in which
young people's lives insistently intersected with concerns about the wars in Iraq
and Afghanistan. Students were alternately encouraged to accept the wars as
being in the best traditions of the nation or to protest them as an act of imperialism, and to enlist in the military and serve their country or resist the efforts
of military recruiters. They endeavored to make sense of the conflicts and the
United States' role in the world as they encountered cultural texts including
pro-war speeches; classes in which the debate over the intervention was either
encouraged or forbidden; the work of military recruiters and those who sought
to thwart them; and their own acts of support, protest, and memorialization.
They also increasingly encountered popular texts about the Iraq War, including
the two novels and memoir mentioned above. And, like all cultural products,
these texts did not simply reflect truths about or an agreed-upon consensus
regarding the war, but rather contributed to the construction and legitimization
of positions within these debates.

"WHAT YOUNG MEN . . . DO WHEN
THEIR COUNTRY IS ATTACKED": READING
THE IRAQ WAR IN ADOLESCENT LITERATURE

Reviewers of Ryan Smithson's memoir and Walter Dean Myers's and Patricia
McCormick's novels have noted that, to varying degrees, these texts do offer
complex portrayals of the Iraq War and meditations on questions of heroism and
masculinity that resonate more broadly with the concerns of recent scholarship.[28]
Certainly this is somewhat true. I argue, however, that in their representation of
the war and the soldiers' experiences, these texts contribute to and perpetuate
the legitimization of the neoconservative interventionist discourse that dominated the early years of the war by insistently constructing the Iraq intervention
as necessary, as related to the September 11 terrorist attacks, and as having the
protection of human rights as their primary purpose. These assertions are buttressed by each text's revision of controversial aspects of the conflict—including
the killing of Iraqi civilians, the Abu Ghraib scandal, the practice of house-
to-house search operations, and the incidence of military sexual trauma—as
legitimate, inconsequential, or having their most significant negative impact
on male US soldiers. In so rewriting events and issues that have accelerated the
Iraq War's decline in popularity, these texts contribute to the inhibition of critiques of US foreign policy by insistently undermining consideration of both the
Iraqis as "precarious" and "grievable" and the troubling policies that underlie the
intervention.[29]

"WE'RE BRINGING THESE PEOPLE AMERICA!" INTERVENTIONIST DISCOURSE IN ADOLESCENT LITERATURE

Reviewers of Smithson's memoir and, less frequently, of Myers's novel note that the 9/11 attacks motivated the protagonists' military service.[30] However, the extent to which these texts affirm the appropriateness of the US intervention in Iraq by evoking and reiterating the interventionist discourse that dominated the early years of the War on Terror has gone unremarked. Smithson, who joined the army reserves after graduating from high school, in fact opens his memoir by recounting his own experience on September 11 in the familiar rhetoric of a mundane existence upset by the attacks: "high school was so typical and predictable," but the attacks were "the atypical, unpredictable kind of real that you never see coming."[31] The juxtaposition of a quotidian middle-class existence with the "atypical" and "unpredictable" attacks reinforces what Sturken has critiqued as a discourse that views the attacks ahistorically.[32]

More significantly, Smithson constructs military enlistment as the only appropriate response to the attacks, writing that as he approached graduation, "I longed for a purpose. The more I agonized, the more I realized that what I'd watched in History class a year before was my purpose."[33] Yet this recognition is quickly qualified by a dismissal of the need to consider any political factors: "I'd heard all about September 11th. I'd watched it happen on television. I'd heard the theories and discussions about foreign policy that were way over my head. I'd bowed my head during tributes and moments of silence. I knew all about 9/11, but I felt like it was my generation's responsibility to do something about it."[34] Echoing Bush's carefully crafted anti-intellectualism, this passage dismisses foreign policy "discussions" as immaterial to the decision to use force and defines "do[ing] something about" terrorism singularly: it demands military service and, by extension, military intervention.

Although such comments may be typical of the opening pages of war memoirs and, particularly, children's war literature, this sentiment persists undiluted throughout *Ghosts of War*.[35] Preparing for his deployment, Smithson writes, "It's time to do my duty, to live up to my promise of service. . . . Because that's what young men and women do when their country is attacked."[36] Once in Iraq, he refers to himself as "an average teenage boy just doing what he can after witnessing the worst attack on American soil since Pearl Harbor."[37] Once again, he mobilizes language that forecloses the consideration of other potentially valid responses or perspectives, constructing a military response as the only thing that "can" be done in response to the attacks.

Smithson's assertions are particularly significant because he is deployed to Iraq, which the memoir positions as a logical and acceptable target in response to "the worst attack on American soil since Pearl Harbor." Smithson, who seems to have forgotten about Afghanistan, makes this assertion explicit by repeatedly conflating Iraq and the World Trade Center site. The lights under which he repairs his equipment are "just like the ones parked at . . . Ground Zero"; in Iraq, "sandstorms throw around enough dust to bury Manhattan."[38] Describing his emotions at a fellow soldier's memorial service—a soldier Smithson confesses to having met only once and hardly remembering—he repeats the language that earlier describes his experience viewing Ground Zero. Of that visit, he writes:

> I didn't know these people. They were not my friends or family. I had never met them. Their existence before that day meant nothing to me. But at this moment their existence meant everything to me. . . .
>
> I shed tears I didn't deserve to shed. I was not entitled to tears but they came nonetheless. These tears for injustice, for impurity, for virtue, for love, for hate, for misunderstanding, for innocence, for guilt, for nothing, and for everything. . . .
>
> We didn't sob; it was respectful crying, like at a funeral.[39]

His reaction at the memorial service is identical:

> I don't know him, the GI Joe Schmo, this hero. He is not my family or close friend. . . . His existence meant nothing to me. And at this moment his existence means everything to me. . . .
>
> ***
>
> I shed tears I don't deserve to shed. I was not entitled to tears but they came nonetheless. They are not quiet, respectful, funeral tears. They are tears for a fellow soldier, a brother I hardly knew, and I sob like a baby. . . .
>
> ***
>
> These tears for injustice, for impurity, for virtue, for love, for hate, for misunderstanding, for innocence, for guilt, for nothing, and for everything.[40]

Although the scenes are transparently parallel, Smithson demands that his readers make the connection, instructing them to "picture a fence in New York City" and describing himself as "feel[ing] as if I'm trapped in rubble."[41] Beyond linking September 11 with the Iraq War, these lines craft the soldier as a victim of an equivalent violence and, in fact, as warranting a more significant expression of grief.

Neoconservative interventionist rhetoric is likewise evident in Smithson's assertion of the intervention's benevolence. Preparing to cross the Iraqi border, he considers, "Maybe I'll be part of an operation that changes an entire country. . . . How many people can find such a sense of purpose? How many people can say that they did their small little part and the result was a whole country full of happier, free people? . . . My deployment, I hope, is allowing me to spread that freedom."[42] Notably, Smithson envisions an unequivocally positive change;

in defining a military invasion as among the most meaningful acts in which an individual can engage and the invasion of Iraq in particular as intended to free the Iraqi people, he echoes the pro-war claims that justified the invasion. He repeats similar sentiments throughout his narrative, particularly in his description of a visit with a recruiter to his high school, a place filled with students whom the recruiter claims "don't have a clue. . . . Because if they did, they'd . . . thank you for what you're doing," before telling Smithson that "the army needs more soldiers like you in Iraq. . . . [because t]hose people deserve to be free."⁴³ Through such remarks, *Ghosts of War* insistently buttresses the discourse of neoconservative intervention that was central to legitimating the Iraq invasion and the escalation of an increasingly unpopular war.

In *Sunrise over Fallujah*, Robin Perry, Walter Dean Myers's more reflective and more ambivalent protagonist, also asserts that military service is the most appropriate means of responding to the crisis of 9/11 and appropriately performing adolescent masculinity. In his first letter to his Vietnam-veteran uncle, Perry writes: "*I felt like crap after 9-11 and I wanted to do something, to stand up for my country. I think if Dad had been my age, he would have done the same thing.*"⁴⁴ Later, he calms his anxiety about the war by reminding himself that "what I did know is that I wanted to do my part," and, after encountering disdainful Iraqis, "reminded myself of my mission in Iraq. I was defending America from its enemies, removing weapons of mass destruction from Iraq, and building democracy."⁴⁵ In a letter home to his parents, he writes: "*I think we are helping the Iraqis, but even more than that, I think we are showing them that Americans are good people. . . . If they respect us and accept democracy, then everything will turn out right.*"⁴⁶ Such comments, published in a moment when the Iraq War was subject to increasing skepticism, contribute to the maintenance of an interventionist discourse.

Perry most stridently resolves his ambivalence in the language of neoconservative interventionism in his own final letter home to his uncle. He initially writes, "*I did what I thought I had to do over here. I did it for my country and for the people I love. . . . But there's a distance between* [that] *and what I'm feeling inside*"; and "*If there comes a day when someone says that we have won this war I know that I'll have doubts inside.*"⁴⁷ Immediately, though, he contradicts this ambivalence by evoking the soldier's service to the Iraqi people: "*If there comes a day that someone says we have lost this war, I'll know that they are wrong, too. Because once you have seen a Jonesy . . . desperately reaching for the highest idea of life, offering themselves up, you don't think about losing or winning so much. You think there is more to life . . . and you want to find that something more.*"⁴⁸

If the American soldier's "reaching for the highest idea of life" negates consideration of larger political questions—"winning and losing"—exactly what constitutes that effort is significant. Jonesy's death, coming as he rescues a wounded blind Iraqi child, constitutes the novel's climactic scene and recalls Bush's frequent allusions to Iraqi and Afghan children. Reflecting on this scene, Perry resolves, "Jonesy giving up his dreams for that child, was what lifted all of this above fear and loathing. In that one last desperate moment, there was actually something for the blind child to reach, some higher point of humanity."[49] The blind, helpless child, an obvious symbol of Iraq, validates the soldiers' presence; in a paternalistic construction of exceptionalist imperialism, the "higher point of humanity" that the child can "reach" is an American soldier.

Rescues of Iraqi children that resonate with Bush's claim that the nation is "feed[ing] the innocents" and "find[ing] those who need help" in fact figure prominently in both texts.[50] Smithson is the more direct, writing early in his memoir, "You don't know what sadness looks like until you've seen children begging for food. . . . This is why we invaded Iraq," and later criticizing Americans as people who, unlike Iraqi children, have "never had tears in their eyes over a bottle of water."[51] In his final pages, he defines the salvation of Iraqi children as the war's central purpose, telling readers that "really, if you ask me why I did it, why I volunteered when so many of my generation ran away, I'll rummage through an old army foot locker. . . . I'll move the Army Commendation Medal aside. . . . Then I'll find [a stuffed] Cat. I'll hold it for a moment . . . remembering the little boy who taught me Arabic."[52] Much like Bush's own rhetoric regarding Iraq, Smithson's answer to "why I did it" is finally divorced from the September 11 attacks, precluding a broader consideration of the invasion, its imperial nature, and, ultimately, the discredited pretexts under which it was waged.

McCormick's *Purple Heart* describes the experience of Matt Duffy, a soldier who, while recovering from an explosion, is plagued by his potential complicity in the shooting of an Iraqi boy.[53] While I will later historicize McCormick's depiction of this incident within contemporary debates about civilian casualties, it is likewise important to note that the trauma is ultimately resolved when Duffy's renewed commitment to an Iraqi future that both supports the American soldier and desires his assistance replaces the recurring traumatic image.

The child in question, Ali, who Matt describes as "so skinny—his belly was bloated and he had legs like a stork" and who subsisted by "picking through the trash heap next to [the US troops'] base," is initially, along with other Iraqi children, the target of the American soldiers' humanitarianism as they "[hand] out candy" and "organiz[e] them into two [soccer] teams."[54] The soldiers' actions thus buttress the interventionist discourse that emphasized the suffering of Iraqi children and presented the military occupation as a solution to it. The presumed benefit of these actions is summed up by Matt's best friend's exclamation, "We're bringing these people America!"[55] Such claims at the beginning of a novel might foreshadow an eventual disillusion, particularly since the child's death and the mysterious circumstances that surround it raise questions about these claims of benevolence. And, even after the details of the shooting have been effectively resolved, a suicide bombing that kills two of his colleagues threatens to leave Matt embittered and skeptical regarding the war and fearing that "every tea seller was an enemy soldier. Every woman was a spy. Every backpack held a bomb."[56]

Yet in the final scene, this suspicion—and, more significantly, the traumatic image that dominates the novel—are finally resolved. The traumatic image appears early on and recurs throughout the book: "There was a silent, silent flash of light and the boy was lifted off his feet. He was smiling. . . . Then he seemed to float, high up in the crayon-blue sky, until all Matt could see were the soles of his shoes as he disappeared, far above the burning city."[57] But on the final page, in a scene that rewrites this image, Duffy symbolically recommits to Iraq's future by returning a soccer ball that has rolled into the street:

> The teacher came to the fence and yelled angrily at him. The bus driver honked his horn. All the kids in the yard gathered at the fence, screaming and pointing frantically.
>
> All except one. She was smaller than the others. . . . Her dark hair hung down in two little braids tied with yellow ribbons.
>
> While all the others were shrieking at him, she'd stuck her arm through the fence to give him the thumbs up.
>
> When the other kids looked at him, they saw just another American soldier. But the little girl with the yellow ribbons in her hair seemed to be saying I see *you*.
>
> And so Matt dashed into the street, gave the ball a gentle kick, and watched as it sailed into the crayon blue sky.[58]

In this scene, key signifiers related to the violent, traumatic image—soccer, the "crayon blue sky"—are reconfigured as symbols of benevolence and gratitude: "yellow ribbons," the "small," vulnerable child, and the American soldier as savior. The novel thus ends by asserting that in spite of whatever chaos might occur in Iraq, and whatever disillusionment it might threaten to produce, Iraqis are nonetheless pro-American and do support and are grateful for a benevolent US military presence. *Purple Heart*, like *Sunrise Over Fallujah* and *Ghosts of War*, thus contributes to the maintenance of pro-war discourse that relies on the language of neoconservative interventionism even amid a prolonged period of anxiety over the Iraq War.

"I REMEMBERED HOW BAD I HAD FELT FOR THEM, ONLY TO FIND OUT THAT THEY . . . PROBABLY WOULD HAVE KILLED ME": REWRITING CONTROVERSIES

Matt Duffy's temporary disillusionment recalls the larger populace's growing cynicism at the moment of the book's publication. When Myers's novel was published in 2008, "63% of Americans [were] saying the United States made a mistake in sending troops to Iraq;" by summer, 2009, when Smithson's memoir first appeared, the numbers were largely the same.[59] They were slightly better by the time McCormick's book appeared in 2009, with "51% of Americans giving a positive assessment of the Iraq war" and more than half still calling the war "a mistake."[60] The causes of this heightened opposition—increasing violence and a rising death toll, reports of scandals and atrocities perpetrated by US troops, and questions about the overall efficacy of the coalition strategy—are well documented, and the publicity that they received raises the question of how these texts can contribute to the maintenance of interventionist discourse in light of them.

The books do acknowledge these issues. However, none invokes them in a manner that critically interrogates the intervention; rather, each insistently constructs these issues and their inherent violence as appropriate or inconsequential. I see this as a rewriting of the Iraq War's troubling history, discursively legitimizing these texts' mobilization of the neoconservative rhetoric that constructs the intervention as appropriate, and further undermining a full consideration of the questionable policies that underlie the larger war and lead to such violence.

The centrality of the Iraqi child's death to McCormick's novel provides a clear example of this revision. The regularity with which Iraqi children have died as the result of US military action has been well documented.[61] As I discussed above, the child is imagined as a sympathetic, precarious character, and over the course of the novel Duffy emerges as potentially complicit in an atrocity that his superiors seem eager to repress, warning him that "you don't want to say something you might rethink later"; condemning insurgents who "hide behind civilians and . . . use civilians"; and declaring that "it's the insurgents who endanger civilians."[62] Matt, recognizing this as "what they always said when a civilian got killed," dismisses it as "classic cover-your-ass language."[63] In thus framing the novel's central conflict in terms of a sympathetic soldier's efforts to acknowledge and repent for egregious violence versus the military bureaucracy's apparent efforts to protect itself, McCormick creates what Butler terms "the conditions for social critique."[64]

However, these concerns ultimately give way to a resolution that absolves the soldiers for their violence. Indeed, it is a detail from within the recurring traumatic image—the protagonist's remembrance of the soles of the Iraqi child's shoes—that confirms his death as appropriate:

Matt sat straight up and opened his eyes. The boy had been wearing shoes. Soccer cleats.

There was only one way a street kid like Ali could have gotten a pair of shoes, especially soccer cleats. From the insurgents.[65]

As Cathy Caruth has shown, in cases of trauma, "what returns to haunt the victim . . . is not only the reality of the violent event but the reality of the way that its violence has not yet been fully known."[66] Here, when that violence *does* become "fully known," it produces the sudden revelation that the Iraqi is not innocent and therefore "grievable," but threatening and therefore justifiably eliminated: "He *was* a kid—until someone gave him a pair of soccer cleats. After that, he was an enemy sympathizer. A spy. A spotter who had nearly gotten Matt killed."[67] In validating the commanding officers' previously suspect statements, the novel asserts that the American soldier is not a perpetrator but a victim and forecloses a thorough consideration of the civilian death toll and an interrogation of the US policies that produce it.[68]

Indeed, even Matt's continued skepticism serves as a vehicle for the assertion of the appropriateness of the soldiers' violence. Having realized that he did not kill the child, Matt worries that "it was his friendship with Ali that had gotten the boy killed."[69] Yet this momentary recognition that the US troop presence endangers Iraqi children is quickly eased when realizing that "by befriending Ali, Matt had actually put the whole squad at risk."[70] When Matt learns that Justin, who had actually shot the child, subsequently became unable to fight and in turn had to be rescued by Matt in a subsequent firefight, he reflects, "What happened in the alley that day . . . had shaken them up so much that they'd nearly stopped being soldiers. But when it had mattered most, Justin still had his back and he had Justin's."[71]

This realization is crucial to the text's larger rejection of political critique, for it identifies the most threatening aspect of combat trauma as the failure to maintain a sufficiently militarized posture and casts the recuperation of that potential as the terms of recovery. The requirement that soldiers protect themselves and their colleagues emerges as paramount, eclipsing the novel's earlier allusion to the possibility that it is, in fact, the US-led occupation itself, and the imperial policies that underlie it, that are largely responsible for creating the conditions for Iraqi civilians' suffering and death. Indeed, in the final discussion of the issue, which comes immediately before Matt's encounter with the young girl seeking the return of her soccer ball, the novel's gesture toward the more complicated realities of American complicity in Iraqi deaths and, more broadly, the benevolence assigned to the US intervention is summarily dismissed: "[G]iving an order," his unit leader declares, "'What happened in the alley, that wasn't your fault'"[72] In making this statement, *Purple Heart* defines civilian deaths as either the fault of the enemy or, perhaps worse, an unavoidable reality of war. In so absolving the soldier from such violence, *Purple Heart* establishes the consideration of that violence as unwarranted.

Purple Heart's construction of Iraqi civilian deaths as simultaneously regrettable but unavoidable and determinedly not the responsibility of the soldier offers the most extensive revision of one of the Iraq War's most controversial issues.

Both Smithson and Myers similarly reconfigure other troubling aspects of the war to justify the US military presence. Smithson, for example, finds himself stationed at Abu Ghraib prison in April 2005. Tellingly, he prefaces this disclosure with the statement "War is dirty and disgusting. . . . But in hindsight, the magical aspects of war are so obvious," and this odd description foreshadows his persistent revision of Abu Ghraib from a site of American shame to a site of US victimization and retribution.[73]

Although Smithson catalogs the now-familiar photographs, he does not condemn the violence; instead, he simply notes that "all this happened at Abu Ghraib prison" and intimates that the controversial issue is not the violence itself but the publication of the pictures.[74] When he describes "an energy" at the site, it is hardly haunting: "This place is alive. Maybe some of it has to do with that whole naked photograph thing. Maybe its fame or infamy is what makes it so interesting, like Times Square in New York City. But there is something deeper. Just like the energy of New York City goes much deeper than Time Square."[75]

Smithson's description of the scandal as "that whole naked photograph thing" reiterates his dismissive minimizing of the torture, but most significant is the geographic metaphor that furthers his efforts to connect Iraq and the World Trade Center attacks. Earlier, he describes New York City as "alive like nothing I've ever seen" and as a place where "the energy of people had a way of spreading."[76] Yet he contrasts Times Square, which he describes as "too big to be real," with the World Trade Center site, the "one spot the energy stood still."[77] In recalling this earlier comparison, Smithson here intimates that its history of abuse is a minor aspect of Abu Ghraib's significance. In doing so, he buttresses the position widely repeated by Bush administration officials and conservative pundits—and equally widely rejected by scholars and more liberal pundits—that the torture was the result of a small cabal of wayward troops and not representative of the wider military presence in Iraq.[78]

This assertion is rather quickly followed by a full-throated celebration of Abu Ghraib as emblematic of the righteousness of the American war effort: "The soldiers stationed at Abu Ghraib are the soldiers fighting the war. This is where the bad guys come to be punished. The genuine bad guys. Even the desk jockeys who live in Abu Ghraib aren't desk jockeys. . . . They run the war; it starts and ends with them."[79] Through the dubious assertion that Abu Ghraib detainees are "genuine bad guys"—most of the tortured detainees were, it has been widely noted, relatively minor figures—and the open admission that punishment, rather than interrogation and intelligence gathering, is the facility's purpose, he emphatically and uncritically posits that what goes on at Abu Ghraib is essential to, and in fact coterminous with, the larger war effort. Perhaps most significant is Smithson's inversion of the US soldiers' experience at Abu Ghraib. The only violence that occurs is directed *at* American soldiers in the form of car bombs and mortars; it is only Americans who suffer there as a result of war's violence.

"Mortar attacks," Smithson asserts, "make me feel like a prisoner."[80] The language here should not be overlooked; in making this assertion, Smithson inverts the narrative of suffering and victimhood, recasting Iraqis not as the subjects but the perpetrators of the violence at Abu Ghraib. This displacement, in turn, contributes to a discourse of aggressive interventionism by simultaneously excusing American atrocity and defining Iraqis as threats that require elimination.

Smithson likewise rewrites the issue of military sexual trauma. As Cynthia Enloe has shown, there was "a significant increase of sexual assaults perpetrated by American male soldiers against American women soldiers" that "never really gained a purchase on the collective consciousness of the American general public as a major issue in the Iraq War."[81] Enloe particularly notes that "women soldiers on service in Iraq were afraid to go to the latrines at night for fear of being attacked—by their male comrades."[82] Smithson, however, ignores an opportunity to recognize this crisis and to critique the policies that enable it. Instead, he turns to adolescent humor. In a chapter replete with scatological stories about stepping in his sergeant's feces and passing gas next to his lieutenant, Smithson relates his accidental intrusion into a female shower trailer. Realizing his error only after a female soldier enters, his thoughts are solely about his own potential for embarrassment:

> I look at the stall to which the female went. Then I look back in the mirror. Back and forth until I decide I might have enough time. I don't want only half my face shaved.
>
> I run the razor over my chin and neck so fast I cut myself twice. . . . and rush out the door. On my way back to the tent I start laughing hysterically.[83]

Smithson's presence in a female shower trailer provokes anxiety only for him, and only because of his potential discomfort, which is so minimal as not to prevent him from completing his shave. Absent from this scene is any acknowledgement or consideration of this woman's vulnerability or, more generally, the risk inherent in unrestricted male access to female shower trailers and the troubling gender politics that dominate the war. In casting this scene as one in which the male is the only actual or potential victim and as a transgression that should be met only with "hysterical" laughter, Smithson reinforces the centrality of homosocial camaraderie within the armed forces and subtly establishes women as marginal figures whose presence in combat zones is either inappropriate or simply the source of slapstick humor. In either case, he negates the potential interrogation of a species of the troubling violence endemic to the Iraq War.

Sexual violence is even more forcefully rewritten in Myers's *Sunrise over Fallujah*. Rather than simply ignoring the problem, he displaces responsibility for it onto Iraqi men and positions the American male soldier as a rescuer rather than a perpetrator. While his unit is tasked with supporting an Iraqi hospital, Robin

Perry discovers two Iraqi men assaulting one of his female colleagues in a bathroom, a scene which culminates in Perry's killing the two men. The female soldier is left wondering, "With all the disgusting garbage that's going on. . . . How can they? How can they?" and declaring, "You stopped them from raping me. . . . But you didn't stop them from ripping up what was left of my soul" before, a page later, thanking Perry for rescuing her.[84] This scene is striking for its reimagining of the source of sexual violence in Iraq. It is the Iraqis who emerge as depraved in their inability to control their lascivious impulses amid the carnage of war, and the American soldier who appears as gallant in a performance of traditional masculinity defined by the rescue of helpless female victims. Although Myers's revision of the history of sexual violence against women is somewhat different from Smithson's, it has the same effect; in casting Iraqis as perpetrators and American men as saviors, *Sunrise over Fallujah* prohibits any consideration of the actual history of and politics surrounding sexual trauma in Iraq, and justifies further violence.

Another revision in Myers's novel counters the notion that the conduct of American soldiers in house-to-house searches unfairly targets, antagonizes, and ultimately alienates civilians. In a scene in which American troops search for bomb-making equipment, Perry describes a house occupied by Iraqis who initially appear sympathetic and, to use Judith Butler's terms, "recognizable to us," and thus "mournable."[85] The occupants include "two women, one of them holding a baby, and three small children"; one woman, Perry reflects, "was pretty. . . . she had huge eyes that I would have loved to have been looking into under different circumstances."[86] This sense of precarity is further heightened by Perry's initial equation of this search with his own experience of racial profiling, which he describes at length:

> I also didn't like searching people. I had been stopped on 136th Street once, just outside the Countee Cullen Library, by two plainclothes cops who had searched me. I knew what it felt like. Embarrassed that I had to stand there with my hands in the air while strangers patted me down and went through my pockets, humiliated because they were assuming power over me and I couldn't do a thing about it. I felt I knew how the Iraqi men felt as I searched them.[87]

It is noteworthy that Perry not once but twice asserts that he "knew" how it "felt." And in this evocation of such searches as invasive and emasculating, the paragraph recognizes their similarities to the racial profiling that dominates domestic urban policing.

And indeed, the search initially appears destructive, terrifying, and fruitless. Perry hears "[t]he older woman . . . crying softly" and the soldiers searching the house "throwing things around"; one of his colleagues asserts, in a claim that calls into question the broader conduct of the US military in Iraq, that "we just

busted up some more damn doors and almost killed some more people for nothing."[88] As in *Purple Heart*, however, the potential critique of US policy and its
devastating impact on Iraqi civilians ultimately is undermined when another soldier discovers the contraband detonators hidden in a container of flour, a revelation that establishes the Iraqis as in fact devious and a "threat to life" that renders
the American aggression appropriate.[89]

With this discovery, Perry's initial ambivalence immediately disappears.
Watching as soldiers "brought out the two males, blindfolded and cuffed, and got
them into their vehicles," he realized that "[i]t was almost a new day," a transpar-
ent metaphor emblematic of the larger transition that Perry makes explicit four
paragraphs later: "I felt good. . . . First Squad had found the detonators. Maybe
we had even saved some lives. But then I started thinking about the Iraqi women,
one crying and one rocking the baby. I remembered how bad I had felt for them,
only to find out that they were in a family that probably would have killed me
if they had had the chance."[90] Rejecting his earlier sympathy for Iraqi precarity, Perry here reaffirms the construction of Iraqis as universally dangerous—
notably, it is not individual bad actors who want to kill Americans, but an entire
family—and deserving not American compassion, but forceful intervention.
Here again, the novel raises a significant controversial issue related to the war
in Iraq, only to imagine it in a manner that buttresses discourse supportive of
the intervention.

Since 2001, the lives of young people have consistently intersected with debates
over the wisdom of the US military interventions waged as part of the War on
Terror, and while those debates have been multivalent and contentious, a significant discourse has presented the interventions as necessary and laudable and has
sought to interpellate adolescents as supporters of a militaristic, interventionist
foreign policy. And as two wars have persisted, the more contentious Iraq War
has become the subject of an emerging body of adolescent literature. Reviews
have lauded these texts as politically neutral and "allow[ing] American teens to
grapple with the Iraq War."[91] However, I have argued throughout this essay that
the work of Smithson, Myers, and McCormick in fact threatens to preclude both
debate over contemporary US foreign policy and an awareness and consideration
of the most troubling aspects of the Iraq War. Rather, in voicing neoconservative
rhetoric that portrays the invasion as simultaneously an appropriate response to
the threat of terrorism and as humanitarian in intent, while systematically obscuring the violence, disruption, and trauma that the war has wrought on both Iraqis
and Americans, these texts insistently buttress a discourse that validates the Iraq
War as necessary, uncritically valorizes the soldiers who fight in it, and condemns
Iraqis as threatening others who require an aggressive, violent response.

It remains unclear whether these particular texts will sustain their cultural
capital and continue to be widely read and taught.[92] Yet it is the case that even

contemporary adolescents increasingly view the war in Iraq as a historical rather than a contemporary phenomenon; as a result, their experience of the war—and, more broadly, their emerging vision of the role of militarism in US culture and the role of the United States in the world—will be constructed increasingly through their consumption of cultural texts such as these. At the same time, it becomes for imperative for scholars to vigorously interrogate young-adult literature's contributions to the political debate over the Iraq War and, more broadly, US militarism and foreign policy.

NOTES

This article copyright © 2012 Children's Literature Association. This article was first published in *Children's Literature Association Quarterly* 37, no. 1 (2012): 4–26. Reprinted with permission by Johns Hopkins University Press.

1. George W. Bush, "Remarks Announcing the 'Lessons of Liberty' Initiative in Rockville, Maryland, October 30, 2001," *Public Papers of the Presidents: George W. Bush, 2001, Vol. 1.* (District of Columbia: Government Printing Office, 2002), 1327. For a photograph of the event, see Tina Hager, *President George W. Bush Announces His Lessons of Liberty Initiative at Thomas S. Wootton High School in Rockville, MD.* 2001. Oct. 2011. http://georgewbush-whitehouse .archives.gov/news/releases/2001/10/ images/20011030-7.html.
2. Bush, "Remarks Announcing the 'Lessons of Liberty' Initiative," 1326.
3. Marita Sturken, *Tourists of History: Memory, Kitsch, and Consumerism from Oklahoma City to Ground Zero* (Durham, NC: Duke University Press, 2007), 16–17. See also Virginia R. Monseau, *Curriculum of Peace: Selected Essays from English Journal* (Urbana: National Council of Teachers of English, 2004), xiii, https://secure.ncte.org/library/NCTEFiles/Resources/ Books/Sample/10061Intro.pdf.
4. William M. Tuttle Jr., *"Daddy's Gone to War": The Second World War in the Lives of America's Children* (Oxford: Oxford University Press, 1993), 115–116, 118.
5. Eric Avila, *Popular Culture in the Age of White Flight: Fear and Fantasy in Suburban Los Angeles* (Berkeley: University of California Press, 2004), 18.
6. Indeed, Myers has remarked, "I don't agree with those who say the war was an horrendous idea from the start." Bob Minzesheimer, "The Somber Realities of War Cross Generations; Myers' 'Sunrise' Transports the Young to Iraq," *USA Today*, April 24, 2008.
7. Tuttle, *"Daddy's Gone to War,"* 148–161; Julia L. Mickenberg, *Learning from the Left: Children's Literature, the Cold War, and Radical Politics in the United States* (Oxford: Oxford University Press, 2006), 7. On antiwar sentiment in children's literature, see, for example, Jonathan Lathey, "Reading War Novels: Seeking a New Heroic Code," *Children and Libraries* 8, no, 2 (Summer/Fall 2010): 45; Judy Brown, "'How the World Burns': Adults Writing War for Children," *Canadian Literature* 179 (2003), 46–47, 49; and Monseau, "Introduction," xvi–xvii.
8. As John Sellers notes, the wars have "been a backdrop to much of their lives." "The War, At Home: Military Conflict in Books for Children and Teens," *Publisher's Weekly*, August 24, 2009, 36.
9. George W. Bush, "Remarks at Booker T. Washington High School in Atlanta, January 31, 2002," *Public Papers of the Presidents: George W. Bush 2002, Vol. 1.* (District of Columbia: Government Printing Office, 2002), 157.
10. Sturken, *Tourists of History*, 8; Bush, "Remarks at Booker T. Washington High School," 157.

11. George W. Bush, "Remarks at Logan High School in Lacrosse, Wisconsin, May 8, 2002," *Public Papers of the Presidents: George W. Bush 2002, Vol. 1*, 742, 743.

12. George W. Bush, "Remarks at Eden Prairie High School in Eden Prairie, March 4, 2002," *Public Papers of the Presidents: George W. Bush 2002, Vol. 1*, 331.

13. George W. Bush, "Remarks at Thurgood Marshall Extended Elementary School, October 25, 2001," *Public Papers of the Presidents: George W. Bush 2001, Vol. 2* (District of Columbia: Government Printing Office, 2003), 1301.

14. George W. Bush, "Remarks at Samuel W. Tucker Elementary School in Alexandria, March 20, 2002," *Public Papers of the Presidents: George W. Bush 2002, Vol. 1*, 460.

15. George W. Bush, "Remarks at East Literature Magnet School in Nashville, September 17, 2002," *Public Papers of the Presidents: George W. Bush 2002, Vol. 2*, 1609, 1610.

16. The closest Bush came to reprising his earlier comments was in Greensburg, Kansas, in 2008. George W. Bush, "Commencement Address at Greensburg High School in Greensburg, Kansas, May 4, 2008," 658, *American Presidency Project*. Ed. Gerhard Peters and John T. Woolley. University of California Santa Barbara, http://www.presidency.ucsb.edu/ws/index.php?pid=77292. For examples of other speakers, see "Gilchrest Will Discuss Iraq Trip with Students from Harford County During Live Webchat on Wednesday," *States News Service*, October 10, 2007; "Graves Speaks to Local Students," States News Service, February 21, 2007.

17. Mary Klaus, "'We Try to Catch the Bad Guys,' Iraq Veteran Says." *Patriot News* (Harrisburg, PA), May 22, 2007; Greg Chandler, "Zeeland Soldier Visits Classroom Full of Pen Pals: Corpus Christi Students Ask About Iraq Experience," *Grand Rapids Press*, May 13, 2007.

18. Michelle R. Davis, "Schools Caught in Draft of War Buildup," *Education Week*, March 12, 2003, 1.

19. Ibid.; Kathleen Kennedy Manzo, "War Lessons Call for Delicate Balance; Experts Advise Teachers to Set Own Views Aside," *Education Week*, March 16, 2003, 1. More generally, see Darcia Harris Bowman, "Principals Walk Fine Line on Free Speech," *Education Week*, March 19, 2003, 1; Catherine Gewertz, "Schools Ready for War and Strive for Routine," *Education Week*, March 26, 2003, 7; Kathleen Kennedy Manzo, "Time an Enemy in Teaching About War," *Education Week*, April 9, 2003, 1; and Monseau, "Introduction," xiv.

20. See Ann Bradley, "Student's Suspension Reduced after Outcry From Ga. Community," *Education Week*, May 18, 2005, 4; Tal Barak, "Texas Teachers Are Suspended for Showing Video of Beheading," *Education Week*, May 26, 2004, 4; Jessica Blanchard, "Teacher Wins Lawsuit on Use of Iraq Prison Photos in Class," *Education Week*, September 8, 2004, 4; Kathleen Kennedy Manzo, "Teachers Tiptoe into Delicate Topics of 9/11 and Iraq," *Education Week*, September 6, 2006, 1; Laura Camper, "Quinn Asks Schools to Recognize Enlistees," *State Journal-Register* (Springfield, IL), May 23, 2007; and Alison Leigh Cowan, "Play about Iraq War Divides a Connecticut School," *New York Times*, March 24 2007.

21. Sean Cavanagh, "Military Recruiters Meet Pockets of Resistance: Handful of Districts Turn 'Opt Out' Rules into 'Opt In' System: Military Says Added Access Helping in Quest to Fill Ranks," *Education Week*, April 23, 2003, 1; Helen Benedict, *The Lonely Soldier: The Private War of Women Serving in Iraq* (Boston: Beacon Press, 2009), 16. On issues of military recruitment in general after 2003, see Beth Bailey, *America's Army: Making the All-Volunteer Force* (Cambridge: Harvard University Press, 2009), 249–254; Cynthia Enloe, *Nimo's War, Emma's War* (Berkeley: University of California Press, 2010), 137–142.

22. Lori Aratani, "Military Recruiters Protested at School: Half-Dozen Decry Visit by Army Van," *Washington Post*, February 3, 2006; Peter Bailey, "Schools to Limit Military Recruiting; School Officials in Miami-Dade and Broward Will Start to Regulate Military Access to Students," *Miami Herald*, March 30, 2006.

23. Edward Colimore, "Army Gives Educators a Taste of Military Life," *Philadelphia Inquirer*, August 2, 2009.

24. Frank Lombardi, "Recruiting OK at Schools: Mike." *Daily News* (New York), November 11, 2006.

25. Jessica Blanchard, "Young War Protesters Demand That Adults Protect Their Future: 'We're the Ones Who Have to Deal' with Consequences," *Seattle Post-Intelligencer*, April 19, 2007. See also Peter Fulham, "War Worries; For High School Students, Iraq Looms Larger Than Ever," *Buffalo News*, March 28, 2007; Elmer Smith, "From These Students, Some Answers on Iraq," *Philadelphia Daily News*, May 18, 2007.

26. See also Hattie Brown, "Prospect of U.S. War Against Iraq Stirs Student Activism: Schools Advised to Examine Issue from Multiple Viewpoints," *Education Week*, February 12, 2003, 6–7; "Students Join National Anti-War Walkout," *Education Week*, March 12, 2003, 16.

27. Karen Maeshiro, "Lancaster High Memorial to Honor Sacrifice: Iraq War Victim Recognized," *Daily News of Los Angeles*, April 14, 2007; Alejandra Molina, "Honoring the Fallen; Banners Featuring Service Members Are on Display in Laguna Hills," *Orange County Register*, October 15, 2007.

28. See, for example, Diane P. Tuccillo, review of *Sunrise over Fallujah* by Walter Dean Myers, *School Library Journal Reviews*, April 1, 2008, 146; Review of *Sunrise over Fallujah* by Walter Dean Myers, *Publishers Weekly*, April 21, 2008, 59. Tina Zubak, "Tales Show Choices and their Consequences," review of *Sunrise over Fallujah*, by Walter Dean Myers, *Pittsburgh Post-Gazette*, April 1 2008; Leonard S. Marcus, "Boys to Men," review of *Sunrise over Fallujah* by Walter Dean Myers, *New York Times*, May 11 2008; Richard Winters, review of *Purple Heart* by Patricia McCormick, *School Library Journal Reviews*, November 1, 2009, 119; and review of *Purple Heart* by Patricia McCormick, *Publishers Weekly*, August 24 2009, 63.

29. Judith Butler, *Frames of War: When Is Life Grieveable?* (London: Verso, 2009), 4, 6.

30. See Eric Norton, "Ghosts of War: My Tour of Duty," review of *Ghosts of War: My Tour of Duty in Iraq* by Ryan Smithson, *School Library Journal Reviews*, March 1, 2009, 169; Elizabeth Floyd Mair, "An American Experience," review of *Ghosts of War: The True Story of a 19-Year-Old GI* by Ryan Smithson, *Albany Times-Union*, August 16, 2007; review of *Ghosts of War* by Ryan Smithson. *Publishers Weekly* 25 May 25, 2009, 59; and Tuccillo, review of *Sunrise over Fallujah*.

31. Ryan Smithson, *Ghosts of War: The True Story of a 19-Year-Old GI* (New York: Collins, 2009), 4, 6.

32. Sturken, *Tourists of History*, 7, 16–17.

33. Smithson, *Ghosts of War*, 8.

34. Ibid., 9.

35. See Judy Brown, "'How the World Burns.'"

36. Smithson, *Ghosts of War*, 51.

37. Ibid., 69.

38. Ibid., 66, 145.

39. Ibid., 17.

40. Ibid., 221.

41. Ibid., 221; for another example of this conflation, see pages 304–305.

42. Ibid., 60–61.

43. Ibid., 236–237.

44. Walter Dean Myers, *Sunrise over Fallujah* (New York: Scholastic, 2008), 2, italics in original.

45. Ibid., 18, 63.

46. Ibid., 85–86, italics in original.

47. Ibid., 280, 281, italics in original.

48. Ibid., 281, italics in original.

49. Ibid., 276.

50. This emphasis, though not its discursive significance, has been noted by several reviewers: see, for example, Norton, review of *Ghosts of War*. Iraq literature is not the first to emphasize such a concern: see Patrick Hagopian, *The Vietnam War in American Memory: Veterans, Memorials, and the Politics of Healing* (Amherst: University of Massachusetts Press, 2009), 309–347.

51. Smithson, *Ghosts of War*, 77–78, 93–94.

52. Ibid., 305–306.

53. Although there is not enough space to discuss it here, this the novel recalls no other text so much as Ron Kovic's *Born on the Fourth of July*.

54. Patricia McCormick, *Purple Heart* (New York: Balzer and Bray, 2009), 29, 28.

55. Ibid., 28.

56. Ibid., 196.

57. Ibid., 4.

58. Ibid., 198–199, italics in original.

59. Jeffrey M. Jones, "Opposition to Iraq War Reaches New High; Sixty-Three Percent Say U.S. Made Mistake in Sending Troops," Gallup.com, April 24, 2008, http://www.gallup.com/poll/106783/opposition-iraq-war-reaches-new-high.aspx; "Iraq: Gallpu Historical Trends," Gallup.com, n.d., http://www.gallup.com/poll/1633/Iraq.aspx.

60. "In U.S., More Optimism about Iraq, Less about Afghanistan: New High of 42% Say War in Afghanistan Was a Mistake," *Gallup.com*, March 18, 2009, http://gallup.com/poll/116920/optimism-iraq-less-afghanistan.aspx.

61. See, for example, Hamid Ahmed, "Iraqi Government Condemns U.S. Raid of Baghdad Slum: Up to 26 Iraqis Killed in Firefight," Associated Press, June 30, 2007; Ellen Knickmeyer and Salih Saif Aldin, "U.S. Raid Kills Family North of Baghdad: Iraqis Say 12 Slain in Airstrike; Americans Believe Targeted Farm Was Shelter for Insurgents," *Washington Post*, January 4, 2006. On civilian deaths more generally, see Enloe, *Nimo's War, Emma's War*, 221–222. In making this claim, however, I do not want to suggest that children have not died as a result of insurgent actions as well: see, for example, Joshua Partlow, "Gunmen Go on Rampage in Iraqi City; Killings Are Revenge for Bombings in Tal Afar," *Washington Post*, March 29, 2007; David Cloud et al., "Truck Bomb Kills 25 and Wounds More than 100 in Baghdad, Foiling U.S. Security Bid," *New York Times*, May 23, 2007. For a more ambiguous example, see "Two Iraqi Children Killed in Baghdad Clash: U.S.," Reuters.com, October 20, 2007, http://www.reuters.com/article/2007/02/24/us-iraq-boys-idUSYAT41936720070224.

62. McCormick, *Purple Heart*, 102, 121.

63. Ibid., 123. On Duffy's attempts to confess, see pages 70–71, 102, 111–113.

64. Butler, *Frames of War*, 34–35.

65. McCormick, *Purple Heart*, 187–188.

66. Cathy Carruth, *Unclaimed Experience: Trauma, Narrative, and History* (Baltimore: Johns Hopkins University Press, 1995), 6.

67. McCormick, *Purple Heart*, 190, italics in original.

68. Regarding veterans' responses to their portrayal as victims, see Greg Jaffe, "Troops Feel More Pity than Respect," *Washington Post*, November 14, 2011, http://www.washingtonpost.com/world/national-security/troops-feel-more-pity-than-respect/2011/10/25/gIQANPbYLN_story.html. Thanks to Elly Lampner for alerting me to this article and its relationship to this point.

69. McCormick, *Purple Heart*, 190.

70. Ibid., 191.

71. Ibid., 192.

72. Ibid., 194.

73. Smithson, *Ghosts of War*, 139.

74. Ibid., 139–140. Notably, this is a perspective for which Susan Sontag criticized George W. Bush in "Regarding the Torture of Others," *New York Times*, May 23, 2004, http://www .nytimes.com/2004/05/23/magazine/regarding-the-torture-of-others.html?pagewanted=all &src=pm. Butler also notes opposition to the photos' display (*Frames of War*, 40).

75. Smithson, *Ghosts of War*, 140.

76. Ibid, 15.

77. Ibid.

78. On Abu Ghraib, see Thomas E. Ricks, *Fiasco: The American Military Adventure in Iraq.* (New York: Penguin, 2007), 290–297. On torture and the significance of "punishment" as it relates to Abu Ghraib, see Michelle Brown, "Setting the Conditions for Abu Ghraib: The Prison Nation Abroad," *American Quarterly* 57 (2005): 976–977. See also Sturken, *Tourists of History*, 17. For an anecdote similar to Smithson's, see Enloe, *Nimo's War, Emma's War*, 190–191.

79. Smithson, *Ghosts of War*, 140–141.

80. Ibid., 152.

81. Enloe, *Nimo's War, Emma's War*, 163, 166.

82. Ibid., 163–64. On the frequency with which women suffer sexual assault in Iraq, see also Helen Benedict, *The Lonely Soldier: The Private War of Women Serving in Iraq.* (Boston: Beacon Press, 2009), esp. 5–8.

83. Smithson, *Ghosts of War*, 258.

84. Ibid., 233–234, first ellipsis in the original.

85. Butler, *Frames of War*, 42–43.

86. Myers, *Sunrise over Fallujah*, 162, 163.

87. Ibid., 163–164.

88. Ibid., 163.

89. Ibid. 164; Butler, *Frames of War*, 42.

90. Myers, *Sunrise over Fallujah*, 165–166. For a similar scene earlier in the book, albeit one that engenders a somewhat more ambivalent response from the narrator, see 52–59.

91. Reviewof *Ghosts of War* by Ryan Smithson, *Publishers Weekly*, May 25, 2009, 59; review of *Sunrise over Fallujah* by Walter Dean Myers, *Publishers Weekly*, April 25, 2008, 59.

92. In a review that included Smithson's memoir and McCormick's novel, *USA Today* reported, "While most of these books don't make the best-seller list, they are becoming increasingly popular in middle- and high-school curriculums" (Carol Memmott, "Iraq War Mobilizes Thoughtful Teen Literature: Sacrifice, Loss, Coping Are Themes," *USA Today*, October 7, 2007).

6 · CALLS OF DUTY

The World War II Combat Video Game and the Construction of the "Next Great Generation"

JEREMY K. SAUCIER

When sergeant major of the United States Army, Kenneth O. Preston, testified before the House Armed Services Committee on Appropriations in February 2005 the United States was engaged in wars in Iraq and Afghanistan—so called battlegrounds in a much broader war against global terrorism. Representing more than one million men and women in the army, Preston reported on the state of the institution, noting the "amazing work" accomplished by soldiers around the globe. "They continue to be ambassadors of democracy," Preston explained. "I am convinced that they are the 21st century's first generation of heroes. We have come to know this generation of heroes as the 'Next Greatest Generation.'" Preston would spend much of his tenure as sergeant major evangelizing the idea of the Next Greatest Generation to soldiers and their families, politicians, and journalists all over the nation. The seventh edition of the army's *Enlisted Soldier's Guide* quotes Preston's declaration "You are the next 'greatest generation.' Be proud of your service to your nation."[1] In August 2011, even the cover of *Time* magazine echoed Preston's words, as a photograph of five military veterans in civilian clothes stood behind the words "The *New* Greatest Generation."[2]

Preston's explicit linkage between the World War II generation and the young men and women fighting in the global War on Terrorism at the beginning of the twenty-first century was part of a much larger effort to remake the image of the US military since the end of the Vietnam War.[3] Yet the roots of the Next Greatest Generation, or the more often called "Next Great Generation," took hold at the end of the twentieth century as Americans remembered, honored, and celebrated what journalist Tom Brokaw dubbed the "Greatest Generation" of World War II.[4]

According to French sociologist Maurice Halbwachs, "collective memories" are social constructions, persisting because individuals located within a specific group context draw on that context to "remember" the past.[5] Halbwachs contended that collective memory could be kept alive and may become "historical memory" through social and cultural institutions such as books, imagery, commemorations, and reenactments. In historian Emily S. Rosenberg's study of Pearl Harbor in American memory, she updates Halbwachs concept of memory, noting that in recent American culture, memory is "inseparable from the modern media, in all their forms." Media, she writes, "provide the matrix that collects and circulates diverse memories in America." It shapes them in a variety of ways keeping some alive while ignoring others and enhancing, and perhaps even implanting memories, through its more rapid widespread circulation.[6]

Historians John Bodnar and Albert Auster (among others) have argued that popular films such as *Saving Private Ryan* (1998) and popular histories such as Stephen Ambrose's *D-Day* (1995) and *Band of Brothers* (1993) and Brokaw's *The Greatest Generation* (1998) helped glorify the sacrifices and heroics of men and women of the World War II generation at the end of the twentieth century.[7] Scholars such as Richard Slotkin and Joanna Bourke (among others) have also demonstrated that combat films have served as vehicles of national mythology, as well as ways for soldiers and potential soldiers to help make sense of their war experiences.[8] At the same time, World War II combat video games emerged as a new site for Americans—particularly young men—to circulate memories through playing a mediated, virtual past. For a new generation of soldiers fighting the War on Terror, combat video games, which drew heavily on the conventions and narratives of the combat film genre, have played a similar role.[9]

This essay traces the construction of the Next Great Generation. It begins by discussing World War II in American memory and the popularization of the Greatest Generation. Next, it explores the intellectual foundations of the Next Great Generation in the work of generational theorists Neil Howe and William Strauss before focusing on the role World War II combat-video games played in establishing this cross-generational linkage between Americans who fought World War II and young Americans potentially fighting in the War on Terror. It examines the ways in which these virtual experiences acted as a lens for youth to view their roles in a global struggle against terrorism in the twenty-first century. Players of game franchises such as *Medal of Honor* engaged in what critic Janet Murray calls "enacted events," which take on the transformative power of being assimilated as personal experiences.[10] That is, World War II combat-video games provided members of the putative Next Great Generation with the opportunity to put theory into practice by embodying virtual World War II soldiers and refighting the Greatest Generation's war.

KEEPING WORLD WAR II ALIVE

Preston's efforts to explicitly link the World War II generation with soldiers fighting around the globe in the twenty-first century rested in part on American's
understanding of World War II in the present. Nearly seven decades after the end
of what documentarian Ken Burns called "The War," World War II continues to
hold a central place in American memory. In the wake of the September 11, 2001,
terrorist attacks on the Pentagon and the World Trade Center in New York City,
World War II analogies saturated American newspapers, websites, and television
screens as politicians and military leaders summoned the memory of Pearl Harbor to articulate the nation's need to mobilize for war.[11]

Indeed, just three days after the terrorist attacks, US president George W.
Bush stood at a podium in Washington's National Cathedral prepared to address
the nation. Like many in the audience, Bush was there to mourn the dead on
a national day of prayer, but he was also there to attempt to make sense of the
horrific images of fire, black smoke, and bent steel on television sets across the
world. Speaking with a somber, though resolute tone, Bush quoted scripture
and former president Franklin D. Roosevelt's call for national unity. In summing
up the attacks on America's economic and military infrastructure, the president
offered a clear response to the pain and injury inflicted on the national imagination. "In every generation, the world has produced enemies of human freedom,"
he observed. "They have attacked America because we are freedom's home
defender. The commitment of our fathers is now the calling of our time."[12] For
Bush, the events of September 11 in many ways mirrored the story that sent an
entire generation of American soldiers, his father among them, across the Atlantic and Pacific Oceans nearly sixty years earlier. As such, evoking World War II
provided Bush, and many Americans, with a way to reduce an impending conflict with Afghanistan in the present to another "good war" to preserve the freedoms and opportunities secured by an Allied victory during World War II.[13]

Nevertheless, the memory of World War II was bitterly contested by those
who fought it and those who wrote or created representations about it. Some
representations of World War II (especially since the Vietnam War) depicted
the war with increasing ambivalence.[14] Many of these memoirs, films, oral histories, and novels questioned the costs, gains, and justness of the war, compli-
cating the nostalgic narratives produced by Ambrose and Brokaw. More than
five decades of war writings and representations demonstrated the myriad ways
that Americans remembered the war. Some, like Norman Mailer's 1948 novel
The Naked and the Dead and marine veteran E. B. Sledge's 1981 memoir *With
the Old Breed: At Peleliu and Okinawa*, unromantically questioned the justness
of war, while depicting cruelty and atrocity in the Pacific.[15] Others—like Mark
Robson's film *Home of the Brave* (1949); Terence Malick's film *The Thin Red Line*
(1998) (the second film adaptation of James Jones's 1962 novel); Paul Fussell's

1989 book *Wartime: Understanding and Behavior in the Second World War;* and James Bradley's 2000 chronicle of the lives of the flag raisers on Iwo Jima, *Flags of Our Fathers*—dealt with the psychological trauma that World War II soldiers endured.[16] William Manchester's 1979 *Goodbye, Darkness: A Memoir of the Pacific War* and Studs Terkel's 1984 Pulitzer Prize–winning and best-selling *"The Good War," An Oral History of World War Two* evinced America's contradictory attitude toward the war.[17] While Manchester noted that his feelings about the marines were "still highly ambivalent, tinged with sadness and bitterness, yet with the first enchantment lingering," many of Terkel's interviewees reflected on both the tragedy and joys resulting from the war.[18] Such representations illustrated a landscape of war memories fraught with the kind of tension some Americans wanted to avoid.

In 1998, director Stephen Spielberg offered yet another interpretation of the war with his combat film *Saving Private Ryan.* The film was Spielberg's second World War II epic in five years, following *Schindler's List* in 1993, grossing an impressive $216 million domestically and $440 million worldwide.[19] The film followed the story of a squad of army Rangers who land on D-Day, and later travel across Europe to locate Private James Ryan—the only one of four brothers to survive the invasion—and bring him home. Although the film immediately raised questions about how Americans remembered the war, its portrayal of the sacrifices made by American soldiers left many viewers wondering whether they had, as Captain John Miller (Tom Hanks) suggested during the film's climax, "earn[ed]" the freedoms and privileges they enjoyed.

Saving Private Ryan resonated with many Americans who found Spielberg's graphic portrayal of the war honest and realistic. Spielberg's depiction of the horrors and the brutality of combat, as Robert Westbrook argues, cast "a complex shadow over the signal triumphant event for Americans of the European War: the Allied invasion of Normandy in June 1944."[20] Indeed, scenes depicting the blood-soaked beaches of Normandy and the callous execution of Nazi prisoners presented American soldiers in ways that complicated popular perceptions of the Good War. Nevertheless, the film, as John Bodnar asserts, also restored "a romantic version of common-man heroism in an age of moral ambivalence."[21] It was this heroism and sacrifice of the "common-man" that struck a chord with many Americans celebrating the veterans of the war.

Sensing the film's resonance with audiences, America Online and Dream Works (Spielberg's production studio at the time) set out to record viewers' responses. They compiled various emails posted on an online message board, and in 1999 published the aptly titled, *"Now You Know": Reactions after Seeing Saving Private Ryan.* While the responses appear to come from people of all ages, some common themes prevailed, including appreciation and guilt. One Gulf War veteran wrote, "There is finally a movie that shows what our fathers and grandfathers had to go through. . . . Freedom comes at a price. It is not, nor has it ever been, free!"[22] Another person explained, "I think it is evident that the great majority of those who watched the film have gained a greater understanding of why we must honor our veterans, why we must honor the memory of the fallen, and why we must honor the debt that we owe them."[23] One teenager criticized his fellow classmates for their lack of appreciation, asking, "Freedom is not free. Have you earned it?"[24] For many Americans who watched the film, *Saving Private Ryan* produced deep feelings of guilt and appreciation for the Greatest Generation.

Although *Saving Private Ryan* evoked a range of emotions, Spielberg described the film as a tribute. He told his cast halfway through the filming not to think of the movie as "something we are going to go out and make a killing on but as a memorial. We are thinking of all those guys, your grandparents and my dad, who fought in WWII."[25] For US secretary of defense William Cohen, the film did more than educate. As he told crowds of people at the opening of the National D-Day Museum in June 2005, *Saving Private Ryan* raised "the existential questions about whether we are really worthy of what all of you, and those who have succeeded you, have sacrificed on our behalf. Who are we? Why are we here? What's the price of freedom? Are we willing to pay for it?"[26] It was in this spirit that Spielberg's film stood at the forefront of a much larger movement to educate people about the quickly fading members of the Greatest Generation while at the same time challenging a new generation to live up to their grandparents' sacrifices. Writers Tom Brokaw and Stephen Ambrose had also urged Americans to appreciate, learn from, and "remember" the heroes of the "the greatest generation any society has produced."[27] Indeed, Brokaw wrote that those who came of age during World War II "had given the succeeding generations the opportunity to accumulate great economic wealth, political muscle, and the freedom from foreign oppression to make whatever choices they like."[28] While these films and books celebrated the common GI and suggested that Americans needed to earn and defend the opportunities they'd been given, generational theory provided the intellectual foundations for political and military leaders to construct and call upon a next great generation of soldiers as the nation went to war.

FORGING THE NEXT GREAT GENERATION

As Americans processed the September 11 terrorist attacks, popular histories and ideologically fueled rhetoric had already framed the nation's new conflict as akin to World War II and therefore a good war for a new generation of Americans. Such an interpretation rested in part on the work of popular authors and generational theorists Neil Howe and William Strauss. During the last decade of the twentieth century, Howe and Strauss developed an influential theory of generations that permeated American business, military, and political culture.

In 1991, the authors published *Generations: The History of America's Future, 1584–2069*—the first book to use the term "millennials" to describe the generation of Americans born after 1982. According to the authors, millennials arrived in an America "awash in moral confidence but in institutional repair."[29] As a result, older generations of Americans asserted greater control over the world of childhood in order to "implant civic virtue in a new crop of youngsters."[30] After publishing two more books, *13th Gen: Abort, Retry, Ignore, Fail?* (1993), an examination of Generation X, and *The Fourth Turning* (1997), an attempt to spell out a kind of American prophecy, Howe and Strauss established themselves as influential cultural observers and authorities on forecasting youth trends for the public and private sector.

In 2000, Howe and Strauss published their first major study of the millennial generation. Their *Millennials Rising: The Next Great Generation* sought to link the nation's youth with Americans from what they called the 'GI,' or what had been already well established as the Greatest Generation. Drawing on statistical and attitude studies and generational theory, the authors argued that Americans born after 1982 were more affluent, better educated, and more racially and ethnically diverse than previous generations. Yet more importantly, they were "beginning to manifest a wide array of positive social habits" that previous generations no longer associated with youth, including a "new focus on teamwork, achievement, modesty, and good conduct."[31] Despite such positive generational traits, the authors asserted that millennials must be led, challenged, and tested nonetheless. Only through older Americans' faith in millennials could they "become a powerhouse generation . . . perhaps destined to dominate the twenty-first century like today's fading and ennobled GI generation dominated the twentieth."[32] If nurtured, the authors contended, millennials could become America's next great generation.

For Howe and Strauss, the Greatest Generation that Brokaw and others saluted was an archetypal hero generation that collectively accomplished "great deeds, construct[ed] nations and empires, and [was] afterward honored in memory and storied myth."[33] Mapping out a generational history of the United States, the authors identified five hero generations, including the "Glorious" (born between 1648 and 1673), the "Republican" (1742–1766), the "Progressive" (1843–1849), the "G.I." (1901–1924), and the "Millennial" (1982–). The authors placed each generation in historical context, arguing that hero generations arrive soon after a period of social and cultural upheaval and grow up during a time of "decaying civic habits, ebbing institutional trust, and resurgent individualism."[34] The authors assert that millennials, a group that grew up during Reagan's America, perfectly fit their mold. Yet millennials played a particularly special role because of their newfound appreciation for their grandparents' sacrifices. The mentality of the next great generation, as they argued, was not only tied to "a grandchild's affection" for the Greatest Generation, but also to a realization that their grandparents were vacating a special role that would need to be filled. Howe and Strauss thus constructed a narrative of an emerging hero generation that if confronted with crisis, as their grandparents were, would answer the call and reshape society.[35]

The authors' generational theories were and are at best questionable, but the influence of their work is undeniable. In 1999, Howe and Strauss founded Lifecourse Associates, a consultant company, which, as they put it, uses "a visionary blend of social science and history" to "interpret the qualitative nature of a generation's collective persona to help managers and marketers leverage quantitative data in new and remarkable ways—and to lend order, meaning, and predictability to national trends."[36] Over the last decade the company's list of clients included an impressive range of influential public- and private-sector institutions, such as Viacom, Hearst Magazines, Paramount Pictures, Nike, Raytheon, Ford Motor Company, J. Walter Thompson, Harvard University, and the US Army.[37]

Indeed, the army found the company's generational approach so useful that they commissioned Howe and Strauss to author a special army handbook outlining who millennials were and how the institution should go about recruiting them. While at least some army officers were already familiar with Strauss and Howe's work, the *Recruiting Millennials Handbook: How to Improve Recruiting, Training, and Retention by Understanding America's New Youth Generation* was prepared specifically to help the army and its recruiters better understand the values and attitudes of millennials and translate that understanding into recruiting success. According to Strauss and Howe, the army could mobilize millennials because they were naturally attracted to organizations whose purpose was to defend their country, community, and family. However, the army needed to replace the image of the "Gladiator" or "solo-warrior" that appealed to Generation X with a more up-to-date "team theme," exhibited in other marketing campaigns such as Team Cheerios, Nickelodeon Nation, and Barbie's Generation Girl.[38] Although other advertising campaigns championed collaboration, there were few more effective examples of teamwork than the mythic World War II generation that collectively saved the world. For the army then, allusions to World War II were expected to be an important part of their recruiting strategy. As the inside cover illustration of a group of adult millennials signing copies of the "#1 Bestseller, The Next Greatest Generation" attested, the army was recruiting and building a force of heroes who fought for and carried with them values associated with the World War II generation, and who would some day be the subjects of future Brokaw-esque books. To make this linkage more explicit, recruiters were even told to hang "a poster or two of the World-War II winning G.I.s" in their offices."[39]

Yet constructing a next great generation also served as a way for members of the Boomer Generation born in the early postwar era to work out their own collective past. If World War II or the Good War seemed to define the Greatest Generation, Vietnam or the Bad War became synonymous with the Boomer Generation. As Boomers themselves, Howe and Strauss's reading of millennials as potential saviors appears colored by the perceived failures of their own generation. Not surprisingly then, framing millennials as having more in common with the World War II generation meant avoiding the moral ambiguity, accounts of combat atrocities, and an antiwar movement that characterized the Vietnam War experience. As "Boomers and Gen Xers" they write, "realize that neither of their generations is likely to be remembered as a generation of heroes. Perhaps, however, both can someday be remembered as the leaders, educators, and parents who *shaped* a generation of heroes."[40] In such a scenario everyone wins: Boomers and Gen Xers teach and prepare a "generation of heroes," while millennial youth, linked to the World War II generation's seemingly less morally ambiguous war, pose ready to take on their own social and economic challenges and military conflicts.[41]

If, as Brokaw and others suggest, the World War II generation had brought order to the chaos of the modern world, some Americans hoped their grandchildren would do the same in age when the nation's enemies could fly airplanes into the New York skyline. And although Howe and Strauss provided the intellectual foundations to justify the forging of the next great generation, World War II combat video games gave that generation the opportunity to enter virtual spaces where they could replay an interactive mediated version of their grandparent's war.

"EARN THIS": THE NEXT GREAT GENERATION PLAYS AS THE GREATEST GENERATION

When Dale Dye, a military technical advisor on such film, video-game, and television productions as *Saving Private Ryan, Medal of Honor* (1999), and *Band of Brothers* (2001) was asked why Hollywood producers and game developers showed so much interest in World War II at the turn of the twenty-first century, the retired marine captain explained, "There has been increasing awareness and empathy for what our forefathers' generation went through during the seminal event of the twentieth century. Films like *Saving Private Ryan* and video games like *Medal of Honor* serve, among other things, as a long overdue salute to the men and women who freed the world from tyranny and oppression."[42] Although Dye's assessment isn't wrong, I contend that these films and games did more than "salute" World War II veterans. They also acted as an important bridge between the so called Greatest Generation and Next Great Generation—a virtual space where a new generation could explore the combat experience, as well as sympathize, and even virtually embody soldiers of the World War II generation as they played a mediated, often fictionalized, cinematic version of the past.

Much like the movies, warfare has been one of video games' principal subjects since their birth during the 1960s and 1970s.[43] Indeed, one of the earliest mainframe computer games, *Spacewar!* (1962), allowed players to fire torpedoes at each other from dueling space ships. Yet unlike films, video games tend to be categorized into genres that prioritize game-play style over narrative content. The vast majority of World War II–themed games are first-person shooters or games that provide the player with a first-person perspective—experiencing a virtual world through the eyes of one's avatar or game character. In many cases, the only part of the avatar's body the player can see are hands (and sometimes forearms) holding a weapon.[44] More than any other video-game genre, the first-person shooter served as the principal means of disseminating the World War II combat experience at the turn of the twenty-first century.

Although the first-person shooter can be traced back to developer Steve Colley's *Maze War* (c. 1973–1974), the genre coalesced nearly two decades later with id Software's *Wolfenstein 3D* (1992). Id programmers John Carmack and John Romero based the genre's archetype on Muse Software's 1981 game *Castle Wolfenstein*. In that game, players view a Nazi castle from a top-down perspective and sneak around killing Nazi guards with the ultimate goal of stealing secret war plans and escaping Castle Wolfenstein. Carmack and Romero remade the game into a revenge fantasy in which player-controlled ally spy B. J. Blazkowicz carried out a one-man search-and-destroy mission to kill German leader Adolf Hitler. Although there's little more to the game's narrative, its backstory or what author Stephen Poole calls its "diachronic story," instantly connects the game to already existing cultural narratives about World War II.[45] As such, any backstory that identifies Nazis as a game's enemy evokes Americans' collective memory of Nazi atrocities and the Holocaust and justifies any violence the player inflicts on his or her enemies.[46] As Rick Giolito executive producer of Electronic Arts game *Medal of Honor* explained, "World War II is automatically iconic. You can pick out who's good and who's bad right away."[47] Whether or not many young people fully understood they were killing "Nazis," the game sold more than 100,000 copies by 1993, making it the best-selling shareware (introduced to consumers through a free demo) game released at that point.[48] Id's decision to license the *Wolfenstein 3D* game engine so that other studios could make their own games using the company's 3D technology and the release of id's space marine first-person shooter Doom (1993) paved the way for improved game engines and the popularization of the first-person shooter.

By the turn of the century the first-person shooter dominated the gaming marketplace and World War II shooters such *Medal of Honor, Return to Castle Wolfenstein* (2001), *Battlefield 1942* (2002), *Call of Duty* (2003), *Brothers in Arms:*

Road to Hill 30 (2005), and their many sequels established the World War II combat video-game subgenre. The video-game industry's production of World War II shooters far outpaced Hollywood films addressing World War II during the first decade of the twenty-first century. However, video games hardly left Hollywood behind. Many of these games drew heavily on the generic narratives, conventions, and imagery established in the Hollywood combat film—packaging the game in a familiar cultural form. In *Brothers in Arms* (a reference to Ambrose's book and Tom Hanks's miniseries *Band of Brothers*) game players led squads from the 502nd Parachute Infantry Regiment of the 101st Airborne Division in a storyline based in part on an actual mission. However, the characters—including Staff Sergeant Matthew Baker, a newly promoted squad leader struggling with his responsibilities; Private First Class Stephen "Olbie" Obrieski, a Polish immigrant who joined the military to prove his commitment to American after the attack on Pearl Harbor; and Private David Muzza, who after saying "I have too much to live for back home to die over in France" is killed by shrapnel on the plane ride over Normandy—follow many genre conventions as well as represent the multiethnic America portrayed in dozens of combat films.[49]

Indeed, *Medal of Honor*, the game which led the surge of World War II combat video games at the end of the 1990s, was the brainchild of *Saving Private Ryan* director and Dream Works Interactive founder Stephen Spielberg. Spielberg wanted *Saving Private Ryan* to educate a new generation, but he also realized that many young people wouldn't have the opportunity to see the violent R-rated film. Inspired by his teenage son's playing of *GoldenEye 007* (1997) on the Nintendo 64 video-game console, Spielberg put his studio to work. Set in World War II Europe, *Medal of Honor* placed players in control of US Office of Strategic Services Lieutenant Jimmy Patterson as he participates in search-and-rescue and search-and-destroy missions against the Nazis. Alongside Valve's *Half-Life* (1998), *Medal of Honor* helped redefine the first-person shooter as the series would generate more than $1 billion in sales over its lifetime.[50] Yet it was the game's 2002 sequel *Medal of Honor: Frontline* that allowed many young Americans to experience the virtual horrors and triumphs of D-Day.

As the opening montage begins, players view authentic newsreel footage of President Franklin Roosevelt, Winston Churchill, tanks, bombers, and Higgins boats, as a voiceover quotes General Dwight Eisenhower's letter to invasion forces on June 6, 1944, "You are about to embark on a great crusade. . . . You will bring about the destruction of the German war machine." Although these historical documents provide authenticity, they also challenge game players to take on the same "crusade" that their grandparents engaged in decades earlier. When play begins, the screen zooms in on a first-person view of a Higgins boat. As the player takes in the hellish seascape through the eyes of Lieutenant Patterson—explosions, battleship cannons, planes on strafing runs, and a soldier vomiting over the side of the transport—the captain yells out, "Stay with me and we'll get through this. We got to take this beach!" Suddenly, a mortar hits the boat, and like *Saving Private Ryan*, players find themselves with an underwater view of machine-gun bullets piercing the water and the flesh of fellow soldiers. As the player finally makes it onto the beach, he or she is met by machine-gun bullets zooming through the air, screams, cries that "we're getting slaughtered," and soldiers disappearing into explosive clouds of smoke. As the player storms the beach and moves inland to carry out a series of missions, the player experiences D-Day through the virtual eyes and actions of a soldier, interacting with an imagined past in ways that even a Spielberg film can't re-create.

Medal of Honor: Frontline's final mission to prevent the production of an experimental Nazi jet bomber, perhaps with the long-range capability of taking the war from Europe to the United States, implicitly links the September 11, 2001, terrorist attacks with the determined evil ingenuity of the Nazis. The game's climax allowed young Americans—who experienced a real "long-range" attack on American soil in the recent past and feared another one—to strike first at a fascist regime. In this way, the game both links the experiences of Greatest Generation with the Next Great Generation as well as suggests a major tenet of the War on Terror: Americans must be willing to engage in preemptive action: fighting the terrorists abroad so Americans do not have to fight them at home. It was this principle of taking preemptive action, and the fear of "weapons of mass destruction" that prompted a US-led invasion of Iraq and the toppling of the Saddam Hussein regime in 2003.

Yet did players respond to World War II games such as *Medal of Honor: Frontline* in similar ways to viewers of *Saving Private Ryan*? Some press and user reviews, and studies of player communities suggest that many people did. Scholar Joel Penney's examination of Medal of Honor and Call of Duty player communities suggests that although game players hold complex and nuanced views of war and politics, some players sympathized and identified with the sacrifices World War II era soldiers.[51] These players take what Penney calls "the 'Strong Defense' interpretation" of World War II combat video games that reinforce an ideology that supports an aggressive foreign policy and holds the military in high regard. As one player in Penney's study noted, "I've gained a greater appreciation of the dedication, effort, and fighting spirit of the previous generation, and came to believe we could learn a lot from them."[52] Penney also documented what he calls a "good war/bad war" comparison among some players who reject Strong Defense because they view the World War II military and its soldiers, rather than the current military and its soldiers, as role models who should be emulated. "For these players," Penney explains, the "World War II-themed content of *Call of Duty* and *Medal of Honor* represents what a 'good war' should look like: soldiers are disciplined, the military is forceful, and the taking of life is morally justified."[53]

Similarly, some press and user reviews of Medal of Honor: Frontline demonstrate that many players viewed the game as more than running around shooting Nazis. Several user comments on the Internet website Internet Movie Database applaud the game for its ability to create an emotional cinematic experience. While one player noted, "It's just like being in *Saving Private Ryan*. Wow!!!," another reviewer explained that "Being an Immigrant and knowing members of my family being involved in World War II it's something truly special when I get to re-live the events that changed the face of the war."[54] Other reviewers noted how the game's cinematic-like score added tension and infused emotion during gameplay. As one reviewer explained, the "masterful score" was very reminiscent of "the music found in HBO's *Band of Brothers* miniseries," while another reviewer wrote, "Some of the music in the game is absolutely haunting. You truly feel like you are part of something bigger, part of the war for freedom, you remember those who have given your [sic] lives. Rarely, if ever, does a videogame invoke this kind of emotion in me."[55] Not everyone experienced or "read" World War II combat video games in quite the same way, but players own comments suggest that some players, whether they support American foreign policy or not, viewed the game as a tool to understand the war experiences of the Greatest Generation within the broader context of the War on Terror.

By the mid 2000s, as the real wars in Iraq and Afghanistan appeared less like World War II and game studios searched for new stories to resonate with players, the World War II combat video-game subgenre declined. Popular first-person shooter franchises such as Medal of Honor and Call of Duty left World War II behind and launched new titles focused on contemporary conflicts. In 2007, Activision published Call of Duty: Modern Warfare, the fourth game in the Call of Duty franchise, and the first to deviate from the World War II combat subgenre. Instead, the game centered on future Middle Eastern and Eastern European conflicts in 2011. Call of Duty: Modern Warfare proved so successful it spawned two best-selling sequels, *Modern Warfare 2* (2009) and *Modern Warfare 3* (2011), as well as the *Call of Duty: Black Ops* (2010 and 2012) and *Call of Duty: Ghosts* (2013) game series, which generated more than $1 billion in sales per title. In 2014, combat video games are as popular as ever, but few game studios seem interested in remaking World War II games. For their part, players appear more attracted to games that address present military tensions and potential near-future conflicts and virtually fighting the Next Great Generation's war.

While popular histories and films elevated the World War II generation to the pantheon of American cultural heroes, World War II combat video games acted as living, virtual memorials where young players could parachute into France, storm the beaches of Normandy, or trace the footsteps of their GI ancestors through a reconstructed digital past. Within the context of the War on Terror and efforts to link American youth to the World War II generation, replaying the war of that generation took on a whole new meaning: have Americans earned and are they worthy of all that the Greatest Generation sacrificed and accomplished? The fact that Americans raised this question during a period characterized by deep anxieties about national insecurity is more interesting than any answer. Millennials were also called upon to fight in the War on Terror as the Next Great Generation because of what took place between World War II and the War on Terror. That is, asking millennials to fight as children of the Vietnam generation proved much more problematic than challenging them as heirs to the Greatest Generation. As Howe and Strauss explained, "Anxiety about the future can be a good thing, when directed to useful purpose, and surely one of history's best purposes is the raising of good and capable children. . . . Whether or not Millennials must ever respond to an epic crisis history will propel them to be and do what Boomers and Gen Xers were not and did not do. That much is certain."[56] As this quote suggests, the construction of the Next Great Generation demonstrates that some Americans feared a nation devoid of a "great" generation, but it also illustrates the variety of ways modern cultures evoke, and even "enact" the past in order to better understand and communicate with each other in the present. Within the context of the War on Terror many of these widely circulated cultural representations and narratives acted as calls to duty, attempts to mobilize young Americans as gamers and grandsons and granddaughters of the Greatest Generation.

NOTES

1. Sergeant Major Kenneth O. Preston, "Written Statement (As Prepared) before the House Armed Services Committee on Appropriations," Washington, DC, February 16, 2005, http://www.army.mil/leaders/leaders/sma/testimony/16Feb05HASC.htm; Command Sergeant Major Robert S. Rush, *Enlisted Soldier's Guide* (Mechanicsburg, PA: Stackpole Books, 2006), 39.
2. Joe Klein, "The New Greatest Generation: How Young War Veterans Are Redefining Leadership at Home," *Time*, August 29, 2011.
3. See for instance, Jeremy K. Saucier, "Mobilizing the Imagination: Army Advertising and the Politics of Culture in Post-Vietnam America" (PhD diss., University of Rochester, 2010).
4. Tom Brokaw, *The Greatest Generation* (New York: Random House, 1998).
5. Lewis A. Coser, ed., *Maurice Halbwachs: On Collective Memory* (Chicago: University of Chicago Press, 1992), 22.
6. Emily S. Rosenberg, *A Date Which Will Live: Pearl Harbor in American Memory* (Durham, NC: Duke University Press, 2003), 3–4. See also Alison Landsberg, *Prosthetic Memory: The Transformation of American Remembrance in the Age of Mass Culture* (New York: Columbia University Press, 2004). Landsberg argues that modernity made it possible for a new form of public cultural memory or "prosthetic memory" in which a person experiencing a representation of the past in a site such as a film or museum takes on a personal, deeply felt memory of the past that they did not live. Landsberg asserts that these prosthetic memories have the ability to shape a person's subjectivity and politics.

7. John Bodnar, *The "Good War" in American Memory* (Baltimore: Johns Hopkins University Press, 2010); Albert Auster, *"Saving Private Ryan* and American Triumphalism" in *The War Film,* ed. Robert Eberwein (New Brunswick: Rutgers University Press, 2004).

8. Richard Slotkin, *Gunfighter Nation: The Myth of the Frontier in Twentieth-Century America* (Norman: University of Oklahoma Press, 1998); Joanna Bourke, *An Intimate History of Killing: Face-to-Face Killing in Twentieth-Century Warfare* (New York: Basic Books, 1999); Michael C. C. Adams, *The Great Adventure: Male Desire and the Coming of World War I* (Bloomington: Indiana University Press, 1990); and Craig M. Cameron, *American Samurai: Myth, Imagination, and the Conduct of Battle in the First Marine Division, 1941–1951* (New York: Cambridge University Press, 1994).

9. See Jeremy K. Saucier, "Playing the Past: The Video Game Simulation as Recent American History," in *Doing Recent History: On Privacy, Copyright, Video Games, Institutional Review Boards, Activist Scholarship, and History That Talks Back, ed.* Claire Bond Potter and Renee C. Romano (Athens: University of Georgia Press, 2012) for a discussion of "combat simulations and the rise of the virtual veteran in recent America."

10. Janet Murray, *Hamlet on the Holodeck: The Future of Narrative in Cyberspace* (New York: Free Press, 1997), 170. For more insight into play itself, see for instance, Johan Huizinga, *Homo Ludens: A Study of the Play-Element in Culture* (New York: Routledge, 2000); Roger Callois, *Man, Play, and Games* (Urbana: University of Illinois Press, 2001); Brian Sutton-Smith, *The Ambiguity of Play* (Cambridge: Harvard University Press, 1997); and Stuart Brown, *Play: How It Shapes the Brain, Opens the Imagination, and Invigorates the Soul* (New York: Avery, 2009).

11. Evan Thomas, "A New Date of Infamy," *Newsweek* extra edition (September 2001), 22–29. See for instance, Rosenberg, *A Date Which Will Live,* 174–189.

12. George W. Bush, "President's Remarks at National Day of Prayer and Remembrance," Americanrhetoric.com, September 14, 2001. http://www.americanrhetoric.com/speeches/gwbush911.memonationaldayofprayerandremembrance.htm.

13. For insight into World War II–themed rhetoric after September 11, see Denise M. Bostdorff, "George W. Bush's Post–September 11 Rhetoric of Covenant Renewal: Upholding the Faith of the Greatest Generation," *Quarterly Journal of Speech* 89 (2003) and David Hoogland Noon, "Operation Enduring Analogy: World War II, the War on Terror, and the Uses of Historical Memory," *Rhetoric & Public Affairs,* 107, no. 3 (Fall 2004).

14. See, for instance, Edward T. Linenthal and Tom Engelhardt, *History Wars: The Enola Gay and Other Battles for the American Past* (New York: Metropolitan Books, 1996); Andrew J. Huebner, *The Warrior Image: Soldiers in American Culture from the Second World War to the Vietnam Era* (Chapel Hill: University of North Carolina Press, 2008); and John Bodnar, "Public Sentiments and the American Remembrance of World War II," in *Public Culture: Diversity, Democracy, and Community in the United States,* ed. Marguerite S. Shaffer (Philadelphia: University of Pennsylvania Press, 2008).

15. Norman Mailer, *The Naked and the Dead* (New York: Rinehart and Company, 1948); E. B. Sledge, *With the Old Breed: At Peleliu and Okinawa* (New York: Oxford University Press, 1990).

16. Paul Fussell, *Wartime: Understanding and Behavior in the Second World War* (New York: Oxford University Press, 1989); James Bradley, *Flags of Our Fathers* (New York: Bantam Books, 2000).

17. Studs Terkel, *"The Good War,"* An Oral History of World War Two (New York: Ballantine Books, 1985).

18. William Manchester, *Goodbye, Darkness: A Memoir of the Pacific War* (New York: Dell Publishing, 1987), 456.

19. Ian Freer, *The Complete Spielberg* (London: Virgin, 2001), 272.

20. Robert Westbrook, "Great Ambiguities, Ghastly Carnage and a 'Good War,'" *Newsday*, August 2, 1998.

21. John Bodnar. "*Saving Private Ryan* and Postwar Memory in America," *American Historical Review*, 106, no. 3 (2001).

22. Jesse Kornbluth and Linda Sunshine, eds., *"Now You Know": Reactions after Seeing Saving Private Ryan* (New York: Newmarket Press, 1999), 69.

23. Ibid., 82.

24. Ibid., 95.

25. Lester D. Friedman and Brent Notbohm, *Stephen Spielberg Interviews* (Jackson: University Press of Mississippi, 2000), 222.

26. William S. Cohen "National D-Day Museum Opening, Award Presentation to Dr. Ambrose," speech presented by US secretary of defense William S. Cohen at the opening of the National D-Day Museum, New Orleans, Louisiana, June 5, 2000, http://www .defenselink.mil/speeches/

27. See Stephen E. Ambrose, *Band of Brothers: E Company, 506th Regiment, 101st Airborne from Normandy to Hitler's Eagle's Nest* (New York: Touchstone, 1993); Stephen E. Ambrose, *D-Day June 6, 1944: The Climactic Battle of World War II* (New York: Simon and Schuster, 1995); Stephen E. Ambrose, *Citizen Soldiers: The U.S. Army from the Normandy Beaches to the Bulge to the Surrender of Germany, June 7, 1944–May 7, 1945* (New York: Simon and Schuster, 1997); and Stephen E. Ambrose, *The Victors: Eisenhower and His Boys, the Men of World War II* (New York: Touchstone, 1998). Brokaw, *The Greatest Generation*, xxx.

28. Brokaw, *The Greatest Generation*, 388.

29. Neil Howe and William Strauss, *Generations: The History of America's Future, 1584–2069* (New York: Quill, 1991), 337.

30. Ibid., 335.

31. Neil Howe and William Strauss, *Millennials Rising: The Next Great Generation* (New York: Vintage Books, 2000), 4.

32. Ibid., 5.

33. Ibid., 326.

34. Ibid., 326–327.

35. Ibid., 335.

36. See, "About Us, Mission," LifeCourse Associates, http://www.lifecourse.com/ about/mission.html.

37. See "About Us, Our Clients," LifeCourse Associates, http://www.lifecourse.com/about/ clients.html.

38. Neil Howe, William Strauss, and Rick Delano, *Recruiting Millennials Handbook: How to Improve Recruiting, Training, and Retention by Understanding America's New Youth Generation* (Great Falls, VA: LifeCourse Associates, 2001), 3.

39. Ibid., 2.

40. Howe and Strauss, *Millennials Rising*, 366.

41. On the memory of the Vietnam War, see, for instance, John Carlos Rowe and Rick Berg, *The Vietnam War and American Culture* (New York: Columbia University Press, 1991); H. Bruce Franklin, *The Vietnam War and Other American Fantasies* (Amherst: University of Massachusetts Press, 2000); Robert D. Schulzinger, *A Time for Peace: The Legacy of the Vietnam War* (New York: Oxford University Press, 2006); and Patrick Hagopian, *The Vietnam War in American Memory: Veterans, Memorials, and the Politics of Healing* (Amherst: University of Massachusetts Press, 2009).

42. "New Appreciation for Combat Soldiers and WWII Vets," *USA Today*, February 3, 2002, http://usatoday30.usatoday.com/life/cyber/tech/review/games/2002/2/01/dye-interview.htm.

43. See, for instance, Ed Halter, *From Sun Tzu to Xbox: War and Video Games* (New York: Thundermouth Press, 2006).

44. On the formal elements and narrative structure of first-person shooters, see Paul Budra, "American Justice and the First-Person Shooter," *Canadian Review of American Studies* 34, no. 1 (2004): 1–12.

45. Poole makes a distinction between the diachronic story or backstory and the synchronic story or the story that happens in the present while playing the game. Stephen Poole, *Trigger Happy: The Inner Life of Videogames* (London: Fourth Estate, 2000), 106–107.

46. See, Peter Novick, *The Holocaust in American Life* (New York: Mariner Books, 2000); Robert B. Westbrook, *Why We Fought: Forging American Obligations in World War II* (Washington: Smithsonian, 2004), especially introduction and chapter 4.

47. Eryn Brown, "Electronic Arts Makes Itself a Hollywood Home," *New York Times*, October 5, 2003.

48. Tristan Donovan, *REPLAY: The History of Video Games* (East Sussex, UK: Yellow Ant, 2010), 258.

49. On the platoon film formula, see Jeanine Basinger, *The World War II Combat Film: Anatomy of a Genre* (Middletown, CT: Wesleyan University Press, 2003), chapter 1; Richard Slotkin, "Unit Pride: Ethnic Platoons and the Myths of American Nationality," *American Literary History* 13, no. 3 (Autumn 2001); and Richard Slotkin, *Lost Battalions: The Great War and the Crisis of American Nationality* (New York: Henry Holt and Company, 2005), chapter 17.

50. Russell, *Generation Xbox: How Video Games Invaded Hollywood* (East Sussex, UK: Yellow Ant, 2012), 198.

51. Joel Penney, "'No Better Way to "Experience" World War II': Authenticity and Ideology in the *Call of Duty* and *Medal of Honor* Player Communities," in *Joystick Soldiers: The Politics of Play in Military Video Games*, ed. Nina B. Huntemann and Matthew Thomas Payne (New York: Routledge, 2009), 191–205.

52. Ibid., 201.

53. Ibid., 202.

54. Marko Djordjevic, "A True Experience" (May 30, 2002) and Tomas Fransson, "It's just like being in Saving Private Ryan . . . Wow!!!" Internet Movie Database, September 8, 2002, http://www.imdb.com/title/tt0289330/reviews?ref_=tt_urv.

55. James Stevenson, review of *Medal of Honor: Frontline*, Mania.com, June 17, 2002, accessed April 1, 2013, http://www.mania.com/medal-honor-frontline_article_35031.html.

56. Howe and Strauss, *Millennials Rising*, 360.

7 · SOFTWARE AND SOLDIER LIFE CYCLES OF RECRUITMENT, TRAINING, AND REHABILITATION IN THE POST-9/11 ERA

ROBERTSON ALLEN

During my ethnographic research among the game developers of *America's Army*, the official video game of the US Army, I spoke at length with many game developers about how they perceived the goals and reasons for the army's development of a free and downloadable first-person shooting video game for military recruitment, training, and soldier rehabilitation purposes. One developer, a friend who I'll call Marcus,[1] explained his rationale for the government-funded recruitment project and his work by asking me a series of questions. He inquired about whether I believed the United States should have a standing military in the first place. "Yes, I think it's necessary, but it's bloated and out of control," I responded, after which he asked, "Do you believe that that standing Army should be all-volunteer?" Perhaps, I replied, less vehemently. Marcus then asked me, "Do you believe that in order to keep an all-volunteer standing army the army should be as accurate in its advertisement as possible?"

"Of course," I told him. Marcus proceeded to bring up the example of military television advertisements to illustrate what he felt that the video game *America's Army* was doing:

So there's this commercial that shows a Marine climbing some crazy cliff with no gear, and then he fights a dragon and converts into a Marine officer with a sword and everything. Now, you tell me which is a more accurate depiction of the military—a Marine fighting a dragon, or a video game that really makes as much effort as possible to be accurate in its depictions of combat and military life? I don't think that [commercial is] a very accurate depiction of what it's like to be a Marine. I think playing a video game is also a far-fetched vision of what it's like to be in the military; however, that being said, our game does genuinely try to portray certain parts of the military. So I do appreciate that, and I think that on some level it is more accurate. But I also feel like there are levels of lying, you know what I mean?[2]

In 2002, *America's Army* became an unanticipated army public-relations and advertising success among the core recruitment demographic of male youth, target age seventeen. The game, still in continuous iterative development as of 2014, achieved a mass appeal to younger gamers following its initial release during its early years, when the wars and Iraq and Afghanistan were both in their infancy. The content of the game evolved with periodic updates, and it consistently ranked among the most played online games.[3] Successive versions of the game and its software modifications, which I explore below, resulted in the expansion of this project to encompass a large network of commercial and military institutions.

America's Army is one example of how a single piece of software has been repurposed and reused for a variety of military goals. Although *America's Army* software is not ubiquitously or uniformly used throughout the US Army, it is one example of how post-9/11 generations of youth have been recruited, trained, and rehabilitated—with games, simulations, and virtual environments as central aspects of these processes (figure 2).

A WIRED ARMED FORCES

America's Army was at the forefront of the "serious games" industry and military entertainment during the post-9/11 decade. Through its business arrangements, the game franchise expanded well beyond the free online game to include commercial console versions of the game, *America's Army* plastic action figures, an arcade game, a cell-phone game, a high-tech cooperative venture in army recruiting and community outreach at the Army Experience Center in Philadelphia, and the Virtual Army Experience, an immersive "mobile mission simulator" for recruitment and public relations.

This entertainment side of the *America's Army* franchise, however, is merely one sliver of the vast expanse of other commercial and military-contracted endeavors that bring together entertainment and defense. Today, industries and organizations devoted to the continuation of a militarized economy now exist at all levels, employ a large percentage of workers, and are central to the overall economic orientation of the United States. The stretch of this economy is vast,

FIGURE 2. A high-school student and future US Army enlistee plays the *America's Army Future Soldier Training System*. This software uses assets from the *America's Army* game to introduce future soldiers army doctrine, tactics, and procedures before they attend basic combat training. Such reuse of gaming software reportedly saves additional money by substantially decreasing dropout rates. (Photograph by the author.)

covering most economic sectors.[4] Marcus understood that everyone working in the *America's Army* franchise is

> definitely part of the military–industrial complex that president Eisenhower warned about. Before he left office [in 1961] he warned us about this very thing. And I don't think he could have imagined at that time this sort of [video-game recruitment] project. I think that this is really close to what he was talking about, the military becoming commercialized. It's almost fashionable, it's really bizarre.[5]

The "fashionable" and commercial nature of the militarized economy is certainly something that has grown since Eisenhower's time. The catchphrases that academics and writers have used over the decades to describe what now exists have built upon Eisenhower's "military–industrial complex." In 1993, science-fiction author Bruce Sterling described the then emergent phenomenon of the "military–entertainment complex" firsthand in the inaugural issue of *Wired Magazine*.[6] In this journalistic piece examining the then operational SIMNET, the first major military simulation used to train units of soldiers collectively, Sterling muses that in the future "a wired Armed Forces will be composed entirely of veterans—highly trained veterans of military cyberspace. An army of high-tech masters who may never have fired a real shot in real anger, but have nevertheless rampaged across entire virtual continents, crushing all resistance with fluid teamwork and utterly focused, karate-like strikes."[7]

Sterling's article, among later pieces,[8] identified the rise of a new kind of militarized media configuration centering on interactive media such as digital games and simulations. First substantially growing around the time of the 1991 Gulf War—dubbed the "video game war"—this arrangement came to life through new institutional and economic practices that reflected a symbiotically profitable relationship between the military contracting and commercial entertainment industries.

Today, the "highly trained veterans of military cyberspace" that Sterling and others from the not-so-distant past envisioned as they witnessed the unfolding of this new form of warfare may seem removed from the realities of the past decade of American war. In Iraq, Afghanistan, Pakistan, and elsewhere, the bodies of soldiers, insurgents, and civilians have been continuously placed at risk, injured, killed, and traumatized. The imagination of a future military deploying its soldiers and weapons through "utterly focused, karate-like strikes" seems to insinuate a long-running military desire for a clean war of "precision bombings" and "surgical strikes." Despite the persistence of such language surrounding the use of new technologies deployed by the military, the clean war has not happened yet.[9] The fleeting promise of healthy, non-injured soldiers and fast, efficient wars nevertheless continues to motivate the investment in and development of new technologies.

Despite this, Sterling manages to capture the essence of what is now a quotidian phenomenon in the lives of not only US soldiers but also a multitude of American youth who have come of age during the decade following the commencement of the so-called War on Terror. For this generation, "the first connected generation, the first generation of Internet natives,"[10] the affordances made available through interactive entertainment and social media have shaped and enabled a wide range of human relationships in institutionalized, public, semipublic, and private settings.[11] Digital games are very much a part of this unfolding of new media in the everyday lives of both youth and adults and have become a hegemonic form of media entertainment over the course of the decade of American war.[12] Although Sterling was not thinking about entertainment media when he wrote his prophetic words, they now perhaps more accurately describe just that. A vast array of military-themed first-person shooting (FPS) games and strategy games (e.g., *Civilization V; Total War: Rome II*) interpellate users to become "high-tech masters who may never have fired a real shot in real anger, but have nevertheless rampaged across entire virtual continents."

Simulations and "serious" games like *America's Army*, concurrent with these consumer uses of digital games, have become adopted into the lives of soldiers and institutional practices of the US military.[13] It would be inaccurate to say that the military has appropriated this technology, since the first digital simulations were developed under projects that received Cold War defense funding. The Internet, to cite a classic example, originated through the military network ARPANET, which was used for defense communications. But the military use of gaming and simulation technologies has in recent years become more apparent and institutionalized. This has been happening as the institutional force of the US military is ever becoming domesticated and normalized, spreading across a mediatized American social sphere through military-entertainment narratives that span multiple outlets. These "societies of control" operate on multiple levels,[14] from domestic security networks for the surveillance of perceived civilian political threats, policing strategies that increasingly adopt military technologies and procedures,[15] and the new unilateral executive practices, such as those adopted by the Obama administration that authorize the targeted remote assassination of American civilians by drones without due process.

Concurrent with these and many other domestic deployments that militarize civilian life,[16] simulation and gaming technologies are now taking a leading role in many parts of a soldier's—or a potential soldier's—military experiences. While this process is, in part, top-down and institutionalized by the military,[17] emergent bottom-up practices of soldiers and civilians also demonstrate how the affordances of interactive media have been used to address the systemic stresses of deployment, the anxiety of separated families, and the trauma of combat.

A hinge concept here is that of the "life cycle," which applies in varying ways to both software and soldiers. In military parlance, the soldier's life cycle is a human-relations concept used in analyzing and managing manpower, employment, and supply. It is an imagined future career trajectory, mapped beforehand according to likely outcomes, demographic modeling, and projected institutional demands. The Human Capital Core Enterprise, the managing army entity responsible for the oversight of soldier life cycles, "develops and deploys a human capital strategy that advises the Army secretary on service-wide personnel issues and priorities that sustain readiness and preserve the All-Volunteer Force. At the operational level, it recruits, trains, educates and develops soldiers, civilians and leaders for the Army to meet current and future requirements."[18]

The application of software such as *America's Army* to help meet these requirements was an intentional decision,[19] as the management offices for the game resided within West Point's Office of Economic and Manpower Analysis for many years. But whereas the ideal life cycle model for a soldier is a perpetual cycling upwards through various stages of training, deployment, post-deployment, and education (and possibly rehabilitation)—gaining experience, skills, and leadership abilities—the software life cycle model is that of a downward degeneration, prolonged as much as possible by updates, fixes, modifications, and repurposing for new uses.

In this chapter I argue that during this post-9/11 era of military entertainment the life cycles of software are intricately, and often intimately, embedded into the life cycles of soldiers, interfacing with and shaping the militarized subjectivities of enlisted, potential, and former soldiers in addition to those who know them. As I detail throughout this chapter, the *America's Army* game software has undergone myriad transformations as it has been reused for basic combat training, situational-awareness training, cultural-awareness education, post-traumatic stress therapy, and vehicle-driving rehabilitation for wounded soldiers, especially amputees. I focus my analysis below through the examples of *America's Army* and similar initiatives and how these operate in the interconnected phases of recruitment, training, and rehabilitation of the post-9/11 generation of American soldiers.

SAVING THROUGH SPENDING

The logic of the life cycle and the rationale for the long-term investment into simulation and gaming software like *America's Army* by military organizations lies beyond the strategic advantage that the repetitive, simulated rehearsal of scenarios and tactics imparts to individual and networked units of soldiers. Despite the bloated (but currently slightly shrinking) defense budget of the United States,[20] the discourse of "cost savings" has been a recurring theme throughout the self-justifying strategies of institutions that produce and purchase simulations. Expensive equipment—missiles, weapons systems, vehicles—are not wasted or jeopardized during simulated rehearsals. The lives of soldiers learning to operate these systems are not put at risk. Military gaming and simulation software assets are furthermore recycled in diverse ways to save production costs by prolonging their utility. Whether or not "cost savings" are actually realized through this practice, the discourse of software reuse by the military is one way in which defense organizations have been able to legitimize their products and preserve government commitments to long-term institutional investment in the games and simulations industry.

From the very outset these logics of cost-saving—and life-saving—procedures were central to the military adoption of simulations. "Affordability," Earl Alluisi writes, "had become a major issue in military departments, and it had a substantial effect on the development and use of simulators for training."[21] Expensive weapons systems could be saved for use in actual combat, and the risk of accidents in training could be mitigated through increased use of training simulations. This was the case even in regards to expensive and stand-alone early training simulators, which were used primarily by individuals, like pilots, whose work depended on the acquisition of specific skills for use in sometimes risky situations, such as ejecting from a plane or crash landing. The late-1980s SIMNET project was a watershed development in military simulation practices because of its ability to network together individual units of combat that were formerly unable to communicate with one another in simulated environments. The design choice to implement "selective functional fidelity" into the simulators—rather than "full physical fidelity" of all parts and nonessential features of the vehicle—was a deliberate measure aimed at producing a large number of low-cost devices.[22] By the late 1980s, SIMNET had enabled the networking of aircraft, tank, and other vehicle simulations together so that, for example, in a virtual environment a navy plane could fly from an aircraft carrier to land in an army refueling station, while communicating with tank crews on the ground. Such interoperability between weapons systems, software, and armed services enabled the large-scale training of not only individuals, but also units, and was a strategic asset that garnered great investments and spurred the growth of the defense simulation industry throughout the 1990s.[23]

One such investment was the Defense Advanced Research Projects Agency's 73 Easting simulation project in 1991, which re-created through interviews, combat action logs, photographs, tape recordings, and a variety of other data a 3-D simulation of one major battle in the 1991 Gulf War. Sterling describes the effort as being "the single most accurately recorded combat engagement in human history."[24] An internal report further identified the areas of historical simulation, training, and combat development as specific future uses for the 73 Easting battle-simulation software.[25] One reporter waxed beyond these potential practical uses of the software and proclaimed that it will enable the conquering of time itself: "It is a step along the way to . . . using advanced simulation technology to fight the past, present, and future. The Battle of 73 Easting project will capture the past with precision, enhance and enliven present training, and be a tool for projecting the future."[26] In addition to these metaphorical and indirect benefits, ideas for direct cost-saving capabilities of the 73 Easting project were, at the time, largely confined the convenient elimination of "up to three tons of book, manuals, and other printed material per battalion and squadron" for briefing and training documents that would come to be archived on CD-ROMs.[27]

The emphases on collaborative training and cost-savings characteristic to both the SIMNET and 73 Easting projects continues in other current military initiatives like *America's Army* that seek to encourage software reuse for games and simulations. One fundamental model driving this expansion is the reuse of software "assets." The array of individual designs and elements that populate a single video game is vast and includes diverse components such as trees, weapons, buildings, textures, sounds, not to mention the underlying programming code. All of these assets take time and money to produce, and the more they are reused in other software products, the less money and time is wasted. Military initiatives that reuse *America's Army* and other digital software for myriad purposes have at their core a logic of cost savings that is simultaneously an apparently

honest desire and a rhetorical strategy for institutional self-preservation and gar-
nering future investment.

AN ARMY OF HIGH-TECH MASTERS

While *America's Army* is an exceptional case in terms of its being an entertainment game directly sponsored by a military organization, the hegemony of
military-themed first-person shooters in the digital games industry already
reflects and perpetuates a kind of "militarized masculinity" that acts as an effective recruitment mechanism for the military.[28] When they are comprehensible,
the narrative themes of military FPS games range across a spectrum, but they are
often vague and heroic dramatizations of historical events that may not always
reproduce the type of messaging required by the US military.[29] American soldiers in commercial FPS games might violate rules of engagement without any
consequences, for instance, or they do not accurately reflect the type of equipment or protocols that is understood by the military as being a "true" reflection
of military culture. Coupled with clichéd actors, the overdramatic elements
found in a majority of commercial FPSes render them more akin to Hollywood
films than any sort of "realistic" vision of the military. As one blogger wrote,
"Modern FPSes *look* and *sound* authentic, but in the process, we've neglected
the intangible aspects of war—the intensity, fear, and crushing sense of finality.
There's no agenda or higher calling beyond pure entertainment."[30]

As a free downloadable game for the PC, *America's Army* was an attempt by
the US Army to intervene in these popular and sensational ludic interpretations
of the military, perpetuated by franchises such as *Call of Duty, Medal of Honor,*
SOCOM, and *Battlefield* among others. In doing so, *America's Army* created its
own discourse of military realism in games by basing their designs on actual
army uniforms, weapons, and procedures, and producing field recordings of the
game's audio at army bases, using actual weapons. Such game-design choices
led to rhetorical claims made by the game that "nobody knows the Army like
that Army" and perpetuated the idea that the game was "as close to the Army as
you can get without joining the Army." Although *America's Army* sought to dif-
ferentiate itself in this way from its commercial competition, the franchise lever-
aged the popularity of commercial military-themed FPS games among the target
demographic of army recruiting—teenage young men—to its own ends by portraying the game as a more "authentic" version of the army than what is reflected
in popular commercial FPSes.

While the discourse of authenticity is, in one sense, a blatant rhetorical strategy belied by the lack of graphic violence, psychological trauma, and social realism in the game,[31] it arises out of a genuine sincerity its developers have held to
represent the army in a more accurate way than the typical fare of Hollywood

military melodrama. This new push toward accuracy and authenticity, they felt, was necessary for multiple reasons. One such reason arose from a desire to reorient the overall army recruiting image in a more positive manner through virtual recruitment centers, moving away from the image of notorious recruiters willing to lie to potential enlistees to meet their recruitment quota. Furthermore, accuracy in depicting idealized army rules and procedures was important to *America's Army* managers in counteracting popular images of "lone wolf," one-man armies who single-handedly destroy the enemy, which is common in most military-themed FPS games. (The failed slogan "Army of One" [2001–2006] did little to help counteract this image.) *America's Army* was deliberately designed to encourage teamwork while punishing violations of army rules of engagement, particularly when players kill or injure enemy prisoners. This, in addition to showing players of the game some of the various jobs available in the army—military occupational specialties—further contributed to a deliberate reorientation through *America's Army* of how the US Army is depicted in video games. Through more efforts at making the game "accurate" and "realistic," players ideally would be able to envision themselves as individual soldiers doing specific, but interrelated and team-oriented, jobs within the broader organization of the army.

In one visit to West Point, where the game's central management was located until 2011, I interviewed Major Mike Marty, the chief financial officer of the Army Game Project, about accuracy and realism in the game. The emphasis placed on "realism" in the game, Major Marty explained, was central to the game's underlying principle,

> because there aren't the opportunities for young kids to learn about the Army other than through pop culture, through intermediaries explaining what the Army is. . . . And because we can't be in every urban city, let's virtually provide them with the opportunity for them to rub shoulders with the Army. That's why we're so focused about everything in the game being real: sound, equipment. It's because when a kid knows that that part of the Army is authentic, when they see the barracks room, when they see how they are going to live when they are deployed, when they see all of these other non-kinetic things in the game, they will know that that is exactly how the Army is, because the Army only puts authentic things in the game.[32]

Such claims to authenticity, of course, can only go so far and have throughout the game's existence invited questioning about the game's relatively sanitized portrayal of militarized violence, in comparison to other commercial games. The army deliberately implemented a game that would achieve a "Teen" rating by the Entertainment Software Ratings Board, and this entailed representing military violence in relatively nongraphic ways, such as through a "puff of blood" appearing when an enemy would be shot. It was a careful line that the army had to toe in using the language of "authenticity": although the audio and visual elements from the game are as realistic as possible, given the software limitations, the game does not by most measures represent the horrors of war, injury, or death.

"But how much is enough?" Colonel Casey Wardynski, director of the Army Game Project, asked me during an interview when I brought up this topic. He invited me to think about the situation from the army's perspective. *America's Army* does implement certain game-design choices that enhance the relative value of in-game lives—both allies and enemies—in comparison to other commercial FPS games. Going too far in the direction of graphically depicting violence and gore would have put forth an undesirable message about the realities of war. It would have also angered the throngs of people still caught up in the "moral panic" of video games as a dangerous social ill, associating the military with the whole host of problems, such as school shootings, regularly blamed on games. Most importantly, though, graphic violence in the game would have limited the player demographic to those within the "Mature" (over eighteen) set of players, who were not the target demographic of users for the game (figure 3).

In appealing to young men who played FPS games, and yet depicting the army as a positive career choice for young men, the directors of the project "want[ed] to get into a kids decision space . . . ," Major Marty told me,

at an age when they are just starting to think about what they can do with their life, what is in their goal set. . . . It takes an exponential amount of more information to change a person's mind as opposed to give them that kind of first impression, to have them think, ok this is doable. The Army should not be a fallback position. I have this very fundamental belief when it comes to recruiting that the Army will sell itself to the right kid. The problem is that there's not enough Army presence in the right formats for young kids to engage with the Army in a platform where they don't feel like they are being sold something by a used car salesman.[33]

The soft-sell affordances of interactive gaming media, thus, were crucial for putting the army forward to a generation of youth more likely to seek out entertainment and information through online and networked formats rather than more traditional media like the TV. "The game is really about changing the way that young people learn about the Army to a format that they are comfortable with," Marty continued,

With the information that they gather, they will believe more than the traditional way of a TV advertisement, which they will either fast forward through on their DVR, go back to their laptop while a commercial is playing, or change the

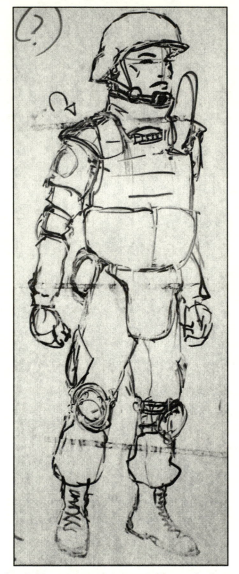

FIGURE 3. Concept sketch for an *America's Army 3* soldier at the former *America's Army* studios in Emeryville, California. (Photograph by the author.)

channel. And even if they do sit through the TV commercial they are much less likely to believe the message because it is being pushed to them. If they go out and seek a message through Google or gaming; if they come upon a message in a way that they feel was on their own; if they structure their path on the internet in a way that they come upon something that they are now reading or engaging with and have some kind of interactivity with, they are much more likely to believe it because they sought it out. So the game and virtual technology . . . allows you to have a much more relevant message to people in a format that they are much more comfortable with.[34]

The interactive nature of games and social media presents a platform for traditional "hard power" institutions like the military to spread their influence through media that are not part of the traditional model of unidirectional media messaging. In this way, the promise of individual agency and empowerment that interactive and social media have for many becomes co-opted by institutions of power, which present their messages in formats that are more easily palatable and less likely to be interpreted as being an "advertisement" or, in a more extreme understanding, "propaganda."

HIGHLY TRAINED VETERANS OF MILITARY CYBERSPACE

As the *America's Army* franchise expanded between 2004 and 2008, during the Bush administration's self-proclaimed "War on Terror," the army invested in other relatively short-lived experimental recruitment projects, such as the Virtual Army Experience (VAE) and the Army Experience Center (AEC), both of which implemented *America's Army* software assets into new simulations that were more explicitly targeted at enlistment and public relations.[35] The Virtual Army Experience toured through the United States to large public events—air shows, NASCAR races, state fairs, and theme parks—to present a free thirty-minute interactive combat simulation to visitors (see figure 4), interpreted by former army soldiers and on-site army recruiters. All visitors were required to enter basic personal information into a database, and those falling within a targeted demographic (which included the then twenty-nine-year-old me, apparently), were approached by army recruiters by phone following their visit.

Closed in 2010 after the completion of a two-year pilot project, the Army Experience Center included the same simulated combat scenarios present at the Virtual Army Experience and combined five Philadelphia-area army recruiting centers into a large, interactive technology-oriented gaming and outreach center inside the Franklin Mills Shopping Mall. Hosting regular regional school and extracurricular events, and with a large number of games on computers and Xbox 360s freely available to use, the AEC encouraged youth to come to the center to simply "hang out," without the experience of the hard sell so common to army recruitment. The AEC itself was the soft sell to join the army, and in efforts to depict the center as a community-oriented place, a curious rhetorical twist occurred. The combined five Philadelphia-area recruiting centers were no longer publicized as being geared toward recruitment; rather, they were all about "educating" the public and youth about the army, especially the various military

FIGURE 4. Interior view of the Virtual Army Experience. (Photograph by the author.)

occupational specialties (MOS) that were available for enlistees. As Scott Johnston, the government project manager of both the AEC and VAE told me,

> We think of the AEC as an education center, not a recruitment center. We see
> the VAE as another education tool, as public outreach. We want to get away from
> all the negative publicity that you have, that everything is blood, guts, and glory,
> boots on the ground and a rifle in your hand. That's just not the way the Army is,
> and we want to show the technical side of the Army, all of the MOSes. We want to
> show that to the public that we are doing things to keep the guys in the field safe.
> And we want to show that there are things that you can do in the Army and come
> out and get great, great jobs and experience.[36]

As I have argued elsewhere, the distinctions between the binary configurations of soldier and civilian, and war and game, is eroding.[37] This is happening
is such a way that media users of games and venues such as *America's Army*, the
VAE, and AEC could be referred to as "virtual soldiers," in the sense that they are
not only playing at soldiering through a virtual interface, but also simultaneously
being encouraged to think of themselves as potential (i.e., virtual) soldiers by the
military and state institutions of power. Players step into the shoes of soldiers
via interactive media on a daily basis and are asked through such media to take
on the subjectivities and attitudes of soldiers. In this manner, the life cycle of

the soldier begins well before actual recruitment takes place and continues on through training. This model became apparent as I continued my conversation with Johnston, who in addition to the VAE and AEC recruitment efforts was also in charge of overseeing the implementation of *America's Army* training systems for actual soldiers.

Johnston explained how extending the utility of *America's Army* software through the recycling of assets was a critical cost-saving mechanism: "Reuse is huge, and it saves a lot of time and money. Most of the time on any project [involving *America's Army*] you have a 50 or 60 percent completed solution before you get started, because all the art assets and everything is basically there. It's just a matter of piecing it all together." A live-fire virtual shoot house for training was one such development that garnered a list of US military customers. This Live Fire Virtual Targeting Program is

> an actual trainer that the military uses to train close-quarter type battle tactics, where teams are going in and clearing rooms, clearing buildings. You typically see static targets with pop-up targets or sliding silhouettes on strings. Well, we go in and retrofit those shooting houses by adding screens, projectors, and thermal cameras that actually allow you to fire live rounds. They have scenarios based on hostage situations, any type of situation based on making split decisions. We take our requirements straight from the customer and build it into the software. Our first project was with the JFK Special Warfare School at Ft. Bragg.[38]

The convenience of such virtual shoot houses, as opposed to older models that do not use virtual technology, lies in the ability to allow

> instantaneous training, and you can push through your guys on a much quicker basis from your old way. Soldiers go through the old way and you have to spend the next half of the day setting the room back up. So now, it's just a click of a button, and boom, you're off. . . . We have five different scenarios now. Three of them have three levels of difficulty. We also have a schoolhouse scenario and a domestic disturbance scenario where you have to make decisions based on what's going on in the environment. [With asset reuse], the great thing, as with any *America's Army* project, is that the software is free to those sites. So everybody benefits. What we try to do is get what functionality we have in there and show [the customers that]. And then have them say, "well from our point of instruction, and our tactics and training, we want to do this, this, and this." So they give us funding to build those types of scenarios. Well, when we build it for one customer, everyone else gets it too, so the entire Army benefits from one customer.[39]

Following this model, *America's Army* developed a whole list of other trainers for teaching soldiers how to use specific weapons systems. These user-friendly training systems did not require previous experience with digital games and made no assumptions about the technological skills of the user. The Javelin Basic Skill Trainer, for example, was a portable system that could be brought with soldiers to areas of deployment to teach individuals how to use the Javelin missile system. The project produced yet other training simulators for robots used to destroy explosives and for remotely operated gun turrets on placed top of armored vehicles. A Convoy Skills Engagement Trainer using *America's Army* assets, according to a brochure, provided "a mobile, flexible and cost-effective simulation experience for training individuals or teams in mission-critical convoy skills"[40] (figure 5).

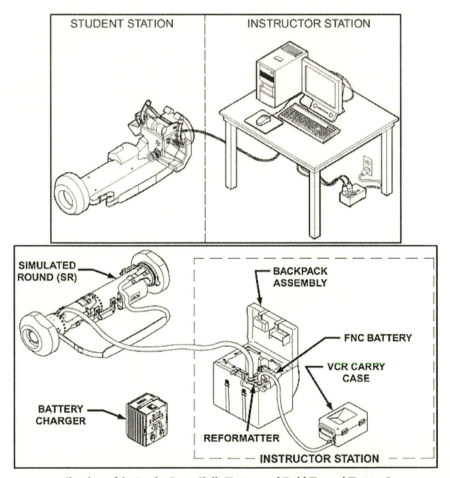

FIGURE 5. Sketches of the Javelin Basic Skills Trainer and Field Tactical Trainer. Images from *U.S. Army Field Manual 3–22–37*, section 3–8. (Washington, D.C.: U.S. Department of the Army, 2003), http://www.globalsecurity.org/military/library/policy/army/fm/3 -22-37

While *America's Army* has specialized in producing such individual- and squad-focused training simulations, the Czech company Bohemia Interactive Simulations has kept the SIMNET tradition of networked military simulation training alive through its development of the official US Army and Marines training simulator, *Virtual Battlespace 3* (*VBS 3*). *VBS 3* also embraces asset reuse, as Bohemia Interactive Simulations contracts its software to the specifications of the militaries of many Western nations, such as Canada, the Netherlands, the UK, Australia, and New Zealand.[41] Here, too, "cost-effectiveness" is a rhetorical strategy used by contractors for acquiring lucrative military investments; multiple e-newsletters from Bohemia Interactive Simulations indicate how their products are "efficient yet cost-effective."[42] The commercial video game, *ARMA 2*, is additionally a kindred piece of software made by Bohemia Interactive (a separate company) and shares many of its assets with *VBS 3*.

Other simulations sought to educate soldiers about basic cultural norms, both in terms of army culture and simplified depictions of cultures with which the army interacted on a large scale, namely Iraq and Afghanistan. The *America's Army* Future Soldier Training System (see figure 2) was one such tool that sought to introduce enlistees who had not yet entered basic training to army procedures and culture with the purpose of decreasing drop-out rates during boot camp due to the unanticipated hardships in a foreign institutional environment. (*America's Army* can also be interpreted as seeking to achieve this goal among a population of potential civilian enlistees.) The Adaptive Thinking and Leadership simulator also "allow[ed] players to discover their strengths and weaknesses in mental agility, cultural awareness, interpersonal adaptability and communication" among a simulated population of non-American civilians.[43] These *America's Army* versions of cultural simulations are but one small aspect of an increasingly large subset of military contracting initiatives. As Roberto González has shown, a vast but underinvestigated industry of military initiatives exists that seeks literally to code human culture and behavior through social-media data-mining techniques, with a *Minority Report*–like goal of preempting and forecasting global insurgent "hotspots" before they get hot.[44]

The small sampling explored here underscores an explosion in the military training software industry currently underway, as actual weapons systems (and their virtual training systems) are procured through military contracts even when relatively modest defense budget cuts are becoming necessary in the global post-recession economy. These trainers accurately reproduce to a high degree of fidelity how specific weapons systems operate, and in cases such as *VBS2* and *VBS3* they enable the collective training of soldiers within computer-generated environments across wide swaths of terrain. Such soldiers do indeed "rampage . . . across entire virtual continents, crushing all resistance with fluid teamwork,"[45] but what these training simulations deliberately lack in their mimetic depictions of war is the real suffering that soldiers and civilians experience when faced with the unforgiving realities of war. Other simulations exist for that.

FULL-CYCLE WARRIORS: POST-9/11 POST-TRAUMA

Psychological and physical trauma suffered in combat by soldiers, civilians, and their families is one of many unaccounted costs of war that the United States will be confronting for years to come.[46] This is particularly the case for families of returning or formerly enlisted soldiers, who are at greater risk of domestic violence, divorce, and the loss of a family member due to suicide.[47] Games and simulations like *America's Army* have come a grim full circle through their growing involvement in the rehabilitation of soldiers and have been a part of new and belated efforts at understanding and alleviating endemic problems suffered by returning injured soldiers. In a sense, such programs seek to treat illnesses and injuries that are, in part, of their own creation; the games-and-simulations sector of the military contracting industry supports the implementation of a "military normal" that perpetuates a government-subsidized militarized economy, which at its core institutionalizes the processes of war, from prerecruitment to post-trauma.[48]

Even remotely stationed drone pilots—harbingers of future mediated war—are not immune to combat injuries, and according to one news report the stress rates among drone pilots are higher than the average rates among other enlisted service members.[49] Perhaps one reason for this phenomenon is perhaps the lack of any formal transition period for drone pilots between the once-distinctive realms of battlefront and home front, as opposed to other soldiers who must at the very least travel across great distances to return to friends and family. But due to the affordances of cell-phone and Internet communication these two realms are becoming ever more connected, even for soldiers deployed overseas. Internet calling services such as Skype have become an everyday way for soldiers to connect with loved ones back home. Such technologies sometimes connect people in unwanted and traumatic ways, as was the case when a soldier accidentally called his family's home phone during a firefight in Afghanistan.[50]

Post-traumatic stress disorder (PTSD) cases among soldiers have skyrocketed over the past decade, and tailored simulations of traumatic events have proven to be successful in alleviating and treating some of its symptoms. One of the first efforts at treating PTSD through virtual environments began through perhaps the most visible and oft-cited example of the kinds of new relationships between the defense and entertainment industries that have emerged over the past two decades. Founded in 1999, the Institute for Creative Technologies (ICT), a US Army–funded research center at the University of Southern California, brought together executives and professionals with backgrounds in Hollywood, software engineering, and the military to produce novel ideas for harnessing emerging media technologies for military purposes. The ICT designed an officer-focused training simulation for combat situations, *Full Spectrum Warrior*, in 2003 and published through Ubisoft a commercial version of the simulation as a game in 2004. Sequels to both the trainer and game quickly unfolded after the software was deemed a success both for training and commercial purposes.

Following this, the ICT invested its resources and research into developing and implementing a form of "virtual reality (VR) exposure therapy" for soldiers with combat trauma and PTSD. Originally developed in 2005, the *Virtual Iraq/Afghanistan* simulation reuses the software assets from *Full Spectrum Warrior* and is now being used for VR exposure therapy in a variety of locations, such as Madigan Army Medical Center in Ft. Lewis, Washington.[51] The software, "designed to use off-the-shelf equipment in order to minimizes [sic] costs and maximize the access and availability of the system,"[52] enables therapists to re-create tailored virtual environments for the purposes of revisiting specific traumatic "trigger" events. In addition to manipulating visual elements, clinicians are able to use auditory, tactile (vibrations), and even olfactory stimuli (ranging from cooking smells, burning rubber, cordite, smoke, and others) to "foster the anxiety modulation needed for therapeutic habituation and emotional processing in a customized fashion according to the patient's past experience and treatment progress."[53]

The designers of *Virtual Iraq/Afghanistan* acknowledge that "the use of VR for clinical care may have some appeal to a generation of [service members] and veterans who have grown up 'digital' and are comfortable with treatment delivered within this computer and information-technology format."[54] The familiarity of the post-9/11 generation of soldiers and veterans with virtual interfaces has improved the accessibility of other forms of treatment that use games, simulations, and virtual environments. One such example involves the presence of soldier and soldier family-therapy communities in online worlds like *Second Life*, an online multiuser virtual world that provides relative anonymity and the ability to craft personal avatars within a persistent, user-created universe. Within *Second Life*, an array of military-support communities exist, such as the Amputee Virtual Environment Support Space;[55] the ICT-developed Transitional Online Post-deployment Soldier Support in Virtual Worlds project, Coming Home;[56] the National Center for Telehealth and Technology's Virtual PTSD Experience;[57] and the Army One-Source Community's Virtual Resiliency Campus, which brings together soldiers and their families for the purposes of communication and support.[58] As a long-popular haven for multiple other communities of support, *Second Life* and similar virtual worlds offer individuals much-needed opportunities to speak with others who have shared, and sometimes traumatic, experiences.

America's Army, too, has contributed to the rehabilitation of injured soldiers through the implementation of a driving simulation at locations like the Walter Reed Army Medical Center, which houses some of the most severely injured soldiers and amputees. The simulation, which reuses *America's Army* assets, teaches veterans with lost limbs how to drive using modified steering and controls. Other applications of the simulation assist soldiers with reintegrating into civilian defensive-driving culture, because driving practices in combat environments are so vastly dissimilar. (Driving in the center of the road to avoid improvised explosive devices (IEDs), speeding through dangerous intersections, tailgating, and making unpredictable turns, accelerations, and decelerations are all adaptive techniques for combat driving.[59])

In this way, *America's Army*, a piece of software that may have had a role in a soldier's decision to join the military, might also have had a role in training him through the *America's Army* Convoy Skills Engagement Trainer on how to drive as a part of a convoy in Iraq.[60] After his deployment the same piece of game software might also enable the soldier's successful transition into civilian driving. The convoy, though, may have been ambushed by an IED, and the soldier would then need to learn via a training simulation how to operate his car back home without any legs.

Nonvirtual settings that nevertheless use video games as focal points for enlisted soldier team-building activities have also proven useful in fostering a sense of camaraderie, as some reports have noted.[61] But soldiers with combat trauma, many of whom remain enlisted, have been warned to avoid playing war games, as unsupervised playing without the contextualization of traumatic experiences for the purposes of healing is potentially dangerous and could trigger flashbacks.[62] I have found through both my ethnographic fieldwork and interactions with veterans at my university that a number of ex-soldiers who grew up playing video games seek out gaming combat experiences in order to "self-medicate" outside of formal clinical supervision. One former army soldier who was working as a tour guide for visitors to the VAE (see above) spoke at length to me about his worldview in ways that left me disturbed and concerned not only for his well-being, but any person with whom he had contact. All the games he played, he said, were

> war-oriented, for the most part. I can play racing games, all these other games, and I get no enjoyment out of it. I get enjoyment out of seeing someone's head get peeled like a fuckin' grape by a .50 caliber round. In a game or in real life. I don't [play military games] for training, I do it for fun. It relaxes me. I mean, I play Madden [NFL football games] and get all pissed off, play baseball and get all pissed off, play a racing game or a flying game and get all pissed off. I play a game where I get a big fucking gun and I can kill people, I'm cool. It's a relaxation thing, where I can just hang out and blow people up.[63]

As is the case with any medium, the context and intent of its use is central to its interpretation. Military games and simulations, as tools, have the potential to recruit, to train, and to educate. They can help people to heal by encouraging them to face their fears and talk through their trauma, and they can enable users to deny that a problem in their lives exists.

CONCLUSION

It is challenging at times to discern exactly how specific software products and development choices about them impact the lived realities of individual software users. Marcus, for one, speculated that nonenlisted players of *America's Army* would not be compelled to join the army from simply playing a video game. If they did, he reflected, "It would be weird. If some kid said to me, 'Yeah, I joined the military because of your game, dude, and I remember those moments playing and hiding behind that [tower that you designed]. That was so awesome. I may have lost my legs but I did it for my country,' I would probably feel terrible."[64] While it is difficult to critique the patently positive function that virtual technologies effect in the rehabilitation of soldiers such as the imagined one described by Marcus, media like the *America's Army* franchise carry with them an institutionalizing force that maps onto the bodies of soldiers an imagined, carefully managed, and violent life cycle career trajectory. It seems to me that the overarching political economy of the military-entertainment complex has not changed so much over the past twenty years and remains, in Bruce Sterling's words, "a complete and utter triumph of chilling, analytic, cybernetic rationality over chaotic, real-life, human desperation."[65] The underlying principle of these technologies is, at its very heart, a militarized logic of biopolitical governance that aims to more efficiently streamline the apparatuses of war, to enable potential soldiers, recruited soldiers, and traumatized soldiers to become more "battle ready." While many American youth who have come of age during the wars in Iraq and Afghanistan have benefited from their military enlistment in some kind of way—in terms of employment, class mobility, and skills training—military-funded games and simulations are merely one evolution of the destructive war machine so entrenched in the post-9/11 American ethos.

NOTES

1. Names with surnames in this and other publications of mine are the actual names of individuals. First names without a surname are aliases. Quotations are actual verbatim comments made by individuals, recorded by me through interviews or field notes. Over the course of twenty months (2007–2009), I conducted National Science Foundation–funded ethnographic fieldwork among the game developers, military officers, government software engineers, and contracting organizations that design and implement not only *America's Army*, but also software based on the game that has become reused for various military training and weapons development purposes. My multisited fieldwork brought me to a range of locations,

like the Virtual Army Experience, a public outreach/recruiting effort using *America's Army* technology that toured the United States to large public events, air shows, and state fairs. My travels were numerous and constant as I visited the Virtual Army Experience's design studios in Alabama and the San Francisco Bay area, its marketing and data offices in Southern California, and any number of military bases, recruiting centers, and elsewhere.

2. Marcus [pseud.], interview by author, audio recording, October 2008, Emeryville, CA.

3. In 2009, *America's Army* was awarded five Guinness World Records, reflecting its once-massive appeal: Largest Virtual Army (9.7 million registered users, about ten times the total size of the actual US Army); Most Downloaded War Video Game (42 million downloads); Most Hours Spent Playing a Free Online Shooter (231 million hours as of August 2008); Earliest Military Website to Support a Video Game; and Largest Travelling Game Simulator. See http://pc.gamespy.com/pc/americas-army/951010p1.html.

4. Nick Turse, *The Complex: How the Military Invades Our Everyday Lives* (New York: Metropolitan Books, 2008).

5. Marcus, interview.

6. Bruce Sterling, "War Is Virtual Hell," *Wired Magazine*, 1:1 (1993), http://www.wired.com/wired/archive/1.01/virthell.html.

7. Ibid.

8. See, for example Jean Baudrillard, *The Gulf War Did Not Take Place* (Sydney, AU: Power Publications, 1995); Manuel De Landa, *War in the Age of the Intelligent Machines* (1991; repr., New York: Zone Books, 2003); James Der Derian, *Virtuous War: Mapping the Military-Industrial-Media-Entertainment Network* (Boulder, CO: Westview Press, 2001); J. C. Herz, *Joystick Nation: How Videogames Ate Our Quarters, Won Our Hearts, and Rewired Our Minds* (Boston: Little, Brown and Company, 1999); Timothy Lenoir, "All But War Is Simulation: The Military-Entertainment Complex," *Configurations* 8, no. 3 (2000): 289–335; and Roger Stahl, *Militainment, Inc.: War, Media, and Popular Culture* (New York: Routledge, 2010).

9. Jeff Sluka, "Death from Above: UAVs and Losing Hearts and Minds," *Military Review*, May–June 2011.

10. Bifo Berardi, *The Uprising: On Poetry and Finance* (Los Angeles: Semiotext(e), 2012), 37.

11. Nancy Baym, *Personal Connections in the Digital Age* (Cambridge, UK: Polity Press, 2010); Nancy Baym and danah boyd, "Socially Mediated Publicness: An Introduction," *Journal of Broadcasting and Electronic Media* 56, no. 3 (2012): 320–329; and Mizuko Ito et al., *Hanging Out, Messing Around, and Geeking Out: Kids Living and Learning with New Media* (Cambridge, MA: MIT Press, 2010).

12. Nick Dyer-Witheford and Greig de Peuter, *Games of Empire: Global Capitalism and Video Games* (Minneapolis: University of Minnesota Press, 2009).

13. The overview of various technologies and institutions presented here is by no means meant to be considered exhaustive.

14. Gilles Deleuze, "Postscript on the Societies of Control," *October* 59 (Winter 1992): 3–7.

15. See Tom Hall, "Killing Civilians Without Due Process," *LA Progressive*, February 12, 2013, http://www.laprogressive.com/killing-civilians-without-due-process/.

16. See Catherine Lutz, "The Military Normal: Feeling at Home with Counterinsurgency in the United States," in *The Counter-Counterinsurgency Manual: Or, Notes on Demilitarizing American Society*, ed. Network of Concerned Anthropologists (Chicago: Prickly Paradigm, 2009), 23–37; Turse, *The Complex*.

17. Timothy Lenoir and Henry Lowood, "Theaters of War: The Military–Entertainment Complex," in *Collection–Laboratory–Theater: Scenes of Knowledge in the 17th Century*, ed. Jan Lazardzig, Helmar Schramm, and Ludger Schwarte (Berlin: Walter de Gruyter, 2005), 427–456.

18. Broderick Bailey, "Soldier Life Cycle," Association of the United States Army, October 10, 2009, http://www.ausa.org/publications/ausanews/archives/2009/10/Pages/Soldier lifecycle.asp.

19. Robertson Allen, "War Games at Work: Networks of Power in the U.S. Army Video Game Project" (PhD diss., University of Washington, 2012).

20. In 2011, the United States allocated more money to its defense budget than the next combined eight countries. See Peter G. Peterson Foundation, April 13, 2014, http://www.pgpf .org/Chart-Archive/0053_defense-comparison.aspx; Lutz, "Military Normal."

21. Earl Alluisi, "The Development of Technology for Collective Training: SIMNET, a Case History," *Human Factors: The Journal of the Human Factors and Ergonomics Society* 33, no. 3 (1991): 346.

22. Ibid., 347.

23. Mark Long, interview by author, audio recording, September 2007, Seattle, WA.

24. Sterling, "War Is Virtual Hell."

25. Gary Bloedorn et al., "73 Easting Functional Description and Guidance Document, 1st Draft." Illusion Engineering, Inc. Report #DA-MDA972-8-91, August 3, 1991.

26. Clifton Berry, "Re-Creating History: The Battle of 73 Easting," *National Defense,* November 1991.

27. *Defense and Aerospace Electronics,* September 9, 1991, Pasha Publications.

28. Stephen Kline, Nick Dyer-Witheford, and Greig De Peuter, *Digital Play: The Interaction of Technology, Culture, and Marketing* (Montreal: McGill-Queen's University Press, 2003), 246–268.

29. Robertson Allen, "The Unreal Enemy of America's Army," *Games and Culture* 6, no. 1 (2011): 38–60.

30. Sam Barsanti, "Realism in First Person Shooters and the Fact that There Isn't Any," Bitmob.com, 2011, http://bitmob.com/articles/the-case-for-realism-in-first-person-shooters.

31. Alexander Galloway, "Social Realism in Gaming," *Game Studies* 4, no. 1 (2004), http:// www.gamestudies.org/0401/galloway/.

32. Mike Marty, interview by author, May 2009, West Point, NY.

33. Ibid.

34. Ibid.

35. Robertson Allen, "The Army Rolls through Indianapolis: Fieldwork at the Virtual Army Experience." *Transformative Works and Cultures* 1, no. 2 (2009), http://journal .transformativeworks.org/index.php/twc/article/view/80/97.

36. Scott Johnston, interview by author, January 2009, Redstone Arsenal, AL.

37. Robertson Allen, "Virtual Soldiers, Cognitive Laborers," in *Virtual War and Magical Death: Technologies and Imaginaries for Terror and Killing,* ed. Neil Whitehead and Sverker Finnström (Durham, NC: Duke University Press, 2013), 152–170.

38. Johnston, interview; see also Kent Harris, "Shoot House Tests Service Members with Video Technology," *Stripes,* September 9, 2009, http://www.stripes.com/news/shoot-house -tests-servicemembers-with-video-technology-1.94614.

39. Johnston, interview.

40. *America's Army* program informational brochure, published by the US Army.

41. Robertson Allen, "Games without Tears, Wars without Frontiers," in *War, Technology, Anthropology,* ed. Koen Stroken (New York: Berghahn Books, 2012), 83–93.

42. Bohemia Interactive Simulations newsletters, emailed November 13, 2012, February 2, 2011.

43. *America's Army* program informational brochure.

44. Roberto González, "Cybernetic Crystal Ball: 'Forecasting' Insurgency in Iraq and Afghanistan," in *Virtual War and Magical Death: Technologies and Imaginaries for Terror and*

Killing, ed. by Neil Whitehead and Sverker Finnström (Durham: Duke University Press, 2013), 65–84; Roberto González, "World in a Bottle: Prognosticating Insurgency in Iraq and Afghanistan," in *War, Technology, Anthropology*, ed. Koen Stroken (New York: Berghahn Books, 2012), 45–61.

45. Sterling, "War Is Virtual Hell."

46. For an excellent exploration of these unaccounted costs of war, see the PBS *Frontline* documentary, *The Wounded Platoon* (2010).

47. As soldiers return, an array of journalistic and academic literature has sought to address some of these issues. For a representative sample of literature on the topic, see Benjamin Karney, David Loughran, and Michael Pollard, "Comparing Marital Status and Divorce Status in Civilian and Military Populations," *Journal of Family Issues* 33, no. 12 (2012): 1572–1594; Robert McLay, *At War with PTSD: Battling Post-Traumatic Stress Disorder with Virtual Reality* (Baltimore: Johns Hopkins University Press, 2012); Michele Sherman et al., "Domestic Violence in Veterans with Posttraumatic Stress Disorder who Seek Couples Therapy," *Journal of Marital and Family Therapy* 32, no. 4 (2007): 479–490; and Timothy Williams, "Suicide Outpacing War Deaths for Troops," *New York Times*, June 8, 2012, http://www.nytimes.com/2012/06/09/us/suicides-eclipse-war-deaths-for-us-troops.html.

48. Lutz, "Military Normal"; Eugene Jarecki, *Why We Fight*, documentary film (Sony Pictures, 2006).

49. Elisabeth Bumiller, "Air Force Drone Operators Report High Levels of Stress," *New York Times*, December 18, 2011, http://www.nytimes.com/2011/12/19/world/asia/air-force-drone-operators-show-high-levels-of-stress.html. The US Air Force reportedly now trains more drone pilots than conventional fighter pilots, according to Rachel Martin, "Drone Pilots: The Future of Aerial Warfare," National Public Radio, November 29, 2011, http://www.npr.org/2011/11/29/142858358/drone-pilots-the-future-of-aerial-warfare; Giles Whittell, "Top Gun Is the Wrong Stuff for the Drone Age," *The Times*, August 2, 2012, http://www.thetimes.co.uk/tto/opinion/columnists/article3496191.ece.

The Obama administration's heavy political and military investment in drones as a solution to fighting Al Qaeda and other insurgents has led to a dramatic increase in the number of air strikes in Pakistan, Yemen, and Afghanistan, a number that only accelerated over the course of the president's first term in office.

50. McLay, *At War with PTSD*, 23.

51. See CNN video report, "Virtual Reality Battles PTSD," CNN, September 23, 2011, http://edition.cnn.com/video/?/video/tech/2011/09/23/virtual-reality-battles.cnn.

52. Albert "Skip" Rizzo et al., "Development and Early Evaluation of the Virtual Iraq/Afghanistan Exposure Therapy System for Combat-Related PTSD," *Annals of the New York Academy of Sciences* 1208 (2010), 118.

53. Ibid.

54. Ibid., 115.

55. See Doug Thompson and Amy Fisher, "Guest Editorial: Amputee Virtual Environment Support Space—A vision for Virtual Military Amputee Support," *Journal of Rehabilitation Research and Development* 47, no. 6 (2010), vii–xi, http://www.rehab.research.va.gov/jour/10/476/pdf/thompson.pdf.

56. See Institute for Creative Technologies, "Coming Home," http://projects.ict.usc.edu/force/cominghome/.

57. See http://t2health.org/vwproj/, accessed February 13,2013.

58. See Army OneSource, "Army OneSource in Second Life," http://www.myarmyonesource.com/communitiesandmarketplace/virtualworlds/secondlife/default.aspx.

59. See Military OneSource, http://www.militaryonesource.mil/crisis-prevention?content _id=268840.

60. Although both men and women are now able to fully serve in combat positions in the US military, the underlying assumed user of all *America's Army*–related software is male.

61. See Kristin Kalning, "Playing 'Outside The Wire,'" NBC, December 2, 2008, http://www .nbcnews.com/id/23114125/ns/technology_and_science-games/#.UZo8MLUsnh5.

62. See Wenda Benedetti, "Vets Warn Soldiers with PTSD to Avoid War Games," NBC News .com, February 10, 2011, http://ingame-discuss.nbcnews.com/_news/2011/02/10/6022663 -vets-warn-soldiers-with-ptsd-to-avoid-war-games.

63. Interview by author, August 2008, Indianapolis, IN.

64. Marcus, interview.

65. Sterling, "War Is Virtual Hell."

PART III

COMING OF AGE STORIES AND THE REPRESENTATION OF MILLENNIAL CITIZENSHIP DURING THE WAR ON TERROR

8 · COMING OF AGE IN 9/11 FICTION

Bildungsroman and Loss of Innocence

JO LAMPERT

[I]t is the insecurity of the present and uncertainty of the future that hatch and breed the most awesome and least bearable of our fears. That insecurity and that uncertainty, in their turn, are born of a sense of impotence: we seem to be no longer in control....

—Zygmunt Bauman, *Liquid Times: Living in an Age of Uncertainty*[1]

Directly after the horrific events of September 11, 2001, many Americans were saying the same thing: the world has changed forever. They were overwhelmed with a sense that "the party was over." It was clear that America had lost its innocence; it now had to "grow up." Much of the fiction produced since 9/11 and with 9/11 at its core provides evidence of the larger cultural belief that September 11 was a turning point (much like adolescence) from which there is no turning back. In this chapter, I examine how three post-9/11 novels—Lorrie Moore's *A Gate at the Stairs*, Joyce Maynard's *The Usual Rules*, and John Updike's *Terrorist*—position readers to understand September 11 as a moment that changed how young Americans come of age.[2] The texts selected for discussion in this chapter, however, represent the variety of ways in which this "new" post-9/11 coming-of-age subject has been conceived in fiction with young adult protagonists. In each case, the grief and profound loss provoked by terrorism prompts a different, but life-changing maturity.[3] While, in these texts, the forms this new maturity takes range from cynicism to optimism to patriotism, the common element, evidence of a larger cultural phenomenon, is this persistent sense of a nation forced against its will to grow up in the wake of an uncertain future.

Because 9/11 equates to a moment when America had to grow up, the prevalence of coming-of-age stories in 9/11 fiction makes inherent sense. The cultural mood particularly suited the bildungsroman genre, which is characterized by fictional coming-of-age narratives that involve protagonists who, provoked by crisis, find the maturity that comes only from suffering. The crises are usually a result of a catastrophe and take the characters on journeys of self-discovery, which, once fulfilled, lead them back home. It is a genre familiar to readers of American litera- ture (perhaps the best-known example is J. D. Salinger's 1958 novel, *The Catcher in the Rye*).[4] With its key elements of loss, suffering, self-awareness, introspec- tion, and growth, the coming-of-age novel also fulfills agendas common to both literature and politics: the literary journey becomes the nation's journey. The quest for restabilization is found through a reassuring explanation for 9/11 that provides an answer to the "why" that consumes adolescence. The loss of Ameri- can confidence and self-worth after 9/11 may also be related to the egocentric preoccupation of adolescence.[5] If the events of September 11 led the nation to a preoccupation with the self, or to develop an even stronger sense of self and a more mature response to a fragile world, it will seem to have had some purpose.

Indeed, John Frow has suggested that 9/11 was particularly ideologically suited to the bildungsroman genre—"nearly perfectly scripted for a revival of coming-of-age and crystallising a set of pre-existing cultural tropes."[6] Authors may have found some comfort in presenting small, personal coming-of-age sto- ries, rather than tackling the big-picture politics of 9/11. Looking at localized, small, and personal struggles may have made the impossible task of understand- ing a changing world more manageable when, Bauman claims, many Americans no longer felt in control.[7] Similarly, examining 9/11 through the eyes of young adults highlights how innocence was seemingly lost overnight and how it might be reclaimed. This preoccupation with reclaiming innocence does important cultural work, reasserting the United States as politically innocent and unjustly wounded and, as Sturken claims, distant from the world of politics and history.[8]

Bildungsromane are always concerned with a passage into adulthood.[9] How- ever, in the past, this literary journey typically involved a maturation that led to assimilation into society—a process by which a young (historically male) hero "discovers himself and his social role through the experiences of love, friend- ship and the hard realities of life."[10] Although many of the features of traditional bildungsromane remain in the three novels examined here, the society into which the protagonists must assimilate (or resist) shifted with 9/11, producing a generation of young people required, at least in the short term, to declare their allegiance to their country. It seems that 9/11 provided a clear link between the growing up of an individual and the growing up of a nation. Like adolescence, 9/11 led its subject to seek new meaning.

The three books chosen for analysis in this chapter are selected both for their similarities and differences. Each of them uses 9/11 as a narrative strategy, and each is concerned with 9/11 as an identity project. In other words, while the ter- rorist attacks of 2001 are used as a pivotal backdrop in each of the books, 9/11 is also constructed as a moment of transition into the adult world. Though similar in this respect, the novels offer up three different options to their readers; that is, different solutions to what is perceived as the inevitability of growing up, or reaching maturity. For Tassie, in *A Gate at the Stairs*, reaching adulthood in a post-9/11 world is tainted with cynicism and despair—this is a resigned subject, older and yet wiser. *The Usual Rules* instead presents the reader with an optimistic subject with a renewed faith in humanity. Different yet again, *Terrorist* privileges the patriotic subject, forced to declare his political and cultural allegiance in a way less previously required of young-adult protagonists. While all three novels declare the necessity for healing as a condition of growing up, they produce the 9/11 subject in different ways, drawing varied conclusions about young citizenship post-terrorism.

A GATE AT THE STAIRS: GROWING UP CYNICAL

The first novel to be discussed, Lorrie Moore's *A Gate at the Stairs*, is set just after 9/11. Strictly speaking, it is not a 9/11 novel because it is not about the terrorist acts themselves; however, the events of that day have a significant impact on the protagonist and her friends and family. Grief, fear, and uncertainty permeate everything in this novel. For the teenage Tassie and her friends, 9/11 is ever present, forcing her generation to grow up in a way they would happily have avoided had they had the choice. But because they are growing up in the wake of the attacks, they face uncertainty and insecurity with every move they make.

A Gate at the Stairs tells the complex story of Tassie, a twenty-year-old farm girl from the Midwest who started university in 2002 in the nearby larger city, Roma. Seeking a part-time job, Tassie finds herself employed by the eccentric forty-five-year-old Sarah and her distant, mildly sleazy husband, Edward, as a nanny for their adopted African American toddler, Mary-Emma. Caught up in the intimate lives of her dysfunctional employers, Tassie finds herself naively drawn into their tragic history and complicit in the inevitable breakdown of Mary-Emma's multiracial adoption. In *A Gate at the Stairs*, things are never what they appear. Tassie's employers claim infertility as their reason for adoption, but it is not until quite near the end of the novel that we discover they once had a biological son, Gabriel. He was killed tragically in a car accident at the age of four. Sarah and Edward—their marriage rotten even then—left him by the side of the road when he was whining, and he was hit by a car and killed.[11] The near-unbearable tension of the scene in which this is revealed is in many ways rivaled in 9/11 literature only by Beigbeder's *Windows on the World*.[12] Both the randomness and the inevitability of Gabriel's death, covered over as it is in lies, denial, sarcastic self-loathing, and even attempted humor, corresponds to the covering up of a multitude of griefs in the novel: national grief over 9/11, the grief of heartbreak, grief over the loss of marriages and children, and ultimately, the grief that is part of growing up in a complex post-9/11 world. When Tassie hears the terrible story, Sarah's earlier strained jokes such as "Remember when we once killed someone and American Express paid for it?" now take on twisted, tragic meaning.[13] What seemed early in the novel like light, amusing repartee between the parents is now understood to have portended something much darker. For the first time, Tassie is faced with America's underbelly, its bleak secrets revealed. *A Gate at the Stairs* makes it impossible to believe in youth as a time of innocence. This growing up, post-9/11, is full of ominous foreboding—a "psychical stew of trauma and denial."[14]

As Tassie becomes a nanny for this privileged family with their seething secrets, she simultaneously embarks on her first love affair with an exotic "Brazilian" boyfriend, Reynaldo. He is ultimately revealed to be Muslim, possibly involved in a terrorist cell, and not Brazilian at all—he is from Hoboken, New Jersey. In fact, little in this novel can be taken at face value and readers are never offered the truth about Reynaldo's identity. When Tassie learns Reynaldo is not who he appears to be, she is both shocked and doubly confused about the extent of his lies:

> "I'm not part of a cell," he said.
> "That never crossed my mind." Though now it did. He had accepted some assignment. That must have been it. There was some manipulative mullah in his life. . . .[15]

Tassie is amazed she was so naive, wondering how she could have thought he was Brazilian: "Of course he wasn't. Why hadn't I figured that out? Where were the bossa novas? Why did he not know a single phrase of 'The Girl from Ipanema'?"[16]

While Tassie is also acutely aware of the stereotypes about Islam provoked by her uncertainly about Reynoldo's identity, her broken heart, commonly linked to a loss of innocence or growing into maturity, is now felt through the lens of terrorism. Reynaldo did not merely betray her heart but may have betrayed her country as well. As in the other novels discussed in this chapter, love of country is a central part of Tassie's identity, and her growing loyalty to her homeland is linked to her maturation. While Tassie remains cynical, this aspect of her identity only strengthens as she tries to understand what is real.

Tassie doubly distrusts Reynoldo now, and indeed, a 9/11 loss of trust infuses everything. There is nothing "true" or permanent about anyone in this novel, and in fact, anyone and anything can change seemingly overnight. For instance, Reynoldo immediately changes how he speaks when he reveals himself as Muslim. Where moments previously he spoke much like Tassie and her other friends, suddenly he lectures Tassie: "As Muhammed said, we do not know God as we should." Tassie is both cynical and threatened by this: "What happened to your voice? You're speaking without contractions."[17] While on one level Tassie's reaction exposes the cultural and religious stereotyping that surfaced after 9/11 and the general suspicion that of anyone potentially "un-American," her loyalty to her own country rarely wavers. Even when, later, Sarah and Edward are revealed as much more deceptive than Reynoldo (whose actual involvement with terrorism remains undetermined) Tassie chooses her "own" over the foreign other. She does not love the choice she makes, but in the end, in a post-9/11 climate of distrust and uncertainty, she (albeit reluctantly and ironically) chooses allegiance to middle-class America, wrapping herself later in the novel in the comforting American flag.

On the path to becoming this American subject, Tassie must sift through the lies told not only by her loved ones, but also by her country, her new Muslim boyfriend, and her white American employers. Sarah and Edward also lie to themselves, and their self-deception is serious. Their foster daughter Mary-Emma is taken away from them and the adoption halted when it is discovered that they were once charged with their own biological child's death. Concern for the innocent toddler and the impact being taken away will have on her is largely bypassed in the horrid moment when she is taken out of Sarah's arms by the adoption agency. Sarah weeps in profound despair, not so much for Mary-Emma, but for herself and her own loss, crying out, "This at long last is our formalized punishment."[18] This is a profoundly, tragically self-absorbed family. Mary-Emma's removal is a complex resolution—one that makes it clear that despite the pretense that things can be returned to "normal," neither personal nor political history can be truly erased. There is no going back to innocence. If one aspect of traditional bildungsromane is that the heroes assimilate, Tassie finds herself in a post-9/11 bind. The society she sees is so grief stricken, dysfunctional, and complex after 9/11 that she sees no moral place in the world where she can fit in. Growing up after 9/11 entails the deepest of sadness and cynicism. Although she does see a future for herself (because "one has to get on with life") at the end of the novel, she assimilates into society more with resigned acceptance of its deep imperfection than with optimism.[19] She thinks, "I've come to realize that life, while being everything, is also strangely not much."[20] If Tassie is representative, growing up post-9/11 is more about grief and resignation than optimism.

For Tassie, maturing also involves confronting the complexities of race and ethnicity brought into focus in the United States after 9/11. In different ways, each of the main characters, Tassie, Sarah, and Edward, find their relationships with the exotic Other untenable in the end. The Brinks couple (their assumed surname after their son Gabriel's death and the court case) thought they could replace one child with another and partly appease their personal guilt by adopting a needy black child. Much is made of Mary-Emma's mixed-race heritage.

Tassie, too, becomes increasingly aware of America's seedy, shaky underbelly, including the nation's uncomfortable relationship with problems of race and social class (as represented by Mary-Emma being the biological daughter of a poor, powerless mother). Although the politically correct Sarah and Edward Brinks host a regular biracial adoption support group (which is treated in the novel with satiric humor), the mothers in the group are forever making startling comments about race: "And don't get me started on Islam!" says one of the moms.[21]

Similarly, Tassie initially thinks race does not matter when she begins her love affair with Reynaldo. When it is revealed, however, that Reynaldo is leaving town in a hurry, the young lovers' political, cultural, and religious differences are all exposed as problems after all. The pretense that post-9/11 America is one big happy family is exposed. In this novel, personal choices are political choices and vice versa. The actions of all the characters, except Tassie, are always tainted with ulterior motives. Again, the journey toward self-discovery after 9/11 involves hard truths with respect to race and a removal of rose-colored glasses. In this novel more than the others examined in this chapter, post-9/11 US culture requires a jaded irony.

Tassie's growing awareness of her own naïveté is highlighted when her beloved younger brother, trying to find meaning in his own life, joins the army and ultimately dies in Afghanistan. With each part of this complex plot, the reader is positioned to see post-9/11 America as being linked with a loss of innocence. The hypothesis that the uncertain world has lost its "natural order" is a central theme in Moore's novel. Tassie's brother (whose death provides Tassie's final entry point to serious adulthood and an end to her frivolity) often mixes up his words, which humorously includes failing a test when he confuses the words Gandhi with Bambi.[22] Her "quasi-farmer" father calls his potatoes "eggs."[23] Early in the novel, Tassie tries to lose her virginity with a friend who turns out to be gay. She jokes that the world has no order; she "wanted to have sex, but ended up baking a cake."[24] Like so much in this novel, nothing is quite the real deal. But Tassie, despite her pretense at being "grown up" is still just a child— her "deepest brain [was] still a cupboard of fairy tales."[25] Tassie, representing a naive America, has based her actions on half-truths and lies. The events of 9/11 and their aftermath (most significantly, the war in Afghanistan) plunge Tassie— who describes herself as sheltered and "cave-raised"—into a forced coming of age. She resists this as furiously as she can, but through a series of accidents and tragedies, understands there is no truth: just post-9/11 anxiety about the future.[26] The loss of control that 9/11 left in its wake is not dissimilar here to the loss of control commonly attributed to the perils of adolescence.

Loss is a major theme of both American bildungsromane and 9/11 narratives, and the gate in A Gate at the Stairs has several layers of meaning, one of which is a loss of access. In this novel, with its constant play on words, a gate at the bottom of the stairs is most closely associated with a baby gate that has a childproof lock, an artifact from the early part of the journey into adulthood. However, the dual function of the gate extends to a sense of opening out and letting in. Further, Moore describes 9/11 as a moment when a door opened. The word "gate" has another very different association as well: in this novel it connects 9/11 with an earlier historical defining moment in America, the Watergate scandal, reinforcing the relationships in this novel between history, politics, and the coming-of-age process. In addition, the reference to Watergate highlights Tassie's youth and her naïveté. The adoptive mother, Sarah, reminds Tassie of her innocence:

> "Babygate! Now, there's a scandal. You're so young, I'll bet you don't even know how the word gate came to mean disgrace."
> "Watergate," I said, though I wasn't positive.[27]

Tassie is on the precipice (or the brink, like her employer Sarah Brink) of great personal and political discovery. But self-discovery is dangerous; if Tassie opens the gate, she may stumble. The combination of invitation, danger, and adventure are all signposts of the personal journey often associated both with bildungsromane and with 9/11 fiction. Like other 9/11 novels, such as Jane Smiley's *Ten Days in the Hills*, Moore's novel posits the surprising premise that two cataclysmic events—the moment when the planes flew into the World Trade Center and the more languid (but equally cataclysmic) summer between childhood and adulthood—ignite both pain and pleasure.[28]

Hence, Tassie must grow up alongside her country. In part, this involves being less flippant and taking things more seriously. Initially in the book, Tassie speaks in a breezy, ironic teenage voice using "terror humor," even when referencing 9/11.[29] When Tassie first hears about 9/11, her college roommate Murph has just lost her virginity. Their conversation demonstrates their "normal" teenage egocentricity, shocking the reader with their irreverence: "I raised my voice in a mock shout. 'You sick slut! People were killed. All you think about is your own pleasure.' Then we fell into a kind of hysteria—frightened, guilty, hopeless laughter I have never actually witnessed in women over thirty."[30]

In their quasi-adulthood ("quasi" being favored by Tassie in her performative attempts at wit and sophistication), the girls mistake the frivolous for the serious, and the personal for the center of the universe. In part, this novel is the story of Tassie's (and hence, America's) sober coming to terms with hard reality. In the process, Tassie is duped at every single step: she mistakes her employers as genuine and she misreads her boyfriend as Brazilian. Behind every wisecracking, quippy retort, she reveals herself as trusting and inexperienced, as naive as the American population. Underneath her defensive exterior, she is wildly innocent.

It is tempting to see the slow reveal of Tassie's vulnerability as parallel to a perspective on America—despite its hard, seemingly confident exterior, America too was slow after 9/11 to wake up to its own self-deception.

While coming-of-age novels often involve loss, 9/11 gives this loss extra weight. Tassie loves the toddler Mary-Emma and grieves when she is forcibly removed from her new foster family. Tassie also mourns her brother's death. Her final understanding of growing up comes from a fortune cookie message: "Bury your unrealistic dreams or they will bury you."[31] The 9/11 disaster injected uncertainty into a previously certain world in which Bauman claimed Americans were no longer in control.[32] In *A Gate at the Stairs*, Tassie's awakening reveals to her that "The earth [is] not perfectly round, but pear-shaped."[33]

When her brother Robert dies, Tassie can truly understand loss for the first time. In a moment of great tragicomedy, Tassie crawls into Robert's coffin, his body covered in an American flag. But despite her deepest wish, that she could "reassemble him with chat," there is nothing she can do to bring him back nor to revive the innocence she felt so short a time before, in her youth.[34] In the spirit of the bildungsroman, she is now well and truly an adult, with every journey leading to a wiser, more serious America. Growing up means leaving the games of childhood behind. But beyond exposing America's rotting core lies Moore's profound belief in goodness, a feature common to American bildungsromane.[35] At the end of Moore's novel, Tassie is both older and wiser and ultimately embraces responsibility and finds goodness within herself as well as her country. *A Gate at the Stairs* is a fine attempt to reconcile cynicism in a weary, wary post-9/11 world.

THE USUAL RULES: GROWING UP AND REGAINING HOPE

Joyce Maynard's young-adult novel, *The Usual Rules*, offers another, more conventional coming-of-age story for the post-9/11 reader, complete with lonely, lost young people, pop-culture references, and the search for family and meaning in a despairing world that once again seems to have lost its way. *The Usual Rules* follows the standard post-9/11 formula (despite its ironic intention to claim in its title that the usual rules no longer apply after 9/11). This is a folksier, less cynical coming-of-age tale than the one in *A Gate at the Stairs*. In *The Usual Rules*, the journey to adulthood involves the humanistic revival of hope, rather than a loss of idealism. In *The Usual Rules*, resolution involves the remaking of a happy family; however, in *A Gate at the Stairs*, the very notion of a happy family is left in question.

The protagonist in *The Usual Rules* is Wendy, a thirteen-year-old girl whose mother dies in the attacks of 9/11. Wendy lives with her stepfather and little brother, but with her mother gone, she decides to go to California to find the biological father she barely knows. In California she tries to erase her past, believing this will heal her. Wendy often lies about who she is but, along the way, makes genuine friends with characters such as the eccentric owner of a bookstore, a teenage mother struggling to raise her baby, and a street kid who becomes her first boyfriend. She also develops a strong relationship with her biological father and his girlfriend. Like *A Gate at the Stairs*, albeit far more hopeful and optimistic, this is a story about family and healing.

The Usual Rules is a story of a motherless daughter who is looking for both her "real" mother and her "true" father. Reminiscent of Dorothy's quest in *The Wizard of Oz*, Wendy's journey comes with wicked witches (her paternal grandmother), fairy godmothers (her mother's friend Kate), and folksy aunts and uncles (her father's girlfriend, Carolyn, and the bookseller, Alan). Wendy discovers that she must take care of numerous wounded people she meets on the road to her own healing. She becomes witness to the suffering of others: her stepfather, Josh; her half-brother, Louie; the teen mother, Violet, whom she stops from abusing her baby; and her new boyfriend, Todd. Though her own mother has died in the World Trade Center, Wendy is rarely allowed more than the "usual" teen angst as she realizes, somewhat predictably, that there are lots of people whose lives are worse than hers. In this way, 9/11 becomes just another teen trial. She learns not to wallow and not to be such a prickly, self-protective "cactus girl."[36]

At first, Wendy thinks her plight is worse than the troubles other people face as she suggests when she muses: "Being stoned might be terrible, but maybe not as bad as thinking about your mother being dead all the time."[37] But ultimately, Wendy's growing up involves empathy. She comes to see that everybody has trials. Her coming-of-age journey involves sharing her feelings; after 9/11, she learns to "disclose." Though the novel makes some fun of the American confessional (for instance, by mocking the Maury Povich television show), it reveals the preoccupation with disclosure as essential to healing. Wendy, who lies to herself and others throughout (even pretending it is her father who has died in the Twin Towers and not her mother), learns, unlike Tassie, that the truth will set her free.

Wendy's journey reverses Dorothy's in *The Wizard of Oz*: she is led away from the Emerald City (the rubble of New York) to farmland (Davis, California), with its "wheat fields in the background and the hills on the horizon."[38] However, it is in most ways the same journey, eventually ending according to the usual rules in "journey home" narratives. As a Ouija board reveals to Wendy early in the novel, she is "looking for a lost parent"; in the end, *The Usual Rules* claims, family is what we are all looking for.[39] Although it is less alienating than *A Gate at the Stairs*, *The Usual Rules* is more typical of traditional bildungsromane. By the end, Wendy embraces humanity and fully integrates into the family of man. Wendy, readers are told, was named after the responsible, maternal Wendy of *Peter Pan*, and from the start, she is more responsible than both her birth father and her stepfather, Josh. After her mother's death, she imagines her family calling out, "Wendy, Wendy, where are you? We're lost without you."[40] In being both youthful and responsible, she confirms a 9/11 proposition: that the fresh optimism of youth in the face of adversity will "heal" the post-9/11 world.

Wendy initially is so steeped in grief as to be paralyzed, as is her stepfather Josh. In a novel replete with intertexual references, she often seeks solace in other coming-of-age texts or "touchstone stories," which she repeatedly compares to her situation. For instance, she admires the optimism of Anne Frank, the "drek" of Cat Stevens, and *A Tree Grows in Brooklyn*, though not so much the brutality of *Lord of the Flies* and *The Butcher Boy*: "*A Tree Grows in Brooklyn* was a wonderful book, but she didn't like *Lord of the Flies*, she told Alan. It could be true that kids would do terrible things like that, she said. But I believe myself more along the lines of Anne Frank. That people are basically good."[41] Wendy reads Stephen King's *Carrie* and Carson McCullers's *The Member of the Wedding*, searching everywhere for the coming-of-age story that might best suit her times. By doing so, she makes 9/11 a universal, nearly generic "feel-good" story, apolitical and unspecific; it is just another version of the usual teenage angst. In *The Usual Rules*, with the spaces of remembrance that come from multiple coming-of-age references, Maynard sets up the binaries of a clear before and after. If it was more like Shirley Temple and Bojangles Robinson in *The Little Colonel* prior to 9/11, it is more like Miles Davis music afterwards.[42] Though 9/11 is the backdrop to the novel, it is no more than a vehicle to revisit the usual solipsism of adolescence; Wendy's self-absorption takes the standard form. If adolescence itself is the acute discomfort about the unknowable, the events of 9/11 have plunged all of America into this familiar (yet unfamiliar) state of limbo in which yearning for the past collides with an uncertain future. Making the historical and political so deeply individual and personal satisfies two post-9/11 cultural imperatives. First, 9/11 thus appears to have prompted no change at all—young people are as self-absorbed as ever, and this problem too shall pass. Second, 9/11 itself is much more manageable—a small personal problem rather than a permanent crisis from which there is no return.

In *The Usual Rules*, 9/11 becomes a rite of passage: the day when "everything changed." Like other Western rites of passage—such as being kissed for the first time, after which Wendy "thought she'd look a little different, but she didn't"—it amazes Wendy that life can appear to go on as normal after 9/11.[43] As she says, "What seemed craziest was all of this regular, ordinary-looking behaviour: shopping, talking about some brand of car, and going to school. Business as usual, they called it. Behaving, at least out in the world anyway, as if nothing had changed, when the truth was, not one thing was the same. . . ."[44]

The moment of 9/11, thus, takes on the before-and-after significance of the onset of adulthood, whereby Wendy is constantly nostalgic, both for her innocent childhood and for a pre-9/11 world. Remembering dancing around the room with her mother, Janet, to songs from *Guys and Dolls* reminds her of her naive younger self and the world before it changed forever. That the "pop culture" references in *The Usual Rules* are almost exclusively from the author Joyce Maynard's teenage era, rather than from a girl Wendy's age, suggests that the older generations' grief is wrapped up in nostalgia for innocent youth.[45]

At the climax of the story, Wendy's father takes her on a hike to Yosemite, where they find themselves in danger, trapped on a rock ledge with no way to turn back. In a genuinely frightening scene, Wendy finds herself in a situation parallel to her mother's: "She thought about her mother on the eighty-seventh floor, standing at the windows, looking out as the offices of Mercer and Mercer filled with smoke."[46] In a final separation from her mother and in her return from the precipice, Wendy realizes, "Nothing for it but to breathe and back up. One step, two. She was at a place where she could turn around, finally. She breathed again."[47]

Wendy's journey, accelerated by her mother's death, signifies the in-between space of adolescence, when one is neither a child, nor yet an adult. Her mother's death represents a moment of uncertainty and, as such, is unsafe. By finding her way back (and not falling off the edge of the cliff), Wendy takes one step toward adulthood, and a step away from the childhood represented by her lost mother.

In the end, Wendy learns lessons about separation and resilience. There is no "true" father or "real" mother. Despite imperfect endings for some of the characters in the book, we are one big family of man, all in it together and taking care of each other. Wendy loves, and is loved by, her stepfather, her father, her little brother, and her new extended family. The single teen mother, Violet, gives her baby up for adoption, but readers are positioned to believe it may be for the best. Though his wife leaves him to raise their disabled son alone, the bookstore owner, Alan, treasures his bond with his autistic son. The street kid, Todd, miraculously finds his lost brother, though this brother soon after tragically dies in an accident. Shit happens, and then Americans get on with it. This version of the coming-of-age moment proposes a useful lesson for America after 9/11. The humanist premise of the novel is concerned with the essential goodness of human beings, and of Americans in particular, being responsible for one other. In this novel, grief also involves the leaving behind of childish things, including the naive belief in "magic," something readers learn from Wendy's little brother Louie, who thought a magic wand would bring his mother back. Wendy (and by proxy, the reader) recognizes her insignificance in the world. She takes leave of the egocentrism that may have consumed her previously and learns the responsibilities that come with the adult world. By letting go, she finds the "usual" equilibrium returned: life after 9/11 is different, yet remarkably the same. *The Usual Rules* does indeed tell the story of return to the usual. Quite differently from Tassie in *A Gate at the Stairs*, Wendy transcends crisis by embracing a belief in goodness. Novels such as *The Usual Rules* make the unknowable future palatable by reinforcing an optimistic belief that time will heal and goodness prevail.

TERRORIST: GROWING UP AMERICAN

The last novel to be discussed is John Updike's *Terrorist*. Unlike *The Usual Rules*, Updike's text is written for and marketed to an adult audience; however, it remains a coming-of-age story with a young male protagonist. In this often-criticized novel, we are provided with an array of regularly misogynistic, ethnically stereotyped characters, and the backdrop of 9/11 is used to explore the notion of a world gone awry.

In *Terrorist*, two plot lines converge. The main story, which takes place soon after 9/11, revolves around Ahmad, a half-American, half-Egyptian adolescent. During the course of the novel, he descends from devout Muslim to fully committed terrorist. He is coerced by his opportunistic and deceptive Muslim brothers, who recruit him to become a "tool of terrorism." The second plot line involves Ahmad's aging school guidance counselor, the Jewish Jack Levy, who is having a midlife crisis. Levy has lost his life's purpose and is slowly sinking into despair, at least in part because his wife, Beth, has gotten "so ridiculously fat."[48] Levy has a brief sexual relationship with Ahmad's artistic Irish American mother, Teresa, who attracts Levy with her free spirit. But for Ahmad, his mother's free spirit is proof of a corrupt and promiscuous America, a nation with "limitless and gluttonous freedom," which he (as both typical adolescent and Muslim) rebels against.[49] Though he was born in America and has lived nowhere else, he feels, as did Holden Caulfield before him, like an outsider. Ahmad disassociates himself with America, believing that it "has no God, it is obsessed with sex and luxury goods."[50] It is only at the very end of the novel, when he accepts his own American identity and stops fantasizing about the Egyptian father he has never known, that he can "grow up." In this novel, Ahmad's sympathy with Islam is ultimately revealed to be naive and un-American. In some ways similar to *The Usual Rules*, this is a novel that equates love of country to growing up.

Though Ahmad is seduced by terrorism, readers are positioned to understand his mixed loyalties and are required, to some extent, to be sympathetic of his misguided choices. Ahmad is teased and bullied at school for being half Arab. He is mocked by Joryleen, the abused African American girl to whom he is attracted (and who, in Updike fashion, ends up more than a mere temptress, but a prostitute). Ahmad is a nice boy, easily manipulated by terrorists who seek to mislead and corrupt him; his motives for a peaceful, just world are pure. Unlike Tassie in *A Gate at the Stairs* and Wendy in *The Usual Rules*, Ahmad is largely a blank slate, trying on identities in adolescence for the first time. His foray into terrorism is ultimately revealed as a false identity. Understanding the error of his ways, Ahmad finds his "true" self (i.e., his American self) at the end of the novel. That growing up is equated with patriotism sets this far more traditional view of coming of age apart from the other two more complicated portrayals both of young adulthood and of a post-9/11 world with its complexities and contested loyalties.

The young Ahmad is immature in a myriad of ways, not the least of which is demonstrated by his virginity, which he does not quite lose when his crude Muslim mentor, Charlie, sends him to be "devirginated."[51] Because Ahmad does not go through with it, he is not yet quite a man, even at the end of the novel. Like Holden Caulfield or Alexander Portnoy before him, Ahmad's main problem sometimes seems that he simply cannot (or in his case, will not) allow himself to get laid. Whereas Tassie in *A Gate at the Stairs* ultimately sees sex as trivial, Ahmad's virginity is proof of his lack of maturity in all respects: he is physically, emotionally, intellectually, and politically virginal. With Updike's suppositions about entry into manhood, *Terrorist* delivers a complex message that links maturation with the American way.

Ahmad is also portrayed as immature in his apprentice relationship with his boss and in his relationship with his counselor (and savior) Jack Levy. As the ultimate initiation into manhood, the Imam asks Ahmad to prove his willingness to die for his beliefs. It is this Imam who initially sets Ahmad up to get his truck-driver's license so he can carry explosives. The task involves driving a truck to a certain destination and "making a certain mechanical connection."[52] But it is, ultimately, Ahmad's decision to give up his childish trust in Islam that pushes him toward manhood. In part, this can be seen in the shift in how Ahmad speaks. It is strikingly odd throughout most of the novel that Ahmad, this boy born and bred in America, forces himself to speak so unlike an American teenager. His conscious decision to express himself in the manner he imagines a pious Muslim would seems proof that he is trying to be what he is not. Even at the very end, as he heads into the tunnel, Ahmad speaks in jarring platitudes: "Sir, I regret to say you will not live. In a few minutes, I am going to see the face of God. My heart overflows with the expectation."[53]

His archaic, Othered discourse feels unnatural, forced rather than genuine. While bildungsromane often require a journey toward acceptance and assimilation, *Terrorist* frames this in a particular post-9/11 way. Ahmad grows up as he accepts himself as a patriotic American, aligning himself, even linguistically, with the "right" team.

It is the equation of Islam with immaturity that complicates the politics of *Terrorist*. Though Ahmad repeatedly tells the counselor, Jack Levy, and his mother of his desire for independence, he is highly dependent on his teacher, Sheikh Rashid. In addition, we see Ahmad's immaturity in his sexual and political initiation by the worldly "big brother," the Lebanese man, Charlie, who speaks to Ahmad like a man but who nearly leads him to his death as easily as he would a child. There's something particularly childlike in Ahmad's boasts. He tells Jack Levy "I am in charge," and he seems boyishly adamant in his protest, "My teacher thinks I should drive a truck."[54] The reader is led to agree with Jack Levy, who sees a little boy when he hears Ahmad's protest that he is old enough to drive a big truck. We also see Ahmad's immaturity in the way he treats his mother, whom he believes to be promiscuous.

Ahmad "grows out" of his relationship with Islam just toward the end of the novel. This is played out when Ahmad and the Imam say their goodbyes in the hotel room the night before Ahmad is to commit suicide by driving his truck full of explosives. In this final scene, which is closely akin to Martin Amis's fictional recount of the 9/11 terrorist Muhammad Atta's last days, the Imam switches roles with Ahmad.[55] As Ahmad prepares both physically and mentally to commit his "glorious act" with his "faith still strong," Ahmad notes of the Imam, "Without his beard and richly embroidered caftan, he appears tremulous in manner, a bit withered, and no longer young."[56] The boy, Ahmad, believes he becomes the man. It is at that moment that he begins to make his own decision, though it is soon understood that proceeding with the plan would be a poor and dangerous choice. Though he is unquestionably "ready" and resolved to die for his faith, it is not much longer before the novel ends, and Ahmad, at the very last second, is persuaded to change his mind, thus truly becoming a man. In the final moments, the reader is required to believe that Ahmad's allegiance to Islam was not a sign of maturity after all—he may have thought he was a man, but was just "a victim . . . a fall guy" who was double-crossed.[57] The jig is up, Jack informs him, suggesting to Ahmad that he had just wanted to prove himself.[58] It is the suddenly paternal Jack Levy, a Jew, who is his symbolic father after all (a case that he has partially proven by sleeping with Ahmad's mother, the relationship that saves Jack, too). Ahmad is skeptical; however, Jack Levy seals the relationship when he says, "We're in this together, son."[59] Finding his lost father allows Ahmad to drive out of the literal and figurative tunnel without blowing it (or himself) up. In its belief in the redemptive role of the American family, *Terrorist*'s version of growing up is similar to that in *The Usual Rules*. Through talking it out, confessing his "problem" (which, like *The Usual Rules*, involves an absent father and missing mother), Ahmad sees the real problem and begins to heal. This endless talking involves what Karen R. Tolchin claims is a unique feature of the American coming-of-age novel: a kind of logorrhea in which everything is talked out ad infinitum in a self-confessional style.[60]

Moore's *A Gate at the Stairs* was a story of a motherless daughter; *Terrorist* is a novel about a fatherless son. The symbolic father/son reunion in *Terrorist* suggests how Ahmad has been deceived by Islam when all he really wanted was love (demonstrated by the fact that he feels he has "never been essential to [his] mother").[61] Thus, in a sense, *Terrorist* infantilizes Islam. While there is some ambiguity about Ahmad's loss of faith at the end of the novel, Ahmad seems to grow out of it, despite his years of study and his (seemingly) deep knowledge of both its history and convictions. Jack Levy certainly believes Ahmad was never genuinely a true believer; to Jack he is just a grieving American, like everyone else. Levy espouses to Ahmad the aspirational dream, "We're all American here. That's the idea, didn't they tell you that at Central High? Irish-Americans, African-Americans, Jewish-Americans; there are even Arab-Americans."[62]

Along with Ahmad's ultimate savior, Jack, it is ironically the fallen Christian, Joryleen, now working as a prostitute, who offers a home truth: Ahmad is no better than her pimp, Tylenol. According to Joryleen, they're both just boys trying to prove their manhood.[63] Between Ahmad's irresponsible Egyptian father (who "couldn't cut it" in America), the powerless Imam, who has lost all students except the innocent Ahmad, and the ill-fated truck driver Charlie, all Muslims are misguided and Islam itself is, in this novel, proof of immaturity. No wonder Ahmad learns, not without some regret, that he must give up his childish beliefs. The book ends ambiguously with Ahmad's despair: "These devils . . . have taken away my God."[64] But, like Jack, the reader thinks, "Thank God [he] chickened out."[65] The plan seemed naive and misguided to everyone except Ahmad, who, in many ways, does not give up his youth (or naïveté) lightly. Growing up is hard and painful. Ahmad is left, at novel's end, liberated and wiser, "like a plane lifting free of gravity," but infinitely sadder. Like Tassie after 9/11, Ahmad is less innocent, more disenchanted, more despairing, but less vulnerable.[66] Unlike Wendy, who remains ever hopeful, Ahmad and Tassie are jaded and worldly.

September 11 is the common reference point in each of the three novels discussed: the young protagonists, Tassie, Wendy, and Ahmad, are thrust into adulthood in a new landscape of uncertainty and national grief, the world in which Americans are no longer in control. Adhering to many of the familiar features of American bildungsromane, each of the three novels involves a coming-of-age process in which the youthful heroes must navigate a journey from innocence to knowledge and find a road that leads to maturity.

Within these post-9/11 bildungsromane, we see both the old and the new. To a degree, the novels draw on familiar American tropes—growing up is associated with loss and healing, disillusion with adulthood, and entrance at the same time into its cynical ranks. In each case, the protagonists must stop telling lies; they must stop deceiving themselves. The novels reinvigorate a particularly patriotic American belief in "healing" as part of growing up with three different portrayals of the post-9/11 subject. Tassie in *A Gate at the Stairs* is most like Holden Caulfield or James Dean (who rebel against society); however, like Wendy and Ahmad, she is also a new version of youth on the cusp of finding a maturity that comes with "fitting in" to an America imagined as an imperfect but romanticized family to which they belong. The three protagonists come to accept their grown-up obligations in a post-9/11 America in which allegiance to country is equated with maturity. This may be the most significant feature of 9/11 bildungsromane. The protagonists are not out to change or save the world; instead, they aim to fit back in and restore it to its natural pre-9/11 order.

NOTES

1. Zygmunt Bauman, *Liquid Times: Living in an Age of Uncertainty* (London: Polity Press, 2007), 26.
2. Lorrie Moore, *A Gate at the Stairs* (New York: Alfred A. Knopf, 2009); Joyce Maynard, *The Usual Rules* (New York: St. Martin's Press, 2003); and John Updike, *Terrorist* (Maine: Centre Point Publishing, 2008).
3. While only one of the novels (Maynard's *The Usual Rules*) is directly marketed as a young-adult novel, all three feature young people affected by the events of 9/11, linking them to the coming-of-age tradition in American literature.
4. J. D. Salinger, *The Catcher in the Rye* (Harmondsworth: Penguin, 1958).
5. Paul Virilio, *Ground Zero* (New York: Verso, 2002).
6. John Frow, "The Uses of Terror and the Limits of Cultural Studies," *Media International Australia* 109 (2003): 16.
7. Bauman, *Liquid Times*.
8. Marita Sturken, *Tourists of History: Memory, Kitsch, and Consumerism from Oklahoma City to Ground Zero* (London: Duke University Press, 2007).
9. Marian Gottfried and David Miles, "Defining Bildungsroman as a Genre," *Modern Language Association* 91 (1976); Roberta Trites, *Disturbing the Universe: Power and Repression in Adolescent Literature* (Iowa City: University of Iowa Press, 2000).
10. Wilhelm Dilthy, quoted in Susan Cocalis, "The Transformation of 'Bildung' from an Image to an Ideal," *Monatshefte* 70 (1974): 399.
11. Numerous 9/11 novels tell the story of lost children or children who have died, including Phillip Beard's *Dear Zoe* (New York: Penguin, 2006). This coming-of-age novel focuses on the process of healing for the family of a little girl, Zoe, after she is hit by a car on September 11, 2001, and her death is overshadowed by the horrific deaths of thousands of people that same day. An individual's personal tragedy, the worst that can be imagined, often comes in these novels to represent the larger national grief as it does in Jonathan Safran Foer's *Extremely Loud and Incredibly Close* (New York: Houghton Mifflin, 2005).
12. Frederic Beigbeder, *Windows on the World* (New York: Miramax, 2003).
13. Moore, *A Gate at the Stairs*, 115.
14. Jane Caputi, "Guest Editor's Introduction: Of Towers and Twins, Synchronicities and Shadows: Archetypal Meanings in the Imagery of 9/11," *The Journal of American Culture* 28 (2005).
15. Moore, *A Gate at the Stairs*, 204.
16. Ibid., 205.
17. Ibid., 206.
18. Ibid., 244.
19. Ibid., 304.
20. Ibid., 321.
21. Ibid., 188.
22. Ibid., 56.
23. Ibid., 23.
24. Ibid., 13.
25. Ibid., 37.
26. Ibid., 11.
27. Ibid., 130.
28. Jane Smiley, *Ten Days in the Hills* (New York: Random House, 2007). In Ken Kalfus's *A Disorder Peculiar to the Country* (London: Simon & Schuster, 2006), 9/11 is again equated

with both grief and surprising pleasure. While watching the second tower come down from the roof of her own office building, the soon-to-be divorced wife, Joyce, feels uncontrolled elation that her loathsome ex-husband may finally be dead: "The building turned into a rising mushroom-shaped column of smoke, dust and perished life, and she felt a great gladness" (3). The courage to express emotional responses other than grief about 9/11 could not appear in fiction immediately: Kalfus's novel was published five years after 2001, and *A Gate at the Stairs* was not published until 2009. Though there were 9/11 jokes immediately after the event, many people did not appreciate these early attempts to view the tragedy in a light-hearted way. Daniel Mendelsohn writes of the literary problems of proximity in his essay "September 11 at the Movies," in *How Beautiful It Is and How Easily It Can Be Broken*, ed. Daniel Mendelsohn (New York: HarperCollins, 2009).

29. E. Wax, "In Times of Terror, Teens Talk the Talk," *Washington Post*, March 19, 2002.

30. Moore, *A Gate at the Stairs*, 5.

31. Ibid., 321.

32. Bauman, *Liquid Times*.

33. Moore, *A Gate at the Stairs*, 321.

34. Ibid., 300.

35. Karen R. Tolchin, *Part Blood, Part Ketchup: Coming of Age in American Literature and Film* (New York: Rowman & Littefield Publishers, 2007).

36. Maynard, *The Usual Rules*, 204.

37. Ibid., 154.

38. Ibid., 142.

39. Ibid., 112.

40. Ibid., 103.

41. Ibid., 99, 359. Incidentally, Maynard does not mention Salinger's *The Catcher in the Rye*. She had an affair with Salinger as a teenager and recently wrote about the relationship in *At Home in the World: A Memoir* (New York: Picador, 1992).

42. Maynard, *The Usual Rules*, 97, 358.

43. Ibid., 305.

44. Ibid., 81.

45. Most 9/11 fiction also identifies grief as a largely middle-class preoccupation. Though some 9/11 novels include a secondary working-class "marginal" character—such as the single mother, Violet, in *The Usual Rules*, Joryleen in *Terrorist*, and the single black mother in *The Gate at the Stairs*—few tell 9/11 stories through working-class eyes. One that does is Chris Cleave's disturbing *Incendiary* (New York: Simon & Schuster, 2005). If 9/11 was perceived mostly as a personal rather than a political journey, it seems it was mostly experienced by the middle class.

46. Maynard, *The Usual Rules*, 340.

47. Ibid.

48. Updike, *Terrorist*, 357.

49. Ibid., 51.

50. Ibid., 48.

51. Ibid., 257. The 9/11 fiction seems abundant with representations on both sides of the spectrum: the youth losing innocence/virginity and the middle-aged in their last throes of virility. In Smiley's *Ten Days in the Hills*, we encounter both father and daughter filling their days with sex to make meaning of the fragmented world after 9/11.

52. Updike, *Terrorist*, 277.

53. Ibid., 357.

54. Ibid., 51, 354.

55. Martin Amis, *The Second Plane* (London: Jonathan Cape, 2008).
56. Updike, *Terrorist*, 318, 319.
57. Ibid., 364.
58. Ibid., 341.
59. Ibid., 349.
60. Tolchin, *Part Blood, Part Ketchup.*
61. Updike, *Terrorist*, 345.
62. Ibid., 355.
63. Ibid., 264.
64. Ibid., 365.
65. Ibid.
66. Ibid., 346.

9 • "ARMY STRONG"

Mexican American Youth and Military Recruitment in *All She Can*

IRENE GARZA

When audiences first meet Luz Garcia (Corina Calderon), the protagonist of the 2011 coming-of-age drama *All She Can*, the teenager is in agony.[1] A close-up shot displays a glossy mask of sweat covering her cherubic face, clumps of perspiration matting the fine baby hairs on her forehead. Her rigid body stands erect, animating with brief spasms of movement. Only her large, wet black eyes stay completely still, fastened upwards on a pair of dim gymnasium lights. The camera pulls back to reveal Luz performing a dead lift, one of three main routines featured in women's competitive power lifting.[2] At 5 feet 3 inches tall and 114 pounds, so diminutive that larger teammates can lift her with ease, Luz presents an unlikely figure for "the strongest women's sport in Texas high school athletics."[3] But in fact, Luz's future hinges on her physicality. The Mexican American teen's longstanding, but improbable dream of attending college via an athletic scholarship remains her singular recourse against military enlistment—the only other option for "escape" available to low-income youth in her small south Texas town, a last resort Luz will do "all she can" to avoid.

Military service, as both motivator and deterrent, haunts writer/director Amy Wendel's feature-length debut, *All She Can*. Originally titled, "Benavides Born," *All She Can* follows Luz, a high-school senior from the tiny town of Benavides, Texas, who dreams of winning the State Powerlifting Championship in order to fund her attendance to the University of Texas at Austin. Without financial assistance, Luz faces the same fate as her older brother JM (Jaime Medeles), a soldier in the US Army who enlisted exclusively to earn money for college—a decision undertaken by countless other young people from their impoverished rural community. In Benavides, where per capita income averages $11,000 and nearly 30 percent of residents, 95 percent of whom are Mexican American, live at or below the poverty line, military signing contracts and enlistment bonuses ranging from $15,000 to $40,000 offer seductive enticements many youth find difficult, if impossible, to reject.[4] In this environment, limited resources and expectations of monetary support to family members render military service not so much a preference, as a mandate. In a Skype session with Luz from his base in Jalalabad, Afghanistan, JM angrily emphasizes this point. Of his decision to enlist, he bitterly remarks, "What choice? What freaking choice did I have?! . . . You know, I don't even think of college anymore. I'm not here for that."[5]

This essay employs the film *All She Can* to trace how discursive themes of escape and advancement inform contemporary military recruitment practices of Latina/o youth, the largest cohort of military age (17–24) young people in the United States and, since 2001, the subjects of targeted recruitment campaigns by the US Armed Forces.[6] As a post 9-11 cultural text, I argue the film contributes an intimately nuanced, accurate exploration of how disparate material, geographic, and cultural factors have compelled a substantial number of Latina/o youth to enter the military in the last decade; a conspicuous, though sometimes contradictory role they have played since the advent of the US-led global War on Terror. In what follows, I examine how the allure of military enlistment and subsequent tactics pursued by military recruiters portrayed in the film, rest on and respond to specific sites of Latina/o youth subjectivity, framed by desires for economic stability, personal dignity, and cultural affirmation. Second, I contend that *All She Can* is one of the few Iraq War–related films released in recent years to treat seriously the geographic dimensions of contemporary American military service. According to director Wendel, she produced *All She Can* partially to capture how "small town rural America is carrying the burden of the war."[7] Statistically, she's right. A 2010 study by the University of Wisconsin-Madison found aggregately higher mortality rates for service members from rural communities than those from metropolitan areas. Of the 3,853 US service members killed in the Iraq War between March 2003 and December 2007, 23 percent were from non-metropolitan counties, an uneven distribution of burden organized not singularly by race, but location.[8] Put another way, though fewer than a quarter of Americans live in rural communities, 40 percent of the war's casualties come from small towns. In regards to race, this same study found that Latina/os from rural areas like those depicted in the film, were 28 percent more likely to die in service than their urban counterparts.[9] Thus, while this essay foregrounds the ethnoracial identity of Latina/o youth, specifically Mexican Americans from south Texas, it also situates them within a broader spatial analysis of the war's impact on rural communities throughout the United States.

Not long after US military entry into Afghanistan (2001) and Iraq (2003), concerns over mission readiness surfaced, centering on the capability of the armed forces to supply adequate troop levels to simultaneous engagements— the first prolonged wars since the establishment of the all-volunteer force. A steady downturn in military recruitment in preceding years underwrote apprehensions over manpower; in 1999, for example, the army fell short of recruiting goals resulting from competition with an expanded civilian job market, robust economy, and increased focus on higher education among young people. The protracted time lines of military involvement in Iraq and Afghanistan have since exhausted military resources and personnel, achingly apparent in the repeated and extended deployments of service members now considered responsible for record levels of post-traumatic stress disorder and suicide among returning veterans. In an otherwise difficult recruiting environment, young Latina/o service members emerged as a bright spot for military planners. Against declining patterns of enlistment by other racial groups, Latina/o military enlistment rose precipitously during the early years of the Iraq War.[10] Within the US Army, the branch represented in *All She Can*, these numbers were especially dramatic. In the first year of the Iraq War, Latina/os accounted for 13 percent of the army's new enlistment contracts—an increase from 10.7 percent from the year before. These numbers continued growing, as Latina/o accessions rose by 26 percent between 2001 and 2005 overall. During these same years, Latina/o enlistment within all branches of the armed forces rose by 18 percent.[11]

Their recruitment numbers notwithstanding, the subject of Latina/o military service has drawn intermittent national attention, given the increasing visibility of Latina/o immigrant soldiers. Soon after the March 2003 invasion of Iraq, Spanish surnames began appearing with frequency in print and television media, spotlighting the principle role played by Latina/o noncitizen soldiers like Guatemalan-native marine lance corporal José Antonio Gutiérrez, widely acknowledged as the first US Army soldier, or in some iterations "American," to die during Operation Iraqi Freedom. In both political and public discourse, the powerful symbolic currency of immigrant soldiers willing to die for the United States, a country they "loved" according to popular rhetorical claims, constituted what media scholar Hector Amaya deems a "metanarrative of nationalism" communicating sympathy for young people whose otherwise invisible lives as immigrants were ostensibly recast into "heroic military biographies" in support of the war and the United States as a repository of democratic values.[12] Conversely this metanarrative managed, silenced, and ultimately disavowed critiques of the structural factors possibly driving their entry into service. The presence of these "green-card" soldiers in the armed forces was hastened by a July 2002 executive order signed by President George Bush amending the US Immigration and Nationality Act, allowing legal permanent residents (i.e., green card holders) to fast track their path toward citizenship, eliminating a three-year wait time. This executive order was followed by HR 1954, the Armed Forces and Naturalization Act of 2003.[13] Although politically and symbolically significant, these legislative acts only moderately account for the upsurge in the number of Latina/o enlisted personnel during the early years of conflicts in Iraq and Afghanistan.

Taking place in south Texas, where military culture constitutes an omnipresent part of daily life, *All She Can*, affirms the heterogeneity of Latina/o military service. Because national media attention largely focused on immigrant Latina/o soldiers, the role of US-born Latina/os who have served in the military for generations was obscured. Since World War II, a significantly high number of Mexican Americans from south Texas have served in the US Armed Forces, promulgating a distinct brand of patriotism among the region's residents. This spirit of allegiance suffuses daily life, inscribing the landscape in multiple ways. Names of hometown war heroes adorn freeways, parks, libraries, and schools throughout the small towns connecting south Texas to the lower Rio Grande Valley—a rural expanse of dry ranchlands, oil rigs, citrus orchards, and cotton fields. For example, travelers passing along Interstate 141 from Benavides to Kingsville, Texas, will inevitably cross Richard E. Cavazos Boulevard, named for a Kingsville native and the US Army's first Mexican American four-star general. In Mission, Texas, Veterans Memorial High School, home of the Patriots, boasts the widely praised Eagle Battalion Junior Reserve Officer Corps program. Military sponsored billboards promoting the Army Advantage Fund or offering other recruiting enticements, flank vast stretches of highways, including Highway 281, spanning Texas from the Oklahoma border to Brownsville at the southern tip of the United States, where it is tellingly renamed "Military Highway."[14] Along that same stretch, sits Brownsville's Veterans Memorial High School, whose official motto, "Home of the Brave" further attests to the region's insistence on celebrating its military heritage and claim to US national identity. Less formally, yellow ribbons, white crosses, and hand-painted murals honoring service members decorate front lawns and telephone poles year round, while trucks and cars outfitted with vinyl banners of American flags, eagles, or military branch decals ubiquitously line neighborhood streets and roads.

Three years into the Iraq War, another Spanish surname permanently joined the statues, memorials, plaques, and other sites publically commemorating military service and sacrifice in south Texas. The National Guard armory in Weslaco, Texas, was renamed the Sgt. Tomas Garces Texas Army National Guard Armory to honor Garces, a nineteen-year-old army specialist killed during his second tour of duty in Iraq. A member of the Texas Army National Guard's 1836th Transportation Company, Garces was killed when his convoy was attacked in Baghdad on September 6, 2004. Described as a religiously devout young man, Garces played bass in his family's Christian-music band, performing alongside his father and two brothers at the church where they attended services in the *colonia* of Llano Grande.[15] A star athlete at Weslaco High School, Garces longed to attend college and pursue a career as a wrestling coach. Similar to the character of Luz, Garces came from a deeply impoverished background and saw few opportunities to escape his life in Weslaco, a town of twenty-nine thousand where the largest employer was a local Walmart.[16] At seventeen, Garces enlisted in the Texas

National Guard to earn tuition money through the guard's State Tuition Reimbursement Program. With his death in 2004, he became the first Texas National Guardsman killed in action since World War II, but not the last casualty south Texas would endure during the Iraq War. In fact, Garces's death came less than one month after fellow Weslaco native, twenty-six-year-old marine sergeant Juan Calderon Jr.'s death in Anbar province of Iraq. Garces and Calderon were just two of the many Mexican American youths from south Texas who have died since the decade-long conflicts began—a testament to their often high concentration in infantry positions.[17]

While many Mexican American youths from south Texas proudly share in the tradition of military service, there are still others who are frustrated by the lack of opportunities available to them in their rural communities. A running joke amongst many teens at south Texas high schools jests that the only employers at their school career fairs are the army, navy, air force, and marines. It is this lack of choices that was explored in a 2009 episode of the television program *60 Minutes* that director Wendel has cited as her inspiration for the film.[18] Concentrating on the tiny south Texas town of San Diego, Texas (population 4,700), "Call of Duty" explored tensions between cultural fidelity to community, including military service, and the individual desires of many teens for more opportunities in their hometowns.[19] Of military service in San Diego, Ignacio Salinas, a grade-school principal remarked, "It's something that we're very proud of." He then added, "There are no jobs here other than the oil industry, and that's very shaky. Finances are very scarce for parents to send their kids to school. And so, for a kid whose parents are not able to send them financially, the military has always been a viable option to get funding to go to school."[20] Though fictional, the character of Luz in *All She Can* offers a complex portrayal of the struggle faced by Mexican American teens like those in San Diego, Texas. In the words of writer Dan Meisel, the film is intended to represent "the culture, the community, what these kids wanted to be doing . . . and what they would need to accomplish to get there."[21]

"GETTING OUT": MILITARY SERVICE AND THE LOGICS OF "ESCAPE"

Bright but temperamental, Luz has only one aim in life, "getting out" of Benavides. She frequently reminds friends, family, and teachers of her goal, and made a childhood pact about it with older brother JM. With less than two thousand residents, Benavides offers its young people very few choices. In a place this small, the only choices for employment are working in nearby oil fields or in service industries where local fast-food restaurants, gas stations, and hotels cater to the numerous commercial trucks carrying goods between the United States and Mexico. Luz herself works evenings at a local hamburger chain, often peering out the drive-through window in between shifts. Neither working in the oil fields or in the service industry offers much promise of exceeding minimum wage, let alone financial solvency. Unpaved roads, overgrown grass, decaying homes, and abandoned storefronts attest to the town's neglect, a marginality shared by inhabitants seemingly "anchored" there, made to watch trucks, highways, and "life" pass them by. Indeed, a recurrent motif throughout the film contrasts Luz's movement, often showing her running along abandoned train tracks and back roads with the town's emptiness as a backdrop, its residents absent from the landscape. The train tracks Luz is often seen jogging along constitute obvious metaphors for escape, denoting the travel, progress, and departure she furiously longs for.

Ambitious young people like Luz ("light" in Spanish) are left with few alternatives but to leave, a choice compromised by their poverty, geographic isolation, and cultural expectations by family to stay in their community, the same factors leaving them ill-prepared for the world outside. During an exchange between Luz's weightlifting coach, Coach Chapa (Julio Cedillo) and high-school principal, Mr. Martinez (Hector Machado), the latter complains, "We just don't prepare our kids for the city. The few that go, they're back here within a year and with loans to pay."[22] While many of these youth aspire to attend college, their concentrated financial hardships prove inhibitive. A telling scene early in the film sees Luz visiting the library to use dial-up Internet, an amenity readily available and often taken for granted in more privileged urban and suburban settings, but one unavailable in Luz's household (and by inference) Benavides generally. In a digital era reliant on e-mail, Skype, instant messaging, and other forms of technological communication, where college admissions processes now rely on electronically submitted applications, Luz's limited accessibility underscores how deeply circumscribed her life chances are.

Even when admitted to top universities, a number of these young people, many of whom are first generation, simply cannot afford the costs of attendance, opting instead for enrollment in community colleges in neighboring towns. Such is the dilemma facing Luz, whose single mother Rosana (Leticia Magaña), refuses to cosign educational loans that would finance Luz's entry into the University of Texas. In an angry confrontation with her daughter, Rosana argues, "You can't start out with all of that debt. It's a noose. You don't have to have the best. If something else can get you what you need. Responsible people think about all possible options."[23] Rosana's reasoning is grounded in her family's significant debt problems. A nurse, Rosana is the primary earner for her household, responsible for Luz, Luz's grandmother (Julia Vera), and Luz's pregnant older sister Yasmin (Amanda Rivas), who suffers from an unnamed health condition accounting for costly medical bills that are a constant source of stress for the family. Luis (Joseph Julian Sora), Yasmin's boyfriend and the father of her child, lives with the family, contributing what he can of his limited earnings as a foreman on an oil rig. Given these circumstances, Rosana fears risking further debt through Luz's loan payments, a liability she feels she cannot incur. More importantly, her admonition for Luz to be less ambitious ("You don't have to have the best"), in her pursuit of attending the University of Texas shames Luz, suggesting that Luz is selfish for having considered taking loans that could jeopardize her family's already precarious financial position.

This argument between Luz and her mother emblematizes generational, class, and cultural differences specific, though not wholly exclusive, to second- and third-generation Latina/o families. Since 2000, the subject of Latina/o youth education has garnered national attention, given their relatively high dropout rates and simultaneous status as the nation's largest racial minority population. At the start of the decade, Latina/o youth led the nation in high-school dropout rates according to a Pew Hispanic Report from 2003, finding Latina/o youth were more likely than other racial groups to discontinue schooling. For example, in 2000, 28 percent of Latina/o sixteen- to nineteen-year-olds were high-school dropouts compared to non-Latino whites at 8 percent and 12 percent for African Americans. In addition to lower levels of high-school completion, the report observed that Latina/o youth in this profile remained underemployed, with lower rates of college attendance.[24] Just a decade later, in 2011 high-school dropout rates of Latina/o youth declined by half, to just 14 percent of what they had been in 2000. Moreover, 69 percent or a record seven out of ten Latina/o high-school graduates enrolled in college, improvements social scientists attribute to the 2008 economic recession encouraging many youth to attend school in lieu of entering the poor job market.[25] However, this same report found that Latina/os are less likely to be at selective institutions, are less likely to enroll full time, and/ or half as likely to attain a bachelor's degree as their white counterparts, 11 percent to 22 percent respectively.

With little exception, public discourse over Latina/o youth education often centers on the role of Latina/o families and presumptions that Latina/o parents, especially immigrants, are not interested in their children's schooling or do not support higher education in lieu of employment. Yet numerous studies contradict this opinion, finding that parents are highly in favor of their children's education and that overall education is a value deeply respected.[26] The exchange between Rosana and Luz crystallizes the disjuncture between parents who support education abstractly but who are often culturally underprepared or unaware of how to help their children achieve this objective and/or who see college as a means to one end: employment. One never gets the sense that Rosana does not want Luz to pursue college, but rather, Rosana's working-class sensibility bounds her understanding of higher education. In her point that Luz "does not have to have the best," she fully distinguishes between the University of Texas at Austin, the state's premiere public university, from Coastal Bend College, a community college in nearby Alice, Texas, that she thinks Luz should attend instead.

Rosana knows and recognizes they are qualitatively different institutions, but her emphasis on "something else that can get you what you need" accentuates her strict correlation between higher education and getting a "good job." She has little sympathy for her daughter's broader yearning for self-actualization and personal development in the urban milieu of Austin or as provided by a more academically rigorous, culturally diverse institution of higher learning. Moreover, Rosana's declaration that "responsible people think about all possible options" explicitly compares Luz to her older brother JM, ostensibly a role model because he made the "pragmatic," self-sacrificial choice to enlist in the military, continually contributing his military salary to help his family and, though Rosana will not verbalize it, thus surrendering his own hopes of attending college.

"YOU KNOW WHERE TO FIND ME": RECRUITERS AS *FAMILIA* AND EMBODIMENTS OF SUCCESS

With Luz's recent admission to the University of Texas at Austin at the outset of the film, her fate looks promising. But in light of her mother's unwillingness to cosign loans, Luz has no other choice but to win the state power lifting competition, the only means of getting an athletic scholarship. To do so, she must successfully win first or second place in regional competition. Required to keep her body weight low (114 pounds exactly) the first half of the film follows Luz's punishing training routines. Various sequences showcase Luz working out in her gym, running at dawn (her stomach bound in saran wrap), consuming laxatives, skipping meals, spitting into water bottles, performing extended handstands, and eventually injecting anabolic steroids.[27] Undertaking these forms of bodily abuse, Luz demonstrates her commitment to leave Benavides; via her strict regimen of corporeal self-improvement, Luz hopes to will into existence a different life for herself. Her determination, as well as self-discipline, is not lost on those around her, especially Sergeant Lopez (Manuel Garcia), a local military recruiter who freely roams the hallways of Benavides High School talking to students between classes and who, it is inferred, recruited JM to enlist in the army. Not long after one of Luz's qualifying matches, Sergeant Lopez approaches Luz and her boyfriend Ray (Jeremy Ray Valdez) in the hallway:

SGT. LOPEZ: Hey Luz, good luck at regionals!

LUZ: Thank you, Sir

SGT. LOPEZ: How's the family? Any news from JM? Tell him I say "hello" [Turns to Ray]. As for you, that phone number you gave me is to a pizza place.

RAY: I must've been hungry

SGT. LOPEZ [sternly]: You know where to find me

RAY [turning to Luz]: That dude told Manuel they have a traveling basketball team.

LUZ: Maybe they do?

This encounter between Sergeant Lopez and Luz effectively captures a number of themes explored in this essay. Aside from this meeting, various scenes show Sergeant Lopez shadowing other young people around Benavides. For example, following Ray's suspension from school for being caught with marijuana, Sergeant Lopez senses an opportune moment to speak to Ray at his family's gas station where Ray works part time. Sergeant Lopez, like military service in south Texas itself, is a ubiquitous presence in the lives of Benavides's young people. Tall, good looking, friendly, and often seen wearing his uniform accented by a black beret, he cuts a striking figure, his visage of success evident in a large, shiny and presumably expensive SUV he drives around town, attracting the notice of young people impressed by possessions largely out of their own reach and that of their parents'. Moreover, Lopez's countenance, and the distinctiveness of his apparel, gives him a bearing that many young people from Benavides—racially suspect, poor, and "small-town" in their knowledge perspectives— rarely see. The appeal of such visibility and indeed admiration was summated by Private First Class Tomas Lomas, a nineteen-year-old marine en route to Camp Pendleton in San Diego, California, from McAllen, Texas, in the spring of 2004. Lomas chose to travel in full uniform on the plane, unlike many of his white peers who preferred jeans and T-shirts, because he felt he could "command more respect than I would normally get" if not in uniform.[28]

Aside from embodying success via his comportment, Sergeant Lopez's mentioning a "traveling basketball team" available to those enlisting in the US Army, alludes to the powerfully inviting and "fun" benefits military recruiters suggest to young people interested in enlistment. Though Ray is skeptical, Luz shows some curiosity about the basketball team, less for her interest in joining and more as a reflection of her own desire for excitement. It is implied, briefly, that she may enjoy such a nicety—she is, after all an athlete. Whether or not the traveling basketball team promised to Ray's friend exists, it is not uncommon for military recruiters to use such tactics and emphasize "amusement" when discussing military enlistment with teens. For example, in 2004, the US Army subcontracted with the San Diego based Latino Sports Marketing firm to create the Hispanic H2 Tour, showcasing a customized black-and-gold Hummer, referred to as a "mobile branded platform" outfitted with a "Yo Soy El Army" logo beneath golden flames, featuring video games, recruitment videos on multiple screens, and speaker systems blaring Spanish language and Latina/o music.[29] That same year, the US Army was also one of the largest sponsors of the *Lowrider Magazine* Evolution Tour, a traveling automotive show featuring customized cars, including the H2 Hummer, and marketed toward African American and Latina/o teenagers. Aside from showcasing the Hummer, the tour also sponsored push-up contests for the chance to win army-branded jerseys, trucker hats, and in some cases, customized dog tags. The tour visited Latino neighborhoods nationwide, often appearing at sporting events, county fairs, and car shows where Latina/o teenagers were likely to be present. Less flashy, but no less important are the daily visual cues Latina/o teens are bombarded with, from recruitment pamphlets in their schools to television commercials dominating Spanish language networks including Univision, Galavisión, Telemundo, Telefutura, and Fox en Español. In south Texas, these cues appeared in the form of billboards. In 2008, seven billboards were erected around south Texas and the greater Rio Grande Valley, featuring a Latina/o solder in fatigues. In large, black script next to the soldier, the ad stated, "Stand Strong, Stand Tall, Stand Out," next to even larger, bolded lettering stating "Win a Wii" framed by a large set of numbers. If a person (presumably a teenager) texted their phone number to the one on the billboard, they would receive a reply message that redirected them to the army's official website and subsequently made them eligible to win a Wii—an expensive, Nintendo video-game console, unaffordable for many lower-income young people in south Texas.[30]

The most significant aspect of this scene's conversation between Sergeant Lopez and the two teenagers, lies not in the promises, but rather, the familiarity and sense of intimacy he shares with them. Though not a teacher or a guidance counselor, his presence in the school and the respect he commands, makes him tantamount to another parental and/or authority figure. However, he can also serve as a proxy friend and older brother to some of these youth. His familiarity with JM, as suggested by his request that Luz "say hello" indicates this might have been the nature of their relationship, perhaps augmented by the fact that JM and Luz's father left the family when they were young, in effect making him a father figure for JM. Within this spectrum, recruiters can simultaneously serve as parental figures replacing absent parents and/or as friends. Thus, its not unusual to see military recruiters court youth by treating them to meals at a favorite restaurant, working out at a gym with them, or even attending movies together, affective gestures bonding these youth with the recruiter, simulating the relationships of friendship and family.

Not surprisingly, Sergeant Lopez's annoyance with Ray for having given him a fake phone number partially stems from the lack of trust and respect Ray has demonstrated. Accessibility to young people is the most important facet of the recruiting profession. While recruiters might pursue students in school with face-to-face contact as seen in the film, they are also entitled to student's phone numbers, sometimes made available by schools themselves, in compliance with the No Child Left Behind Act passed in 2001, which stipulates that public schools who receive federal funding must allow reasonable access for military recruiters. To Sergeant Lopez, Ray's prank constitutes a betrayal, though it is not an uncommon tactic many youth employ to evade being contacted by or even harassed by recruiters they feel are "chasing them down," a sentiment expressed by students in San Diego, Texas.[31] Lopez, it appears, feels not only a sense of camaraderie, but also "ownership" over and investment in Ray; however, the young teenager does not reciprocate. Frequently, the relationship between Sergeant Lopez and Ray appears to be one of predator and prey, and indeed, it can be argued that *All She Can* illustrates the uneven power relationships between these adolescents and military recruiters, who seemingly exploit the vulnerabilities of young people with whom they are in frequent contact. This point is emphasized twice when both Luz and Ray have made poor decisions, which further erode their prospects for "escaping" Benavides, leaving military service as their *only* option. After Ray's initial suspension for marijuana, he is later caught during a routine drug search on school grounds in possession of one of Luz's steroid syringes. Rather than confess that the syringe belongs to Luz, Ray claims it as his own and is permanently expelled from school. At the end of the film, Ray is shown training in the gym of the army recruitment center with Sergeant Lopez. Luz, whom Ray has been estranged from, sees him in the window of the gym as she is driving by. She parks her truck and runs to him:

LUZ: What are you doing?

RAY: I was going to tell you the other night. I got my GED. I signed up.

LUZ: What are you talking about?

RAY: I realized something Luz. When I took the heat for you . . . it felt good. I'm not going to get that working at the gas station.

LUZ: Then be a cop or something.

RAY: I can't! Not with my pot record. The Army doesn't care.

LUZ: What about your parents?

RAY: They couldn't be happier.

LUZ: You've been thinking about this for a while, haven't you?

RAY: I don't know, Luz. You finish school you start thinking about stuff. How about you? What are you going to do?

LUZ: I'm going to stay here and try to help my family if you really care!

Ray's remark that he's "not going to get that at the gas station" encapsulates a purposefulness otherwise unavailable to him in Benavides and a subjective reason many young people from rural areas cite as compelling their enlistment. It is a motivation that Sergeant Lopez has seemingly crafted, encouraged, and fostered, evident in Ray's language, gesturing toward a futurity he now feels is possible, contrary to the "impossibility" of life in Benavides. For her part, Luz is disqualified from competing in the state championship because of her steroid use. Not long afterward, while hanging out with friends at a ranch, Luz experiences a fit of rage over her poor judgment in using steroids and then proceeds to set an old barn on fire. Her actions are inexplicable to her friends, who quickly flee the scene, while Luz stands in front of the fire, seething with anger and waiting for the police to arrive. She is arrested and sentenced to serve several weeks in a juvenile-detention facility for the incident. After her release, she takes a job working with Luis at the oil rig, driving the company supply truck. One day, Luz returns home from work to find Sergeant Lopez parked in her family's driveway. Concerned, she jumps out of her truck and runs toward him:

LUZ [worried]: Is JM okay?
SGT. LOPEZ: Oh hi Luz. Yeah, yeah, everything's fine. I just stopped by to see how your family is doing. Glad I caught you too. I want you to know the Army has a new college program called College First . . . you do a little training over the summer then you can go to college for two years and the Army pays for your tuition. After your deployment, the Army pays for you to finish college. It's a great deal.
LUZ: I don't know. I'll think about it.
SGT. LOPEZ: That's okay, just want you to know about it. Give my best to JM.

Sensitive to Luz's predicament, but conscious of his own agenda, Lopez approaches Luz in an upbeat, positive manner. Unlike his tense, sometimes coercive relationship with Ray, his style toward Luz is much more intimate, caring, and sentimental. For Luz, he frontloads the possibility of college, treating military service as an addendum to her education. He also eerily echoes Luz's mother, in suggesting the military is that "something else" that can get Luz what she needs. In this regard, he, like the military, constitutes a site of redemption—delivering a way out, though one with a very steep cost. Although both Ray and Luz made very poor decisions, arguably shaped by frustrations over their limited life choices, the army, in Ray's words, "doesn't care" about their mistakes. It not only offers a way out, it offers a way over—a means of recovering, transforming, and surpassing the lives they have lived in Benavides. Far more than a physical escape, the army offers a psychological one, an opening through which young people can intellectually and emotionally emancipate themselves from the boundaries of life in small town, rural America.

This scene, though brief, also hints at the important relationship between recruiters and families especially in small towns. In the idiom of military recruitment, family members, clergy, and school officials are often referred to as "influencers" for their ability to influence a youth's decision to join. This was especially the case in the early years of the conflicts in Afghanistan and Iraq, during which market research suggested that parents, especially mothers, would be the dominant obstacles to enlistment and, therefore, needed careful attention by recruiters.[32] Thus, recruiters can just as likely be found having dinner with a potential recruit's family and/or chatting with parents on the phone as they can spending time with a recruit; a closeness that Sergeant Lopez has with Luz's family. It is unclear how often he sees Luz's family, the degree of his history with them, or how sincere he is. What is key in the scene, and earlier ones between Luz and Sergeant Lopez is the projection of care, understanding, and place within the Garcia family he occupies. For many recruiters targeting Latina/o teens, this means respecting the input, contributions, and perspectives of family members, especially in places like south Texas, where those very same family members including uncles, cousins, and siblings have also served in the military. According to Staff Sergeant Jose Diaz of the Miami East Recruiting Station, recruiting within Latina/o communities "becomes a major family event," noting that "most of the time, I not only have to sit down with the potential candidate, but also his parents, grandparents, uncles, and siblings."[33]

"AND GIVEN THE THREE, IT'S THE ARMY FOR ME"

While Luz is in the juvenile detention center, she encounters her classmate Carlos (Julian Works) a vibrant young man, noted troublemaker, and self-styled rapper. Lively and charming, Carlos assures Luz she needs to hold on to her dream of attending college, reminding her that everyone has a dream. Carlos's own dream is to become a rapper, and while optimistic, he is all too aware of how unrealistic his goal is. During a class activity in which he is asked to share his written thoughts, Carlos instead performs "Benavides Born," a self-authored song about his hometown:

> You come in on the flat road, no trees around or grass mowed
> Your doors are locked, your windows are up, you jam on through and don't stop
> You see the past and move your ass 'cuz nothing's here you want to last.
> But me? This is my whole world
> My crib, my hood, my Hollywood
> I'm proud of it, yeah, but I want out of it—too bad
> 'Cuz the train no longer stops here, don't even blow its horn
>
> I'm Benavides Born, I'm Benavides Born
> Bump Bitta Bump Bump
> I'm Benavides Born Bitta Bump Bump
>
> I got no ride, I won't lie, but look at where I am, where'm I gonna fly?
> So dónde estoy? You'll find me chillin' at the car wash talkin' to a tall boy
> 'til my uncle appears and when he sees the beers, he drags me off to school with
>   his finger in my ear
> So I'm in theater arts class
> This could be my hall pass
> I'm bustin' a rhyme, got the kids all in line when the narc dog arrives and hones
>   in on my hash pipe
>
> So it's back to Juvie for a while, school just isn't my style
> If and when they let me be, it's oil fields, fast food and Top Gun on a Humvee

And given those three, it's the Army for me, traveling for a living and your meals
  are free
And when my welcome there is worn, back I will come, in a coffin, you
  will mourn

I'm Benavides Born
Bump Bitta Bump Bump
I'm Benavides Born[34]

While the song captures the desperation of a town on the margins and the
ironic sense of pride Carlos feels in being from a place "where the train no longer
stops," it is the final four lines in which he highlights the "choice" of military service that distills how complex the desires for military service are by young people
in south Texas. He boldly asserts that life in the army can offer stability ("meals
are free") and adventure ("travelin' for a livin'"), before ending on a more serious
note. Presciently aware of the possibility of his own mortality in the army during
wartime, he cheekily asserts, "back I will come, in a coffin you will mourn." For
Carlos, "given the three" he exerts some, however limited, agency in choosing a
life in the military, even if it means his own expendability.

"OH, THAT'S THE REAL DEAL": FICTION AND
REALITY IN SOUTH TEXAS MILITARY SERVICE

Before Luz's disqualification from the state championships, she has an outburst
in her high-school gym class during which she throws a large piece of weightlifting equipment at a stereo, shattering it. Sent to the principal's office for detention, Luz encounters Carlos. After a brief discussion about their frustrations
with school, Carlos defiantly declares, "Whatever! If they kick me out, I'll just
join the Army, get me an AK 47 and drive a crazy tricked out Hummer." Luz,
slightly bemused, corrects him by noting the Humvee "is called an MRAP[35] and
you have to graduate or get a GED to enlist." When Carlos asks how Luz knows
this, she references her older brother JM, offering that he is currently stationed
in Afghanistan. Humbled, Carlos adds, "Oh, that's the real deal."[36]

Military service by young Mexican Americans from south Texas since the
start of the Iraq War has been all too real. As discussed earlier, director Amy
Wendel credits the film's genesis to a news report exploring military service by
young people from San Diego, Texas. She notes:

The idea for this film came from a *60 Minutes* segment that Dan [Meisel] and I
had seen years ago. And this segment was about this small town in South Texas
called San Diego, TX where two young men ... youths died in the first year of the
war in Iraq. ... And that piqued our interest, but what we found most interesting

was how this small town that's predominantly Mexican American who have been there for generations and generations and are more American than my family and what that version of America looked like.[37]

The two young men Wendel is referring to are Jose Amancio Perez III, and Ruben Valdez Jr., childhood friends who died eleven months apart.[38] Perez, a twenty-two-year-old army medic and member of the 6th Battalion, 27th Field Artillery died March 28, 2003. His death was followed by that of Marine Lance Corporal Ruben Valdez Jr. Just twenty-one years old, Valdez Jr. was killed while serving in Operation Iraqi Freedom—one of five Marines from the 3rd Battalion, 7th Marine Regiment killed the same day.[39] Valdez was also the subject of a handwritten note left at the base of the shrine at the Basilica of our Lady of San Juan de Valle, located in McAllen, Texas, seven miles north of the United States–Mexico border. The note reads:

In loving memory of our brother Lance Cpl. Ruben Valdez Jr. He served our country and fought for our freedom. We lost him on April 18, 2004, but always in our hearts he will live. I am grateful for having angels like him that defend our country. May he rest in peace. From all our hearts I can say thank you to all of our U.S. troops and God Bless them and bring them home safely.[40]

This note left for Valdez Jr. was part of a set of memorial panels dedicated to military servicemen and women, located at the Basilica. Since 2001, thousands of visitors, primarily Mexican nationals and Mexican Americans have left items paying homage to the Virgen de San Juan de los Lagos, while simultaneously asking for her protection of their family members serving in Iraq and Afghanistan.[41] The eleven acrylic panels themselves feature hundreds, if not thousands of photos of primarily Mexican American armed services members left by family members and south Texas residents who have made a *peregrinación* or pilgrimage to the Virgen, offering her *promesas* (promises) and requesting her blessing. Sometimes, they are accompanied by handwritten notes, funeral notices, prayer cards, sonogram images from expectant wives or other family members, dried flowers, and *trensas* (braids of human hair offered in worship to the statue). The image of worshippers praying for loved ones in the military is uncannily re-created in *All She Can*, in a scene during which Luz attends church with her grandmother. Toward the back of the church, a small table draped in white lace cloth holds the framed portrait of JM, Luz's older brother, as well as several dozen other young men and women serving in the military. Luz's grandmother lovingly caresses the photo before taking her seat in the pew.

As the note exemplifies, particularly the author's use of the endearment "brother," Valdez was a metaphorical family member. Whether because he originated from the same town as the author of the note or perhaps even because he represents the hundreds of young people from the Rio Grande Valley and from south Texas who have served in the wars in Iraq and Afghanistan, Valdez is an *hermano* (brother) to some or an *hijo* (son) to others. This concept of *compadrazgo* or *compadrismo*, a type of fictive kinship, common throughout south Texas, is rooted in Mexican and Mexican American cultural practices as well as small-town regional identity. During the early years of the Iraq War, the *Valley Morning Star*, one of the most widely circulated newspapers in south Texas, published a section called, "Sons and Daughters of the Valley, Sacrifice of Honor" reporting on the deaths and/or activities of young people serving in the wars in Iraq and Afghanistan. Again the extension of *compadrazgo* to these young people is reflected in the familial terms of "sons" and "daughters"—the region's, and by extension, the nation's children.

Toward the end of *All She Can*, Luz makes a last minute choice to drive to the University of Texas in Austin, seven hours away. After forcing her way into a meeting with Augustin Garza, director of freshman admissions, she learns her admittance has been revoked in light of her arrest and suspension from school. Unlike Ray, and presumably Carlos, she chooses not to enter the military and enrolls in classes at Coastal Bend College instead. Whether or not she will eventually enlist in the military as a means of financing her way through the university is left up for the viewer to decide. As made clear in the film, it is a choice made by many young Mexican Americans from south Texas, alternately described as, "America's heroes," "our brave soldiers," and "*nos hijos*" (our children) throughout their hometowns. In places like Benavides, San Diego, and other forgotten south Texas towns so small they aren't on county maps, residents offer testimony through parades, charity drives, and backyard barbecues, bearing witness to the costly impact of military service on the lives of their young people. It is an impact that Mexican American adolescents from south Texas have felt acutely in the last decade. For example, during the early months of Operation Iraqi Freedom, forty of the first one hundred Texans killed in service were Latina/os, a casualty rate 18 percent higher than their overall representation within the state. Put another way, although accounting for 30 percent of Texans in the armed forces, the casualty rates of Mexican Americans were 33 percent higher overall.[42] Though two thousand miles distant, the events that took place on September 11, 2001, in New York, Washington, DC, and Pennsylvania have irrevocably shaped the lives and possibilities of young Mexican Americans in south Texas, now engaged in the Global War on Terror. Though geographically on the periphery of the nation they serve, and often symbolically rendered as "non-American" given their ethno-racial identity, Spanish surnames, and accented English, Mexican American youth from south Texas have given all they can in service to the US military.

NOTES

1. *All She Can*, directed by Amy Wendel, written by Amy Wendel and Daniel Meisel, SDB, LLC. Distributed by Maya Entertainment and New Video Group, Inc. 2011.

2. The other two events are bench presses and squats. The dead lift is so named for the dead weight of beginning from a fixed, stable position, requiring participants to bend forward, engaging their entire body to lift a heavily loaded barbell from the floor to the middle of their frame.

3. Texas High School Women's Powerlifting Association, http://www.thswpa.com/.

4. Martin Donell Kohout, "BENAVIDES, TX," *Handbook of Texas Online*, http://www.tshaonline .org/handbook/online/articles/hjb04, published by the Texas State Historical Association.

5. *All She Can.*

6. Throughout this essay, I use the term "Latina/os" interchangeably with "Mexican American." "Latina/o" is a pan-ethnic term referring to both US and foreign-born populations from Spanish speaking countries and/or the Caribbean, while "Mexican American" refers explicitly to Americans of ethnic Mexican descent. Owing to their numerical dominance in South Texas and nationally, Mexican Americans constitute the largest percentage of the US Latina/o populace. Finally, it is worth noting that this is a departure from US Army's official terminology, which employs "Hispanic" when referring to either of these groups.

7. Wendel, DVD commentary, interview, *All She Can.*

8. Katherine J. Curtis and Collin F. Payne, "The Differential Impact of Mortality of American Troops in the Iraq War: The Non-Metropolitan Dimension," *Demographic Research* 23 (July 6, 2010).

9. Ibid., 55.

10. As Latina/o enlistment within the military rose, percentages of African American recruits dropped from 23 percent in 2000 to 12 percent in 2006; their numbers began steadily declining before the occupations of Afghanistan and Iraq. Beth Bailey, *America's Army: Making the All-Volunteer Force* (Cambridge: Harvard University Press, 2009), 258.

11. In hard numbers, the Latina/o population within the US Army increased from 31,000 in 1991 to 50,000 in 2004. Jason K. Dempsey and Robert Shapiro, "The Army's Hispanic Future." *Armed Forces & Society* vol. 35, no. 3 (2009): 526–538. See also, Lizzette Alvarez, "Army Focuses on Recruitment of Latinos," *New York Times*, February 9, 2006.

12. Hector Amaya, "Latino Immigrants in the American Discourses of Citizenship and Nationalism during the Iraqi War," *Critical Discourse Studies* 4, no. 3 (December 2007): 238.

13. Hector Amaya, "Dying American or the Violence of Citizenship: Latinos in Iraq," *Latino Studies* 5 (2007): 4.

14. The Army Advantage Fund was a 2008 recruiting incentive program by the US Army, aimed at providing recruits with a down payment for home ownership or seed money to begin their own businesses. It was advertised in only five US cities, including San Antonio, Texas. San Antonio is home to the San Antonio Battalion, the most successful recruiting unit of the US Army's forty-one national recruiting battalions, and directly responsible for coordinating recruitment efforts throughout south Texas. "Army Testing 'Advantage Fund' Recruiting Incentives," Recruiting Command Public Affairs, February 12, 2008, http://www.army .mil/-news/2008/02/12/7405-army-testing-advantage-fund-recruiting-incentives/.

15. Situated primarily along the US-Mexico border, *colonias* are unincorporated townships, often lacking basic infrastructure including plumbing, sewage, electricity, and paved roads. Texas leads the nation in *colonias*.

16. Amy Smith, "Remembering Spc. Tomas Garces." *Salon*, October 30, 2004. http://www .salon.com/2004/10/30/spc_garces/.

17. According to a 2004 study, of Mexican American Texans killed in the Iraq War, 62.5 percent were concentrated in the lower enlisted ranks. Brian Giffords, "Combat Casualties and Race: What Can We Learn from the 2003–2004 Iraq Conflict?," *Armed Forces and Society* 31, no. 2. (2009): 201–225.

18. Wendel, DVD commentary, interview, *All She Can.*

19. San Diego, Texas, is located fifteen miles north of Benavides, Texas. *60 Minutes*, "Call of Duty in San Diego, TX," CBS, February 11, 2009, hosted by Vicki Mabrey.

20. Ibid.

21. Dan Meisel, DVD commentary, interview, *All She Can.*

22. *All She Can.*

23. Ibid.

24. Richard Fry, *Hispanic Youth Dropping out of U.S. Schools: Measuring the Challenge* (Washington, DC: Pew Hispanic Research Center, 2003).

25. Richard Fry and Paul Taylor, *Hispanic High School Graduates Pass Whites in Rate of College Enrollment* (Washington, DC: Pew Hispanic Research Center, 2013), 4–5.

26. Bernadette Sanchez and Yari Colón, "Explaining the Gender Disparity in Latino Youth's Education: Acculturation and Economic Value of Education," *Urban Education* 45 (May 1, 2010).

27. To keep or maintain their body weight within their weight class, female weight lifters resort to spitting to dehydrate themselves, often able to lose one to three pounds in a day. Handstands are used to redistribute weight in advance of weigh-ins if a lifter suspects they might exceed weight limits.

28. Tomas Lomas, interview by author, March 24, 2008.

29. The "Yo Soy El Army" campaign was a Latino directed recruitment initiative of the US Army that ran from 2001 to 2005 and was designed to appeal to Latina/o youth.

30. Author's personal notes, spring 2008; see also, Christopher Sherman, "Army Offers Texas Recruits Chance to Win Wii," *Army Times*, April 9, 2008.

31. *60 Minutes*, "Call of Duty in San Diego."

32. Bailey, *America's Army*, 251.

33. Alberto Betancourt, "Yo Soy El Army," *Soldier*, August 2003, 38.

34. "Benavides Born," written by Daniel Meisel, Amy Wendel and Kevin Affleck.

35. Mine-resistant ambush proof vehicle.

36. *All She Can.*

37. Wendel, DVD Commentary, interview.

38. *60 Minutes*, "Call of Duty in San Diego."

39. Jose Luis Martinez. "Ruben Valdez Jr. Found Himself in a 'Full Blown War.'" *Corpus Christi Caller Times*, April 22, 2004.

40. Handwritten note left by Joanna Cadena on one of the panels at the shrine at San Juan Basilica in San Juan, Texas. Undated.

41. The San Juan shrine is a replica of the Our Lady of San Juan de los Lagos figurine in Jalisco, Mexico, founded in 1542. Manuel A. Vasquez, Globalizing the Sacred: Religion across the Americas (New Brunswick, NJ: Rutgers University Press, 2003).

42. *All She Can.*

PART IV

POLITICS AND
PEDAGOGY

10 · IN THIS WAR BUT NOT OF IT

Teaching, Memory, and the Futures of Children and War

BENJAMIN COOPER

On the heels of teaching a course on the Civil War and American literature a few semesters ago, I felt compelled to offer a counterpoint course on modern war and American culture, one that I hoped would burn within my students and, to paraphrase Oliver Wendell Holmes Jr., touch their hearts with fire.[1] Teaching the Civil War is an essay unto itself, but in brief, that class was a typical course on nineteenth-century American literature and culture. That is to say, our experience was largely registered as "history," with our assigned purpose to study a long-ago time, populated with Americans who, it seems, grow increasingly difficult to recognize as Americans by students today. Nonetheless, we tried, and often succeeded, and I give my students all the credit for when we connected. Yet even then there was often a gulf of feeling between me and them from which I wanted to learn, especially because I consider the Civil War fundamentally to be "my war"—a conflict central to my academic identity and also to the ways in which I tend to interpret American culture more broadly. But for my students, a group of earnest and engaged and conscientious undergraduates, the Civil War was not their war even despite the hoopla of the ongoing sesquicentennial celebration. I wanted to go find and teach what they themselves considered to be the wars of their generation. Consequently, I designed Children and War, a course that considered representations of war in American children's literature from World War II through the current conflicts in Iraq and Afghanistan.

In what follows, I want to express what modest lessons I took from twice teaching that course. I have observations to make about what wars are of the current generation and which are not, and I have some arguments to make about why some are in and some are out. I have reflections to offer about the specific challenges of teaching children's literature to readers who are themselves emerging from their own childhood, and of teaching contemporary warfare to readers who have lived through the wars under study (unlike the Civil War). But first, an important disclaimer must be made. The students with whom I have worked with over two iterations of Children and War and in other courses on the War on Terror cannot be considered an exhaustive sample, although I believe in many ways they are typical of today's undergraduate. Washington University in St. Louis, where I taught these courses before recently moving to another university, draws students who are highly motivated and want to succeed. As many of my students would readily admit, they also tend to arrive in my classroom sheltered by academic and socioeconomic privilege. None that I have taught within this context have directly engaged in warfare, served in the military, or had their immediate families displaced or destroyed by armed conflict (at least none that have said as much to me). And yet they, like all undergraduates in the United States today, have been the witnesses to war their entire lives. This generation was born after the First Persian Gulf War and before 9/11. The first years of the first decade of their life were colored by the resurgent strength of American military power and the "kicking of the Vietnam syndrome" once and for all, courtesy of a seemingly endless supply of Tomahawk and Patriot missiles.[2] The waning years of their first decade, in contrast, went terribly wrong following 9/11, an event that disabused them of the certainties of America's fate and the clarity of war's purpose, which were supposed to be their ideological birthrights at the close of the twentieth century. Today, this generation of undergraduates has lived more of their years after 9/11 than before it, by a margin of more than two to one.

In whatever class you might be teaching related to the War on Terror, these demographic facts should be embraced rather than ignored because they allow you to identify and contrast the different layers of knowledge we have about war. I frame these systems of knowing as a competition between overlapping forms of memory that allow us (as observers) to be in the wars we study but not necessarily of them. The goal of this premise is to foreground the incompleteness of our understanding of the War on Terror and to ask direct questions about the ethical consequences of "knowing" war in an academic setting. Students tend to feel strongly about their own subject positions. Indeed, in the beginning of a course, teasing out what students personally know about war generally, and the War on Terror specifically, turns out to be a key pedagogical strategy. I label this knowledge—what students think they know about the War on Terror—as their *living memory* of violent group conflict. Ask a class where they were on 9/11 or what they remember about it, and everyone has a personal story to tell (they were in school that day, someone from their high school went on to fight in Iraq), even if the details of those stories grow increasingly remote and removed from their immediate world. While there are points to be made about the unreliability of personal memory and how eye-witness accounts are prone to suggestion and misremembering, I try to suggest to the class not that their experience with 9/11 and the subsequent War on Terror are wrong, but that they are once again incomplete. War, and the War on Terror in particular, is defined by other "operations of memory" (to borrow Carol Gluck's term)[3] such as *generational memory* and *collective memory*. To understand the former term, at various points throughout a course I ask the group to identify and explain what causes them, the present generation, to gravitate their interests toward certain wars and toward certain aspects of those wars at the expense of other wars and other aspects of "their" wars. The Holocaust, for example, feels to many of my students like it is their experience on par with 9/11, whereas the Vietnam War (and even more so the Korean War) seems much more unavailable. Why this might be is tied up with what Maurice Halbwachs, Jan Assman, and Jay Winter (among others) have theorized as collective or cultural memory, which I try to frame as the grand narratives that endure over time. The calcification of collective memory is not necessarily a benign process since some discursive practices benefit at the expense of others. (I would recommend theorizing as much or as little as you see fit, but by way of example, David Blight's work on the "Lost Cause" in the South following the Civil War can be a quick and effective baseline demonstration of the power and bias of collective memory.[4]) Layering memory in this way allows you to pose a tripartite question at every stage of the course: what ideas, values, and ideologies profit from the different ways we remember war over time? "We" must be understood first as a mélange of individuals; second, as a crowd of different generations; and third, as a collective yet fragmented culture.

The assumptions I took with me about my particular class's living memory of war were that their unexamined halcyon days of early childhood soon gave way to an unrelenting anxiety and uncertainty following 9/11. I sought to mirror that progression in the course's narrative trajectory, which began with the Japanese attack on Pearl Harbor on December 7, 1941. Regardless of the generation of Americans—be it this one or the next one—there is an enduring and unquestioned clarity to Pearl Harbor. Even though perhaps it should, Pearl Harbor does not register in our collective memory as a category for critique (one might say the same about the bombing of Hiroshima and Nagasaki). Ambiguity is reserved for the incarceration of the more than 120,000 Japanese Americans (the majority of them citizens) that Pearl Harbor helped set in motion, but "why we fight"—as retaliation for Japanese aggression and, once we came to learn about places like Dachau and Auschwitz, to liberate the death camps—seems on its face intractable. Wartime children's literature such as Esther Forbes's *Johnny Tremain* (1943), a historical novel set in the days leading up to the Revolutionary War about a young silversmith who suffers a grave injury to his hand and, having no other way to make a living in Boston, becomes a messenger boy for the likes of John Hancock and Paul Revere, often was complicit with the moral certainty inherent in World War II nationalism. "Why are we going to fight? Why, why?" asks James Otis during a secret assembly of the Sons of Liberty. We fight "for something more important than the pocketbooks of American citizens. . . . For men and women and children all over the world." Those children are "the peasants of France, the serfs of Russia," and notably also "Italy. And all those German states."[5] Neither Italy nor Germany would even exist politically by those names until their respective nationalist movements in the middle of the nineteenth century, but the anachronism of Forbes's wartime generational memory is representative. More often than not, students come to recognize in World War II, and in *Johnny Tremain* specifically, the fantasy within such a Whiggish version of American history. "We fight, we die, for a simple thing," Otis concludes. "Only that a man can stand up."[6] Liberal democracy and self-determination will vanquish all tyrants, be they British or Japanese or Taliban. America will make new nations in its own image to the gratitude of all the peoples of the world.

The plan was to establish the jingoism of World War II and then gradually dismantle the subsequent ideological certainties of the United States at war by marching through the existential unease of the atomic age, the dissent and distrust produced by Vietnam, and the contemporary drift of military policy in the Middle East. The fault lines of collective memory would be revealed, I hoped, by the various and divergent generational memories that formed over the last half century. My assumption, once again, was that I was reproducing for students on a historical scale the same pattern from confidence to fear they had unconsciously witnessed in their own childhood. What I came to learn was that American power did not ring as true for the class as I had assumed. In *Johnny Tremain* and in Helen Wells's popular *Cherry Ames, Army Nurse* (1944), students recognized the total-war narrative of World War II that emphasized universal sacrifice and service by every American, even children, who could sell war bonds door-to-door, plant victory gardens in their backyards, and count the days until they could become a soldier or nurse themselves. Students recognized this argument intellectually, but they were also wary of "The Happy War Child" as a normative narrative of the war similar to "The Greatest Generation," each intent on consolidating nostalgia for patriotic ends.[7] In her 1944 acceptance of the John Newberry Medal for *Johnny Tremain*, Forbes notes that in her characterization of Revolutionary boys and girls, she knew she wanted

to show the boys and girls of today how difficult were those other children's lives by modern standards; how early they were asked to take on the responsibilities of men and women. They were not allowed to be children very long. Then came Pearl Harbor [in the course of drafting the novel] and once again we were at war. In peace times countries are apt to look upon their boys under twenty as mere children and (for better or worse) to treat them as such. When war comes, these boys are suddenly asked to play their part as men. Our young fliers today have much in common with the nineteen-year-old boys who served as captains of armed ships during the Revolution. . . . The twentieth-century boys and girls are by the very fact of war closer now spiritually, psychologically, to this earlier generation [of the Revolution].[8]

In Forbes's estimation, the true war of the World War II generation was the Revolutionary War: "I really wanted young people today to think of the British in Boston—and the Nazis in, say, Rotterdam."[9] The association Forbes wanted to make in the 1940s between the Nazis and the British was a surprise to many students because her implicit warrant—that both the Revolutionary War and World War II were experienced by their respective generations as total wars with epic consequences—was incompatible with students' own lived experience of war, which has been more quotidian than revolutionary.

The first lesson I took was that living memory has the most gravity in the classroom, followed closely by generational memory; and both will become normative unless they are constantly acknowledged and, when appropriate, undermined. Interpreting war is unique for every person and for every generation, which may sound obvious, but what I mean is that war does not register as timeless or in the abstract in the classroom. "Total war" is a case in point. Total war signifies the (near) complete mobilization of a country's resources. Within the context of World War II, American manufacturing and private industry coordinated with government to build planes and manufacture ammunition and other war matériel; young men and women volunteered their bodies for military service at an extraordinary rate; even machines of popular culture from Hollywood to comic books collaborated with the national propagandistic mood.[10] Such a set of affairs is foreign to the current generation, who cannot connect with the magnitude of collective will required to maintain such war frenzy. In the mindset of *Johnny Tremain*, America was "all in," and so was the larger world. Complex international alliances formed during the 1940s as if on a Risk board game, and Carl von Clausewitz's famous nineteenth-century theory of warfare seemed to dictate the military strategy of the geopolitical map: "War is nothing but a duel on a larger scale. If we would unite in one conception the countless duels of which it consists, we should imagine two wrestlers. Each seeks by physical force to overthrow the other, render him incapable of further resistance, and compel his opponent to do his will. *War is thus an act of force to compel our adversary to do our will*" [emphasis in original].[11] Total war and duels are abstractions, relics really, of an unfamiliar past for students that we now assume (maybe at our peril) will never again come back to life. I, too, began to see myself as a bit of a relic. The assumptions I had made about my students' collective starting point with the First Persian Gulf War as a site of patriotism, pride, and security—the very reasons why the course started with World War II to provide a corollary—were actually *my* experiences with the First Persian Gulf War as a child, which I erroneously assumed students shared. They might have inherited that war, but I was the only one to internalize it in my youth as the high-water mark of American power. Despite my best intentions to be objective, I had told the truth but told it slant viz my own living memory.

The second lesson I took was the inevitable consequence of the first, namely, that definitions of war are biased and personal, and, like a person, evolving and unresolved. My subsequent strategy became to highlight how war memory changes at each level. For example, from a foreign-policy and cultural-memory perspective, war's development is certainly noticeable. Whereas Clausewitz claimed nearly two hundred years ago that armed conflict is the desire "to compel our adversary to do our will," in 1957 amid the height of the Cold War, Henry Kissinger would offer an alternative to total war in what he and other government strategists coined "limited war . . . fought for specific political objectives which, by their very existence, tend to establish a relationship between the force employed and the goal to be attained. It reflects an attempt to *affect* the opponent's will, not to *crush* it, to make the conditions to be imposed seem more attractive than continued resistance, to strive for specific goals and not for complete annihilation" [emphasis in original].[12]

Within Kissinger and Robert McClintock's *The Meaning of Limited War* (1967), students quickly saw how the philosophies and strategies of war are relative and historically situated. The anxieties of the Cold War differed from those of World War II, especially after 1949 when the USSR developed the atomic bomb and Mao Zedong won the Chinese Civil War. The threat of mutually assured destruction softened war's hard lines, and consequently, the United States now sought containment rather than complete destruction, to "*affect*" the enemy's hearts and minds rather than "*crush*" them. This attitudinal shift toward limited war in the 1950s and 1960s helped in part to explain the different affect in children's literature of the Korean and Vietnam Wars, a literature largely riddled with fear, skepticism, and dissent.[13]

Such a bird's-eye view of how war has adapted over previous generations, however, needs to be reconciled with the constant adjustments being made to students' current generational memory. Near the end of the last semester, we were talking about the War on Terror and I had put up on the board two columns with separate headings—"War" and "Terrorism"—and asked the class to throw out words and phrases that defined each concept. "War" solicited a comfortable enough response: "front lines," "violence for political objectives," "two enemies, usually nations," "organized and led by governments." While I quickly would try to complicate these descriptions (What about the "War on Drugs"? Korea and Vietnam? Syria today?), students had a much more comfortable time with "War" than with "Terrorism." As soon as one student would argue for "foreign radical extremism," another would back away from the religious implications of that phrase. Does terrorism *have* to be religious? Does it *have* to be "with the purpose of creating fear"? Or when another student struggled with how to say terrorism is usually a symptom of racial and cultural conflict, others were quick to retort that terrorism didn't *have* to fit Samuel P. Huntington's "clash of civilizations" thesis. The class struggled with its own guilt (justified or not) about how the current generation remembers 9/11. Indeed, the criteria for "Terrorism" was intimately tied with the images of 9/11, but I had not asked them to define 9/11; I had asked them to define terrorism. No one wanted to say "Arab" or "Muslim" or "al-Qaeda" out loud, but the subtext was clear that for this particular group at least, terrorism was defined through the faces of the nineteen hijackers. 9/11 was terrorism and terrorism was 9/11.

As time ran out, no one could offer a counterexample to the list on the board, i.e., instances of terrorism that did not ostensibly derive their motivation from religion, race, and foreign sources (What about cyberterrorism? The assassination of President Kennedy? The Los Angeles Riots of 1992?). As it happened, our discussion transpired on April 15, 2013, at exactly the same time two pressure-cooker bombs exploded near the finish line of the Boston Marathon. At our next class, the identities of Tamerlan and Dzhokhar Tsarnaev were not yet known. The unidentified but media-labeled "terrorists" could have been anyone—any race, any religion, from any country in the world. Unsettled as the students were to realize we had tried to define terrorism at the same time a terrorist event was unfolding, they still felt the need to return to our previous exercise. Without them seeming to realize it, every demographic now became a suspect. Suddenly domestic attacks orchestrated by white males entered the conversation, notably the Oklahoma City bombing in 1995 and the Sandy Hook Elementary School shootings in 2012. To teach war to the current generation is to be obsolete at the moment you teach it because this generation, like all generations, interprets and defines war on a daily basis.[14] Obsolescence was the third lesson, which is not a problem unless you fail to recognize it as a underlying condition of teaching the War on Terror. Semantics shift and definitions are amended, and students learned a great deal when they recognized themselves in relation to such change.

War might not even be the right word anymore. When asked explicitly to locate what wars they did in fact feel to be their own, students tended to give two responses: 9/11 and the Holocaust. I will address each of these categories in greater depth in a moment, but for now let me note that students did not say Iraq and Afghanistan or World War II. Instead, the words they chose call up particular images of immense horror and suffering. They are the experiential subsets to the larger "official" events of war: the campaigns, the operations, the boots on the ground. One student for her final project wanted to understand why 9/11 felt so intimate while the Vietnam War seemed so distant. Her solution was to create scrapbooks for each scenario, with the charge that the objects she crafted would teach future generations of children about Vietnam and 9/11. The Vietnam scrapbook was page after page of facts, dates, and watershed moments in the course of the conflict. The 9/11 scrapbook, however, was page after page of stories, anecdotes, and personal remembrances from her friends and schoolmates whom she surveyed. As for why she memorialized each war differently, "To me, Vietnam is an event—not an experience. . . . To me, Vietnam is one story within a history textbook. A story faded in the memory of society, and therefore lacking in the minds of my generation." If Vietnam was an event—i.e., one story inert and indistinguishable among many—9/11 was a seemingly infinite series of the same story, told by different voices yet somehow similar, a shared generational memory rather than an impersonal historical record.

While certainly not every student would have the same estranged relationship with Vietnam, this anecdote nonetheless reveals how living memory and generational memory tend to appropriate only those wars and those narratives that benefit the images that both the generation and the individual would like to maintain. Unless they have taken a specific class on the Vietnam War, most students are troubled to learn about gross misbehavior such as the massacre at My Lai or the Pentagon Papers, in part because such events construct a narrative that bothers us out of our preconceptions and ideals, namely, a defeated America that has lost its putative moral authority. Even though there are rough analogies to be made to contemporary war—between My Lai and Abu Ghraib, the Pentagon Papers and Edward Snowden—such connections tend to be ineffective because they construct an uncomfortable present underscored by loss and disillusionment. Memories of 9/11 are colored by loss and disillusionment as well, yet they, like a dominant strand of Holocaust memory that I will analyze at the end of the essay, tend to focus on resiliency and survival in the midst of loss rather than on succumbing to it. Books such as Don DeLillo's *Falling Man: A Novel* and Jonathan Safran Foer's *Extremely Loud and Incredibly Close* are not "salvation" stories exactly, yet they represent how 9/11 despair is countered by the voices of survivors searching for purpose. The kinds of violence with which this generation identifies (be that violence a declared war, an episode thereof, a police action, or a terrorist act) is heavily determined by the degree to which the representations of that violence—within cultural texts such as children's literature but also in national customs and institutions—conforms to the dominant preexisting discourses of American war, e.g., the United States as resilient, exceptional, superior, the world's reluctant police force, an innocent victim. The pedagogical goal is to demonstrate for students how the larger forces of collective memory, which have existed since well before they and their generation were born, coerce their generational and living memories. They are not as independent and self-determined as we might assume.

My generation had family members and friends during the Vietnam War who served in theater (including my own father), who dodged the draft, who protested on college campuses. To me, Vietnam is an experience, but I sympathize if to some undergraduates today it is an event. Indeed, many wars in my various classes tend to register as events: Korea, Vietnam, Iraq, and Afghanistan never vibrated with the same sense of community that the shared traumatic experience of 9/11 produced, in large part because there is no strong living memory of these wars for the current generation.[15] This absence did not go unnoticed and, in fact, bothered many students. After all, Afghanistan is still an active armed conflict (as was Iraq until quite recently) being fought by American men and women of the very generation in question.[16] Shouldn't *they* be the wars of utmost concern? Before the War on Terror had its name, Canadian author and activist Deborah Ellis wrote the children's book *The Breadwinner*, the first in a popular series of novels about the displacement of an Afghani family under Taliban rule, in 2000; it was first published in the United States immediately after 9/11 in November of 2001.[17] The protagonist, Parvana, is an eleven-year-old girl whose father is kidnapped by the Taliban in the opening pages. With the only working-age male in her family imprisoned, Parvana is forced to support her mother and four siblings by working in the local market dressed in boy's clothes (so as not to arouse the Taliban's misogyny). Parvana will subsequently scavenge in a graveyard, witness the public severing of thieves' hands, and save a woman who has fled a neighboring region after the Taliban murdered her entire family in the street as she watched.

Reading about Parvana's gruesome world dredges up a dormant guilt within some students, one of whom asked in an essay, "Am I so far removed from the atrocities in the Middle East that I cannot even grasp that these events are happening in the same world I'm living in?" Teaching contemporary war to contemporaries of those wars can produce a brand of ethical crisis almost equivalent to survivor's guilt, which is not a desired effect, but it nonetheless can be instructive. It was not simply that other young people their age suffer, fight, and die, while we were sitting in the comfort of Midwest America; moreover, my classes struggled with what it meant for their generation cumulatively to have survived 9/11, what their responsibility to uphold that memory was, and what the legacy of the War on Terror ultimately would be. Parvana's suffering transpires (i.e., is published, or "in the can" ready to be published in the United States) before the events of 9/11 ever take place. She actually is not "in the same world I'm living in," as the student author presumed. Ellis imagined Parvana within a quantitatively different living memory of war that was *pre*-9/11, in contrast to us now who read about her after having lived through the events. Moreover, an eleven-year-old American child reading *The Breadwinner* today would have been born after 9/11, and like Parvana and Deborah Ellis when she wrote the novel, he or she would have no living memory of the events of 9/11 despite the class assumption to the contrary (a similar assumption to how I believed students would "remember" the First Persian Gulf War). Suddenly students began to worry that for the next generation of Americans, 9/11 and the War on Terror would not be the same war, at least not in the way it was for them.

The anxiety that has to be managed in the classroom is that 9/11 will eventually become the "event" of the Vietnam scrapbook, relegated to the quaintness of a previous generation who "all remembered" when the world was a different place. Immediately after 9/11, adults such as Mitch Frank worried about this inevitable oblivion of living and generational 9/11 memory. A journalist at *Time* magazine, Frank opens *Understanding September 11th: Answering Questions about the Attacks on America* (2002) with the personal clarity of his own recollection—"I can still remember the boom of the first explosion"—and ends the book with his fear that today's and tomorrow's children will lose the clarity of what he physically witnessed. He invites his children readers to consider, "What can *you* do? You can learn about other countries and cultures. Read books to find out more about the topics covered in this book. . . . You can also resolve never to forget 9/11."[18] "Never forget" as a slogan of 9/11 has always puzzled me because 9/11 never seemed in danger of being forgotten. It is a defining moment of modern history. You might as well instruct Americans not to forget to breathe or pay their taxes. Yet after teaching the War on Terror several times, I realize that the mandate worries not about the current generation but about the unborn. "Never forget" admits its own tragedy insofar as it both resists and acknowledges the probable oblivion of 9/11 from every level of memory at some distant future date.

But does the erasure of this generation's memory of 9/11 *have* to be unavoidable? As with any question about what the future holds, it is probably best to say as little as possible.[19] Rather than speculate, I would simply point out that the inherent optimism of the question is striking, and the recurring hope among this generation that 9/11 will not fade helps to explain why a significant population of this generation also considers the Holocaust their own.[20] Indeed, the Holocaust often registers in the classroom as an "experience" (as opposed to the "event" of World War II), and there is perhaps an odd comfort in the fact that memories of the Holocaust have not seemed to have passed, even though most of its survivors have. Art Spiegelman drew his Pulitzer Prize–winning graphic novels *Maus I: A Survivor's Tale: My Father Bleeds History* (1986) and *Maus II: A Survivor's Tale: And Here My Troubles Began* (1992) at a time when Holocaust survivors were increasingly passing away and observers began to worry about the prospect of losing their living memories forever. This testimony "rush" produced Claude Lanzmann's *Shoah* (1985, but begun in 1974), Elie Wiesel's *Night* (1982), and Steven Spielberg's *Schindler's List* in 1993, the same year the United States Holocaust Memorial Museum was dedicated in Washington, DC. At the same time in the academy, trauma theory began to take hold with Shoshana Felman and Dori Laub's *Testimony: Crises of Witnessing in Literature, Psychoanalysis, and Literature* (1991) and Cathy Caruth's *Unclaimed Experience: Trauma, Narrative, and History* (1996), each an effort to entangle past traumas such as the Holocaust into the present because "history is precisely the way we are implicated in each other's traumas."[21]

Related to Caruth's definition of history as traumatic memory, Marianne Hirsh theorized "postmemory" as "the relationship of the second generation to powerful, often traumatic, experiences that preceded their births but that were nevertheless transmitted to them so deeply as to seem to constitute memories in their own right."[22] In *Maus*, Art Spiegelman records the experiences of his father Vladek, a Holocaust survivor, but he also finds himself in a struggle with his role as the keeper of another generation's memory. At one point, Art confides to his psychiatrist, "No matter what I accomplish, it doesn't seem like much compared to surviving Auschwitz."[23] As Hirsch notes, the ethical risk to the endurance of generational memory is to have "one's own stories and experiences displaced" by the traumatic memories of others, to in effect abdicate the primacy of one's own living memory to the secondhand traumas of past generations.[24] That may be asking a lot of future generations, but the persistent presence of Holocaust memory seems to satisfy many students that the sorrows of war have an unknown and unwritten fate. As these students are the present descendants of the Holocaust, so they will be the future guardians of the War on Terror.

Postmemory, or "post-9/11 memory," might be a dominant model for this generation's relationship with 9/11, which is not to equate 9/11 with the Holocaust (an argument I am very deliberately trying *not* to make), but rather to pose the question that started this essay somewhat differently: what memory strategies are attractive and efficacious for this generation to preserve their experiences of the War on Terror? The real work ahead lies in teaching the available strategies of remembrance to this generation—living, generational, collective, post-9/11— and in discovering and articulating additional strategies. Children's literature is a productive context to explore because it tends to resist the painful passing of generational memory. The genre often can be susceptible to propaganda and nostalgia (e.g., *Johnny Tremain*), and yet studying children's literature within an academic framework interferes with such wistful reminiscence. Students are themselves emerging from their own childhood, and they cannot help but look back at their own youth and revise their relationships with childhood and war (e.g., many had read *Johnny Tremain* and Orson Scott Card's *Ender's Game* (1985) in elementary or middle school and were shocked by how differently they read now). Our students are products of their childhood yet not still in it, similar to how the War on Terror increasingly feels to them like a war that is becoming not their own. Whether or not this generation remains in the War on Terror or of it depends in part on the memory work still left to be done.

NOTES

1. "In our youth our hearts were touched with fire" is a phrase from Holmes's 1884 Memorial Day speech. For a discussion of this speech and Holmes's relationship with Civil War memory, see Louis Menand, *The Metaphysical Club* (New York: Farrar, 2001), 49–69.

2. Variations of this slogan appeared in contemporary media accounts of the First Persian Gulf War, as well as in the memoirs of military commanders such as Colin Powell. See Heonik Kwon, *Ghosts of War in Vietnam* (New York: Cambridge University Press, 2008), 12.

3. See Carol Gluck, "Operations of Memory: 'Comfort Women' and the World," in *Ruptured Histories: War, Memory, and the Post-Cold War in Asia*, ed. Sheila Miyoshi Jager and Rana Mitter (Cambridge: Harvard University Press, 2007) 47–77. Gluck's terminology is different from my own and may be a useful alternative or supplement in conceptualizing memory in the classroom.

4. See in particular chapter 8, David W. Blight, "The Lost Cause and Causes Not Lost," in *Race and Reunion: The Civil War in American Memory* (Cambridge: Belknap Press of Harvard University Press, 2001).

5. Ester Forbes, *Johnny Tremain* (Boston: Graphia, 1971), 209–210.

6. Forbes, *Johnny Tremain*, 212.

7. For a more thorough discussion of the harsh reality of being a child during World War II, see Steven Mintz, *Huck's Raft: A History of American Childhood* (Cambridge: Harvard University Press, 2004), 254–274; William M. Tuttle Jr., *"Daddy's Gone to War": The Second World War in the Lives of America's Children* (New York: Oxford University Press, 1995).

8. Quoted in Jack Bales, *Esther Forbes: A Bio-Bibliography of the Author of* Johnny Tremain (Lanham, MD: Scarecrow Press, 1998), 145.

9. Quoted in Bales, *Esther Forbes: A Bio-Bibliography*, 145.

10. Popular culture certainly got on board with the war effort, including propaganda cartoons by Looney Tunes and the short film by Walt Disney, *Education for Death* (1943). See Michael S. Schull and David E. Wilt, *Doing Their Bit: Wartime Animated Short Films, 1939–1945* (Jefferson, NC: McFarland, 2004). Marvel Comic's *Captain America* first appeared in 1941 to fight Hitler, as would DC Comics' popular *Blackhawk*. Superman visited the Japanese internment camps in a series that ran from June through August 1943.

11. Carl von Clausewitz, *War, Politics, and Power: Selections from* On War, *and* I Believe and Profess (Chicago: Regnery, 1962), 63.

12. Henry Kissinger, *Nuclear Weapons and Foreign Policy* (New York: Harper, 1957), 140, emphasis in original. For more on limited war from a policy perspective, see also Robert McClintock, *The Meaning of Limited War* (Boston: Houghton Mifflin, 1967).

13. A full analysis of the Korean and Vietnam Wars is too digressive for the body of this essay. The aforementioned World War II novel *Cherry Ames, Army Nurse* contrasts with Eloise Engle, *Dawn Mission: A Flight Nurse in Korea* (New York: John Day, 1962), in which the apparent comfort of World War II seems to have disappeared by the Korean War. To complicate theories of limited war, I offer in class the possibility that Vietnam was in fact unrestrained. Originally published in 1985, the science fiction novel by Orson Scott Card, *Ender's Game* (New York: Tor, 1992), can be read as a Cold War reaction to Vietnam. See also Vietnam veteran Joe Haldeman's science fiction novel *The Forever War* (New York: St. Martin's, 1974) and, in the context of the Afghanistan war, Dexter Filkins, *The Forever War* (New York: Knopf, 2008). For more on how children were an integral yet contested image in the American memory of the Vietnam War, see Patrick Hagopian, *The Vietnam War in American Memory: Veterans, Memorials, and the Politics of Healing* (Amherst: Massachusetts University Press, 2009), 309–347. For a useful survey of Vietnam War children's literature, see E. Wendy Saul, "Witness for the Innocent: Children's Literature and the Vietnam War," *Issues in Education* 3, no. 3 (1985): 185–197. For an example of political dissent in American children's literature during the Vietnam War, see Betty Jean Lifton and Thomas C. Fox, *Children of Vietnam* (New York: Atheneum, 1972).

14. A case in point of how students sense their own relativity is from a student's essay responding to Jean Baudrillard's contention that the First Persian Gulf War was mere "trickery, hyperreality, simulacra" in *The Gulf War Did Not Take Place*, trans. Paul Patton (Bloomington: Indiana University Press, 1995), 67. In a way that represents many of her peer's feelings, this student reflected, "According to Baudrillard and other adults who have lived through Vietnam, an 'actual war,' the Gulf War and most wars since may not be real wars. However, children growing up now, who have only lived through the [Second Persian] Gulf War or the War on Terror where advanced technology is so prevalent, will grow up to redefine war as something where human contact is not necessary nor are the emotional reactions such as guilt or passion that accompany it."

15. Not every dynamic or demographic can be anticipated, but I want to make a special note about teaching veterans, who absolutely have a strong living memory of contemporary war. I have written at length about veteran literature and culture elsewhere, but let me recommend that veteran experience should be acknowledged but not necessarily privileged in discussions of the War on Terror. Inevitably the living memory of students who have served in the military take on a certain polish and authority during class discussion, but other students should be encouraged not to abandon their own "civilian" responsibility to the conversation.

16. By the time this essay went to press in late 2014, President Obama had announced the continuation of American combat troops in Afghanistan through at least 2015. The rise of the Islamic State in Iraq and Syria (ISIS) also raises the question of whether American troops will return to Iraq.

17. Deborah Ellis, *The Breadwinner* (Berkeley, CA: Groundwood Books, 2011).

18. Mitch Frank, *Understanding September 11th: Answering Questions About the Attacks on America* (New York: Viking, 2002), 1, 123–124. Even the youngest of children are targets for securing generational memory. See, for example, the young children's coloring book published by N. Wayne Bell, *We Shall Never Forget 9/11: The Kids' Book of Freedom* (St. Louis: Really Big Coloring Books, 2011). The copyright page announces, "Children of America! As you grow, Do Not Forget. This is your world now." Kids who color this book today would, like readers of *The Breadwinner*, be born well after the events of 9/11.

19. While I think it is best to end a course with the question of the future of the War on Terror, it can be very useful to include professional military strategists who make predictions. At the time of this printing, the most engaging text is David Kilcullen, *Out of the Mountains: The Coming Age of the Urban Guerilla* (New York: Oxford University Press, 2013). Kilcullen argues that counterinsurgency theory's rural focus to "win the hearts and minds" of a population—the dominant way of thinking about the war in Afghanistan—is already obsolete. Future war will become instead incredibly urban in coastal and technologically "connected" megacities such as Mumbai, Kirachi, Lagos, and San Pedro Sula.

20. My criteria for making these judgments is admittedly subjective. Students had limited options about which wars they wished to write about and what their final project could be, and yet the preponderance of interest was around 9/11 and the Holocaust.

21. Cathy Caruth, *Unclaimed Experience: Trauma, Narrative, and History* (Baltimore: Johns Hopkins University Press, 1996), 24. This list is necessarily incomplete, but see also Judith Herman, *Trauma and Recovery* (New York: BasicBooks, 1992); Bessel A. Van der Kolk et al., eds., *Traumatic Stress: The Effects of Overwhelming Experience on Mind, Body, and Society* (New York: Guilford Press, 1996); and Kali Tal, *Worlds of Hurt: Reading the Literatures of Trauma* (New York: Cambridge University Press, 1996). For a rebuttal of this constellation of criticism, see Dominick LaCapra, "Trauma, Absence, Loss," *Critical Inquiry* 25, no. 4 (Summer 1999): 696–727.

22. Marianne Hirsch, "The Generation of Postmemory," *Poetics Today* 29, no. 1 (Spring 2008): 103. See also Marianne Hirsch, "Family Pictures: *Maus*, Morning, and Post-Memory," *Discourse* 15, no. 2 (Winter 1992–93): 3–29; and Marianne Hirsch, *Family Frames: Photography, Narrative, and Postmemory* (Cambridge, MA: Cambridge University Press, 1997).

23. Art Spiegelman, *Maus II: A Survivor's Tale: And Here My Troubles Began* (New York: Pantheon, 1992), 44.

24. Hirsch, "The Generation of Postmemory," 107.

11 · "COFFINS AFTER COFFINS"

Screening Wartime
Atrocity in the Classroom

REBECCA A. ADELMAN

In the spring of 2004, a number of American high-school teachers were reprimanded for pedagogical choices that seemed to demonstrate poor judgment about the visual. A Massachusetts current-events teacher was briefly removed from his classroom after assigning his students to view and write about the Abu Ghraib photos; he was subsequently reinstated after the American Civil Liberties Union (ACLU) intervened on his behalf. In Texas, two teachers were suspended for the remainder of the school year after showing their classes the Internet video of the beheading of Nicholas Berg. Similar screenings were reported in high schools across the country (including one, allegedly, during a pizza party). All such screenings caused controversy in their communities, with the stories following a common pattern in which teachers expose their students to this troublesome content, parents become concerned and complain, and school administrators reproof or censure the teachers. But the debate over educators' judgment and students' maturity distracts from the rights of the people pictured in the images and obfuscates the real significance of these visual events and the kinds of spectators and citizens they train students to be.

For concerned parents or anxious school administrators, the main worry is that the teachers forced the students to confront graphic images for which they might not be intellectually or emotionally prepared. But those perspectives overlook the visual complexities of each document of wartime atrocity and recast scattered spectatorial events as an epidemic of bad teacherly decisions about pictures. Although the superficial similarities between these controversies might overshadow their incommensurability, the torture at Abu Ghraib and the politically motivated murder of Nicholas Berg are not comparable violences. Consequently, the goal of this paper is not to compare the specific classroom screenings and resultant controversies or to assess the motives of the teachers who orchestrated them or to simply judge whether these images are appropriate for classroom use. Nor am I suggesting that everything should be shown; rather, I am hoping to make the case that there is much more at stake than what American teenagers see. Following Ariella Azoulay's call to rethink photography as a dynamic "encounter" between myriad "protagonists,"[1] I want to account for the various forms of agency, empowerment, and violence operative in these educational visual cultures. Consequently, I explore the implications of this kind of educational display and student spectatorship and consider the relationships they establish between teachers, students, and the subjects of the images they viewed together.

Focusing narrowly on the rights of the teachers or students establishes a problematic hierarchy of entitlement that cannot account for the messy ethics of looking at images of atrocity, while an emphasis on the vulnerability of the students risks crowding out other, arguably more important, questions about the subjectivity of the people pictured in the images or the accountabilities that students as spectators might have to them. Predominant media accounts of what transpired in these classrooms mislead by stabilizing the meaning of the images, defining them only by their putative graphicness and wrangling over who should have visual access to it. But graphicness is not a self-evident property of an image. It is relative and context dependent; Barbie Zelizer contends that it is a "moveable, serviceable, and debatable convention, dependent on those who invoke it and for which aim."[2] Far more significant than the question of whether or not students should see (or teachers should be allowed to show) "graphic" wartime images in class is the matter of who assumes the authority to decide what images are graphic, or unacceptably so. Hence, the far more important project is trying to recapture what gets lost in the process, like the specificities of the harm that such images document and the status of the people it befalls within their frames. While most observers were preoccupied by the notion that students would not be able to cope with the sight of such violence and suffering, I suggest that the more urgent questions are whether they would be able to apprehend the significance of what they are seeing and to empathize with the people at whom they are looking.

Debates around these screenings of atrocity images tend not to account for these issues, oscillating in their focus between the rights of the teachers or the status of the students, a constricted vision of citizenship that reinscribes certain blindnesses bound to privilege, a narrative of risk that defines Americanness in terms of vulnerability. This chapter proposes an alternate view of these adolescent spectatorships. I begin by providing a brief account of the visual cultures of Abu Ghraib and the beheading of Nicholas Berg. From there, I consider the dilemmas inherent in the process of turning these images into objects of study in the high-school classroom and attend more specifically to the 2004 visual controversies. Common justifications for such displays include assertions that they are necessary for increasing students' civic and media literacies; I critique the latter premise directly, exploring the insufficiencies of the media literacy model for deciphering images of atrocity. I subsequently reconsider the scandalous classroom screenings, exploring the unnecessary antagonisms that they generated between students, teachers, and the community, and demonstrating the inadequacy of the free-speech paradigm for conceptualizing the teachers' behavior. I conclude by offering a range of suggestions for engaging images of atrocity differently and responsibly in the classroom, strategies that encourage students to consider their own status as spectators and practical steps toward the cultivation of spectatorial habits attentive and responsive to the ethical complexities of militarized looking at suffering bodies.

JUST ANOTHER STORY, DIMLY REMEMBERED: ON ABU GHRAIB AND THE BEHEADING OF NICHOLAS BERG

The spring of 2004 was an extended public-relations nightmare for the Bush administration, as a series of image scandals seemed to contradict all of its assertions about the necessity, progress, and justness of its Global War on Terror. Prior to this, the most visible images of the war—like the endless loop of footage from the September 11 attacks, the abstracted violence of Shock and Awe in March 2003, and the coverage offered by embedded journalists—had been relatively easy to manage (and noncontroversially adaptable for classroom use), even if they were violent, graphic, or frightening. But then there was the battle of Fallujah and subsequent photos of the charred bodies of American contractors; Ted Koppel's roll call of the American war dead; the release of the so-called coffin photos of the flag-draped remains of American military casualties returning to Dover Air Force Base; the revelation of torture at Abu Ghraib and the photos that illustrated it; and rabid circulation of the Internet video showing Nicholas Berg being beheaded. All of these images threatened to undermine public faith in the "mission" that had already gone on eleven months beyond the declaration that it had been "accomplished" on May 1, 2003; by this point, public opinion was beginning to turn against the war.[3] In this context, the images aggregated into a visual environment that forced American spectators to confront new and potentially disturbing sights on a regular basis and to reconcile them somehow with extant visual and ideological paradigms.

Prior to the spring of 2004, perhaps the greatest visual controversy of the war was that surrounding the suppressed photos of the people falling from the World Trade Center towers, most famously Richard Drew's *Falling Man*. If most of the images from September 11 and the early phases of the War on Terror were arresting, they were also rather discursively uncomplicated, with the stark exception of this image. If other photos from that day were readily assimilated into what

Karen Engle describes as "patriotic or hopeful narratives," this photo bespoke nothing but "uncertainty and death."[4] Widely circulated on the day after September 11, but then speedily and thoroughly excised from most popular news media, the photo quickly acquired a status Engle compares to pornography, as it circulated primarily through less-legitimate channels; moreover, she writes, because viewers now had to seek it out to find it, the visual curiosity that motivated those searches seemed "lewd" or prurient.[5]

Indeed, in the case of the falling man, news agencies seemed to take for granted that to look at him would be tantamount to a violation, that perhaps the picture should not have been taken in the first place. At the same time, many commentators suggested that looking at the falling man might have been a profoundly unsettling or disorienting experience for the spectators themselves. Susan Lurie argued that Americans had a tendency to "predicate embodied national strength on difference from rather than vengeful identification with the intolerably vulnerable, trapped, and falling figures," while David Friend surmised that the controversy was elicited in part because "because the viewer saw himself too clearly in the frame: a man who had been propelled to his death for having chosen to go to work that morning in an American office building."[6] All of this amounted to a widely accepted prohibition on circulating or looking at the image (Drew himself describes it as "'the most famous picture nobody's ever seen'"[7]), which was quite the opposite impulse than that which was generated by the initial revelation of the Abu Ghraib photos.

The first Abu Ghraib photographs appeared before the American public on April 28, 2004, in a story on *60 Minutes II*. Almost immediately, they became iconic and ubiquitous, and for a time, it seemed that these scenes of American military personnel presiding over tableaus of debasement and sexualized torture might prove fatally damaging to the Bush administration or its war effort. But once the official apologies were blandly issued, the few token punishments were meted out, and sufficient time passed, Abu Ghraib receded from public view, memory, and concern. It barely even registered, as Nicholas Mirzoeff observes, as a factor in the 2004 presidential election.[8] Before the attention dissipated though, Abu Ghraib provoked a range of questions about the facts of what had happened and how, about the legal status of the prisoners and the abuse they had suffered, about the culpability of their torturers and the people who commanded them. But beyond these relatively straightforward issues, there were abiding uncertainties about the significance of the photographs and what they depicted, what they meant and how they mattered.[9]

Images of atrocity are uniquely, and sometimes contradictorily, generative; Elizabeth Dauphinée observes that because their meanings are not inherently stable, "the image of the body in pain animates and makes possible a whole host of political activities, from torture to military intervention to anti-war activities to critical social science scholarship."[10] The photos from Abu Ghraib dramatized this potentiality vividly, as they traveled across institutions and discourses. Various critics have extrapolated from the images theories about the vapidness of contemporary American culture,[11] or the cravenness of the state, or the wantonness of the military as a whole.[12] Searching for causal explanations, authors have attributed the torture to everything from video games to homophobia in the American military, though in the process of querying the significance of the photos for American culture, the non-American bodies in them often got lost.

Appearing as they did at the end of a series of visual scandals, the images of Berg's beheading "surfaced in a context already filled with contradictory images offering alternate interpretive cues about the war's direction, legitimacy, and salience."[13] However, because the story broke at the peak of the debate about Abu Ghraib, the two visual events seemed to form a kind of intertext, each inflecting the interpretation of the other. The American public had been familiarized with the new genre of the beheading through the story of Daniel Pearl in February 2002, but Berg's death was far more visible.[14] Whereas news organizations treaded carefully around the grisly details of Pearl's beheading, the Berg video was widely available on the Internet before any news organizations reported it. While those institutions "scrambled" to figure out how to handle the video of Berg's execution, scores of people were already viewing it independently, underscoring the extent to which the public's news-gathering habits had changed to favor the digital,[15] and Berg's beheading became the second-most-popular search on the internet in May 2004, after *American Idol*.[16] Moreover, his killers filmed his death with a global audience in mind. While the centerpiece was his decapitation, it was not merely a happenstance recording: as Zelizer describes it, "this formulaic video used fade-ins and full motion graphics referencing Palestinian refugee camps, 9/11 and other images central to Islamic fundamentalism."[17] As was the case with Abu Ghraib, what initially registered as a radically disruptive visual event ultimately amounted to very little. For a moment, the beheading seemed to encapsulate the full brutality of warfare, but as Julia Kristeva observes about the new trend of mass-mediated beheadings, "global opinion, initially shocked, eventually shuts its eyes" as this form of violence starts to seem commonplace, merely endemic to certain regions and conflicts.[18] Over the coming months, Berg's death became just another story, dimly remembered.

While many spectators seemed unsure about the true or full significance of the Abu Ghraib photographs, there was very little equivocation about how vividly the beheading of Nicholas Berg testified to the depravity of the enemy. Although some curious observers questioned the authenticity of the video and others tried to assert that it was not an equivalent event to Abu Ghraib,[19] these challenges did not really amount to much. There is something singularly unnerving about the visual documentation of death; for Vivian Sobchack, the "representation of the event of death is an indexical sign of that which is always in excess of representation and beyond the limits of coding and culture. Death confounds all codes."[20] But spectators nonetheless try to make sense of what they see within extant paradigms. And so while Berg's circumstances were far more complicated than those of his predecessor Daniel Pearl, narratives about his innocence gained traction through the generic and visual similarities between his beheading and Pearl's. This made it easier for the beheading to serve, discursively, as a belated exoneration for what had happened at Abu Ghraib.[21]

Against the common assertion that the torture at Abu Ghraib and the beheading of Nicholas Berg were comparable, or that they somehow cancelled each other out, Lila Rajiva makes the provocative claim, "The stories are clearly in entirely different classes of newsworthiness and political importance. The Berg story was a single killing while the prison story involved the detention and ill treatment of tens of thousands . . . as well as the torture or killing of several hundreds of civilians in a country ravaged by the most powerful state in history."[22]

Both are documents of atrocity, but positing an equivalence between them partakes of a grim calculus that accepts dozens of torture victims in trade for one American life as if such a thing could be measured. Certainly, there are superficial connections between the images: the men who murdered Berg explicitly claimed their actions as retribution for Abu Ghraib, while both the perpetrators at Abu Ghraib and the masked assassins who killed Berg apparently realized the staggering power of images. But the initial intended audiences for the Abu Ghraib and Berg videos were different, and even more important than the content of the images is how they circulated and who sought to repurpose them.

Both sets of images were targets of intense regulation as various actors— including the US government, news agencies, and even high-school teachers— tried to control public access to them, their circulation, and the debates about their meaning. In its confrontation with the Abu Ghraib images, the US government variously sought to censor them, to disavow them, and to apologize for them. News agencies have made decisions about whether and how to republish them, choosing which photos to use, appending disclaimers to warn spectators about their graphic content, or modifying the images themselves by pixelizing or otherwise digitally obscuring the faces or genitals of the detainees. While these modifications might be concessions to the sensibilities of American spectators, they do not protect the detainees in any significant way, rendering them visible only as abused bodies rather than full human subjects. More broadly, many different individuals and institutions have sought to exercise discursive control over the images, asserting their authority to determine what they mean and whether or how they matter.

Relative to the discursive, political, and epistemological crises provoked by Abu Ghraib, the Nicholas Berg video was easily managed and cohered readily with post-September 11 images and narratives of American victimization and injury. As Dora Apel recalls, "Many Americans, in a form of circular reasoning, · pointed to the images of Fallujah and to the videotaped murders of Americans such as Daniel Pearl and Nick Berg, to suggest that such images and the events they represented constituted reasons for continued occupation and war."[23] With these logical feats accomplished, the only decisions left to be made were about whether and how to show them; it simply became a matter of editorial decision making. In 2002, most networks made an "easy call" not to show footage of the beheading of Daniel Pearl; CBS showed a segment of the tape before the execution itself and was roundly condemned for doing so.[24] Just over two years later, perhaps because so many other searing images had appeared in the interim, all major television news outlets showed footage from the Berg video, usually, as Susan Moeller notes, editing it just "up to the moments of his execution."[25] Ultimately, efforts by the American media to censor graphic combat images are often, in Jan Mieszkowski's terms, "largely symbolic," because curious spectators can simply find the unredacted images through European media, Al Jazeera, or quick Internet searches.[26]

Neither set of images in question here is transparently or self-evidently meaningful; their import varies by context and audience. For this reason, it may be impossible to ever fully understand or finally interpret them; there is no stable meaning to discover. Instead, we might ask how they are used, how they are circulated, and how they are made to mean. W. J. T. Mitchell reminds us, "Images are certainly not powerless, but they may be a lot weaker than we think. The problem is to refine and complicate our estimate of their power and the way it works."[27] In the high schools where teachers showed the photos from Abu Ghraib and the video of Nicholas Berg, everyone seemed to agree in advance that the images were overwhelmingly powerful in myriad ways, that they demanded to be shown, that the teachers were compelled or obligated to display them, that the students were defenseless against them. Participating in this fiction about the omnipotence of the images requires ceding human agency to these documents of atrocity and obscures a dense and tangled network of relationships in the process, refusing to acknowledge the way the classrooms function as vectors in the visual landscape of the Global War on Terror. This conceptualization of teachers as mere transmitters of the images and students as passive consumers of them promotes an oddly helpless vision of citizenship in which Americans are assailed by grisly images at which they can do nothing but look.

FROM DOCUMENTS OF ATROCITY
TO OBJECTS OF KNOWLEDGE

None of the news stories offered any indication that students were discomfited by what they saw in these spring 2004 lessons. Brian Newark, who taught in Bellingham, Massachusetts, assigned his students to log onto either CNN or MSNBC to look at the Abu Ghraib archive. He reported allowing students to choose whether or not to participate and insisted that he gave them the option of an alternative assignment and none took it. Still, a parent complained, and the high school responded by barring him from teaching his (apparently very popular) current-events class in the fall. With the support of the ACLU, he sued on the grounds that being thus prohibited was a violation of his civil liberties; he won and was reinstated to his classroom in a decision deemed a victory for free speech.[28] This ruling was made, ostensibly, to protect Newark's rights to show these images as a form of protected speech (or, perhaps indirectly, on the basis of a claim that the students had a right to see them). However, such a paradigm cannot account for the rights of the people pictured in the images, so that citizenship in this case is predicated on their supersession, while the discourse of free speech resignified the harms in question to prioritize the transgression against Newark. In *Frames of War*, Judith Butler explores the way in which certain human lives are "framed" in discourse as being valuable, and hence certain deaths are deemed grievable or not—this is a legal manifestation of this process and a misallocation of sympathy onto Newark and off of the tortured people whose pictures he insisted on circulating.

Whereas this Abu Ghraib controversy was apparently isolated, there were widespread accounts of teachers showing the Berg beheading.[29] A Google search turned up instances in California, North Carolina, Nebraska, Pennsylvania, Alabama, Washington, South Dakota, Oklahoma, Ohio, and Canada. The case of Michelle White and Andy Gebert, both teachers in Justin, Texas, garnered the most attention. The special assistant to the superintendent for their school district opined that "these staff members exercised poor judgment," by choosing to expose their students to this imagery.[30] Suspended for the remainder of the school year, they wrote apology letters to parents, while the *Washington Times* reported that they got the video from their students and that the teachers themselves were sent to counseling (for what, precisely, is unclear).[31] All of these controversies have in common a narrow focus on students' feelings and teachers' actions, to the exclusion of the rights of the people at whom they are looking and against a collaborative vision of education in the classroom.

The teachers who assigned the Abu Ghraib and Nicholas Berg images took for granted, apparently, their status as objects of knowledge, their capacity to convey some kind of bodily truth about the war. But the images are not inherently pedagogical; someone must endow them with that capacity, designate them as such. And if the goal was simply to get students to see the images, to engage visually with "current events" (a weirdly apolitical name for the present), then the project of utilizing spectatorship as a potential mode of political engagement was left incomplete. Indeed, even if the intent was to cultivate care or empathy among the students, simply having them look at the images is no guarantee of that outcome; course content that is affectively or visually difficult "is often met," as Jessica Heybach comments, "with profound silence, guilt, and defensiveness rather than understanding."[32] Observing that we already know how to manipulate images and to be cynical about the suffering they show, Susie Linfield laments that "what we have lost is the capacity to *respond* to photographs, especially those of political violence, as citizens who seek to learn something from them and connect to others through them."[33] Simply displaying the images as things students ought to recognize does nothing restore the rights of the people pictured within the photos nor to remedy the social and political conditions that deprive us of such a capacity.

Worrying excessively about harm done to students overemphasizes their vulnerability. This concern is well-intentioned, but specious because of their proximity to adulthood and, more importantly, their status as American citizens, which places them in a privileged position relative to the detainees at Abu Ghraib and most of the suffering others at whom they will look. Emphasis on student vulnerability rearticulates a post-September 11 fantasy of generalized American vulnerability, re-centering American suffering—which is always framed agonistically, exclusively, and superlatively—at a visual moment when it was threatened with eclipse. As Don Pease argues, "The state's representation of a vulnerable civilian population in need of the protection of the state was fashioned in a relation of opposition to the captured Taliban and Iraqis who were subjected to the power of the state yet lacked the protection of their rights or liberties."[34] The relative privilege of American spectators, even pre-adult American spectators, over the detainees at Abu Ghraib makes it easy to objectify them and hence dismiss their suffering; on the other hand, the highly visible death of Nicholas Berg makes it easy to revert to the notion that all Americans are at risk.

The adolescent spectators in this case inhabit a liminal place, on the cusp of adulthood and the full citizenship linked to reaching the age of majority; their proximity to legal adulthood, though based on a somewhat arbitrary number, is a not insignificant variable.[35] Their technical status as children has legal implications and does raise questions about what kinds of reasoning and discernment can be expected of these students, what kinds of political subjectivities they can be said to have.[36] But citizenship is a matter of both rights and obligations, and there is not broad cultural consensus on what sort of either can be attributed to adolescents.[37] While all humans have a common vulnerability to violence by virtue of our mortality, children are uniquely helpless.[38] Adolescents have partially outgrown this, and so their agency is lopsided or uneven, but it is agency nonetheless. Even if they are not yet old enough to vote or serve in the military, they are already political subjects defined by much more than vulnerability.

Concern about the students overshadows the subjectivity of the people pictured within the images and the ethical and political status of the photos themselves. The images from Abu Ghraib are explicitly corporeal, and the teenage body is the locus of the intense cultural anxiety about the mismatch of physical maturity with emotional and cognitive inexperience, while the sexualized content of the photos resonates with common concerns over teenagers' exposure to violent or sexually explicit media. Realistically, because the Abu Ghraib photos are likely "the most widely circulated photographs ever made,"[39] it is unlikely that the students would have arrived at their current-events class being totally ignorant of them, but the comforting fiction that such obliviousness was possible might be difficult to relinquish.[40] Misplaced faith in the students' innocence obscures their agency and the geopolitical dynamics in which spectatorship enmeshes them. Because the images were created with the specific intent of humiliating and objectifying their subjects, they implicate the teenagers who view them and the teachers who display them in a thorny visual relationship. Article 13 of the Third Geneva Convention relating to the treatment of prisoners of war mandates that prisoners of war be shielded "against insults and public curiosity," and so recirculating these photos before a curious public, even one in need of education, places everyone at least a little askew from international law and the ethical precepts on which it is founded.[41]

Recirculating the Nicholas Berg video raises a slightly different set of ethical questions. Barbie Zelizer suggests that the discussion of what to do with beheading videos like Berg's "overwhelmed [their] capacity to visualize the war's brutality."[42] CBS News ran a story about classroom showings of the beheading and offered this commonsense observation that "the reality of course is none of the students needed a teacher to see the video."[43] But the likelihood that students would have already seen the video does not mean that showing it to them again is ethically uncomplicated or neutral. There are, as ever, the abiding questions about exposing young people to the sight of such gruesome violence, and the film likely would have been otherwise inscrutable to most of these students, as the killers read their statement in unsubtitled Arabic. But this is not the most important issue, as concern about the students' sensibilities risked crowding out consideration of Berg's privacy, which apparently did not figure in the public debate about the classroom screenings. The result is a vision of citizenship that is terrorized but also solipsistic, in which Americans (whether Berg himself in the video or spectators of it) are wantonly victimized and under no obligation to be self-reflexive about the cost of exercising their putative rights.

Susie Linfield characterizes scenes like Berg's beheading as "Abu Ghraib's mirror," an intensely reactive and hypervisual retribution marked by an "intimate relationship between the acts of violence and their documentation; it is hard to distinguish between the two."[44] These images do not only document violence, but also enact it and so implicate us in it. Consequently, spectatorship bears witness to that violence but also partakes of it as the lines between violence and image, reality and representation, are blurred. Berg's killers avowed: "The dignity of the Muslim men and women in Abu Ghraib and others is not redeemed except by blood and souls. . . . You will not receive anything from us but coffins after coffins . . . slaughtered the same way."[45] Classrooms thus become another institutional feature of this image landscape, sites where this visuality is propagated. Viewing such images means participating, howsoever passively, in their visual economy.

But the issue is not so much that students might be traumatized by these sights, or even that they would become inured to this sort of violence; rather, my concern is that there is no mechanism in these displays for promoting students to think through their relationships to them or to attend to the intricacies and obligations inherent in their roles as spectators. The possibility that classroom displays might encourage or vindicate careless looking—the kind of spectatorship that is passive, uncritical about the circumstances of consumption, unconcerned about the people whom it regards, and unwilling to explore connections to them—is the primary reason why they are profoundly questionable, essentially problematic. Even if the teachers had hoped to foster compassion (which was not a stated motivation in anything that I read), simply showing the images and asking the students to reflect on them does not guarantee it or excuse the decision to recirculate them. Dauphinée offers the important reminder that "the 'ethical' use of the imagery of torture and other atrocities is always in a state of absolute tension; the bodies in the photos are still exposed to our gaze in ways that render them abject, nameless, and humiliated—even when our goal is the use of that imagery to oppose their condition."[46]

Right intention alone does not justify making these photos available for scrutiny. One version of the story of Nicholas Berg in the classroom alleges that a teacher in Texas showed the beheading video during a pizza party.[47] This is obviously gratuitous, self-evidently unjustifiable, a perversion of the possibility that spectatorship can ever be ethically or politically meaningful. Azoulay writes that regarding photographs thoughtfully is a "civic skill,"[48] a notion that might be applied to spectatorship more generally; such a screening clearly does nothing to propagate it. Beyond the obvious reasons to critique this teacher's actions, they are worthy of comment because they are predicated, fundamentally, on a presumption of authority over, or even ownership of, these images. This notion, that mere access to the images entails some kind of entitlement to use them for any chosen purpose or in any circumstance ignores or disregards the possible rights claims of the people pictured within them. This presumption desperately needs to be undone.

As a companion to the *Frontline* documentary about Abu Ghraib, *The Torture Question*, PBS developed a lesson plan for grades nine through twelve, which I believe represents a semi-official approach to the images.[49] In this module, students watch the documentary and subsequently participate in a range of complementary activities, like reading the Geneva Conventions, deliberating about what counts as torture, and engaging in thought experiments about the sort of counterterrorism policies they would enact. The multipart curriculum is thoughtful and layered but does not include any structured invitation for students to reflect on their own status as spectators; insofar as the curriculum is concerned with questions of American and global citizenship, this omission suggests that there is no link between these different roles, when in fact they are intimately connected. There is a warning to teachers that the subject matter might be difficult and a statement that the photographs are "unquestionably repulsive," but no advice on how to talk about what that means. There are factual questions about how the photographs became public, a reference to "humiliation and ridicule" of prisoners, but no suggestion that students need to be introspective about looking or that teachers need to be self-reflexive about showing. Certainly, some teachers may be doing this work on their own, but the oversight in this prominent resource is telling.

While the PBS curriculum addresses images somewhat incidentally, media literacy as an educational paradigm focuses intently on spectatorship with the goal of training students to be critical consumers of images and texts circulated by mass media industries. Crusading against corporate control of images and information, proponents of media literacy endeavor to empower students as audience members and citizens who must be trained to decode images and so to uncover the stable or knowable truth presumably lodged within or behind them. Images, in this model, are understood as deceptive and powerful; students are instructed in how to outsmart them. The media-literacy model positions images as teachable objects; exemplary in this regard is Henry Giroux's work on education and Abu Ghraib. He suggests that the photos served as a stark counterpoint to the "mythic representations" of the war, and speaks of the necessity of "rendering them intelligible." We need an education, he asserts, that will train everyone to view them with a gaze that is not pornographic and ultimately inspires students to "dialogue," "dissent," and "agency" rather than mere visual consumerism.[50] Doubtless, there is much to be lauded about the media-literacy platform, and its critiques of the profit orientation of the news media and the complicity between media industries and the government are well-taken, especially in a context where the state often actively tries to obstruct citizens' access to potentially damaging images and to interfere in the rights of citizens to visually document what they see.[51]

While the media-literacy approach might be a potentially useful one for addressing images like those produced by embedded journalists under the aegis of the government, there are a number of problems with the media-literacy model as well, particularly around images of suffering. It encourages students to take a dubious stance toward images, which risks sliding into a dismissal of the suffering they see within them. It objectifies images as mere targets of inquiry and, relatedly, tends to overlook the rights of the people pictured within them. It situates the spectator as the most important agent, while also locating her as a victim, or potential victim of a deceitful media apparatus, instead of identifying the spectator as an active participant who occupies a sometimes problematic position in various visualities.[52] When spectators are children or students, they might seem even more like victims, particularly on questions of militarization, from which they seem to be exempt. J. Marshall Beier writes that in the discourse about children's participation in wartime national cultures, "complex subject positions collapsed into juridical categories and the rhetorically necessary construction of victimhood insisted on children's separation from politics and the denial of their agency."[53] In the case of high-school students viewing images like the ones in question here, these conceits are unsustainable. And so, as an alternative to media literacy, I propose a different objective: classroom enactment of the practice of ethical witnessing, which Wendy Kozol characterizes as "the process of critically engaging with the historical complexities of representing social violence, including the ways in which the viewer is implicated in those complexities."[54] All citizens, even young ones, are ensnared in this visualized violence, if only by their (perhaps unchosen) role as spectators to it; ethical witnessing requires moving beyond the simple consumption of images to consider the consequences of that very act.

Media discourse about the screenings generally presumes that the students would have been traumatized by the encounter with graphic depictions of torture by Americans or, alternately, the sight of an American being viciously murdered; either way, these stories are predicated on assumptions about lost innocence, and the conclusions are based on the need to manage the students' unpleasant feelings that might result. For example, the CBS News story took for granted that students would see wartime atrocity in the media; the journalist reframed the question as a matter of whether it was better for them to witness the "horrors of the war on terror" at school or at home (where, presumably, they could be better insulated from difficult realities). But what students see (or don't) is not the most important thing to consider here; the far more substantive issue is who they look at and how they understand and interpret—how they are *taught* to understand and interpret—these scenes. Contrary to prevalent depictions of them, the images in question are more than merely affronts to their senses.

Emphasizing the students' vulnerability primes these young people for two differently problematic forms of citizenship. Lorraine Macmillan analyzes the "many inconsistencies" about the militarization of childhood in Anglophone cultures, which allow students to be recruited and trained for future military service, encourage them to participate in nationalist projects, while fretting about the deleterious influence of violence in their lives (especially violence in mass media) more generally.[55] The emphasis on their vulnerability eclipses the suffering of others at whom they look, reducing it only to a threat to their own visual security. Relatedly, it underscores their susceptibility to danger while making it seem entirely random and apolitical. The idea that students might only or first encounter graphic representations of violence in the high-school classroom is comforting but unlikely, and the clamor to protect them from such images emphasizes their own fragility while also assuming (hoping?) that they would be sensitive enough to find it upsetting and that such unsettlement is an undesirable outcome. Against this perspective, Heybach argues for the importance of such "difficult knowledge" as an antidote for the "anesthetizing" and "desensitizing" visual culture outside of the classroom,[56] which underscores the need for a different kind of lesson.

RE-ENVISIONING VULNERABILITY

This is not to suggest that we should be unconcerned about students; rather, I argue that their vulnerability is the wrong place from which to begin their education. The preoccupation with students' fragility is rooted in a deeply flawed assumption of equivalence between their spectatorial suffering and the bodily, often mortal suffering to which they bear witness. Prioritizing their susceptibility to visual harm also establishes a host of agonistic relationships and defines their citizenship in solipsistic terms. The Americanness of the perpetrators in the Abu Ghraib photos imbues them with the potential to be even more politically traumatic, as the teenage students will encounter this brutality when they are on the verge of becoming full citizens; it is reasonable to assume, therefore, that part of the anxiety about their exposure to such sights is rooted in concern about the effect they will have on the political perspectives of the students. Lauren Berlant writes of "infantile citizenship" as a favored mode of participation in the US nation-state; infantile citizens are naive and loyal, loving their nation like they do their parents, while also clinging to a vision of its goodness.[57] In the narratives of infantile citizenship that Berlant describes, the fledgling citizen always encounters some sort of revelation of the nation-state's imperfection; crucial to the fetishization of infantile citizenship, however, is the idea that it is so pure and genuine that even after this potential crisis, it can be restored to its original earnestness and intensity. Cultural concern over the sight of militarized violence in the classroom is rooted in worry about the tenuousness of the students' protocitizenship, a fear that it can be visually undone. Preemptively, then, the blame for this potential undoing is foisted onto the teachers who showed the images, and onto the images themselves.

Simultaneously, it presumes that students' responses to the sights of torture or beheading would be negative or unpleasant. Many young people regularly, habitually consume media that "disembody" war and violence, that encourage them to see these phenomena as spectacularly intense.[58] Worrying that students might be overwhelmed by the documentary evidence of violence ignores the possibility that they might feel nothing at the sight of it and denies the chance that they might feel a kind of pleasure. It presumes that they are already compassionate, empathetic to a fault. But the history of photography is crowded with examples of the failure of even the most searing images to stir compassion. Photography has made violence visible, but Linfield underscores "just how limited and inadequate such exposure is: seeing does not necessarily translate into believing, caring, or acting."[59] Even if high-school students are disturbed by what they see, that perturbation can be teachable; we need, as Kozol argues, to move beyond our instinctive "recoil" at graphic images, to think about its mechanisms and implications.[60]

The widespread concern with student vulnerability establishes an agonistic relationship between them and their teachers, a framework within which teachers wield the images that harm their students. In some ways, this narrative exaggerates educators' power, making them the primary source of the images and the arbiters of what students see. At the same time, by positing that the teachers function only to display the images (and students act only to consume them), this interpretation of the events also understates their function as agents and subjects within these militarized visual cultures, as they invest and reinvest the images with meaning every time they invoke them in the classroom. In such a model, the solution starts to look bureaucratic, a matter of better teacher training, as opposed to highlighting the need for a critical reevaluation of the role of images in the classroom. At the same time, orientation toward the students places teachers and their communities at odds, with each faction trying to demonstrate their superior concern for the children.[61] From the perspective of the teachers and their advocates, it becomes a matter of free speech exercised or impeded, so that the images become little more than instruments in this grander drama.

Most troublingly, this configuration places students in an antagonistic relationship to the images, which risks devolving into a lack of concern with or even enmity for the people pictured within them. In a context where teachers are reprimanded for showing such pictures, images are refigured as weapons with the capacity to unsettle or unnerve students and interrupt their progression toward uncomplicatedly patriotic adult citizenship.[62] The images are recast as obstacles, the people pictured within them rendered incidental or perhaps the cause of all the unpleasantness; they are never recognized as victims or subjects. Ultimately, this approach excludes students' feelings from the realm of the pedagogically relevant or the domain of the teachable, rather than integrating a consideration of those feelings into the curriculum itself with an eye toward critical reconsideration of spectatorship and the nature of their discomfort. It ignores the possibility that discomfort can be instructive for students and teachers alike.[63] The greatest risk inherent in showing these images in such an educational regime is reinforcing the idea that the most important thing about them is how they make students feel, with the implied corollary that they should never have to feel anything unpleasant.[64]These controversies place free speech in a predicament, situating the classroom as its limit case rather than the site where it is most crucial, thus limiting its potential to introduce students to lively participation in the messiness and complexity of democracy in the contemporary moment. While education has long been a realm of contestation about the limits of free speech, these dilemmas are particularly acute in the context of the Global War on Terror. Elisabeth Anker traces out what she believes to be a "key paradox" of the post-September 11 political landscape: "In the name of freedom and liberty, many Americans legitimated violence, coercion and surveillance over others as well as themselves, and circumscribed their own already restricted access to political power. These expansions in state power often worked at the very expense of the civic participation of the people who authorized them."[65]

She continues that the solution to this dilemma requires more than the "attempt to experience individual mastery over lived experiences of social powerlessness,"[66] more, therefore, than remedying it at the level of individual students, teachers, or classrooms. It entails a broader rethinking of the conditions and consequences of that powerlessness, considering how it is dramatized and reinforced by difficult images.

A simple defense of free speech is not a resolution; it simply privileges the rights of the already privileged, rather than foregrounding a network of vulnerabilities and complicities. As Pease contends in his analysis of the debasing photographs of detainees released from Guantanamo Bay, "The state proffered this spectacle of sublegal persons being stripped of all rights and liberties as symbolic compensation for the Patriot Act's drastic abridgement of civil liberties."[67] Free speech is critically important in its own right; it just might not be the most important thing here. Of course, it is cause for concern that, as Charles Garoian and Yvonne Gaudelius report, more and more young adults say they support restrictions on free speech during wartime and in general.[68] But stridently defending free speech, carelessly enacting it, will do nothing to reverse that trend. "In most cases," as Ariella Azoulay demonstrates, "the struggle over the right to see disavows the duty to behave as spectators and by this spectatorship to criticize government power, reflect on its actions, and impose constraints."[69] In these cases, the particular struggle over the right to show such images might actually undermine the cause of free speech more broadly.

The most potentially productive lesson to be drawn from the Abu Ghraib and Berg images is their illustration of the common vulnerabilities between students, teachers, and the people pictured within them. There is the simple, biological fact that all humans are vulnerable to violence, and the political one that all citizens (particularly in conditions of militarization) are vulnerable to having their rights radically impinged. But the limited defense of teachers' free speech establishes an agonistic paradigm for understanding the circulation and consumption of images. The same is true of a pedagogy of media literacy, which simply emphasizes our own disempowerment and a more individualized form of agency. It may be difficult to get high-school students to apprehend, in Judith Butler's terms, "our radical substitutability and anonymity in relation both to certain socially facilitated modes of dying and death and to other socially conditioned modes of persisting and flourishing."[70] But it may be possible to lay the groundwork for that potentially radical revelation, to read the images as documents of that common human precariousness, rather than an imagined singular vulnerability unique to the students or Americans in general. For, as Sharon Sliwinski optimistically conjectures, "the circulation of representations of distant events creates a virtual community between spectators and, moreover . . . this virtual community . . . is one location where the ideal of a shared humanity literally comes into view."[71]

TEACHING OUT OF THE THRALL

To conclude, I want to offer some pedagogical strategies for engaging atrocity images in ways that are more politically productive and ethically nuanced.[72] Crucially, this pedagogy must address questions of photography and violence together. Media literacy tends to isolate pictures from their material referents, while the myopic focus on questions like what constitutes torture or what might motivate someone to beheading obscures the essential role of the visual in those events. Increasingly, militarization and the visual are overlaid and co-constitutive, and so must be thought together.[73] This requires a direct confrontation with the exceedingly complex social and ethical relationships that photography ushers in. In Azoulay's words, "The capacity to look can no longer be seen as a personal property, but is a complex field of relations that originally stems from the fact that photography made available to the individual possibilities of seeing more than his or her eye alone could see, in terms of scope, distance, time, speed, quantity, clarity, and so on."[74] Beyond inviting students to make sense of single atrocities, such teaching might help prepare them for a lifetime of engaged spectatorship.

This might begin with querying of spectatorship itself, before anyone looks at anything, so students might understand that, as Kelly Oliver asserts, "Seeing is an activity that like any other brings with it responsibilities. When it involves other human beings, then it brings with it ethical, social, and political responsibilities."[75] Students need to think, in a sustained way, about what those might be. Teachers can facilitate a critical and candid discussion of students' spectatorship, its conditions and consequences. Before showing atrocity images, teachers might ask whether students have seen them before, under which circumstances, and what enabled them to look; a consideration of the role of electronic media would necessarily be part of this discussion. Students could verbalize how the images made them feel; teachers could ask them why that matters.

With that background in place, conversation could turn to the specific images in question. Teaching early undergraduates, I have often asked them to consider a photograph and list all the various actors who have a stake in it, from the person being represented to the photographer who took it and the editor who will eventually publish it and the advertisers who will underwrite wherever it appears, and so on. Invariably, students are surprised at the tabulation of how many actors are involved and how relatively powerless the actual subjects of the images are. By attending more to the vulnerability of the other, students can begin to think about what it means to be photographed in duress, rather than focusing on their own unease. This is key because, as Carrie Rentschler asserts, "Victim identity allows people to claim their own sense of injury . . . in a way that forecloses their own accountability for the violence they help perpetrate, often unknowingly, but not always."[76] In her course on photography and writing, Janet Zandy describes the process of working toward the goal of cultivating in her students "a double-seeing—a consciousness of the past in the present—and a self-consciousness about not participating in a voyeuristic pornography of violence."[77] Tracing out the various agents involved in every image might help demystify those relationships and so prevent students from stepping too carelessly into the role of spectator or severing that role from its political context.

Another possibility would be to have the class decide, collectively and intentionally, whether they ought to view such images in the classroom. In a high-school setting, teachers might have ultimate authority and may rightfully use their judgment to make the final decision about what happens. Such a decision would not preclude, however, giving students the opportunity to comment on it, for example, by writing an essay in which they reflect on the educational experience and their peers' spectatorship, and then argue for or against the use of such images in the classroom in light of this evidence. If everyone agrees that looking is necessary and valuable, it should be done in such a way that, as Sliwinski puts it, "the spectator is allotted a fragile but critical task: that of judgment," of reasoning about what they see, how they are implicated in it, and what to do with that new awareness.[78] It is important nonetheless to encourage students to conceptualize spectatorship as a matter of choice rather than accident and so to reflect on all the responsibilities that attend it while debating questions of access and visual entitlement.

If the teacher does decide to show the images, subsequent looking ought to be a matter of individual choice. Before displaying the photos or screening the video, teachers might ask students to anticipate what they are going to see, decide whether or not to look, and then justify their choice. Subsequent questions could encourage students to consider who their looking affects and how, and also how they themselves might be changed by the sight; these questions could be posed again after students have acted on their choice to look (or not). Shoshana Felman claims that "the burden of the witness—in spite of his or her alignment with other witnesses—is a radically unique, noninterchangeable and solitary burden."[79] Students need a chance to think about whether or not to assume it, and to be reminded that they make these sorts of decisions all the time, often unthinkingly. Moreover, slowing down and disassembling the act of looking might help to defuse that problematic frisson that spectators sometimes experience at the sight of violence.

Such teaching is not so much a matter of deciphering the pictures as objects of knowledge, but a process of articulating students' positions with respect to them. Most adolescents are likely to be cognitively equipped to participate in this kind of reasoning; ideally, they would begin from that self-reflexive place and move beyond it. In his brilliant and haunting reflection on the relationship between education and Auschwitz, Theodor Adorno states simply, "The only education that has any sense at all is an education toward critical self-reflection."[80] This is the foundation for a meaningful and ethical engagement with the image; after all, as Sliwinksi argues, "The photograph is the exemplary site for encountering the painful labour of facing responsibility to others and the world."[81] The work begins with naming what that is. As war becomes increasingly and essentially a visual phenomenon, students will be required, continually, to partake in this kind of reasoning, especially if they end up actually fighting these battles. Minimally, they need to be aware of their status as visual consumers, to understand that their choices are constrained but are choices nonetheless. The grim and likely possibility is that students will confront a visual landscape populated with "coffins after coffins," for the foreseeable future. Consequently, they will need to know how to look at them, which requires first finding a vantage outside of their thrall.

NOTES

1. Ariella Azoulay, "What Is a Photograph? What Is Photography?," *Philosophy of Photography* 1 (2010): 9–14.

2. Barbie Zelizer, *About to Die: How News Images Move the Public* (New York: Oxford University Press, 2012): 22.

3. Pew Research Center, "Public Attitudes Toward the War in Iraq, 2003–2008," March 19, 2008, http://www.pewresearch.org/2008/03/19/public-attitudes-toward-the-war-in-iraq -20032008/.

4. Karen Engle, *Seeing Ghosts: 9/11 and the Visual Imagination* (Montreal: McGill-Queen's University Press, 2009), 47. Chapter 2 is a detailed consideration of the various visual lives of this figure.

5. Ibid., 31, 30.

6. Susan Lurie, "Falling Persons and National Embodiment: The Reconstruction of Safe Spectatorship in the Photographic Record of 9/11," in *Terror, Culture, Politics: Rethinking 9/11,* ed. Daniel J. Sherman and Terry Nardin (Bloomington: University of Indiana Press, 2006), 50; David Friend, *Watching the World Change: The Stories Behind the Images of 9/11* (New York: Picador, 2011), 140.

7. Quoted in Friend, *Watching the World Change,* 136. Certainly, it's possible that images of these 9/11 casualties made their way into American classrooms, but my searches yielded no stories about a resultant controversy, which suggests that the implicit and explicit prohibitions around these images had some effect.

8. Nicholas Mirzoeff, "Invisible Empire: Visual Culture, Embodied Spectacle," *Radical History Review* 95 (2006): 21–44.

9. Part of the difficulty of interpreting the images, as Peggy Phelan notes, is that they appeared in multiple contexts, and their meaning varied accordingly. Peggy Phelan, "Atrocity and Action: The Performative Force of the Abu Ghraib Photographs," in *Picturing Atrocity: Photography in Crisis*, ed. Geoffrey Batchen et al. (London: Reaktion Books, 2012), 54.

10. Elisabeth Dauphinée, "The Politics of the Body in Pain: Reading the Ethics of Imagery," *Security Dialogue* 38, no. 2 (2007): 139–155.

11. See, for example, Kelly Oliver, "Innocence, Perversion, and Abu Ghraib," *Philosophy Today* 19, no. 53 (2007): 343–56.

12. See, for example, Elizabeth L. Hillman, "Guarding Women: Abu Ghraib and Military Sexual Culture," in *One of the Guys: Women as Aggressors and Torturers*, ed. Tara McKelvey (Emeryville, CA: Seal Press, 2007); Lila Rajiva, "The Military Made Me Do It: Double Standards and Psychic Injuries at Abu Ghraib," in McKelvey, *One of the Guys*.

13. Zelizer, *About to Die*, 284.

14. It also seemed to inaugurate a whole slew of beheading videos that would be released in the subsequent months.

15. Zelizer, *About to Die*, 286.

16. Susan D. Moeller, *Packaging Terrorism: Co-Opting the News for Politics and Profit* (Malden, MA: Wiley-Blackwell, 2009), 160.

17. Zelizer, *About to Die*, 285.

18. Julia Kristeva, *The Severed Head*, trans. Jody Gladding (New York: Columbia University Press, 2012), 26. Comparing the contemporary media representations of beheadings to their sculptural predecessors, Kristeva notes that those had been "a meditation on the precariousness of their condition, which does not seem to faze modern warriors."

19. For an overview of these challenges, see Lila Rajiva, *The Language of Empire: Abu Ghraib and the American Media* (New York: Monthly Review Press, 2005), 56–60.

20. Vivian Sobchack, *Carnal Thoughts: Embodiment and Moving Image Culture* (Berkeley: University of California Press, 2004), 233.

21. Rajiva, *The Language of Empire*, 55–56. She writes, "The beheading immediately deflected attention from the burgeoning torture scandal and allowed apologists for the administration to claim that Abu Ghraib was fully justified by the barbarism of the enemy."

22. Ibid., 68.

23. Dora Apel, *War Culture and the Contest of Images* (New Brunswick: Rutgers University Press, 2012), 125.

24. Moeller, *Packaging Terrorism*, 156.

25. Ibid., 158–159.

26. Jan Mieszkowski, *Watching War* (Stanford: Stanford University Press, 2012), 100.

27. W. J. T. Mitchell, *What Do Pictures Want? The Lives and Loves of Images* (Chicago: The University of Chicago Press, 2005), 33.

28. Parenthetically, there is a confused element of this story that relates to the Berg video; the superintendent accused Newark of also assigning the Berg video, which Newark denies, while one parent from the community argued that he should have also assigned it in tandem with the Abu Ghraib images, to provide a more balanced view of wartime atrocity. For a detailed account, see Michael Kunzelman, "Teacher in Flap over Iraqi Prisoner Photos Files Lawsuit," *Milford Daily News*, August 24, 2004, http://www.milforddailynews.com/news/x349379805.

29. This lopsidedness is worthy of further investigation.

30. Quoted in Tal Barak, "Texas Teachers Are Suspended for Showing Video of Beheading," *Education Week*, May 26, 2004, 4.

31. Washington Times, "School Suspends Teachers for Video," *Washington Times*, May 20, 2004, http://www.washingtontimes.com/news/2004/may/20/20040520-115221-3528r/.

32. Jessica A. Heybach, "Learning to Feel What We See: Critical Aesthetics and 'Difficult Knowledge' in an Age of War," *Critical Questions in Education* 3, no. 1 (Winter 2012): 23–34.

33. Susie Linfield, *The Cruel Radiance: Photography and Political Violence* (Chicago: University of Chicago Press, 2012), 24.

34. Donald E. Pease, *The New American Exceptionalism*, (Minneapolis: University of Minnesota Press, 2009), 171. This vision also had the potential to reconcile one of the earliest spectatorial dilemmas of the War on Terror that was prompted by Richard Drew's photo of the September 11 "falling man." Describing the awkward position in which the photos placed American citizens, who might have wished simultaneously to identify with and distinguish themselves from this victim of the attacks, Susan Lurie writes, "Such tension between identification with and repudiation of 9/11's most horrifying sights—those of the trapped and falling people—is central to reconstruction of secure national identity after 9/11" ("Falling Persons and National Embodiment," 45). This ambivalence veers closest, perhaps, to what some spectators might have experienced in the encounter with the images from Abu Ghraib.

35. The age of the students here is significant, as the capacity for ethical deliberation and action varies by age, as does their relative vulnerability. For example, the visual assignments I consider here are qualitatively different than the assignment, reported in fall 2012, to have fourth-grade students draw their visions of the September 11 attacks. "9/11 Assignment Outrages Texas Elementary School Parents," ABC News, September 14, 2012, http://abcnews.go .com/US/video/911-assignment-outrages-texas-elementary-school-parents-17239839.

36. For more on the complexities of adolescence as it relates to militarization, see Anna M. Agathangelou and Kyle D. Killian, "(Neo)zones of Violence: Reconstructing Empire on the Bodies of Militarized Youth," in *The Militarization of Childhood: Thinking Beyond the Global South*, ed. J. Marshall Beier (New York: Palgrave Macmillan, 2011), 17–42.

37. I am especially appreciative of Chandra Talpade Mohanty's definition of citizenship: "that particular form of belonging to the nation-state that is based on rights, participation and obligations and anchored in historical geographies of racial and cultural identities," (Chandra Talpade Mohanty, "U.S. Empire and the Project of Women's Studies: Stories of Citizenship, Complicity, and Dissent," *Gender, Place, and Culture* 13, no. 1 (February 2006): 7–20).

38. Adriana Cavarero, *Horrorism: Naming Contemporary Violence*, trans. William McCuaig (New York: Columbia University Press, 2011), 20ff.

39. Linfield, *The Cruel Radiance*, 151. Other images of wartime atrocity have not acquired the same iconicity.

40. In the nine years intervening since the release of the Abu Ghraib photos, this may have changed. Anecdotally, it seems that increasing numbers of my undergraduates are unfamiliar with the story of what happened at Abu Ghraib and the resultant images. At the time, however, this would have been a difficult story to miss.

41. International Committee of the Red Cross, "Convention (III) relative to the Treatment of Prisoners of War, Geneva, August 12, 1949," 2012, http://www.icrc.org/ihl.nsf/FULL/375 ?OpenDocument.

42. Zelizer, *About to Die*, 291.

43. CBS / AP, "Berg Video Shown in Classrooms," CBS.com, December 5, 2007, http://www .cbsnews.com/2100-500257_162-616842.html.

44. Linfield, *The Cruel Radiance*, 162, 163.

45. Quoted in Maria Newman, "Video Appears to Show Beheading of American Civilian," *New York Times*, May 11, 2004, http://www.nytimes.com/2004/05/11/international/ middleeast/11CND-BEHE.html.

46. Dauphinée, "The Politics of the Body in Pain," 145.

47. "Teachers Disciplined for Showing Beheading," *New York Times*, May 24, 2004, http://www.nytimes.com/2004/05/24/us/teachers-disciplined-for-showing-beheading.html.

48. Ariella Azoulay, *The Civil Contract of Photography*, trans. Rela Mazali and Ruvik Daniell (New York: Zone Books, 2008), 14.

49. "Teacher Center—The Torture Question," *Frontline*, October 2005, http://www.pbs.org/wgbh/pages/frontline/teach/torture/hand2.html.

50. Henry A. Giroux, "From Auschwitz to Abu Ghraib: Rethinking Adorno's Politics of Education," in *Iraq War Cultures*, ed. Cynthia Fuchs and Joe Lockard (New York: Peter Lang, 2011): 182–185 passim.

51. On the final point, see Daniel Palmer and Jessica Whyte, "'No Credible Photographic Interest': Photography Restrictions and Surveillance in a Time of Terror," *Philosophy of Photography* 1, no. 2 (2010): 177–195.

52. For example, it overlooks the ways in which all citizens are hailed to do the work of surveillance; for more on this, see Louise Amoore, "Vigilant Visualities: The Watchful Politics of the War on Terror," *Security Dialogue* 38, no. 20 (June 2007): 215–232. In general, the media literacy model positions all spectators (especially but not exclusively young people) as victims, or at least potential victims, of deceptive images or manipulative image makers.

53. J. Marshall Beier, "Introduction: Everyday Zones of Militarization," in *The Militarization of Childhood: Thinking beyond the Global South*, ed. J. Marshall Beier (New York: Palgrave Macmillan, 2011), 6.

54. Wendy Kozol, "Battlefield Souvenirs and the Affective Politics of Recoil," *Photography and Culture* 5, no. 1 (March 2012): 21–36.

55. Lorraine Macmillan, "Militarized Children and Sovereign Power," in Beier, *The Militarization of Childhood*, 75.

56. Heybach, "Learning to Feel What We See," 23.

57. Lauren Berlant, *The Queen of America Goes to Washington City: Essays on Sex and Citizenship* (Durham, NC: Duke University Press, 1997), 27–28.

58. Lesley Copeland, "Mediated War: Imaginative Disembodiment and the Militarization of Childhood," in Beier, *The Militarization of Childhood*.

59. Linfield, *The Cruel Radiance*, 33.

60. Kozol, "Battlefield Souvenirs," 23.

61. In the university setting, cases like these are generally adjudicated in terms of "academic freedom." On the wartime complexities of this, see Richard Falk, "John Yoo, the Torture Memos, and Ward Churchill: Exploring the Outer Limits of Academic Freedom," in *Speaking about Torture*, ed. Julie A. Carlson and Elisabeth Weber (New York: Fordham University Press, 2012).

62. On the hostility toward people and things that disrupt the idealized happiness that seems to indicate peaceful coexistence with one's political context, see Sara Ahmed, *The Promise of Happiness* (Durham, NC: Duke University Press, 2010).

63. Heybach, "Learning to Feel What We See," 26.

64. Ann Cvetkovich offers a compelling defense of the potential personal and cultural importance of lingering in bad feelings. See *Depression: A Public Feeling* (Durham, NC: Duke University Press, 2012), 14.

65. Elisabeth Anker, "Heroic Identifications: Or 'You Can Love Me Too—I Am So Like the State," *Theory and Event* 15, no. 1 (March 2012): paragraph 1.

66. Ibid., paragraph 2.

67. Pease, *The New American Exceptionalism*, 184.

68. Charles R. Gaoroian and Yvonne M. Gaudelius, *Spectacle Pedagogy: Art, Politics, and Visual Culture* (Albany: SUNY Press, 2008), 84.

69. Azoulay, *The Civil Contract*, 343.

70. Judith Butler, *Frames of War: When Is Life Grievable?* (London: Verso, 2009), 14.

71. Sharon Sliwinski, *Human Rights in Camera* (Chicago: University of Chicago Press, 2011), 5.

72. For a consideration of engaging images of atrocity in the undergraduate classroom, and the vexed politics of transparency that surround such action, see my article, Rebecca A. Adelman, "Atrocity and Aporiae: Teaching the Abu Ghraib Images, Teaching against Transparency," *Cultural Studies<->Critical Methodologies* 14, no. 1 (February 2014): 29–39.

73. For a discussion of how such work might be accomplished in art education specifically, see David Darts, Kevin Tavin, and Robert W. Sweeny, "Scopic Regime Change: The War of Terror, Visual Culture, and Art Education," *Studies in Art Education: A Journal of Issues and Research* 49, no. 3 (2008): 200–217.

74. Azoulay, *The Civil Contract*, 113.

75. Kelly Oliver, *Witnessing: Beyond Recognition* (Minneapolis: University of Minnesota Press, 2001), 157.

76. Carrie A. Rentschler, "Witnessing: U.S. Citizenship and the Vicarious Experience of Suffering," *Media, Culture & Society* 26, no. 2 (2004): 296–304.

77. Janet Zandy, "Photography & Writing: A Pedagogy of Seeing," *Exposure: The Journal of the Society for Photographic Education* 41, no. 1 (Spring 2008): 30, 32–36.

78. Sliwinski, *Human Rights in Camera*, 47.

79. Shoshana Felman, "Education and Crisis, or the Vicissitudes of Teaching," in *Testimony: Crises of Witnessing in Literature, Psychoanalysis, and History*, by Shoshana Felman and Dori Laub (New York: Routledge, 1992), 3.

80. Theodor W. Adorno, "Education after Auschwitz," in *Critical Models: Interventions and Catchwords*, trans. Henry W. Pickford (New York: Columbia University Press, 1998), 193.

81. Sharon Sliwinski, "A Painful Labour: Responsibility and Photography." *Visual Studies* 19, no. 2 (October 2004): 150–161.

AFTERWORD

Scholarship on Millennial and Post-Millennial Culture during the War on Terror

A Bibliographic Essay

DAVID KIERAN

The eleven essays in this collection provide an introduction to millennial and post-millennial culture in the aftermath of the September 11 attacks and during the War on Terror. They illustrate that the members of these groups have had a range of experiences, consumed a multitude of cultural products, been exposed to a variety of pedagogical practices, and embraced diverse political positions. They show how young people's ages, region, ethnicity, and class have informed their experiences and positions, and reveal that quite often young people have been encouraged to embrace discourses that encourage patriotic orthodoxy and support for the military interventions central to the War on Terror. In addition, they identify some of the challenges inherent in teaching this diverse population.

These essays thus offer fertile ground for thinking about young people's engagement with what are arguably the most important foreign and domestic policies of their lives. This collection, however, is not comprehensive; indeed, no single collection could be. Some aspects of young people's experiences and genres of cultural production are not discussed here, not because they are unimportant but rather for one of three reasons. First, some topics, particularly popular music and popular film, have been ably discussed by other scholars within the growing body of literature about the September 11 attacks and their aftermath. Much of this work is cited in the notes to each chapter, and readers interested in particular topics are advised to begin their search for additional materials there. Second, some popular culture about these events, despite being consumed *by* young people, is not created explicitly *for* them, and thus falls outside the parameters of this collection. For example, various genres of popular film and music have appeal across generations but are not understood specifically as "children's" or "young-adult" materials. Finally, some very important topics, such as commemoration and anti-war protest, have yet to receive the scholarly attention that they deserve.

This afterword offers a brief bibliographic overview of some of the best scholarship that documents millennial and post-millennial experience, analyzes popular culture popular with millennials and post-millennials, and explores the pedagogical challenges of teaching this population. As well, it suggests avenues for further research. Like the collection itself, it is not comprehensive, but we hope that it offers a useful starting point for students, teachers, and scholars interested in further research on these topics.

The exploration of young people's lives and political investments after September 11 has been studied most thoroughly by scholars of ethnicity, education, and psychology. Any examination of these issues would do well to start with the work of Sunaina Maira, whose essay on youth organizing appears in this volume. Her book *Missing: Youth, Citizenship, and Empire After 9/11* offers an ethnography of South Asian youth living in a working-class Massachusetts city in the early twenty-first century. In addition to offering useful theorizing about youth as a socially constructed category, her book provides "a focus on the everyday experiences of young people [that] reveals how they grapple with the meaning of the state's role in their lives with the implications of war, violence, and racism for an ethics of belonging."[1] Similarly, the experiences of Muslim American youth is the topic of Moustafa Bayoumi's *How Does It Feel to Be a Problem: Being Young and Muslim in America*, which provides an ethnography of Muslim millennials living in New York City. Bayoumi recognizes that "many young Arabs or Muslims have no adult experience of the world prior to September 11" and that many of these young people have "an acute kind of double consciousness that comprehends the widening gap between how they see themselves and how they are seen by the culture at large."[2] An additional profile of the Sikh Coalition in *Amerasia Journal* details the organization's efforts to reduce the bullying and harassment of Sikh children in schools across the nation.[3]

Muslim and Arab youth are not, of course, the only young people to confront the political changes of post-9/11 US culture. Other writers have explored similar issues from different perspectives. Richard Brent Turner has examined the experience of college-aged African American converts to Islam after September 11, finding that "their 'masculine identity,' that is their religious and political consciousness, is mediated through the interaction between Islam and hip-hop culture" and that they embrace "hip-hop's emphasis on the black urban landscape as a site for political and social discourse and the tensions between African American Muslims and new Arab and Asian immigrants in the country, especially in the wake of 9/11."[4] Gina Perez's work on Latinos and Junior Reserve

Officer Training Programs explores how the Army has sought to recruit Latinos and notes that "in Chicago . . . JROTC has enjoyed unprecedented expansion in the public schools, with more than ten thousand students, largely Latina/o and African American, participating in the program."[5] For many of these students, Perez shows, JRTOC membership offers a means of gaining both the "respect" that their otherwise marginalized social positions often deny them and develops habits that they believe will allow them greater educational opportunities.[6] Perez has also analyzed the gender and sexual politics of JROTC, arguing, "For young Latinas . . . participating in JROTC programs offers both a way for them to contribute to their household economies as well as the possibility of creating a space for them to exercise some autonomy . . . in ways that conform to cultural expectations of young women."[7] Similarly, Hector Amaya has theorized about the links between Latino military service, citizenship, and efforts to reaffirm American nationalism and masculinity by exploring the cultural and political responses to the death of Latino millennials in Iraq.[8]

As Holly Swyers's essay points out, schools and school curricula have shaped young people's robust engagement with these issues. Scholars of school and society have explored these issues in education journals. Simone Schweber, for example, has analyzed how religious faith shaped how teachers and students in a fundamentalist Christian school discussed the September 11 attacks in the context of learning about the Holocaust.[9] Likewise, Katharyne Mitchell and Walter C. Parker found in their case study of five Seattle schools that most students did not maintain the extreme patriotism that marked the immediate aftermath of the September 11 attacks and were more globally engaged than many adults assumed.[10] Cooper's essay that explores college students' use of the Holocaust to make sense of the September 11 attacks and Swyers's analysis of some young people's reluctance to embrace the vibrant patriotism that followed the attacks build usefully on such work.

Psychologists and social workers have also explored the impact of the September 11 attacks and the War on Terror on young people in clinical journals. A useful overview of this research with an extensive bibliography can be found in Nancy Eisenberg and Roxane Cohen Silver's essay "Growing Up in the Shadow of Terrorism: Youth in America After 9/11," which appeared in *American Psychologist*.[11] Also useful are works that detail how young people processed the attacks, were traumatized by them, or learned about them from their parents and caregivers.[12] Additional work has been done by political scientists and media-studies scholars to examine how children and adolescents responded to media coverage of the attacks and subsequent wars.[13] Shereen Ismael's "The Cost of War: The Children of Iraq," published in *The Journal of Comparative Family Studies*, offers a grim perspective on how the Iraq War impacted children living in that country.[14]

There are, however, important topics that the existing literature on young people's engagement with September 11 and the War on Terror does not cover.

Although, as the introduction notes, young people have been frequent visitors to the memorials in New York and Pennsylvania and have helped construct memorials and participated in remembrance ceremonies in a variety of settings, there has yet to be a study on how children and adolescents have worked to remember September 11. The same is true for their activities protesting or supporting the war, including on how students have engaged in anti-war protests, reacted to military recruitment in schools, or participated in the construction of war memorials and efforts to support deployed troops. As well, ethnographies of the children of military personnel would be a welcome addition to the growing body of research on military families during the Iraq and Afghanistan Wars; at the moment, only one article treats these issues by focusing largely on children.[15] These are important topics that are necessary to a complete history of the twenty-first century, and they are thus deserving of thorough scholarly treatment.

The second section of *The War of My Generation* examines old and new media about the War on Terror and US military recruitment that was produced specifically for young people. As with the first section, these essays do not offer comprehensive treatment of millennial and post-millennial culture, partly because members of these groups frequently consume cultural products that are not specifically marketed to "children" or "adolescents." Scholars interested in popular culture of this sort would do well to consult the growing body of more generalized scholarship about 9/11 culture, but in this section I provide an overview of recent scholarship about post-September 11 popular culture that is popular with millennials and post-millennials but not specifically created for them.[16]

As I note in the introduction, some work has been done on comic books and graphic novels, and a worthwhile addition to that scholarship is Cord Scott's survey of post-September 11 comic books, which he juxtaposes with those that appeared during the Second World War. He shows that while some comics valorize the first responders, amplify narratives of trauma, and encourage pluralism while discouraging ethnic discrimination, others present more familiar revenge narratives.[17] Stacy Takacs's *Terror TV* discusses, though briefly, programs popular with millennials and post-millennials, including *South Park, The Mickey Mouse Club, The Colbert Report, The Daily Show with Jon Stewart, Lost, The Simpsons, Generation Kill,* and *Over There.*[18] Additionally, useful essays on late-night television, *South Park,* and *The Colbert Report* can be found in Ted Gournelos and Viveca Greene's edition on comedy after September 11, which also contains interesting work on other forms of popular culture of interest to millennials and post-millennials, including jokes and internet memes, African American stand-up comedy, and the satirical newspaper *The Onion.*[19]

Film represents another genre that this collection only partially covers but which is significant within millennial and post-millennial culture. It is, however, a genre that has received considerable attention from scholars of 9/11 culture.[20] Two texts offer good starting places. Tom Pollard's *Hollywood 9/11: Superheroes,*

Supervillains, and Super Disasters offers a comprehensive overview of science fiction, superhero films, among others, and discusses for example how the title character of *The Incredible Hulk* (2003) is "a perfect post-9/11 superhero because his superpowers flow from his anger" and illustrates that destruction of Gotham in *The Dark Night* (2008) or of New York in *Cloverfield* (2008) recalls media coverage of the September 11 attacks.[21] Pollard argues that in post-9/11 US culture, "horror films . . . provide symbolic reflections of today's unpleasant realities," a topic taken up in greater detail in Aviva Briefel and Sam J. Miller's *Horror after 9/11: World of Fear, Cinema of Terror.*[22] Also important is Shilpa Dave's recent work on the *Harold and Kumar* series, particularly her analysis of *Harold and Kumar Escape from Guantanamo,* which she argues "reinvents the fear and terror embodied by brown and yellow bodies and through the use of comedy proves that brown and yellow bodies can be harmless, normal, and patriotic."[23]

The War of My Generation also does not analyze popular music after September 11, largely because that topic has been ably covered in two excellent collections and in the work of other scholars. Jonathan Ritter and J. Martin Daughtry's collection *Music in the Post-9/11 World* includes essays on music as varied as Top 40 hits, Bruce Springsteen, and Darryl Worley's "Where Were You When the World Stopped Turning."[24] Equally useful are the essays collected in Joseph P. Fischer and Brian Flota's *The Politics of Post-9/11 Music: Sound, Trauma, and the Music Industry in the Time of Terror,* which includes essays on artists as varied as Nine Inch Nails and Carrie Underwood and genres that range from hip-hop to Christian heavy metal.[25] Jeffrey Melnick's *9/11 Culture: America under Construction* provides useful discussions of several varieties of popular music, but offers particular insight into hip-hop, which Melnick argues, was one way in which African American artists sought to "connect up the suffering of inner-city people of color with the suffering of the victims of the 9/11 attacks."[26]

Literature represents one area in which studies of millennial and post-millennial popular culture about the September 11 attacks and the subsequent War on Terror have fallen short. Almost all of the work by literary scholars has focused on novels with lesser appeal to young people. Yet a search of Amazon .com reveals a growing number of books for children and adolescents about the attacks (from Joan S. Dunphy's *The Mouse Family's Most Terrible, Terrifying Day* to Lauren Tarshis's *I Survived the Attacks of September 11th, 2001*); the wars that followed them (*The Iraq War: A History Just For Kids!*); and young people living in Afghanistan (N. H. Senzai's *Shooting Kabul,* Suzanne Fisher Staples's *Under the Persimmon Tree,* Malala Yousefzai's *I Am Malala: The Girl Who Stood Up for Education and Was Shot by the Taliban,* and Deborah Ellis' series of books about life in Afghanistan under the Taliban). Texts like these, their reception by young people, and their place in school curricula are worthy topics of discussion and analysis as the post-millennial generation begins to grapple with the legacies of these events.

The question of how to teach September 11 and the subsequent wars has also been taken up by scholars and educators, but a considerable amount of work remains to be done. The works by Melnick, Shihade, Potter, and May cited in the introduction offer important insights into what and how to teach about these topics. An additional useful essay is an early piece by Michael W. Apple, "Patriotism, Pedagogy, and Freedom: On the Educational Meanings of September 11th," which argues that "the politics of patriotism made it much more difficult for schools at all levels to engage in social criticism or meaningful dialogue about U.S. policies and economic power" and that "9/11 had powerful and worrisome effects that are often hidden in our rush to use schools for patriotic purposes."[27] Apple concludes that teachers need to be aware of the tensions between the sometimes implicit imperative to cultivate patriotism and the goal of encouraging students to think critically and historically about their world.[28] In a piece that appeared in the *OAH Newsletter* around the same time, James McGrath Morris made a similar argument for teaching the attacks in their historical context, writing that "a solid grounding in history can help [students] see how the attacks are part of a bigger, unfolding story that dates back hundreds, if not thousands, of years" and arguing for "history-based lessons [that] empower students to make up their own minds about the meaning of events" rather than those designed to "produce a particular result, namely patriotism and loyalty."[29] These essays reveal that from the beginning historians and educators at the secondary and post-secondary levels were deeply concerned about how to help their students make sense of these events.

However, the study of what and how to teach about the attacks and their aftermath remains incomplete. Hopefully in the near future, scholars will take up the question of how these events are portrayed in secondary and post-secondary history textbooks and in the educational materials and lesson plans offered by memorials and government agencies. As well, more discussion is necessary regarding what resources and approaches will allow students to engage in the sophisticated, historically grounded thinking that Apple and Morris called for in the event's immediate aftermath.

This admittedly brief overview of the existing scholarship on millennial and post-millennial attitudes and culture in relation to the September 11 attacks, the Iraq and Afghanistan Wars, and the broader War on Terror reveal that it is a vibrant field. Yet while much has been written, there clearly remains much more to be said. The essays collected in *The War of My Generation* raise provocative questions about young people's engagements with and attitudes toward the most important historical and political questions of the twenty-first century. But this collection, like the work that I outline here, is hardly the last word on these generations' engagements and activism. Analyzing these questions will this be central to the larger project of understanding the culture and politics in the twenty-first century and the legacies of the September 11 attacks and the War on Terror.

NOTES

1. Sunaina Marr Maira, *Missing: Youth, Citizenship, and Empire After 9//11* (Durham, NC: Duke University Press, 2009), 13–15, 22.
2. Moustafa Bayoumi, *How Does It Feel to Be a Problem: Being Young and Arab in America* (New York: Penguin Books, 2008), 6–7, 12.
3. "The Sikh Coalition," *Amerasia Journal* 40, no. 1 (2014): 102–105.
4. Richard Brent Turner, "Constructing Masculinity: Interactions between Islam and African-American Youth since C. Eric Lincoln, *The Black Muslims in America*," *Souls: A Critique of Black Politics, Culture, and Society* 8, no. 4 (2006): 38, 40.
5. Gina M. Perez, "Hispanic Values, Military Values: Gender, Culture, and the Militarization of Latina/o Youth," in *Beyond El Barrio: Everyday Life in Latina/o America*, ed. Gina M. Perez, Frank R. Guridy, and Adrian Burgos Jr. (New York: New York University Press, 2010), 177.
6. Ibid., 177–179.
7. Gina M. Perez, "How a Scholarship Girl Becomes a Soldier: The Militarization of Latina/o Youth in Chicago Public Schools," *Identities: Global Studies in Culture and Power* 13–53–72 (2006): 64.
8. Hector Amaya, "Latino Immigrants in the American Discourses of Citizenship and Nationalism during the Iraqi War," *Critical Discourse Studies* 4, no. 3 (2007): 253; Hector Amaya, "Dying American, or the Violence of Citizenship: Latinos in Iraq," *Latino Studies* 5 (2007): 3–24.
9. Simone Schwebber, "Fundamentally 9/11: The Fashioning of Collective Memory in a Christian School," *American Journal of Education* 112, no. 3 (2006): 392–417.
10. Katharyne Mitchell and Walter C. Parker, "I Pledge Allegiance to . . . Flexible Citizenship and Shifting Scales of Belonging," *Teachers College Record* 110, no. 4 (2008): 789, 797.
11. Nancy Eisenberg and Roxane Cohen Silver, "Growing Up in the Shadow of Terrorism: Youth in America after 9/11," *American Psychologist* 66, no. 6 (2011): 468–481.
12. Rose Latino, Barbara Freidman, and Victoria Belluci, "Treatment with Children and Adolescents Traumatized by the September 11th Attack," *Clinical Social Work Journal* 34, no. 4 (2006): 447–466; Tara M. Stoppa et. al., "Defining a Moment in History: Parent Communication with Adolescents about September 11, 2001," *Journal of Youth and Adolescence* 40, no. 12 (2011): 1691–1704.
13. Karyn Riddle et. al., "'People Killing People on the News': Young People's Descriptions of Frightening Television News Content," *Communications Quarterly* 60, no. 2 (2012): 278–294; Stacey L. Smith and Emily Moyer Guse, "Children and the War on Iraq: Developmental Differences in Fear Responses to Television News Coverage," *Media Psychology* 8, no. 3 (2006): 213–237; Kathrin Horschellmann, "Populating the Landscapes of Critical Geopolitics— Young People's Responses to the War in Iraq (2003)," *Political Geography* 27, no. 5 (2008): 587–609; and Marinella Garatti and Rose A. Rudnitski, "Adolescents' Views on War and Peace in the Early Phases of the Iraq Conflict," *Adolescence* 42, no. 167 (2007): 501–523.
14. Shereen T. Ismael, "The Cost of War: The Children of Iraq," *Journal of Comparative Family Studies* 38, no. 2 (2007): 337–357.
15. Patricia Lester et. al., "The Long War and Parental Combat Deployment: Effects on Military Children and At-Home Spouses," *Journal of the American Academy of Child and Adolescent Psychiatry* 49, no. 4 (2010): 310–320. This body of work includes James S. Krueger and

Francisco I. Pedraza, "Missing Voices: War Attitudes among Military Service-Connected Families," *Armed Forces and Society* 38, no. 3 (2012): 291–412; Kenneth MacLeish, *Making War at Fort Hood: Life and Uncertainty in a Military Community* (Princeton: Princeton University Press, 2013).

16. Of this large body of work, three texts stand out as starting points: Andrew Schopp and Matthew B. Hill, eds., *The War on Terror and American Popular Culture* (Madison, NJ: Farleigh Dickinson University Press, 2009); Stacy Takacs, *Terrorism TV: Popular Entertainment in Post-9/11 America* (Lawrence: University Press of Kansas, 2012); and Jeffrey Melnick, *9/11 Culture: America under Construction* (Malden, MA: Wiley-Blackwell, 2009). The last two of these are useful not only for the comprehensive and wide-ranging analysis that each provides but also for their useful bibliographies of television programs, films, and music about September 11 and its aftermath.

17. Cord Scott, "Written in Red, White, and Blue: A Comparison of Comic Book Propaganda from World War II and September 11," *The Journal of Popular Culture* 40, no. 2 (2007): 336–338.

18. Takacs, *Terrorism TV*, 54–55, 102, 120, 170–175, 200–203, 240. For additional analysis of *The Daily Show* as well as coverage of the War on Terror by *The Onion*, see Ian Reilly, "Satirical Fake News and/as American Political Discourse," *Journal of American Culture* 35, no. 3 (2012): 258–275.

19. Ted Gournelos and Viveca Freene, eds. *A Decade of Dark Humor: How Comedy, Irony, and Satire Shaped Post-9/11 America* (Jackson: University Press of Mississippi, 2011).

20. For overviews of post-September 11 film, see John Markert, *Post-9/11 Cinema: Through a Lens Darkly* (Lanham, MD: Scarecrow Press, 2011); Wheeler Winston Dixon, ed. *Film and Television after 9/11* (Carbondale: Southern Illinois University Press, 2004).

21. Tom Pollard, *Hollywood 9/11: Heroes, Supervillians, and Super Disasters* (Boulder, CO: Paradigm Publishers, 2011), 82, 89, 45.

22. Ibid., 58. Aviva Briefel and Sam J. Miller, eds. *Horror After 9/11: World of Fear, Cinema of Terror* (Austin: University of Texas Press, 2012).

23. Shilpa Dave, *Indian Accents: Brown Voice and Racial Performance in American Television and Film* (Urbana: University of Illinois Press, 2013), 130.

24. Jonathan Ritter and J. Martin Daughtry, *Music in the Post-9/11 World* (New York: Routledge, 2007).

25. Joseph P. Fisher and Brian Flota, *The Politics of Post-9/11 Music: Sound, Trauma, and the Music Industry in the Time of Terror* (Farnam, UK: Ashgate, 2011).

26. Melnick, *9/11 Culture*, 96.

27. Michael W. Apple, "Patriotism, Pedagogy, and Freedom: On the Educational Meanings of September 11th," *Teachers College Record* 104, no. 8 (2002): 1761.

28. Ibid., 1770.

29. James McGrath Morris, "Using History to Teach about 9/11," *OAH Newsletter* 30, no. 4 (2002): 5.

CONTRIBUTORS

REBECCA A. ADELMAN joined the Department of Media and Communication Studies at the University of Maryland, Baltimore County as an assistant professor after earning her PhD in comparative studies from The Ohio State University in 2009. Her research and teaching interests include visual culture, citizenship, and cultural studies of terrorism and war. She has published on spectatorship; transparency; and visual ethics, methodologies, and pedagogies as they intersect with militarized violence. Her first book, *Beyond the Checkpoint: Visual Practices in America's Global War on Terror* (University of Massachusetts Press, 2014), maps the visual circuits linking the terrorized American nation-state, its citizens, and its enemies by exploring the practices of image creation, circulation, and consumption that animate these relationships.

ROBERTSON ALLEN is a cultural anthropologist and research fellow at the Institute for Advanced Study in Media Cultures of Computer Simulation at Leuphana University, Germany. His research focuses on the militarization of digital media, the military-entertainment complex, and military cultures and institutions of gaming and simulation. His work also examines the electronic-entertainment industry and emergent forms of post-Fordist game labor. His forthcoming book, *America's Digital Army: Games at Work and War,* connects these salient topics. His work has appeared in *Games and Culture, Transformative Works and Cultures, The Journal of Gaming and Virtual Worlds,* and in the anthologies *War, Technology, Anthropology* (Berghahn Books, 2012) and *Virtual War and Magical Death: Technologies and Imaginaries for Terror and Killing* (Duke University Press, 2013).

LAURA BROWDER is Tyler and Alice Haynes Professor of American Studies at the University of Richmond. She is the author, among other works, of *When Janey Comes Marching Home: Stories of American Women at War* (with photographs by Sascha Pflaeging) (University of North Carolina Press, 2010), *Her Best Shot: Women and Guns in America* (University of North Carolina Press, 2006), and *Slippery Characters: Ethnic Impersonators and American Identities* (University of North Carolina Press, 2000).

CINDY DELL CLARK does interpretive research focused on children's experiences and vantage points, unpacking the substantial part that children play in sustaining and shaping larger social dynamics. She has research skills honed both as an applied qualitative researcher and as an academic anthropologist. She is the author of *In Sickness and In Play,* which describes how children and their families cope with childhood diabetes and asthma. She is also the author of *Flights of Fancy, Leaps of Faith,* a child-focused ethnography of the American childhood rituals, Santa Claus, the Easter Bunny, and the Tooth Fairy. Her book, *In a Younger Voice,* provides an accessible methodological toolkit for those who seek to do child-centered ethnographic inquiry. Clark, who is a fellow in the Society for Applied Anthropology, holds a PhD in human development from the University of Chicago. She currently is visiting associate professor of anthropology at Rutgers University, Camden.

BENJAMIN COOPER is assistant professor of English at Lindenwood University. His teaching and research interests center largely around veteran literature and memory studies, and he is presently at work on a book about the unheralded rise of the veteran authorship from the early republic through Reconstruction. A graduate of Washington University in St. Louis (PhD), Northwestern University (MA), and Davidson College (AB), he has published most recently in *Arizona Quarterly.*

IRENE GARZA is a doctoral candidate in the Department of American Studies at the University of Texas, Austin. Her dissertation is entitled, "The Stuff of Which Heroes Are Made: Latina/os, the Armed Forces, and Discursive Productions of Patriotism, 1971–2006." She is the recipient of a Ford Foundation Dissertation Fellowship and University of Texas Powers Fellowship. Irene holds a BA in American studies and ethnicity, race, and migration from Yale University.

DAVID KIERAN is assistant professor of history at Washington and Jefferson College. He is the author of *Forever Vietnam: How a Divisive War Changed American Public Memory* (University of Massachusetts Press, 2014). His current project is *Signature Wounds: Mental Health and the Iraq and Afghanistan Wars.* He has also taught at Washington University in St. Louis, Franklin and Marshall College, and at Skidmore College. He is the cofounder of the War and Peace Studies Caucus of the American Studies Association.

JO LAMPERT has a long history of teaching, publication, and research in both social justice and children's literature. Jo's book *Children's Fiction about 9/11: Ethnic Heroic and National Identities* was published by Routledge in 2010, and she continues to work in the area of children's books and child sexual abuse. Jo is associate professor in the faculty of education and codirector of the National Exceptional Teachers for Disadvantaged Schools Program at Queensland University of Technology.

SUNAINA MAIRA is professor of Asian American Studies at the University of California, Davis. She is the author of *Desis in the House: Indian American Youth Culture in New York City* and *Missing: Youth, Citizenship, and Empire After 9/11.* She coedited *Contours of the Heart: South Asians Map North America,* which won the American Book Award in 1997, and *Youthscapes: The Popular, the National, and the Global.* Maira's recent publications include a monograph based on ethnographic research, *Jil [Generation] Oslo: Palestinian Hip Hop, Youth Culture, and the Youth Movement* (Tadween), and a volume coedited with Piya Chatterjee, *The Imperial University: Academic Repression and Scholarly Dissent* (University of Minnesota Press). Her new book project is a study of South Asian, Arab, and Afghan American youth and political movements focused on civil and human rights and issues of sovereignty and surveillance in the War on Terror.

JEREMY K. SAUCIER is assistant director of the International Center for the History of Electronic Games at The Strong Museum in Rochester, New York. He is the author of "Reconstructing Warriors: Myth, Meaning, and Multiculturalism in U.S. Army Advertising After Vietnam," in Jimmy L. Bryan Jr., ed., *The Martial Imagination: Cultural Aspects of American Warfare* (Texas A&M University Press, 2013) and "Playing the Past: The Video Game Simulation as Recent American History," in Claire Bond Potter and Renee C. Romano, eds., *Doing Recent History: On Privacy, Copyright, Video Games, Institutional Review Boards, Activist Scholarship, and History That Talks Back* (University of Georgia Press, 2012). He is currently revising his manuscript on the history of army advertising for publication. The author thanks Robert Westbrook and members of the Albion Tourgée Seminar in American Cultural History for their thoughtful feedback on an earlier version of his essay in this book.

HOLLY SWYERS is an associate professor of anthropology at Lake Forest College. She earned her PhD in anthropology at the University of Chicago for her work on how American high-school culture sets the terms and conditions by which young people understand their connection to the American nation-state. She has subsequently researched the way community is formed and maintained in the United States, using the bleacher regulars at Wrigley Field as a case study. The results of this research are available in the book *Wrigley Regulars: Finding Community in the Bleachers.* Swyers is currently heading up the Adulthood Project, a team-based ethnographic project investigating American adulthood. This project seeks to contextualize apparent trends in education, career building, household management, marriage and family life within US history, tracing changes in the experience of race, class, and gender and how they are interpreted and shaped by the lens of American culture.

INDEX

CPSIA information can be obtained at www.ICGtesting.com
Printed in the USA
LVOW11s2311231115

463845LV00002B/478/P